Studies in Employment and Social Policy

VOLUME 56

Editors

Objective

Studies in Employment and Social Policy series seeks to provide a forum for highlighting international and comparative research on contemporary areas of significance for evaluation and regulation of the world of work.

Introduction

Launched in 1997, the Studies in Employment and Social Policy Series now boasts over fifty titles, addressing key policy and development issues in the fields of industrial relations, labour law, social security, and international labour regulation.

Content

With contributions from leading figures in the field, the series brings together key policymakers, academics, and regulators, providing a unique context in which to analyse and evaluate the rapid and dramatic work and social policy developments taking place around the globe.

The titles published in this series are listed at the end of this volume.

The Future of Work

The Future of Work

Labour Law and Labour Market Regulation in the Digital Era

Edited by
Adalberto Perulli
Tiziano Treu

Wolters Kluwer

Published by:
Kluwer Law International B.V.
PO Box 316
2400 AH Alphen aan den Rijn
The Netherlands
E-mail: international-sales@wolterskluwer.com
Website: lrus.wolterskluwer.com

Sold and distributed by:
Wolters Kluwer Legal & Regulatory U.S.
7201 McKinney Circle
Frederick, MD 21704
United States of America
Email: customer.service@wolterskluwer.com

ISBN 978-94-035-2853-3

e-Book: ISBN 978-94-035-2861-8
web-PDF: ISBN 978-94-035-2865-6

Editors

Adalberto Perulli, Full Professor of Labour Law at Ca' Foscari University of Venice.

Tiziano Treu, ISLSSL Honorary President, CNEL (National Council for Economics and Labour) President, Professor Emeritus of Labour Law at Catholic University of Milan.

Contributors

Edoardo Ales, Full Professor of Labour Law at University of Naples Parthenope.

Janice R. Bellace, Professor of Legal Studies and Business Ethics at the Wharton School - University of Pennsylvania.

Michele Boldrin, J.G. Hoty Distinguished University Professor in Arts and Sciences at Washington University in St. Louis.

Valentina Cagnin, Research assistant of Labour Law at Ca' Foscari University of Venice.

Giuseppe Casale, ISLSSL Secretary-General, ITCILO Deputy Director.

Simone D'Ascola, Assistant Professor of Labour Law at University of Pisa.

Michele Faioli, Associate Professor of Labour Law at Catholic University of Milan.

Mario Fasani, Senior Research Coordinator at the Turin School of Development (TSD) of the ITCILO.

Federico Fusco, Assistant Professor of Law at Prince Mohammad bin Fahd University.

Philips Jennings, UNI Global Union.

Ceren Kasım, PhD Candidate in Labour Law at Georg-August University of Göttingen.

Antoine Lyon-Caen, Professor of Labour Law at Paris Ouest Nanterre La Défense University.

Marcella Miracolini, PhD in *Economics, Business and Law* at 'Kore' University of Enna.

Pasquale Monda, Researcher of Labour Law at University of Naples Federico II.

Kamila Naumowicz, Assistant Professor of Labour Law at University of Warmia and Mazury in Olsztyn.

Alberto Pizzoferrato, Full Professor of Labour Law at University of Bologna.

Iva Bjelinski Radić, PhD Candidate and Teaching Assistant Professor of Labour Law at University of Zagreb.

Luigi Salvati, PhD in Economics at University of Roma Tre.

Iacopo Senatori, Researcher of Labour Law at University of Modena and Reggio Emilia, Marco Biagi Foundation.

Pasquale Tridico, President of the Italian National Institute of Social Security (INPS), Full Professor of Labour Economics at University of Roma Tre.

Céline Wattecamps, PhD Candidate and Teaching Assistant at University of Louvain (UCLouvain).

Manfred Weiss, Professor Emeritus of Labour Law at Johann Wolfgang Goethe University of Frankfurt.

Summary of Contents

Table of Contents

Introduction

Adalberto Perulli

The centenary of the International Labour Organization (ILO) was celebrated in a historical phase characterized by profound changes in the economic and social system, both nationally and globally. This is a complex and ambivalent evolutionary process in many respects, which is having a frontal impact on labour law systems, which are naturally very sensitive to changes in the sphere of production, the rationality of the market and new business strategies.

On the one hand, the rapid development of a particularly pervasive technological and digital revolution has posed new problems and new challenges to labour law, which mainly concern the transformation of production systems in the direction of the so-called Industry 4.0, with significant changes in the organization of work, such as the spread of artificial intelligence, detrimental for many jobs but also a harbinger of new perspectives in human-machine interaction, the development and dissemination of digital platforms, with the problems (especially related to precariousness and exploitation of work) raised by the Gig Economy and the consequent need to rethink the problem of the qualification of employment relationships and, above all, to provide social protection to the new workers intermediated by platforms, even beyond their formal qualification as subordinate.

On the other hand, the new turbulence in the world economy which has highlighted the social limits to the development of a globalization without rules, with a return to policies of economic nationalism (also by some European countries) and a growing difficulty in the development of international trade relations, leading to hypothesize a trend towards de-globalization and neo-protectionist tendencies. In this context, the role of the ILO is weakened on the one hand due to tensions between States and opposing interests, and on the other, it becomes even more necessary due to the peculiar tripartite structure of the organization and its historically tested capacity to combine – in naturally compromising terms – the different dyads that affect labour law (State and market, individual and collective, economic rationality and socially sustainable development). This movement of 'tectonic plates' has raised a series of questions which the doctrine is innovatively trying to answer, both in the sense of valorizing what benefits we can derive from the digital technological revolution (e.g., in the sense of freeing unspoken professional energies, creating new employment opportunities, making work more independent and less linked to hierarchical logic), both in the direction of rethinking some basic elements of labour law, focusing on the development of the people's 'skills', expanding the boundaries of work, rethinking the distinction between subordinate work and self-employment in a perspective of greater universalism of protections, etc. In this scenario, which is already complex and ambivalent in itself, the global health crisis of COVID-19 hit the world, not only put the systems of labour law and social security in a completely new perspective, but also made it urgent to understand in depth an economic system, based on global value chains, which has basically represented the channel for the spread of the virus.

The pandemic is still ongoing, and the long-term effects of this unprecedented situation – which, however, highlighted the 'systemic' importance of labour law in dealing with the emergency – are still to be analysed. However, some basic evidence seems to have already been acquired: from the importance of social dialogue in the definition of safety protocols in the workplace to contain the infection and protect the health of workers, to the great resource constituted by tele-work and smart working, which allowed companies and public administrations to continue operating during the lockdown. Some of these issues will probably be overcome with the end of the pandemic, which we hope will happen soon; but many other social issues, which emerged during the crisis, are destined to remain on the table (one for all: the protection of the workplace of employees in the phases of suspension of the activity, as well as the protection of the income of the self-employed, who do not have social protection systems comparable to those of subordinate workers).

This book intends to contribute to the debate on these issues, analysing some aspects of the ongoing transformation, starting from the role of international labour law in the task of adapting labour law systems to changed social and economic conditions. The choice is not only linked to contingency (the centenary of the ILO) but also to the awareness that only an international perspective can make it possible to face the challenges of the present (and the future), thanks to the indications that the ILO is able to provide to States, starting with the report 'work for a brighter future' produced by the Global Commission on the future of work.

Part I is dedicated to this topic, with a series of chapters inspired by the ILO report on the future of work. Tiziano Treu's chapter retraces the role of the historic ILO, highlighting the challenges for the future. After recalling the cornerstones of the subject, from the principle of universality of social rights to regulatory techniques for social standards also through international trade law, Treu's study focuses on the ILO agenda centred on the human person and on the development of his/her abilities, concluding with a reminder of the need to strengthen the 'social pact' that underlies our societies, in the face of the fragility – and, one might add, the failures – of many economic policies. Antoine Lyon-Caen's chapter also concerns the theme of the future of work in the perspective of the social investments that the report suggests making. According to Lyon-Caen, the report helps to forge a common opinion on the phenomena analysed, as well as on the evolution of the problems to be addressed, with particular reference to three key words: work (emploi), platform and algorithm. The first argument recalls the constant (and dating back over time) debate on the creation-destruction of work by technologies, highlighting the need to adapt, especially through the right to training, work and professionalism with respect to the new technological context; the platform economy invites workers' and employers' organizations to reinvent themselves, and suggests a new form of global governance based on eighteen decent work principles applied to platforms; the algorithm recalls the need - indicated by the report - of a responsible use of the algorithms by the employer, but for the Author this is not enough, as it is important to make the very concept of the algorithm consistent with some basic guarantee rules, in order to avoid that behind the apparent neutrality/objectivity of the algorithm there are hidden work management choices based on a purely mercantile rationality.

Giuseppe Casale's chapter is on the same line of thought. According to Casale, the digital economy has emerged as a major feature of the future of work and underlines the rise of online business as work opportunities. But the existing rules and practices in many countries are not fully capable to deal with this new economic reality. As the European Parliament suggested, policy makers at national level should focus on areas where regulatory needs are becoming more obvious, especially in reaction to court judgments that highlight ambiguities and gaps with regard to the employment status of platform workers, their social protection and labour rights, cross-border issues (notably in taxation field and dispute resolution) and consumer protection in a broad sense. According to the ILO, reforms should also be adapted to cover 'workers in all forms of employment' regardless of the type of contract, to use 'technology to simplify contribution and benefit payments' and to strengthen tax-financed mechanisms of social protection. In a perspective of overcoming the strict notion of subordinate worker in order to respond to the regulatory challenges of the present, we have the chapter by Janice Bellace. After having carried out a historical analysis on the inception of labour law and on the transition from the master-servant relationship to the relationship between employee-employer as an effect of the changes in the social relations of production, Bellace projects his survey on the current world of work, on the Gig Economy, and on the difficulties of using the old category of employee, linked to a production model that is now being overcome. Labour law must have as a reference a broader notion, that of a worker, making its scope more universal and guaranteeing what, despite everything, remains the most important fundamental social right: that of trade union association and collective bargaining.

According to P. Jennings, a member of the Global Commission on the Future of Work, the report refers to the despair facing millions of workers and, at the same time, concludes that drastic and comprehensive policy changes are required, intending to trigger significant policy change. The Commission calls clearly for every Member State of the ILO to get national tripartite talks underway to debate a national action plan on the implementation of the report's recommendations. So, it is important that Unions demand involvement in the elaboration of national action plans, in order to help people through the coming transformation. The Commission report looks to create better times and a new lease of hope, and Unions are called to participate to the change. The chapter of Pasquale Tridico suggests that, perhaps due to the lack of so-called complementary investments, it seems that the technological revolution has not yet affected all sectors and all countries in a uniform way. In fact, a particular category of workers, the so-called medium-skilled workers, seems to be the most penalized by new technologies. Italy still seems substantially far from full participation in the new production methods made possible by the revolution in the Information and Communication Technologies (ICT) field but the Italian Government is implementing a mix of policies aimed at favouring the adaptation process to Industry 4.0, such as pushing firms in human capital investment rather than exploit labour cost and flexibility as levers for competitiveness and to protect low skilled workers.

Regarding the industrial policies, there is an almost unanimous agreement that industrial policies must have the aim of accompanying economies on the 'green transition' path; support for workers in difficulty should take the form of financial support for the unemployed and training for those whose skills are made obsolete by technological developments; and a gradual reduction in working hours, combined with work-family conciliation and forms of smart working, would be positive.

Part II investigates some very problematic profiles relating to the qualification of employment relationships in the face of new technological contexts. Adalberto Perulli deals with the issue of the connection between work and technology, wondering whether the latter, as an instrumentum, indicates a possible path to liberation of work, or if, on the contrary, technology, as an imposition, once again manifesting itself as a device that is functional to the subordination of the worker to economic rationality. The problems of qualification of the employment relationships, in particular those with digital platforms, are addressed by the Author from the perspective of a renewed need for axiological rationality, and not just a formal correctness and an 'instrumental' rationality of the qualification processes. In fact, beyond the qualification quarrel (subordination/autonomy), what really matters is that labour law is capable of responding positively to the requests for protection that arise in the new production contexts. In this perspective, the qualification dilemma can be partially overcome by adopting remedial regulation techniques, or by protection thresholds, i.e., extending in a selective way – but with a universalistic spirit – the protections also to self-employed/economically dependent employment relationships, as done, albeit with different levels of intensity, by the French and Italian legislators with an ad hoc discipline of self-employment through digital platforms.

The issue of the qualification of employment relationships, in this context, is particularly relevant, considering that self-employed workers, at least in Europe, risk not being able to benefit from the right to collective bargaining, considered incompatible with European competition law. Vania Brino's investigation focuses on this topic, which highlights the error of approach of the Court of Justice in automatically assimilating, for the purposes indicated, the self-employed worker with the company (e.g., in *FNV Kunsten*), and proposes to reserve the same 'exception' for the self-employed as already provided for subordinate workers since the famous Albany ruling (the Irish antitrust legislation has recently moved in this direction).

The chapter of C. Wattecamps, using as theoretical basis the conception of social law that Supiot develops in his essay *Critique du droit du travail*, suggests that in view of the emergence and development of platform work we should reflect on the relevance of the current institutions and categories of social law. It highlights that, due to the fact that many platform workers are considered as being self-employed, physical and economic security, collective and individual identity are not guaranteed to platform workers. So, the institutions of social law related to the distinction between self-employed workers and employees should be questioned. However, a reconsideration of the institutions of social law requires us thus to see the broader picture. Although the regulatory practices also play an important role, we should keep in mind that the growth of atypical forms of employment should also be seen as a voluntary or involuntary outcome of regulation: it can be attributed to other factors such as the impact of global trade, the decline of the manufacturing sector, the massive expansion of the service sector in industrialized countries, as well as technological innovation.

According to Valentina Cagnin, the incapacity of a traditional labour law to adequate its regulatory and cognitive structures to a new economic, social and cultural context could be an occasion to find a new reference paradigm to define the founding values of a new 'sustainable' labour law. It is thus time to rethink labour law, to switch from the industrial to the digital era, and this could possibly rediscover its historic values of universalism, community and solidarity. A way to act this re-modulation of labour law could be the adoption by the legislators and judges of a new paradigm of reference for labour law: that of sustainable development that considers economic and social development and environmental protection as equally important, interdependent and mutually reinforcing. The adoption of this new paradigm should lead to a revision of the conditions of access and the conditionality of social protections, because what digital workers need is a sort of hard-core of basic protections, unrelated from the contractual qualification.

Part III is dedicated to the analysis of the changes in labour law in the face of the transformations of the company, which takes the form of the Industry 4.0. The production model, highly informed by the principles of artificial intelligence and digital technologies, radically changes the perspective of the old Taylor-Fordist labour law. According to Manfred Weiss the need for adaptation to the new circumstances created by new technological developments is also due to the fact that it has not yet come to its end but is continuing to rapidly provide further innovations, which, moreover, will lead to new challenges for labour law. The Author also wants to demonstrate that, although satisfying solutions are not yet in place, many efforts are made towards this goal. Digitalization leads to dangers as well as to new chances for the workforce, and the aim of the labour law is to guarantee that workers profit from new technological developments, for example, by providing them life-long training opportunities. Michele Faioli points out that, in the new organizational model applied to work, there are new and wider prospects concerning the impact of technology on work organization in the factory of the future. Technology can be considered as a third subject, as it is a 'third element' that takes part in the legal matters of the contractual pattern involving the employer and the worker. Thus, the Author examines the impact of technology on work organization in the factory of the future and how labour regulation – including the European Union (EU) labour regulation – is changing and will change and is taking shape further, adapting to technology.

The chapter of Iacopo Senatori examines the link between the digital transformation and the work organization in order to find the path for a win-win regulation approach that increases the quality of work going beyond the established standards.

The Author considers that the managerial decisions referring to digital transformation not only do not have to threaten the fundamental rights of workers, but also do not have to shift towards the workers the responsibilities and the risks normally linked to the exercise of an economic activity. Rather, the managerial decision should present an added value for the worker, and specific arrangements should be in force to ensure that the decision is the outcome of a genuine negotiation, or at least it should be accepted by the worker in the context of a free appreciation of his/her interests. Crucial is the role of collective bargaining in the involvement of employees in the company's strategic and operational decisions, also for its regulatory potential.

Also I. Bjelinski Radic focused his analysis on the impact of digitalization on individual labour relations in traditional businesses and industries. This chapter, in particular, focuses on the specific working time issues arising in the digital era: digitalization significantly affects working time organization in traditional businesses and industries, because working schedules are becoming more and more flexible, and this implies blurred lines between work and private life. From a working time perspective, the ineffective enforcement of the existing regulations and/or inadequate regulations was identified as the main issue for the ICT-based mobile workers. However, the permanent availability of modern workers does not seem to fit easily into the existing mutually exclusive categories, namely working time and rest periods.

Part IV concerns some aspects of institutional regulation, with reference to European sources and collective bargaining. It opens with a reflection conducted by Edoardo Ales, who deals with the subject in a European key, discussing whether labour law can be adapted by way of judicial or scholarly interpretation or if a legislative intervention at EU level is needed. In fact, the 'digitalization' of the employment relationship poses to labour law some adaptation problems related to its scope of application, that is, the entitlement to individual and collective rights. He concludes that a legislative intervention or a strong action by the European Social Partners are necessary; such intervention is vividly longed for also by the Commission, in order to assure to platform workers fair and just working conditions and the adoption of a new Digital Service Act, announced by the European Commission, could be a huge chance to regulate not only technical and competition aspects but also labour law issues.

The theme of collective bargaining and its possible articulations is at the centre of the analysis of Alberto Pizzoferrato. This chapter shows that at the moment – due to the exclusion of the platform workers from the setting of employment relation, as well as that EU competition law cannot prevent from collectively contracting for dependent self-employed – the only way of providing answers to gig-workers is through collective bargaining at a company stage; but it is necessary to think and implement a specialized collective bargaining, in order to assure, on the one hand, decent work and decent life conditions to platform workers and on the other hand, flexibility in labour supply, rebalancing at the same time the existing asymmetry of information between contracting parties. The chapter of Marcella Miracolini analyses some effects that the process of digitalization has had upon traditional relationships and their management in indus tries, focusing mainly on the job polarization effect, as resulted from the strong interaction between the work performance and the technologies applied to the existing productive processes, which, for instance, could be explained in terms of substitution or complementarity. The chapter investigates also the innovations through the lens of collective bargaining - and the role of involved sources - as a tool to deal with changes, not only to ensure the adaptability but also to provide for the safety of workers.

The role of the social partners should be considered as crucial, to the extent that they are able to take into account the variability of the possible models and find suitable solutions to effectively balance the needs of the company and of work with those of workers.

In Part V, some scholars contribute to research by analysing their own national system. The chapter of Federico Fusco analyses the phenomenon of the gig work in Sweden, focusing on the description of its dimension and on the legal challenges linked to its regulation, thanks to the comparison of two different methods, the former based on the collection of data via surveys and the latter on the measurement of the activities of the major crowd-work web portals. This chapter shows that the classification of the work relationship becomes relevant mostly in relation with the fiscal obligation. Because of the lack of a Labour Inspection Authority, the only control on the juridical status of the gig-worker is performed by the Tax Authority. For this reason, as long as the due taxes and fiscal contribution are paid, the classification of the working relationship of the gig-workers remains an untouched issue. Therefore, the Author investigates the opportunity of dealing with the problem resorting to new systems of allocation of labour protection among people performing economic activities, together with the possibility of qualifying some of the gig-workers as temporary workers. The chapter of Ceren Kasim deals with the question of the protection of employees or independent contractors working in new forms of work in the light of the existing international labour law protections. In particular this chapter examines the ILO law in the context of discriminatory dismissal from a comparative perspective, namely by comparing German and Turkish law.

The ILO system is based on the responsibility of individual States. So its scope is limited, not only in terms of standard-setting activity, or the low rate of ratification, but also in view of the weakness of its supervisory mechanisms and the lack of effective sanctions. However, with respect to Turkish industrial relations and the Turkish legal system, these limited monitoring mechanisms are more frequently used compared to Germany. The ILO's tripartite system allows social partners to seek support in the ILO mechanisms, even if they are poorly enforceable and they serve as a place to make the voice of others heard; voices that cannot be heard in the national systems for various reasons.

In her chapter, dedicated to the figure of 'digital nomads', Kamila Naumowicz underlines that we are witnessing a significant transformation in the way work is performed, being different from the classical concept of the employment relationship. The dominant form of cooperation on the digital market is a so-called freelancers' contract. But the employer-employee relationship has a completely different nature compared to the seller-client relationship on which the activity of freelancers is based (also referred to as 'giggers' or digital nomads). The chapter presents the status of

Polish freelancers and the characteristics of this type of employment on the digital market in Poland. By examining and analysing the forms of work performance, legal solutions adapted by the parties of the agreements, their mutual rights and obligations as well as the results of the surveys, the Author aims to present the reality of digital nomads on the Polish labour market and tries to find an answer to the question on how the chosen form of employment corresponds to elements of traditional employment contracts.

The Italian case is dealt with in the chapter by Simone D'Ascola, suggesting that the idea of 'double alienness', as a paradigm of subordination, can still produce interesting heuristic results with regard to the work through digital and web platforms; the Author tries to verify if is it possible to use this Italian theory as a relevant contribution to the debate about the uncertain salaried nature of the work given in the Gig Economy. In Italian Labour Law it is possible to state that the qualification process is the 'access gate' to the whole set of protections, so the question about how to apply qualification categories to platform work is crucial. The double alienness approach should at least be taken into consideration (from judges and scholars) for the contribution it can give.

The chapter of Pasquale Monda analyses the role of Unions in the era of the fourth industrial revolution in the Italian dimension, a role that is extensively discussed, due to the tendency of disintermediation that overcomes the intermediate bodies of the production process, which does not consider the collective representations of the workers and due to the difficulty of Unions in carving out their role within the change, above all within the organizational changes in progress.

Also, as highlighted by some documents of European Institutions, the EU is trying to give a role to Unions in the context of the European social dialogue, promoting a widespread social dialogue on the social aspects of digitalization, due also to the fact that digitalization, far from being solely a technological issue, has broad implications in the social, labour and economic spheres.

I think I can say, at the end of this short introduction, that the issues addressed in this book really represent a condensation of the challenges that labour law is currently called to respond to. On the one hand, there is a mix of the institutional capacity of national States in dealing with global issues (because as Rodrik rightly said, it is up to States now to face global problems), valorizing the ILO indications and respecting international social standards; on the other hand, there is the classic problems of labour law (being rational in the application of protections, guaranteeing social rights to all those who need them, even regardless of the formal status of subordinate worker) sharpened and made more complex by the new forms organization of production and work made possible not only by the technological transformation in progress but also by the strategies of companies as well as by the difficulty of collective actors in influencing the subject matter in a significant way, as it happened in the Fordist era. We should reconsider the methods of qualifying relationships, relaunch the right mix between universalism and selectivity in the distribution of protections, deepen the links between work and technology to grasp the possible fruits of the new relationship between man and machine and to not only release energy and create new capabilities but also relaunch the institutional dimension of regulation, from the supranational and national State to the new forms of aggregation of collective interests, which digitalization on the one hand tends to deny (disintermediating work from traditional collective arenas) but on the other, it enables them in new forms (opened by digital communication systems to keep together even virtually dispersed workers and try to aggregate their collective interests through digital platforms and applications). The scenario is so complex and uncertain that it requires additional attention and dedication on the part of scholars; this book is intended as a contribution in this direction.

PART I The Future of Work in the ILO Perspective

CHAPTER 1

The ILO and the Future of Work

Tiziano Treu

1.1 THE HISTORY AND THE MISSION OF THE ILO

The effectiveness of the ILO, the role it can play and its ability to respond to the demands that are put upon it depend on major world events: economic crisis, social conflicts, war and in recent years globalization policies which are inimical to ILO values. But in all these extreme situations, the ILO is an indispensable partner because of the balance it brings between state and markets, between society and individual and today between economic, social and environmental policies for sustainable development.

This is the most significant sentence by which J. Somavia Director of the ILO, summarizes the experience of the Organization throughout the last century (Lee, Rodgers, Swepston, Van Daele, 2009).

The centennial of the ILO in 2019 has been the occasion for many of us not only to remember the key role plaid by the Organization in helping to achieve progress and social justice but also to consider some teaching for the future of work which may be drawn from its long experience (Treu, 2019).

The history of the ILO is significant in many respects of the evolution of our discipline, because its activity and regulations have been tested through the many dramatic and tragic events which characterize the last century. The fundamental principles of the Constitution of 1919 have resisted the turbulence of times.

They have been developed and adapted many times in response to the challenges of the events, while the ILO has been acting often in isolation and against the tide. In fact, many decisions of the Organization, particularly when they were anticipatory, have been taken against the opposition of dominant economic powers and of the established cultural and legal traditions. In addition they had to meet often the resistance of the national states, which have always reaffirmed, even when weakened by globalization, their exclusive competence in labour and social matters.

For a century the ILO has greatly contributed to frame and to diffuse among the countries of the world a set of international labour standards and social rights many of which have been embodied in the law and practice of what are considered the developed societies.

Initially its regulations have been mainly derived from the experience of the industrialized countries and shaped after the type of employment prevailing in their manufacturing. But the enlargement of its constituency in the process of time has confronted the ILO with the economic and institutional diversities of the developing world (Trebilcock, 2009; Supiot, 2010).

1.2 A BASIC PRINCIPLE: THE UNIVERSALITY OF SOCIAL RIGHTS

The need to reflect these diversities has been decisive for the choice of the ILO to emphasize the role of basic social rights and standards, as fundamental instruments of promoting the universal cause of work and of meeting the needs of workers operating in a multitude of different conditions. The often detailed regulations present in the ILO Conventions were proving inadequate or counterproductive, and inapplicable to the extreme diversity of the ILO constituent national members, even when the Conventions were ratified.

For the same reason the ILO has adopted the view that some rights and labour regulations present in the acquis of Member States should be recognized to all employees regardless of the legal status of their work contracts and has started the search to identify those principles and rights which were most fit to reach the objective of granting 'a common core expressing the universal principles of the dignity of human labor' (Trebilcock, 2009; Ghai, 2003).

The concrete translation of these principles into the different legal systems was indicated as an essential policy objective to be pursued by the states, in order to provide a unifying basis for the fragmented jobs of the future and free them from the danger of deregulation.

This perspective was rather anticipatory, but in the following years was to become common and to attract the attention of modern labour lawyers, even though their application in the national legal system is still lacking or at most incomplete (Du Toit, 2015; Casale, Treu, 2018).

The decision to adopt a universal core of social rights was widely discussed in the general assembly of the ILO in 1998. Fundamental objections were raised from opposite sides, on the one hand by some developing countries which feared that it might be detrimental to their competitive position, and on the other by those who were afraid that shifting the emphasis on core rights and principles rather than on the specific regulations of the ILO Conventions might open the way to a regression from hard law to soft guidelines (Alston, 2004; Langille, 2005; Maupain, 2005).

But this criticism may apply to all the instruments of the ILO which are not backed by direct sanctions. In fact the interventions of the Organization have always privileged promotional rather than imperative regulatory techniques, considering that the former are realistically more fit than the latter to approach the objectives proclaimed in the diversified and changing international scenario.

The issue discussed in that assembly is still open and has different implications in the changed context of present times. The approach of basic rights and principles has proved to be important to meet the needs of the diversified types of workers originated by new technologies and operating in the globalized economic. But at the same time the guarantee of basic standards for these workers does not exclude the necessity of further measures aimed at protecting and promoting the conditions of standard employees which have represented the core workforce in advanced economies.

The approach followed by the ILO and the variety of working conditions present in the economies of its broad constituency has made evident to the governing bodies of the Organization the necessity to go beyond the regulations and the categories framed after the characters of the industrial workforce which are the original imprint of traditional labour law.

1.3 HOW TO REGULATE THE INFORMAL ECONOMY AND INFORMAL EMPLOYMENT

A major area where ILO has tested the limits of its regulations has been the widespread phenomenon of the informal economy and of the multitude of informal jobs which are legally non-compliant with those regulations or borderline.

Here again this is still an open issue even though in a completely different scenario. In fact the most recent developments of the gig economy have accelerated the diversification of working patterns in ambivalent directions, not only combining aspects of freelance and subordinate status but also giving rise or favouring new forms of informality.

The ILO has been the first organization to be confronted with the task of formalizing the informal, to which many national legislators have been subsequently committed even though with uneven results (ILO Conference, 2014).

The research and the experience of the ILO suggest the necessity to face the many challenges of the informal world of work by adopting an integrated policy approach and by providing interventions which go beyond employment related measures. This set of interventions is required to combine different targets for influencing the economic context in which the informal economy develops, also due to the fact that this context comprises not only backward areas but also modern sectors affected by the new technologies (Villasmil Prieto, 2018).

Some policy measures may be required in all these contexts, such as supporting legality and the formation of human capital, strengthening of social networks and all economic measures necessary to promoting a sustainable development.

Other initiatives need to be specific and related to the different types of informality or irregularity. Among those the ILO has suggested the importance of removing the obstacles in the way of formalization and of growth of the activities in question: e.g., the simplification of bureaucratic procedures for setting up and running a business, the forms of workers management, as well as measures to facilitate access to the instruments needed for this purpose; financial services, information and consultancy on business and employment opportunities; advice on how to compete to public contracts; support for managerial training.

In areas directly connected with employment, major interventions are required to improve inspection services which are almost everywhere understaffed, and to train their employees to the challenge of preventing and monitoring illegal and irregular activities, even though this intervention is in itself insufficient and needs to be supplemented by preventive measures and incentives to encourage irregular activity to emerge.

A specific kind of measure is necessary to contrast the forms of irregular employment common in decentralized production processes (contracting and subcontracting) which are widespread even in advanced sectors of the economy. Many states member of the ILO have introduced forms of more or less extensive co-responsibility on the lead firms in these decentralized contractual arrangements, with penalties for non-compliance with labour and social security standards on the part of the contractors and subcontractors (Treu, 2018).

The international experience the ILO shows that the processes of regularization of informal work need to be adapted to the specific economic and social context. They may require a gradual approach and possibly different degrees of harmonization of the rules, aiming at the enforcement of the basic labour standards rather than at an unrealistic alignment to the wages of the established sectors of the economy. Acceptance of a certain degree of regulatory differentiation may be necessary to achieve effective results with the possibility of making improvements over time.

1.4 THE PRINCIPLES OF FAIR GLOBALIZATION: UNEVEN IMPLEMENTATION

At the beginning of this century the ILO, like all the institutions and the collective actors of the world, was confronted with the two major factors of transformation of our societies, namely the explosion of globalization and of new digital technologies.

The ILO has been involved rather late in the issues of the internationalization of the economy, a delay which is rooted in the historic separation between the sphere of its competence with those of the WTO.

This separation has been a major obstacle to promote common efforts in facing the negative and positive aspects of globalization. Indeed it has been detrimental to both institutions, because the WTO has become, also due to this separation, the main object of the social protest against globalization, and the ILO has been left to elaborate its social norms in isolation, without the links with and the sanctions of the international commercial treaties.

The expansion of international trades and their growing influence on the world economies made clear to the ILO that the international projection of the principles of the decent work agenda was a necessary step for adjourning its mission in the new global scenario.

Indeed the pervasive influence of globalized economies and even more of international finance was in itself challenging the traditional separation of the two spheres because it was altering the precarious balance by which national states had tried to conciliate for a century the economic imperatives with the social and personal interest of their citizens. The altering of this balance has exposed millions of people and of enterprises to the risks of global competition and to growing inequalities which appeared to be the dark side of globalization.

Following the explosion of the 2007 world crisis, the ILO General Assembly of 2008 approved the document 'social justice for a fair globalization', which is the third major statement of principles and policies of the Organization since the Constitution of 1919.

Its fundamental assumption is that the basic tenet of the ILO whereby economic growth has to go hand in hand with social progress must be affirmed and effectively implemented also in international relations and trade. The objective to be pursued to this end implies the need to ensure a strong social dimension of globalization.

Accordingly the Member States are committed to mobilize all available means of action necessary to promote a globalization based on the universal principles of the decent work agenda. It is worth noticing that the document stresses to the same end the importance of promoting sustainable enterprises able to create good employment and income opportunities for all.

The diffusion of the principles of fair globalization in the following years has been promoted by a variety of instruments and strategies. Parallel principles were adopted by other international institutions: the United Nations which approved the global impact of shared value and the Guiding Principles on the responsibility of transnational corporations, the OECD which approved the Guidelines for Multinational Enterprises. Social rights and standards have been introduced by the European Convention on Human Rights and by the European Charter of Fundamental Rights.

Another important instrument to connect global trade with social rights has been the so-called generalized system of preferences by which a country recognizes preferential treatment on tariffs or on other benefits to developing countries on the condition that they respect certain social standards.

A major source of international social regulation has been the social clauses included in international trade and investment agreements (Vogt, 2014; Perulli, 2018).

These social clauses have not only grown in number so as to become a common trait of these agreements but also have acquired great substantive and procedural complexity.

The rationale of the various systems of international social regulation has been interpreted differently. While originally the promotion of social rights in international trade was seen as an instrument to regulate competition, according to a broader vision, present already in the ILO document on fair globalization, it was considered as a means also to promote a sustainable growth. This wider approach has influenced to a different extent the contents of trade agreements and contributed to insert the social clauses in the same chapter with the clauses on sustainable development and on environmental protection.

The same evolution is reflected in the terminology adopted by these clauses which has changed from labour standards to human rights at work.

The diffusion and the impact of these forms of international social regulation, in particular of the social clauses, have been objects of many analysis and comments, to which I have myself contributed (Treu, 2018; Compa, 1993; Bellace, 2014; Perulli, 2018).

The evidence is partial also due to the scarce transparency of the sources and indeed of the entire negotiation process of trade agreements. But the accredited results on the efficacy of these instruments are at best uneven and variable according to the national contexts.

The ILO reports indicate that the most widely implemented parts of the labour chapters of the treaties, particularly by developing countries, are those concerning capacity building programmes, exchange of good practices, promotional activities, social and public communication. More uncertain is the impact of the procedures of the social clauses on the actual improvement of labour standards.

In fact, in spite of the importance attributed to the procedural aspects of the treaties and of the social clauses, these procedures, and in particular the instruments of enforcement, are the weakest links of the agreements. This weakness is only in part procedural, because it reflects the fact that the entire process of enforcement depends on the initiative of the negotiating states and indeed of their bureaucracies.

The ILO has been involved in the implementation of these clauses but mainly with promotional functions as those mentioned above. Recently some agreements, like the CETA, have entrusted to the ILO a significant task of monitoring, fact-finding and mediation. The ILO could contribute more directly to the enforcement of these clauses if it could be indicated as arbitrator by the parties to the treaties, but some proposals advanced to this extent have not been accepted.

Indeed also the role in these procedures of the major social stakeholders, beginning with the labour unions and the ONG, has been so far limited. Even though the experience of some international cases has demonstrated that the initiative of these collective actors can greatly increase the effectiveness of the clauses and compensate for the inertia of the states (Treu, 2018).

1.5 THE ROLE OF THE NATIONAL STATES: PROTECTIONISM AND LEGITIMATE DEFENCE OF SOCIAL STANDARDS

The difficulties in implementing social standards in international trade and the weakness of the ILO, even more than that of other international institutions, are part of a wider problem which has to do with the role and the strategies of the national states vis-à-vis globalization and its regulation.

This has been always a contested area, even more so in recent years when the recurrent international crisis and turbulences have shown the fragility and the negative aspects of globalization.

The slowing down of growth and the increase of inequalities have obscured the good economic performances of the past; have caused to reconsider the excessive optimism concerning the future of globalization and confirmed the need of specific regulation. More worrying is the fact that protectionist reactions have grown in many states, including some of those traditionally devoted to free trade and lately among the various sovranistic governments which have come to power in Europe. These reactions have resulted in a series of measures introduced unilaterally by many states which have imposed limits to the flow of international trades and denounced bilateral and multilateral treaties.

The democratic states, D. Rodnik reminds us, have the right, and I may add the duty, to defend their values and the welfare of their citizens from the negative influence of the global markets. The borders between these legitimate reactions and protectionist measures unduly restricting commerce may not be easy to identify and should be a matter of public discussion and open deliberation.

The principles indicated in the ILO document on fair globalization can offer a valuable guideline for national decision-making in this respect, because they have been built on the basis of a wide process of international consultation according to the established method of the Organization, and they have taken into account the opposing reasons, economic and social, involved in the regulation of international relations.

The events of the recent years, marked by continuous turbulence and recurrent crisis, have clearly demonstrated the precariousness of the rules governing international relations and indeed the inherent fragility of the whole globalization process.

The health emergency caused by COVID-19 has shown with dramatic evidence a further critical aspect of globalization, i.e., the fact that the intensity and dimensions of international exchanges of goods and people have been the major vehicle of diffusion of the virus.

The breaking down of the supply chains caused by the pandemic has blocked entire sectors of world production which they had greatly contributed to boost.

The implications of the pandemic not only on the economy but on all aspects of our lives are uncertain. This crisis may not lead to the end of globalization, but the signs are visible that the speed and dimensions of its growth will be reduced. A possible consequence may be that the range of international commerce and of production will be reduced to more restricted areas, possibly within regions of variable size according to economic and geopolitical variables (Treu, 2020).

This sort of regionalized globalization will impact not only on the material dimensions of the traffic but also on the institutions and the social actors involved in the government of the processes events. The European Union will be required to respond to this evolution using its institutions and experience of economic and social governance to influence the future trends of world trade according to the principles of fair globalization.

The threat posed by the world pandemic has increased the defensive reactions of national states, from the closing of their borders to the imposition of strict controls and limitations to the movement of people and goods, to the reinforcement of public and private health systems of prevention and cure.

The measures taken by the various states have been different also in the relatively homogeneous space of Europe, and this diversity has contributed to different performances of the nations in the control and fight of the health crisis. This divergence goes against the goals pursued since the foundation of the European community and may prove to be negative for the welfare of the Europeans as it has been experienced in other social and economic fields. That is why many experts and representatives institutions like the EESC are advocating the need to promote a direct initiative of the European Union in the matter of public and private health which has been so far outside the Union competences.

This initiative should be connected and integrated with the vast body of European rules already existing in the field of health and safety of work. Various European states, including Italy, have taken detailed measures to prevent contagion and to guarantee safety in the workplaces, usually according to special protocols agreed with the social parties unions and then sanctioned by legislative and administrative regulations. These measures have been framed with the objective to counter the general risk of contagion taking into account the forms and content in which it is transformed or specified in the various working environments.

For the same reasons a similar combined approach will be necessary in the regulation of international relations, whatever the forms and the intensity in which they continue. The techniques and procedures used in the practice of social clauses may be useful, but they will have to be adapted in order to face the different risks of contagion involved in the international traffic and to protect the health and safety of the millions of people concerned.

Joint efforts by national states and international institutions will be needed in order to find common standards which can respond to the general and specific risks for health provoked by the pandemic, suitable to be recognized and applied by all the participants in international trades. The ILO and the World Health Organization will have to use their expertise and their international experience, with the participation of all the stakeholders, in developing these common standards.

1.6 THE HUMAN-CENTRED AGENDA: INVESTING IN PEOPLE'S CAPABILITIES AND IN THE INSTITUTIONS OF WORK

The most recent contribution of the ILO on how to respond to the great transformations brought about by the digital and the green transition is given in the report 'work for a brighter future' produced by the Global Commission on the future of work, composed of experts coming from different geographical regions and having different professional and governmental experience.

The main political message of the report is a strong appeal to seize the opportunities offered by technological advances and by the greening of the economy to promote the main objectives long promised by democratic societies and promoted by the ILO: economic security, equal opportunities and social justice. A second message indicates that forging a new path towards this end requires committed action by governments, workers and employers' organizations directed to reinvigorate a social contract aimed at putting people and the work they do at the centre of economic and social policy and of business practice.

The three pillars of action which compose the 'human-centred agenda' proposed by the Commission build on the major strategic guidelines elaborated in the history of the ILO, but are renovated by a vision which includes specific suggestions and raises open questions.

Some of them are particularly relevant and challenging for the present debate on the role of labour law and social policies.

The most significant innovation, which is far from formal, is that all the three pillars of the agenda are worded not in terms of regulatory standards and of protective rules, as is usually the case in these documents, but in terms of investments: investments in people' capabilities, in the institutions of work, in decent and sustainable work.

This wording corresponds to the approach followed by the ILO that considers labour standards and regulations as part of more complex policy package finalized to pursue the main strategic objectives of employment, social protection, social dialogue and rights at work; all of which are inseparable and mutually supportive and where the role of the international standards are a useful means of achieving all of them.

In line with this vision the first recommendation of the report is to establish a universal labour guarantee including fundamental rights to all workers regardless of their contractual arrangements or employment status and is named under the title 'increasing investments in the institutions of work'.

This wording suggests that the guarantees provided by labour standards are not only a means of protection but also an investment in people and that they must be conceived more than a static set of rules but rather as an institution of work which may evolve so as to include new rights and which may be enriched by collective agreements.

This conception represents a useful tool of analysis for understanding the transformations of work in the present digital era and for guiding us in the research of suitable forms of regulation.

The disruptive effects of the new technologies have so profoundly altered the forms of employment on which labour law has been built as to make inadequate not only the traditional rules applied to it but also the categories on which our discipline is founded, beginning with the contract of subordinate work (Eurofound, 2018; Hepple, Veneziani, 2009; Ales, Deluert, Kenver, 2017).

The uncertainty in the categorization and regulation of the varieties of work present in the modern labour markets has affected not only the interpreters but also the courts, the social partners and even the legislators.

The result is that the formerly compact body of labour law has become diversified due to a multitude of modifications of the established legal patterns introduced by various sources of law. The attempts to reflect the diversity and fluctuations of work in the digital era have not only introduced variations within the individual types of employment thus destroying their unity but also produced partial forms of osmosis of regulations between the different types.

The different, often divergent, positions concerning the possible regulations of the many atypical forms of employment and lately platform-based work are a matter of unresolved debate in most legal systems. We all are involved (Araki, Laloum, 2018; Weiss, 2018).

The debate is still open but the proposals advanced by the ILO, in the decent work agenda and lately in the report of the global commission, to identify and implement a universal guarantee for all types of employment, seem to indicate a most convincing policy perspective. Similar principles appear to be adopted with different variations in some legal systems with respect to platform-based workers, e.g., by the French and Italian legislators, and by many judges in civil and common law systems.

A common trend in these solutions is that they focus on a number of essential rights and protection, to be granted to these workers, even without providing a legal definition of their forms of employment, and at the same time that they abandon the all-or-nothing logic inherent in the traditional legal categories.

This general line of policy will require further analysis and specifications adapted to the different employment and business situations, as the ILO suggests and now is indicated also by the European Commission. Recently the Commission has initiated a procedure for a directive to make mandatory for multinational enterprises the adoption of procedures of due diligence on the respect of human rights and of environment protection rules in their global supply chains.

This is an open field of research for jurists and lawmakers who are called to identity principles and criteria suitable for guiding these specifications. As I have discussed in other occasions (Treu, 2017 and 2018) the main criteria to be followed should consider on the one hand people's needs to enjoy fair working conditions and adequate protection, and on the other hand, the environment in which they operate, including the new forms of organization of work present in the smart factories and the innovations introduced by the diffusion of the smart work.

The speed and variety of these innovations may suggest to leave to collective bargaining the task of specifying the regulations best suitable to the workers' needs and the work environment and of identifying both the characters of the various forms of employment and the borders between them (a similar solution is adopted by the Italian legislation in the decrees 81/2015 and 34/2020).

The report of the ILO Commission gives another important suggestion in this matter by proposing to establish an international governance system for digital labour requiring the platforms which organize the work of their clients to respect minimum rights and protection for them.

The new digital work activities may be organized in a great variety of forms, from types of organization which control and direct employees with equivalent although different intensity than that common in traditional subordination, to extremely loose business relations which may leave significant margins of autonomy to the platform client while at the same time indirectly determine the conditions of work and of life of the same client.

This variety makes extremely difficult to identify the concrete characters of each type of arrangement and match them with the appropriate regulation; precisely this difficulty accounts from the persistent uncertainty of the regulatory solutions adopted by the various legal systems.

The digital platforms, when they act as an employer, and they are often recognized as such, are the most concrete and unitary object of regulation. Imposing on them the duty to grant fundamental rights and protections to their clients/workers, as the ILO proposes, is the most effective way to guarantee that these rights and protections actually reach all these clients/workers.

This technique of regulation has been used with good results in many legal systems and recently by a directive of the European Union in the case of temporary employment agencies. Future research should be devoted to adapt the requirements and rules applied to these agencies and for the operation of the digital platforms and for the regulations of their relations with the clients/workers taking into account of the multifaceted characters of digital work.

1.7 EXPANDING TIME SOVEREIGNTY: WORK-LIFE BALANCE AND SMART WORKING

The second pillar of action proposed by the ILO report is titled rather emphatically 'expanding time sovereignty'.

Appropriately it includes not only the theme of working time flexibility, with the specification that real choice and control on working schedule should be guaranteed, but also it stresses the need to achieve a better balance between work and personal life.

The conditions of work created by the new flexible forms of work organization, which are often more demanding than in the past, and the new aspirations of the employees have stimulated an increased demand of quality of working life. In response to this demand various measures have been introduced by legislators and more often by collective agreements, not only for improving health and safety at work but also for promoting a better work-life balance (Treu, 2018).

The report stresses the fact that revising this balance is made more necessary than in the industrial era also in order to address the pressure that comes from the blurring of boundaries between work and personal life made possible by the digital technologies as exemplified by the diffusion of smart working.

Indeed these problems are being considered in various ways by legislators and social actors. Many states have introduced specific regulations aimed at preventing any use of digital devices that are capable of violating the employees privacy and finalized to guaranteeing the right of the employees to disconnect, i.e., to cease to be available on line in certain time of the day and night.

The search for a better work-life balance has been promoted by the legislation of many countries with various measures (family and parental leaves) and by an extensive activity of collective regulation at the national and decentralized company levels which have introduced a variety of personal and family friendly working arrangements. This kind of contractual welfare, which is directed to supplement the public welfare, has expanded its scope by providing many benefits aimed at promoting the wellbeing of people at work (care services for children and aged relatives of workers, support to children education, supplementary pensions, medical prevention and assistance, now intensified to meet that impact of the pandemic).

The number of these welfare agreements has been growing (in Italy company-wide agreements are counted by the thousands) also because they have been supported by considerable fiscal advantages.

The impact of digital technologies on the organization of production has changed, among other aspects of work, the arrangements of working time.

The diffusion of the various forms of smart working, now accelerated by the pandemic, is a major aspect of a new conception of working time made possible by digital technologies.

Those forecasts which envisage an irrelevance of time in the future of work are probably illusory and dangerous; but the abolition of physical distances in the execution of work made possible by these technologies will imply new ways of organizing work and of evaluating its performance. These implications are still undefined like those of other aspects of digitalization.

The smart working presents a variety of possible utilizations. The simplest and widely used version, which consists in delocalizing the activity outside the place of work, often to the employees premises, does not imply any innovation; and it may have negative impact on family life, particularly on women who have increased difficulties in reconciling this type of work with their commitment to the family, as demonstrated during the COVID lockdown.

But some experiences, particularly in technologically advanced firms, show that smart working may be instrumental to changes of the organization of work and of the production which can allow more space to workers autonomy and participation, and contribute to develop Human Resource practices based on mutual trust among the parties.

Indeed the application of this type of work to a large part or even to the majority of the workforce, which is envisaged particularly in many service activities, may imply a deep transformation of the structures of the firms and of the relations between those workers and managers who continue to operate within these structures and the 'new outsiders'.

1.8 THE INDIVIDUALIZATION OF WORK AND THE FUTURE OF COLLECTIVE ACTION: REDUCTION OF WORKING TIME?

A similar evolution would equally impact on the activities of workers representatives, and on the functioning of collective labour relations, which has been negatively affected by many adverse factors, including the impact of globalizations and of the new technologies (Pedersini, 2014).

The organizations of collective interests, beginning with the unions, are also confronted with the process of individualization which has invested many aspects of our societies and which is to be emphasized by the various transformations of the working patterns. Meeting the challenge posed by this process to the established fabric of our society requires a reappraisal of the balance between collective and individual interests in many social activities, including the various forms of industrial relations.

The social parties have just begun to face this problem by reframing the content of some collective agreements in order to leave room for the various individual interests present in the groups once homogeneous and now differentiated of workers represented by them.

The ILO report, being aware of the problem, urges the social parties to use their convening power to bring diverse interests to the table, underlining that this is also a way to strengthen their representative legitimacy. At the same time the report calls on the public institutions to ensure the collective representation of workers and employers through the social dialogue as a public good which deserves to be supported.

The impact of the digital revolution on the future quantity of jobs is still controversial. But it is certain that the impact will be profound on the quality and the distribution of work. The awareness of this problem should determine, as the report clearly mentions, two major areas of policy for the future of work: more and better finalized investments in education and training, and reinforced active labour policies to support people in the transitional labour markets of the future. Whatever the possible impact of technologies, the key challenge is to innovate public and social policies as to make them effective in influencing the use of technologies in the directions mentioned.

With respect to working time it is significant that the digital threat has reopened, at least in Europe, the debate not only on work time flexibility but also on the reduction of working time.

The recent German collective agreement of the metalworking industry has recognized the right of workers to reduce temporarily their weekly working time to twenty-eight hours and the parallel right to return to the number of hours previously worked. The employers in exchange are allowed greater flexibility in the distribution of the weekly working time. Other collective agreements, particularly in the sectors most exposed to the digital revolution, have provided that a certain number of working hours, regularly paid, must be devoted to training and retraining of the workers directed to adjourn their skill and prevent technological obsolescence.

These collective innovations are an initial contribution of the social parties to a much wider policy perspective that is recalled by the ILO report. Its first pillar of action calls for the recognition of universal entitlements to lifelong learning as a fundamental investment in people capacities necessary to enable them to thrive in the digital era.

The prospects of work time reduction are still controversial and have to pass a difficult test of feasibility. Past experiences seem to suggest that the most practical approach is not to legislate on the issue but to experiment possible solutions by collective agreements beginning from the company level.

A few pilot agreements reported in Italian firms using advanced technologies have adopted with some success certain forms of work time reduction, mainly to thirty-five-thirty-eight hours weekly, coupled with flexible work time schedules (Pero, 2019 and 2020).

Another controversial evolution, partially linked to new technologies, is the growth of part time. In a country like the Netherlands it accounts for around half of the working population and has become a common way of distributing work often within the family. It may be used as a favourable way of conciliating work and family life, if it were not for the fact that the majority of part timers are women, and that such an arrangement contributes for them not to conciliate but to sum up their family roles with external work.

Recently in many countries, beginning with Italy, there has been a considerable increase of involuntary part time, which amounts in fact to a form of disguised unemployment or of underemployment. This trend is one aspect of the crisis of employment, which is particularly worrying because it has been so far disregarded or under evaluated also due to the fact that it concerns mostly women workers or youngsters, who are still considered secondary wage earners.

The need to face this problem with specific policies is urgent because part timers are disadvantaged in many respects. First of all they are affected by a reduction of their wages, unfavourable working conditions and diminished possibilities of career, since the principles of equal treatment sanctioned by many national legislations and by a European directive are not fully respected.

Moreover these unfavourable working conditions are reflected in the lack or in the reduction of many provisions of public welfare, like unemployment protection and old age pensions, and often of welfare benefit provided in collective agreements.

1.9 SOCIAL SECURITY: BEYOND INSURANCE SCHEMES

This last remark raises a much wider problem, which I can only mention here, namely the negative consequences of the various kinds of atypical and precarious work on public welfare systems.

The ILO report stresses the need to apply to this problem the same principle of universality proposed by the basic guarantees of employment relations; it advocates a social protection floor for everyone in need, complemented by contributions to social insurance schemes that provide increased levels of protection.

The social security schemes applied in many countries, including Italy, were established in the past on the assumption of stable labour markets and stable jobs. Keeping these schemes unchanged has negative consequences on the social protection for non-standard job, due to the fragmentation and frequent interruptions in their work records.

Some countries have begun to introduce changes aimed at correcting their insurance based social protection systems, from unemployment benefits to old age pensions, by extending some basic protections to non-standard types of work. These changes have parallels with those introduced in the regulation of other conditions of the individual employment relationship.

The progress of reforms in this area is slow and is meeting the same obstacles encountered in the extension of basic social rights and fair conditions of treatment to all workers. A further difficulty is that the reforms of social security have to cope with the reduction of financial resources available for spending which is caused by the diminished tax base caused by the increased volatility affecting employment.

The extension of this approach to part time work is the most difficult case because the tax base for their contributions linked to wages is greatly disproportionate to their needs of social protection (Ferrera, 2009; Marhold, 2018; Treu, 2018; OECD, 2017; European Commission, 2018).

1.10 TO COPE WITH AN UNCERTAIN FUTURE: REINVIGORATING THE SOCIAL CONTRACT

The transforming forces of technologies and of international competition that have brought about the great transformations of work also have profoundly influenced the international scenario and the relations among the nations. The national responses to the challenges posed by this new scenario have been diversified, even polarized in many respects, and these different reactions have contributed to increase the distance among the social and economic conditions of the various countries and of their citizens.

While these responses reflect the different conditions of each national community, they are increasing the divergences and dualisms in the world economy. This trend contradicts the mission of the ILO and of our discipline to promote social justice and progress for all workers and citizens and is bound to create social and geopolitical tensions which may contribute to destabilize the international scenario. The risk is increased by the fact that the divergences among the nations add up to the inequalities which have been growing among individuals and social groups.

The contradictory pressures of the various forces which are transforming the world make for an extremely uncertain international scenario. The ILO has been directly affected by these tensions. It has been weakened by the distancing of some Member States (United States in the first place), like other international institutions (the World Health Organization); moreover it has suffered from the disaffection of the employers' associations which have resisted to the proposal to reinforce the powers of the ILO in the composition of international disputes concerning the interpretation of the conventions.

The recurrent crisis and lately the health emergency have demonstrated the fragility of many economic arrangements which have brought prosperity in the past and also of the systems of social and civil rights on which democratic welfare societies are based. The democratic states and their social actors are called to react to the challenges which are threatening the global social and economic stability.

These states and their constituent social partners should take the lead not only in supporting the role of international institutions like the ILO but also in taking action to strengthen the social contract in their respective countries as advocated by the global commission on the future of work.

REFERENCES

Ales E., Deluert O., Kenver J. (eds), 2017, *Core and contingent work in the European Union: A comparative analysis*, Hart Publishing.

Alston D., 2004, *Core labour standards and the transformations of the international labour rights*, EJIL, vol. 15, f. 471 ss., e ID, f. 478 ss.

Araky T., Laloum S., 2018, *Report to the ISLLSS Turin World Congress*, in G. Casale, T. Treu (eds), *Transformation at work*, Kluwer.

Bellace J., 2014, *Human rights at work: The need for definitional coherence in the global governance system*, Int. Journal of comparative Lab. Law Ind. Rel., vol. 30, f. 175 ss.

Compa L., 1993, *Labour rights and labour standards in international trade*, Law and Policy, Intern. Business, vol. 25, f. 165 ss. e ID., f. 167.

Du Toit D. (ed.), 2015, *Bulletin of comparative labour relations*, debates at the ISLLSS World Congress, Cape Town, *Labour law and social rights*, f. 96.

Eurofound, 2018, *Automation, digitalization and platforms implications for work and employment*.

European Commission, 2018, *Pensions adequacy report*, vol. I.

Ferrera M., 2009, *From the welfare state to the social investment state*, Riv. Italiana Scienze Sociali, pp. 513 ff.

Ghai D., 2003, *Decent work: Concept and indicators*, International Labour Review, vol. 122, no. 2, f. 125.

Hepple B., Veneziani B., 2009, *The transformation of labour law in Europe, a comparative study of 15 countries*, Hart Publishing.

ILO Conference, 2014, *Transitioning from the informal to formal economy*.

ILO, 2015, *Recommendation*.

Langille B.A, 2005, *Core labour rights: The true story*, EJIL, f. 425 ss., e ID f. 423, 426, 437.

Lee E., Rodgers G., Swepston L., Van Daele J., Introduction, 2009, *The international labour organization and the quest for social justice*, 1919-2009, Geneva, f. X.

Marhold F., 2018, *New forms of labour: New solidarity?*, Report to the Turin Congress ISLLSS, in Casale G., Treu T. (eds), *Transformation at work*, Wolters Kluwer.

Maupain F., 2005, *Revitalization not retreat: The real potential of the 1998 ILO declaration for the universal protection of workers' rights*, EJIL, vol. 16, f. 440 ss.

OECD, 2017, *Pensions at a glance*.

Pedersini R., 2014, *European Industrial Relations between old and news trends*, Stato & Mercato, f. 345 ss.

Pero L., 2019, *Organizzazione, lavoro e tecnologie 4.0*, in Sviluppo e Organizzazione, f. 192; e ID, 2020, con L. Campagna, L. Erlicher, *Agire in piccolo e pensare in grande*, Mondoperaio, n. 5, f. 10.

Perulli A., 2018, *The perspective of social clauses in international trade*, Report to the Turin Congress ISLLSS, in Casale G., Treu T. (eds), *Transformation at work*, p. 105 ss.

Supiot A., 2010, *L'esprit de Philadelphie. La justice sociale face au marchè total*, Seuil, Paris.

Trebilcock A., 2009, *From social justice to decent work: An overview of the ILO's guiding ideals 1919-2008*, f. 11 ss.

Treu T., 2017, *Rimedi, tutele, fattispecie: riflessioni a partire dai lavori della Gig Economy*, Lav. Dir., f. 367.

Treu T., 2018, *Sustainable social security*, Rivista Italiana Sicurezza Sociale.

Treu T., 2018, *Transformations of work: Challenges to national system of labour law and social security*, in Casale G., Treu T. (eds), *Transformation at work*, Wolters Kluwer.

Treu T., 2019, *Employment for a sustainable society: What is to be done?,* Report to the ILERA Seoul World Congress, in Kim Dong-One, Rönnmar M. (eds), *Global labour and employment relations: Experiences and challenges*, Parkyoung.

Treu T., 2020, *Diritto del lavoro tra due crisi*, DRI, n.2.

Weiss M., 2018, *Challenges for labor law and industrial relations*, Paper presented to the ILERA World Congress, Seoul, now in Kim Dong-One, Rönnmar M. (eds), *Global labour and employment relations*, Parkyoung.

Villasmil Prieto H., 2018, *World report on informal workers*, in Casale G., Treu T. (eds), *Transformation at work,* Wolters Kluwer, f. 61 ss.

Vogt S., 2014, *Trade and investment arrangements and labor rights*, in Bechler L., Stafford N.K., Bellany G. (eds), *Corporate responsibility for human rights impact: New expectations and paradigms,* ABA, Chapter 5, f. 121 ss., e ID, f. 127 e f. 146 ss.

CHAPTER 2

Technology and Decent Work: Observations on the Report of the Global Commission on the Future of Work

Antoine Lyon-Caen

The report of the Global Commission on the Future of Work has a section devoted to 'technology for decent work'. Such section basically represents a synthesis exercise, but it is clarified by the analysis presented in various preparatory documents, including the initial report realized with the support of the International Labour Organization (ILO)[1] and two briefing notes.[2]

The title of this section should not be abused; its purpose is not generic. It focuses on the modern versions of technology: namely digital technologies. However, digital work platforms are not the only subject considered: a keen eye is focused on artificial intelligence, robotics, sensors and the data they generate.

The considerations in this section have, at least, a twofold interest.

The Commission's Report helps to forge a common opinion on the phenomena, the developments and the problems it evokes, which is, moreover, one of the expected functions of such a report. Thus, we can surely say that the general position adopted in the report concerning technologies in the production system and the vanity of the resistances which could be opposed to them should contribute to the generalization of this discourse.

There is, of course, another reason to pay special attention to this section. It is a matter of seeking the paths of evolution that the report traces and, in particular, those which would eventually find a normative translation. Synthesis has merits. It makes it easy to identify the themes that the report has chosen to promote technologies for

1. ILO, *Inception Report for the Global Commission on the Future of Work, Geneva*, 2017.
2. ILO, Global Commission on the Future of Work, *Job quality in the platform economy*, Issue briefs no. 5, 2018; *The impact of technology on the quality and quantity of jobs*, Issue briefs no. 6, 2018.

decent work. These themes can be introduced by three words: employment, platform and algorithm.

2.1 ON EMPLOYMENT

The interest and the concern regarding the impact of 'automation' on employment are not a recent fact: they date back to the first resistance of workers to the introduction of machinery. Are these machines called upon to replace human labour? This old question finds a new topicality with digital technologies. But according to the report of the World Commission on the Future of Work, the terms of this issue have not basically changed.

The spread of digital technologies not only causes the destruction of certain types of jobs but also promotes the creation of other jobs. Given this twofold phenomenon, what should be the results?

This depends on the skills of current workers and the skills required to carry out the jobs that would actually be created. The deviations likely to be observed and to be corrected are part of the professional training system.

The ILO began its studies and research concerning this dual movement of job destruction and creation in the early 1980s. The resulting ILO reports underlined the positive effects of robotics and numerical control machines on workers' health and safety. However, they also specified that the workers capacities (or skills) should be improved and that attention should be paid to the risks of accentuated imbalance between Countries where new technologies contribute to development and Countries where their diffusion is low.

The report of the Global Commission on the Future of Work recalls and extends these analysis and reflections. One of the preparatory papers reported various estimates of the effects on employment that have emerged from recent works. The Commission expresses no preference regarding such estimates.

It conforms to the double face of technological progress which, on the one hand 'does not only widen choices about where and when to work [and] also create new and better jobs', and, on the other hand, destroys jobs and marginalizes workers, who can no longer claim access to this new labour market. The Commission also insists on the imbalances caused by the digital economy. This favours multinationals, who are at the core of this system.

For the Global Commission for the Future of Work, the balance is positive. However, it insists on the need to provide training adapted to these technological changes and to ensure that the resulting benefits are better shared.

2.2 ON PLATFORMS

It was difficult for the Commission not to mention work platforms in its report, although one of the preparatory documents reported that the importance of the work provided by the mediation of mobile apps[3] remains modest.

Within the field covered by work platforms, the report mainly refers to those offering the performance of 'micro-work', to use the expression mentioned in the preparatory documents and borrowed from a previous study requested by the ILO. These 'micro-work' services most often correspond to fragmented, repetitive tasks, which do not require specific capacities. According to the Global Commission for the Future of Work, these platforms 'hold the potential for creating job opportunities'. The ILO further observed that 'the digital labour rate is expected to increase in the future'.

The Commission does not stay with these quantitative predictions. It points out that there is a need to be sensitive to 'the quality of the jobs created in the digital platform economy'. So, it reflects the observations of one of the preparatory documents which observed the low remuneration, the defaults of payment and the lack of social security.

The Commission is therefore fully aware of the criticisms addressed at 'micro-work'[4] platforms.

It is in the light of this balanced assessment that its recommendations must be valued. Its first recommendation is addressed to workers' and employers' organizations. It encourages them to 'strengthen their representative legitimacy' and, to do so, to undertake actions directed towards workers in the platform economy. The Commission does not appear, however, to ignore the profound difficulties encountered in organizing these workers, who are isolated, helpless and very often are not willing to join any organization. Aware of these difficulties, the Commission suggests that workers' or employers' organizations should use 'innovative organizational techniques' and, in this regard, it advocates the use of technology.

The platform economy, in its own way, invites workers' organizations to reinvent themselves.[5]

Another recommendation is addressed as much to organizations of workers and employers as to States. The Commission advocates 'the development of an international governance system for digital work platforms that establishes a base of rights and protections and forces platforms (and their clients) to respect them'. The Commission even outlines a way forward, which would be to follow the example of the Maritime Labour Convention adopted on 23 February 2006, which sets a base of rights applicable to seafarers and establishes the regulation of relations among people who fall within different rights and jurisdictions. Eighteen principles intended to ensure decent work

3. The data provided therefore relates only to one of the forms of work carried out through the mediation of digital platforms.
4. V.J. Prassl, *Humans as Service: The Promise and Perils of Work in the Gig Economy*, Oxford University Press, 2018.
5. On a first assessment of union reflections and initiatives, J. Freyssinet, *Les syndicats et les plateformes*, *Chronique internationale de l'IRES*, n° 165, 2019, p. 34.

on digital work platforms have already been identified following a survey carried out by the ILO.[6]

2.3 ON ALGORITHMS

The subject of algorithms is not exclusive to labour law. But labour is not immune to the double movement of multiplying the data produced by digital technologies and multiplying the controls resulting from the exploitation of data by mining algorithms.

It is therefore not surprising that the Global Commission on the Future of Work devotes substantial observations and proposals on data processing and algorithms. In each issue dealt with, the Commission performs an act of balancing, pointing out the merits that the growing capacities of data processing can present. All the protagonists of labour relations can expect certain advantages from it. In this way, the labour administration can find in data and its ever-expanding processing a means of better detecting irregularities. The social partners can rely on this to strengthen the control of working conditions. But what draws particular attention is the path offered by the collection and data processing for the exercise of the duty of vigilance which weighs on mother companies and contracting companies with regard to the entire value chain.

Even the technique of the blockchain can bring improvements, in particular to the security of the payment of wages and the payment of social security tax.

This picture, positive at first glance, should not conceal the risks that go along with the proliferation of data, their processing by implementing algorithms and the controls that are thus made possible. The Commission underlines the risks to the privacy of workers. It also highlights the specific risks that affect recruitment procedures which may lead to discriminatory biases.

For this reason, the World Commission on the Future of Work calls for the 'responsible use of algorithms in the world of labour'. It is a prodigal exhortation; however, it is too general to be perfectly satisfactory, because the Commission does not explicitly take the further step that, on the other hand, its wish to 'manage technology and … put it at the service of decent work' would no doubt authorize itself to take. In actuality, it does not go so far as to consider the design of algorithms. Should not their design be subjected to certain standards, so that it is not only the use of algorithms that should be at the service of decent work, but also their programming?

Moreover, the design and the use of algorithms raise a question whose importance will only increase in the future. Many of the decisions that are taken by the management come from the implementation of algorithms. The 'micro-work' services provided by digital platform intermediation offer a simple example: the allocation of a job, the determination of the price paid by the client, the evaluation of the work and of the workers are the result of an algorithm use.

---

6. J. Berg et al., *Les plateformes de travail numérique et l'avenir du travail- Pour un travail décent dans le monde en ligne*, ILO, 2018.

It is this pervasiveness of what must be called an algorithmic decision, which vividly manifests the extension to the field of labour of a market rationality that thrives in websites.

But the question is, precisely, that of knowing whether management, and the management of the human capital in particular, can give rise to algorithmic decisions. The algorithmic decision does not come in the form of a decision based on a choice, but of a technical decision, as such unquestionable. The choices that are integrated into the algorithm are no longer perceptible, nor *a fortiori* questionable, when the algorithmic decision is executed. Even the author of the decision, which itself is no more than the result of a technical device, dissolves.

Is it in the end conceivable that the management decision, which is at the heart of labour law, is erased and disappears behind the algorithmic decision?

Putting 'technology at the service of decent work' requires, as stated by the Global Commission on the Future of Work, that 'workers and managers negotiate the terms of labour', and that management choices are therefore always perceptible and subjects for discussion.

CHAPTER 3

Rethinking Labour Law for the Twenty-First Century

Janice R. Bellace

3.1 INTRODUCTION

For the past two decades, there has been discussion over the relevance of labour law. Much of this scholarly commentary reflected recognition that somehow traditional labour law regulation was not protecting workers as it once did. Moreover, the primary mechanism for setting terms and conditions of employment, collective bargaining, could not assist many workers because the percentage of the labour force that was unionized was declining, precipitously so in some countries. Over the last decade, various articles have been written about the 'gig economy' and the problems this creates for labour law. Most scholars view the problem relating to the legal concept of employment, namely that these gig workers do not fit the mould of traditional employees, as fashioned by statutes and court decisions. As a result, they fall outside the perimeter of the area deemed employment and in many countries, beyond the scope of labour law. Responding to a situation viewed as dire, some have used dramatic language, to the extent that there have even been references to the 'death' of labour law.[1]

It is widely acknowledged that modern labour law is a product of industrialization. When exactly it appeared in any one country depended on the political system in the country and the stage of industrialization. Those countries that first experienced significant and widespread industrialization, such that a working class formed, were the first to respond with legislation. Britain and Germany are the most prominent

1. In reviewing Davidov, G. & Langille, B. eds (2011). *The Idea of Labour Law*. Oxford: Oxford University Press, Professor Matthew Finkin emphasized this tendency he detected among the thirty chapter authors. He titled his review, The death and transfiguration of labour law. *Comparative Labor Law and Policy Journal* (2011) 33, p. 171.

examples, and their legislative responses served as a model for many other countries. Often, though, these legislative responses were simply that: responses to demands rather than part of a comprehensive policy on how to regulate and/or support this new working class.

Before one can reach the grim diagnosis that labour law is in a critical state, or in terminal decline, one must consider what the purpose of labour law is and whether that still has relevance in the twenty-first century.

3.2 THE PURPOSE OF LABOUR LAW

In a 1972 lecture Sir Otto Kahn-Freund observed that the principal purpose is 'to regulate, to support, and to restrain the power of management and the power of organised labour.'[2] Here one sees a definition influenced by the conditions of a particular era or a very narrow view of labour law. Today if labour law only regulated organized labour, it would cover a very small percentage of working people in some countries. It must be recalled, however, that Kahn-Freund's focus was the inherent inequality in the bargaining relationship between companies and workers, a factor that is even more prominent today in the gig economy. Although he believed law could be used to change the balance existing between labour and management, he stressed that the primary force in labour relations is economic. He emphasized that the law is secondary,[3] and cautioned that the legislator must be alert to those economic forces when fashioning legislation and regulations.

Yet Kahn-Freund did not articulate expressly what the purpose of labour law is beyond the restraint of the inherent power of management (or more accurately capital, as management acts on behalf of the shareholders). Wedderburn subsequently confronted this issue when the arrangement he and Kahn-Freund had favoured[4] came under strain during the Thatcher era.[5] Wedderburn saw Thatcher's embrace of Friedrich Hayek's economic views[6] as antithetical to labour law, as Hayek placed strong emphasis on individual choice and abhorred collective action. Wedderburn realized that judges, trained in the common law and steeped in property and contract law, would be predisposed to Hayek's views and would find it difficult to discern any

2. Kahn-Freund, O. (1972). *Labour and the Law*. London: Stevens and Sons, p. 5.
3. *Ibid*., p. 8.
4. Kahn-Freund died in 1979. Both Kahn-Freund and Wedderburn had lauded the approach which in Britain is referred to as 'collective laissez-faire'. The term is used to describe the system whereby the State stays out of industrial relations and leaves the determination of terms and conditions of employment to employers and autonomous unions through the process of collective bargaining. Prior to the 1970s, there was very little legislation relating to collective labour relations and none granting affirmative collective labour rights.
5. For a discussion, *see* Ruth Dukes, Wedderburn and the theory of labour law: Building on Kahn-Freund. *Industrial Law Journal* (2015) 44(3), pp. 357-384.
6. The Austrian-British economist was one of the most prominent academic critics of collectivism in the 20th century, in part because of his firm adherence to classical liberalism and in part because of his political conviction that all forms of collectivism (even those arising in social democracies from voluntarily chosen policies) led to socialism which in turn led to an authoritarian State. He expressed these views in *The Road to Serfdom*, first published in 1944, a book which became highly influential far beyond academic circles.

ideology of labour law.[7] At this point Wedderburn looked for the 'values' that 'lay behind' the collective laissez-faire approach of British labour law and declared that these were:

> a passionate belief in democratic values, alongside a clear vision of the subordination and injustice to which the worker is committed by the very act of selling his labour. From that very subordination springs the moral right of ordinary men and women to associate together, to speak freely, and to act collectively.[8]

Wedderburn identified a core value of British labour law which is more commonly known as freedom of association, a value which was enshrined in international labour law in 1919, when the International Labour Organization was established by the Treaty of Versailles.[9] This is more than a core value. It is the foundational value of labour law, something that is often not recognized.

In looking at the current era, Davidov has commented that labour laws are often under attack because they are viewed by some 'as impediments to efficiency, flexibility and growth.'[10] In so doing Davidov pinpoints the core values of those opposed to collective labour law. This is not a new phenomenon. In fact, it dates back to the very beginnings of labour law which arose as a reaction to the harsh judicial view of collective action. Although expressed in somewhat different ways in different countries, judges who utilized economic reasoning in their decision generally viewed workers' collective action as distorting the market and condemned it as anti-competitive and in restraint of trade. Workers who joined together to seek higher wages or better conditions of work were viewed as harming society because prices for finished good would rise. While judges may have expressed the view that it was understandable that workers would seek better terms and conditions of employment, they could find no recognized right in law that would justify their collective action. What is startling today is that many judges still embrace the values and goals of property, contract and anti-competition law, now buttressed by neoliberal, free market orthodoxies but even after a century of labour law, they fail to place much weight on the values expressed in labour law.

The foundational value of labour law is freedom of association; namely, that working persons have the right to associate with each other, to join together, to

7. Although Wedderburn was thinking of the British courts, an American scholar came to the same conclusion at the same time. In analysing American judicial decisions in labour cases, Atleson detected five underlying assumptions that revealed the thinking of judges. These were that continuity of production must be maintained; employees, unless controlled, will act irresponsibly; employees owe a measure of respect and deference to their employers; the workplace is the property of the employer and primarily under management's control; employees cannot be full partners in the enterprise because that would interfere with inherent, exclusive managerial rights of employers. Atleson, J.B. (1983). *Values and Assumptions in American Labor Law.* Amherst: University of Massachusetts Press, pp. 7-9. These assumptions all flowed from basic legal concepts of private property and freedom of contract.
8. Wedderburn, 'Otto Kahn-Freund and British Labour Law' in Lord Wedderburn, Roy Lewis & Jon Clark, eds, *Labour Law and Industrial Relations* (Clarendon Press, Oxford, 1983), pp. 68-69.
9. For a discussion of the history, *see* Vogt, J. et al. (2020). *The Right to Strike in International Law.* Hart Publishing.
10. Guy Davidov, Articulating labour law's goals: Why and how. *European Labour Law Journal* (2012) 3(2), p. 132.

deliberate, to speak out, and to take action together with regard to their working lives. *Why* working persons should have this right speaks to the deeper meaning of freedom in society and whether it exists at work. The critical point is to bear in mind that the bargaining relationship between capital and labour is inherently unequal because of economic forces. Workers need to provide for themselves and their families and in most societies over the centuries this has compelled them to work for others.[11] Prior to labour law, individual workers had no bargaining power and had to 'accept' whatever terms were offered them. To change this situation, workers needed the right or the freedom to act together. Wedderburn was correct in calling this a 'moral right' although today we would term this a 'human right'.

This moral or human right rests upon the concept expressed in Article 1 of the Universal Declaration of Human Rights: All human beings are born free and equal in dignity and rights. Moving from that fundamental concept, Article 2 declares: Everyone is entitled to all the rights and freedoms set forth in this Declaration, without distinction of any kind, such as race, colour, sex, language, religion, political or other opinion, national or social origin, property, birth or other status. The question that arises is whether a person's human rights apply 24/7, everywhere, including the workplace.[12] This may seem an odd question because one would assume the answer is yes. But in most work situations, the worker is in a position of subordination and typically did not possess the bargaining power to negotiate a better position. Moreover, there is a tension, between property rights expressed in Article 17 and the Article 23 rights relating to remuneration, conditions of work and the worker's right to form and join a trade union in order to further his/her interests. One purpose of labour law is to resolve this tension.

3.3 THE COLLECTIVE VERSUS INDIVIDUAL DICHOTOMY

Depending on the country, the law that applies to people at work is divided into parts with each part having a label. This may not be as a matter of law but it is fairly common in popular usage. Law schools may have a course on 'labour law' and another course on 'employment law' and yet another course on 'discrimination law.' Although this may be a useful division for teaching the various laws and regulations that apply to people at work, it lulls many people into thinking that they are quite separate and

11. It is sometimes said that those who own companies or large blocks of shares have achieved this position because of hard work and their own ingenuity or entrepreneurial abilities Historically, wealth was based on land and land often had been given by a ruling power to certain individuals, and generations of descendants would benefit from inheriting the family's wealth. In an agrarian economy those who worked on the land had no say in the terms and conditions of work, and usually would never have been able to acquire land themselves. In the early stages of industrialization, it was landowners who had the financial assets to invest in the new factories, coal mines and railways.
12. *See* Mundlak, 'The Architecture of Human Rights at Work in Israeli Law' in Janice R. Bellace & Beryl ter Haar, eds, *Labour, Business and Human Rights Law* (Elgar, Cheltenham, 2019), Ch. 9. *See also* Janice R. Bellace, 'Perspectives on Labour and Human Rights' in Janice R. Bellace & Beryl ter Haar, eds, *Labour, Business and Human Rights Law* (Elgar, Cheltenham, 2019), Ch. 1, pp. 8-9.

distinct from each other. But this is an artificial distinction. A person at work is at the same time both an individual and part of a collective. If a woman wants to receive equal pay for work of equal value, she does not consider whether her right flows from a statute or from a collective agreement. Nor if it is a statutory right does she consider whether she will be deemed to be an employee within the meaning of the statute. What she knows is that she is working and she wants to be paid the same as the men doing work which seems to require similar skills and knowledge as her job. In a given country, this right might be achieved through a statutory guarantee backed up by an enforcement mechanism or by a collective agreement.[13]

The main reason for considering this individual right versus collective right dichotomy relates to those who see labour law as increasingly irrelevant. Generally those who voice this concern view labour law as mainly regulating collective rights and unions. If this is the case, labour law is becoming irrelevant because an increasingly smaller proportion of the labour force is covered by a collective agreement. But one can view labour law as encompassing both the individual and collective dimensions, and such a broad view is necessary if one considers the practical implications of freedom of association.

As ILO Convention No. 87 declares, all workers have the right to full freedom of association, to form and join organizations of their own choosing. In the industrial era all trade unions were formed with the aim of having the workers engage in collective bargaining. Without legal support the only unions that could bargain successfully with employers were those members could strike or engage in other industrial action such that they had leverage in bargaining. It was obvious, however, that some types of workers had little or no bargaining power. As a result they would be in no position to improve their terms and conditions of work. Thus, sole reliance on collective bargaining would be inadequate to achieve result embodied in the phrase 'labour is not a commodity.'[14] The Webbs in the seminal work on trade unionism had provided the classic definition of a trade union as 'a continuous association of wage-earners for the purpose of maintaining or improving the conditions of their working lives.'[15] They had noted that there were two main ways by which trade unions could achieve this: collective bargaining and legislation. By 1900 it was recognized that it would be

13. In the late 1970s the country with the smallest gender wage gap was Sweden, even though Sweden had no statute on the subject. The Swedish trade union movement had accepted the principle of equal pay for work of equal value and had negotiated wage rates in collective agreements accordingly. At the time, Sweden had a very high unionization rate (with 90% of manual workers and 70% of white collar workers in unions) with collective agreements were negotiated on a sectoral basis.

14. This phrase first appeared in the American statute, the Clayton Act, in 1914 which was enacted in response to the American Federation of Labor's lobbying for relief from draconian court judgments against unions. In 1919, it was the first principle listed in the Labour Charter that became part of Part XIII of the Treaty of Versailles. This motivating concept was repeated in 1944 in the ILO's Declaration of Philadelphia (now part of the ILO constitution).

15. Sidney and Beatrice Webb. (1920). *The History of Trade Unionism 1666-1920* (Self-published, London), p. 1. The authors noted that in the 1894 first edition, they had said conditions of their 'employment', but in 1920 they modified this to reflect that fact that they did not want to imply that trade unions contemplated a perpetual continuance of the capitalist or wage system, p. 1, fn 1.

impossible for unions to achieve certain norms for all workers through collective bargaining, for instance, a limitation on the length of the working day. Legislation applying to all workers was the efficient way to obtain that.

Why the individual versus collective dichotomy has arisen, and with many persons seeing individual rights as superior to collective rights, is unclear. It may be that the post-World War II human rights movement has contributed to the individual rights thinking that has viewed 'labour law' as regulating only collective labour relations and thus relegated it to a corner of the work law landscape. Yet, if one considers what human rights apply in the work context,[16] it quickly becomes evident that most such rights, arguably individual, are applied through the group to which the individual belongs.

3.4 LABOUR LAW IN THE STRAITJACKET OF 'EMPLOYMENT'

It is generally accepted that labour law arose as a reaction to industrialization. Often commentators point to the harsh conditions of factory life in the first stages of industrialization. That is undoubtedly true, much of the early labour laws focused on working conditions. But the need for such laws arose from a paradigm shift. Before industrialization, the term 'employer' was basically unknown. Most persons who worked engaged in agricultural labour or worked as household servants. There was no 'employer' but the 'owner' (of the land, of the house). Although these workers might receive some cash compensation, their remuneration package was complex. Most lived on land and in housing that was the property of the owner. The worker may have paid some rent, but it did not equate with a market rate. Rather, the financial arrangement under which they lived in a house was tied to their work for the owner.

The relationship between owner and worker was constrained by notions of status, and of obligations to the other party, albeit with the owner setting the rules which the worker was obliged to follow. The notion that a worker had bargained with the owner as the basis for a 'contract of employment' simply did not exist. Generally, the relationship was expected to be of some considerable duration unless the worker broke the owner's rules. The predecessor of labour law is known by the label 'master-servant' law which aptly describes the relationship judges were called on to review.

Much labour law scholarship looking back at early labour law cases focuses on the highly skilled worker, such as stone masons and carpenters who performed work or those who made and sold their own products, such as silversmiths and cordwainers. These were the exceptional cases. Typically these workers performed specified work over a short term for a fee. The highly skilled were not in a long-term status relationship with an owner.[17] Industrialization changed the way in which capital organized itself for the purpose of acquiring the necessary labour to make the products. Although a person

16. For a discussion of what human rights do apply in a work context, and how different countries interpret the applicability of rights to the work setting, *see* Bellace and Haar, *supra* n. 12.
17. The words used to describe these workers, such as 'journeyman' and 'master,' indicate the lack of a long-term relationship with an owner.

may have owned a factory and was viewed as the owner of the company, to the workers he was no longer their 'master.'

The major differentiating factor was remuneration. Those who worked were paid wages, and nothing else. The employer felt no obligation to provide housing or food.[18] Employment was viewed as a cash-only transaction. There was no status relationship. Industrialization raised workers' awareness that capital *buys* labour (the work-for-cash transaction). Heightened competition and the lack of a status relationship led factory owners to cut costs, buying no labour than needed, and shifting risk to labour where possible. This made industrial workers' lives in the early stages of industrialization much more insecure and unpredictable than those of earlier generations. An employer might offer only a few hours work a day, or maybe demand fourteen hours work per day depending on how many orders the factory owner had. Not even a day's employment was guaranteed; dismissal could be instantaneous. There was no promise of employment tomorrow, let alone the following week. As workers came off the fields to the factories, the surplus of labour permitted employers to offer very low wages, often on a piece-rate basis, which in turn caused workers to work very long hours in order to make enough to be able to afford housing and food. The risks inherent in manufacturing, such as the risk of delay from machinery malfunctioning or delays in receiving goods, or injury were all placed on the workers.

3.4.1 The Emergence of Labour Law

Accepting the economic reality of the new factory system, the law moved from a master-servant orientation to an employer-employee orientation. In so doing, the law accepted that there no longer was a status relationship where certain obligations on both sides could be assumed, but the courts had to decide how to conceptualize the new arrangement. Falling back on contract law, the judges now saw a bargain whereby the employee agreed to work for the employer for a certain wage even though there was rarely any indication that the worker had negotiated with the employer on any term. Bowing again to reality, the courts held that beyond the promise to pay for work performed, there was no other enforceable promise in the contract unless expressly stated. Since factory workers individually usually had no bargaining power, the contract of employment served as a legal fiction locking in the workers' weak position.

It was not until the latter half of the nineteenth century in Britain and Germany, and later in many other countries, that the legislature intervened and sought to regulate working conditions. The drafter of any statute must delineate the statute's coverage, and by this point the legislature was reacting to judicial decisions that had focused on the contract of employment. The result was that labour legislation for the most part covered only those deemed 'employees.'

18. Where the factory was located in some remote location, or in the case of mines, the employer might provide housing, but usually the employer charged the workers for this housing. Also the employer set the rent (with the employees having no other rental options). It was not until the late nineteenth century that some companies, in an early manifestation of corporate social responsibility, decided to build decent, subsidized housing.

The nature of production during the height of the industrial age typically required workers who would arrive at a factory at the beginning of their shift and stay there the entire time. They would be assigned tasks by their supervisor who would also monitor their performance. They might be compensated on a piece-rate basis or an hourly basis. There were many exceptions to this, but in general the typical worker was a full-time, year-round, male employed in a factory or other industrial setting. Even during the post-war boom times, 1945-1973 in many countries, the persons who did not fit this mould either were not covered by labour statutes or were not protected by existing legislation. The primary example would be women workers, because they often worked part-time or because of pregnancy-maternity they would exit the labour force periodically (and would lose their job or at best lose seniority). Those who worked in service jobs, such as domestic workers or restaurant servers, often were not covered.

Once a statute was enacted that gave rights or entitlements to 'employees,' there would be litigation over who was covered.[19] For certain types of workers, there was the legal issue of whether they worked under a contract of service or a contract for services. Most statutes did not attempt to delineate the line between the two, leaving the issue to judges who usually relied on multi-factorial tests derived from other branches of law. A 1935 US Supreme Court case, with modern day parallels, illustrates this. In *National Labor Relations Board v. Hearst Publications, Inc.*,[20] newsboys (persons who sold newspapers to the public) wanted to have union representation. The company claimed that they were not employees, and as such, the National Labor Relations Act did not apply. The company argued that these persons were independent contractors, who each day would arrive at a certain location and pick up copies of the daily newspaper, for which they would pay a set price per copy. Then they would go to some location in the city, such a street corner, and sell the papers. The company pointed out that the newsboys could decide how much they wanted to work, and that they took the entrepreneurial risk because their compensation depended on how many papers they could sell. The NLRB had determined that their total compensation was determined in large measure by the company, who determined the price at which the newsboys bought and sold the paper, who fixed the area in which they could sell the paper, who controlled the allocation of papers, and who preferred those who worked regularly on a five-day/week schedule. The Supreme Court agreed with the company that the principal question was whether the newsboys were employees and that common law standards should be applied since the legislature had not defined who was an employee in the statute, but observed:

> The argument assumes that there is some simple, uniform and easily applicable test which the courts have used, in dealing with such problems, to determine whether persons doing work for others fall in one class or the other. Unfortunately

19. For a discussion of this issue, *see* Gerald M. Stevens, The test of the employment relation. *Michigan Law Review* (1939) 38:2, pp. 188-204. The first major federal labour relations statute granting employees the right to form, join and assist labour organizations had been enacted in 1935. Anticipating that the question of who would be deemed an employee would arise in labour cases, Stevens went back a century and reviewed British and American cases, most in non-labour cases, in order to explore factors judges considered.
20. 322 U.S. 111 (1944).

> this is not true. Only by a long and tortuous history was the simple formulation worked out which has been stated most frequently as 'the test' for deciding whether one who hires another is responsible in tort for his wrongdoing. But this formula has been by no means exclusively controlling in the solution of other problems. And its simplicity has been illusory because it is more largely simplicity of formulation than of application. Few problems in the law have given greater variety of application and conflict in results than the cases arising in the borderland between what is clearly an employer-employee relationship and what is clearly one of independent entrepreneurial dealing.[21]

In upholding the NLRB's determination that the newsboys were employees within the meaning of the statute, the Supreme Court observed that '[u]nless the common law tests are to be imported and made exclusively controlling, without regard to the statute's purposes, it cannot be irrelevant that the particular workers in these cases are subject, as a matter of economic fact, to the evils the statute was designed to eradicate.'[22] The Court then looked at the factors the NLRB had considered in reaching its determination:

> the Board found that the designated newsboys work continuously and regularly, rely upon their earnings for the support of themselves and their families, and have their total wages influenced in large measure by the publishers who dictate their buying and selling prices, fix their markets, and control their supply of papers.[23]

The Court upheld the Board's determination that the newsboys were employees within the meaning of the statute after discussing what the legislature had intended when it passed the statute. Significantly the Supreme Court pointed to the inequality of bargaining power and noted that the legislature intended to give those who worked freedom of association and the right to collective bargaining. Not expressly stated but strongly implied was that the legislature had sought to alter the balance between capital and labour, and the newsboys were definitely labour since they relied upon earned income.[24]

3.5 RETHINKING LABOUR LAW

Many labour law statutes today are seen as irrelevant, although anachronistic may be more accurate. There continue to be people who work in factories and mines, and the statutory rights and protections are still relevant to them. But the arrangements regarding how work is done and how these workers are directed and compensated have changed radically over the decades such that decades-old statutory coverage based on a worker being an 'employee' or the statutory rights is inadequate. More

21. *Ibid.*, pp. 120-121.
22. *Ibid.*, p. 127.
23. *Ibid.*, p. 131.
24. The Court had no need to discuss Hearst Publications, Inc. as capital. At the time it was one of the largest publishers of newspapers in the world. In 1944 it was an extremely well-known company at the time, especially since Orson Welles' film, *Citizen Kane*, had premiered in 1941, and it was widely said to be based on the life of William Randolph Hearst, the founder of the company.

importantly, much of labour law revolves around unions and collective bargaining. But the main vehicle traditionally utilized for exercising freedom of association – collective bargaining – is no longer suited to purpose for many workers. In the twenty-first century, with the advent of the digital economy, it is difficult to stop production of many goods and many types of services. Collective bargaining as a means of tackling the inequality of bargaining power fails when the workers lack strike power. Without the ability to carry off a successful strike such that terms and conditions of work improve, workers generally view joining or being active in a union as fruitless or irrelevant.

Freedom of association has never been expressed as limited to workers' deciding to join a union and engaging in collective bargaining. Admittedly, for most of the twentieth century whenever one spoke of freedom of association, the references were solely to unions and collective bargaining. In the twentieth century that may have been the main way workers exercised their freedom of association, but other ways may be better suited to the twenty-first century.

Worker voice, as a value in itself, dates back to 1897 when Sidney and Beatrice Webb deemed it an aspect of democracy that should exist at the workplace.[25] Their view accepted that employers and workers have shared interests and conflicting interests and that workers should have the right to assert their interests individually or collectively to influence the conditions under which they worked. In the twentieth century, legislation in many countries recognized the right of workers to exercise collective voice through collective bargaining. Only a few countries provided another mechanism for the exercise of collective worker voice, generally through works councils.

Recent research in the United States indicates that workers believe they should have a voice on a broad set of workplace issues, but substantial gaps exist between what they expected and what they actually experience at work.[26] Describing these findings, Kochan finds that there is a 'voice gap'.[27] Until recently those workers who had not joined together formally in a union or association had no way of making their voice heard. Individuals may not have realized that others felt as they did, and even if they did realize this, there was no mechanism provided for expressing collective voice. The prevailing view from management may have been 'if you don't like it, you quit,' an unacceptable alternative for most workers. Within the past decade, new technologies have opened up new possibilities for collective voice. Familiar with social media, workers are beginning to come together to share information and express their voice. For instance, *Turkopticon* allows those who do work on Amazon Mechanical Turk to give and leave reviews on those who post tasks to be done. *Coworker.org* permits

25. Sidney and Beatrice Webb. (1897). *Industrial Democracy*. London: Longmans, Green, and Company.
26. Although the research was limited to the United States, there is no reason to suspect that the results would be different for other advanced market economies, especially for those countries where there is no alternative mechanism for collective worker voice.
27. Professor Thomas Kochan and researchers at MIT recently updated survey research on worker voice, and in particular what workers expected, what the reality was, and what they want. Thomas A. Kochan, et al., *ILR Review* (2019) 72(1), pp. 3-38.

workers to sign on and give information about their organization, to link up with similarly minded coworkers, and to learn online how to organize campaigns targeting their employer. *Glassdoor* is a website where current and former employees anonymously review companies, and where they can submit and view salaries at a given company. Websites such as *Glassdoor* has led to more locally based groups forming online (such as using Facebook groups) and sharing information on wages and other working conditions.

The use of social media and worker-oriented websites has improved the position of workers in that they have increased knowledge of terms and conditions of employment in specific companies, but whether that can lead to change and whether the effort can be sustained over time is another question.

3.5.1 Timeless Values but Changing Modes of Application

Recalling the purpose of labour law as articulated by the Webbs in 1897 and by Wedderburn in 1983, we see that belief in democratic values extending to work and not simply the political sphere, a recognition of the subordinate or unequal position of the worker, and a conviction that workers had a right to associate together, to speak freely, and to act collectively.

Another driving force in twentieth century labour law was the concept of social justice,[28] which was articulated in the Treaty of Versailles outlining the urgent matters on which the new ILO should take action. This meant not only the right of workers to freedom of association but the right of workers to just conditions of work. These might be achieved through collective bargaining, but they could also be gained through legislation and regulation. In this regard, if labour law is to remain relevant in the twenty-first century many statutes and regulations relating to minimum wage, hours of work, minimum wages for entry into work, occupational safety and health must be reviewed to ensure that they cover all workers, and not simply 'employees'.

It is difficult to anticipate how capital, through the medium of companies or platforms, may seek to utilize labour and the terms on which they will offer work. For instance, zero hours contracts would have been unthinkable fifty years ago. Today they are common in some countries. The practice of just-in-time scheduling, whereby the company tells the worker the day before whether they will be needed the next day, is now a common practice in retail shops. The labour law value though is that workers should be treated with dignity, and that they are not a commodity. Workers need some stability and predictability, in order to live a decent life and be able to manage their affairs. Those who do not know of Friday if they will be working Saturday, and who do not know how many hours and when they will be working the next week cannot manage their life. They cannot arrange for childcare, they cannot plan when they might take an evening course, they are not able to budget and cannot calculate whether they

28. For a discussion, *see* Supiot, 'What International Social Justice in the Twenty-First Century?' in Darcy du Toit, ed. *Labour Law and Social Progress Holding the Line or Shifting the Boundaries?* Bulletin for Comparative Labour Relations (Wolters Kluwer, The Netherlands, 2016), Ch. 1, no. 92, pp. 1-18.

can afford the rent on an apartment. To remain faithful to the values underlying labour law, legislation and regulations must continually be reviewed. For this abuse, a Fair Work Week regulation may be needed, requiring the scheduling unit to give the worker five-day notice of a schedule of work.

The description 'independent contractor' must be tightly regulated, and the law must be changed to presume that a worker is not an independent contractor. The burden of proof must be on the party insisting on that categorization. The key factor must be 'who sets the price'. An independent contractor decides what price he/she will accept for certain work. By this standard, the drivers and bike delivery persons for Uber and various delivery services are not independent contractors. They do not set the price. They are controlled by the company who has received the order from a customer. The claim by certain companies that they are only platforms that connect the costumer (who needs a ride or needs a meal delivered) with the driver rings hollow. Old-fashioned taxi companies were the platforms of their day; they connected customers who needed a ride with a driver using the telephone instead of the internet. Their drivers were deemed employees. The claims made today by companies such as Uber are not new; they are the same as the claim made by Hearst Publications in the early 1940s.

Yet, the focus on 'employee' is dated. The function of labour law is to support workers. If one is labour, not capital, the person should be covered by labour law. This relates especially to social safety net and social security programmes. In the twentieth century, certain workers were not covered. Often these were women workers on the theory that their husbands or fathers would take care of them. This is outdated. In the twenty-first century, all workers need social safety net and social security coverage. Even those with atypical working patterns can be covered. Decades ago unions devised ways of having such coverage for those who worked for many different entities in a year. Musicians were the original gig workers (they would play a 'gig'). The union determined a way that the employer could make the pension and sickness/disability contribution that an employer would make for an employee on a pro-rated basis. Similarly, the employer contribution to the national social security/pension fund could be pro-rated to the entity that utilizes the worker's services even if only for a day. Here the worker could be required to list those entities for which he/she has worked during a certain period, and those entities would be charged. With online entry and high-speed data transfers, it would not be difficult or expensive for government agencies to keep records, unlike the situation decades ago.

Labour law should remain vital so long as people work, and so long as people need to work to support themselves and their families. The challenge is to remain faithful to the enduring values of worker voice as a fundamental element of freedom in society, and of social justice.

CHAPTER 4

Labour Law and Digital Platforms

Giuseppe Casale & Mario Fasani

4.1 INTRODUCTION

One of the major transformations in the world of work over the past decade has been the emergence of digital platforms. Digital platforms are regarded as a potentially important driver of innovation and economic growth, giving rise to new methods, techniques and data that increase efficiency and productivity and allow for the conception of new products and services.

When dealing with labour law, the digital platform has raised the question about the qualification to be given to the workers who carry out such activities. As pointed out by the ILO, work on digital labour platforms can provide workers with the opportunity to work from any place, at any time and take up whatever jobs suits them. However, the main question remains whether these types of jobs will be 'decent'.[1] Work on digital platforms is new and symbolises somehow the work of the future. It consists of both web-based, digital labour platforms (commonly referred to as crowd-work) and locally based labour platforms where work is allocated through software applications (apps).

With the growth of the Internet and the need for human input in tasks needed for the smooth functioning of web-based industries, new jobs have been created. They range from sophisticated computer programming, data analysis and graphic design to straightforward 'micro-tasks' of a clerical nature.[2]

1. The ILO defines decent work as work that is productive; ensures equality of opportunity and treatment for all women and men; delivers a fair income, security in the workplace and social protection for families; provides prospects for personal development; and gives workers the freedom to express their concerns, organise and participate in decisions that affect their working lives.
2. Silberman, M.S., *Human-centered computing and the future of work: Lessons from Mechanical Turk and Turkopticon*, Dissertation, Irvine, University of California, 2008-2015.

Although digital labour platforms are a product of technological advances, they can also represent a manifestation of casual labour. At a closer look, the platform phenomenon has grown mostly on the margins of regulations applicable to the mainstream economy. This might cause various distortions at national and local level.

Today, estimating the size of the workforce engaged in digital labour platforms – or in the gig economy more generally – is difficult to be done.[3] However, experts estimate that in countries such as the United States the so-called contingent workers will account for nearly half of the country's workforce by 2020, with 11% of these expected to be working for online platforms. In any case, the digital platform phenomenon is set to expand further in an exponential manner over the coming years, with a significant impact on society at large.[4]

4.2 DIGITAL PLATFORM

Nowadays, a remarkable amount of uncertainty still surrounds the concept of digital platform. This is mainly due to the conceptual confusion that results from a lack of a single definition. Under the circumstances, a clear-cut definition would probably be too narrow, or conversely apply to a very wide range of Internet services.[5] According to common understanding, the variety of digital devices such as e-commerce platforms, ad networks, social media or search engines are part of what are considered digital platforms. The latter function as dynamic websites. In fact, digital platforms of this kind involve a dynamic element of interaction or exchange of some kind. Some authors like to describe them as digital 'marketplaces' or 'public squares'. Not only they can become the method of organising the delivery of goods (e.g., food delivery apps; transport apps), but also they can be used for organising the work of workers. In addition, they can be considered the product or service itself, such as the search engine or the social media.[6]

In other words, if crowdsourcing is the act of outsourcing work to 'the crowd', then digital labour platforms are the digital services (websites or apps) that facilitate crowdsourcing. These digital labour platforms provide the technical infrastructure for requesters to advertise tasks to large numbers of potential workers spanning geographic and economic circumstances – 'the crowd' – to retrieve and evaluate the results of completed tasks, and to pay individual workers for services rendered.[7]

At the same time, these platforms also provide services and infrastructure to workers, offering a centralised location for workers to identify tasks from many

3. Smith, R. and Leberstein, S., *Rights on demand: Ensuring workplace standards and worker security in the on-demand economy*, New York, National Employment Law Project, 2015.
4. ILO, *Non-standard employment around the world: Understanding challenges, shaping prospects*, ILO, Geneva, 2016.
5. Martens, B., *An economic policy perspective on online platforms*, JRC/IPTS Digital Economy Working 5F, 2016, available at: https://ec.europa.eu/jrc/sites/default/files/JRC101501.pdf.
6. European Commission, *Online platforms, accompanying the document Communication on Online Platforms and the Digital Single Market*, SWD, 2016.
7. Schmidt, F.A., *Digital labour markets in the platform economy: Mapping the political challenges of crowd work and gig work*, Bonn, Friedrich-Ebert-Stiftung, 2017.

different requesters characterised by the method of submitting work products as well as the technical and financial infrastructure to receive payment for work completed.

When considering labour services provided via digital labour platforms, one distinction can be drawn between services performed digitally and those performed on-location. In the first set of services, there are those dealing with micro-tasks, clerical and data entry; in the second set, one could find services dealing with delivery, transport or housekeeping. The common element for both categories of services is that the platform mediates and administers the provision of services. However, it should be noted that the on-location services require a direct interaction - that is to say, the delivery of services is a physical one - while the digitally performed services are electronically transmittable services and potentially global.

It should be noted that the locus of provision (digital or on-location) has implications for the employment relationship and whether or not national labour legislation is applicable for that specific service provided.

In this regard, a group of researchers has advanced the hypothesis that specific tasks can characterise the labour services via online platforms. Such tasks are:

(1) online clerical and data entry tasks (e.g., customer services, data entry, transcription and similar);
(2) online professional services (e.g., accounting, legal, project management and similar);
(3) online creative and multimedia work (e.g., animation, graphic design, photo editing and similar);
(4) online sales and marketing support work (e.g., lead generation, posting ads, social media management, search engine optimisation and similar);
(5) online software development and technology work (e.g., data science, game development, mobile development and similar);
(6) online writing and translation work (e.g., article writing, copywriting, proofreading, translation and similar);
(7) online micro-tasks (e.g., object classification, tagging, content review, website feedback and similar);
(8) interactive services (e.g., language teaching, interactive online lessons, interactive consultations and similar);
(9) transportation and delivery services (e.g., driving, food delivery, moving services and similar);
(10) on-location services (e.g., housekeeping, beauty services, on-location photography services and similar);
(11) on-location ancillary services (e.g., housekeeping, cleaning) specifically to short-term rental accommodation (e.g., apartments listed on Airbnb and similar).

From such a list of tasks, two broad categories of labour services can be provided: professional tasks (high skills and high education, legal and accountancy, writing and translation) and non-professional tasks (micro-tasks, clerical and data entry tasks, sales and marketing support). Within the latter category is also present a sub-category of on-location tasks which are physically provided and which require, in general, low or no-specific skills.[8]

What distinguishes the provision of labour services through digital platforms is the online services utilised. In general, there are three online categories providing labour services: (a) online freelancing platforms, which enable the access to high and specialised services; (b) microwork platforms, which match independent workers to mini-tasks; (c) platforms that mediate local and physical services (e.g., Uber, Task-Rabbit).

4.3 REGULATORY, POLICY CHALLENGES AND OPTIONS OF DIGITAL LABOUR PLATFORM

From a legal viewpoint, online platform companies have generally proven difficult to regulate, for a variety of reasons.

The online platform sector is constantly in evolution. The creation of new online platforms and the realisation of new business ideas are due to the influence of younger generations (the millennials) and to the emerging of a new labour market after the financial crisis of 2008. The rapidity in which the digital platforms and business progress has characterised this sector since its appearance, and this provokes difficulty in applying rules and regulations.[9]

In the last decade, we have noticed that online platform companies have started their activities without asking for official permission through administrative procedures. This has ignited a phenomenon characterised by a speedy increase of activities with a view to confronting the public authorities or regulators only afterwards. Consequently, the regulators would find themselves with a de facto situation characterised by a major influence gained by the digital platforms/companies and by a majority of customers, clients, enterprises and workers being more and more dependent on them, and hence supportive of the action of such digital platforms. Even though, they were not complying with the current administrative regulations.

An additional argument brought forward by the online platform companies is that they should not be treated as the traditional companies. They claim to represent the new as opposed to the old. Therefore, they need to be treated differently. In this regard, there are also public authorities who fear negative economic consequences if they do not please the request of these online platform companies.

At the same time, a good number of online platform companies try to make existing regulations, where possible, not applicable. Their main argument is that they consider themselves as mere intermediaries, and their main function is to bring people together. It is those people that they bring together who interact with each other and engage in the real economic activity. In this context, they consider themselves only as online platforms. In fact, many online platforms often stated in the agreements or

8. Pesole, A., et al., *Platform workers in Europe*, EUR 29275 EN, Luxembourg, Publications Office of the European Union, 2018.
9. Degryse, C., *Digitalisation of the economy and its impact on labour markets*, ETUI Working Paper 2, Brussels, 2016.

contracts they conclude with users that there is no employment relationship between the platform and the user. Moreover, it is specified that workers are independent contractors and that the platform as intermediary has no liability for anything related to the transaction between users that it has connected with each other.

Against this background, it is quite difficult for public authorities to intervene and make sure that the basic labour law is complied with. In addition, it is difficult for online platform workers to engage in a collective action with a view to engaging in collective bargaining with their online platforms. Even more difficult is to bring a court case by the platform workers.

At a closer look, the increased variety and complexity of the non-standard forms of employment facilitate the way the online platform workers are organised. Regulators, including labour courts, are often not sure which rules apply in some of these cases. This is also because it is difficult to apply the same rules of the pre-established categories of workers. In other words, it is objectively difficult to apply a 'one-size-fits-all' approach to the online platform workers. It seems that each case should be treated after a careful assessment. However, from the fact itself that many activities of the online platform companies by their nature are transnational, therefore creating complex questions about conflict of laws, one could wonder whether a sound response could be a transnational policy instead of, or in addition to, national ones.[10]

4.4 DIGITAL PLATFORM AND THE EMPLOYMENT RELATIONSHIP

The application of existing regulation, such as labour law and Occupational Safety and Health (OSH) legislation, is particularly challenged by the almost inevitably triangular (or multilateral) nature of the online platform work arrangements characterised by the temporary nature of the services provided and by the autonomy of the worker in carrying out the tasks, especially in terms of working place and organisation of working time.

It should be noted that a major feature of the employment relationship is the hierarchical power of employers over employees. The hierarchical power consists mainly of three interrelated elements: (1) the power to assign tasks and to give orders and directives to employees (directional power); (2) the power to monitor both the performance of such tasks and the compliance with same orders and directives (control power); (3) the power to sanction both the improper or negligent performance of the assigned tasks and disobedience to given orders and directives (disciplinary power).

In the online platform sector, the labour service provided introduces a triangular aspect into the relationship between the work provider and the work recipient. The online platform company brings together the person or entity who request work for them and the person or entity performing work following the request. It is only when the online platform is used within a company as a tool of work organisation or when the platform is used as end-user that the relationship is a dual one.

10. Dagino, E., *Labour and labour law in the time of the on-demand economy*, Revista Derecho Social y Empresa, 2016; *see also* Maselli, I., et al., *Five things we need to know about the on-demand economy*, CEPS Essay 21, 2016.

Also for online platform workers, the presence of hierarchical power in a working relationship is a distinctive element of employment in contrast to self-employment. However, the parcelisation of work activities due also to the use of information technology in business has challenged the traditional legal categories of working relationships based on such models as the blue-collar employee working in an assembly line of a big and vertically integrated company. New working practices testified now by the digital platform workers did not easily fit into either employment or self-employment. In particular, they embodied new forms of integration of work in business organisations whereby the coordination exerted by companies upon relevant workers did not match all the elements of hierarchical power as construed by legal experts and case law.

Today, significant problems of classification emerge with reference to a growing number of digital working activities in which directional power and hierarchical organisation were loosened, or in which at least they displayed new features. The risk is either an exclusion of the employment relationship deserving the legal protection afforded to the workers by the legislator from the scope of the employment, or an inclusion in the same scope of workers that did not deserve such protection. Neither exclusion nor inclusion could be determined taking into account the mere written or oral declaration of the parties, since labour courts must rely principally on the factual circumstances and characteristics of the relevant employment relationship.

The criteria of directional, organisational and disciplinary control of the relevant employer (in our case the digital platform) are difficult to depict in reality. Consequently, many digital platform workers are in a grey area between employment and self-employment, for their working relationships only partially fulfil the requirements of the employment relationship under the relevant laws. Such a situation is becoming a serious one, due to the increasing variety of digital platforms. In this regard, in many countries there is no protection or at least no significant protection for self-employees who operate in a grey area that is not covered by any legal structure, with no 'middle' legal category covering the area between employment and self-employment.[11]

A further element to be considered is the temporary nature of the work provided in the digital platform sector. Usually there is a distinction between the temporary nature of the relationship between the digital platform and the digital platform worker, on the one hand, and the temporary nature of the tasks performed, on the other hand. Yet the fact that many online platform working arrangements can be similar to open-ended contracts without any fixed-hours (much like the zero-hours contract), or to on-call contracts or casual employment in terms of their temporary and intermittent nature, does not resolve all the problems of application of labour law and OSH legislation. After all, these non-standard forms of employment continue to create problems for the application of labour legislation.[12]

11. Casale, G., *The employment relationship: A comparative overview*, Oxford, ILO, Geneva, Hart Publishing, 2011.
12. De Stefano, V., *The rise of the 'just-in-time workforce': On-demand work, crowdwork and labour protection in the 'gig-economy'*, ILO Geneva, ILO Conditions of Work and Employment Series 7, 2016.

When looking at the nature of the work performed by the digital platform workers, it is evident that they enjoy larger autonomy when carrying out their tasks; this makes online platform work most resemble self-employment, and this complicates the application of labour law. However, it should be noted that in reality such autonomy might be much constrained.[13]

For example, to ensure their efficient operations, some online platforms oblige or strongly incentivise platform workers to have a certain amount/timing of online presence. In certain cases, accounts may be deactivated because of 'prolonged' inactivity.

Most of the time, the worker is under pressure to complete the task within the agreed timeframe or sooner, in order to maintain high ratings and thus ensure future work, or even to be able to obtain payment for the task itself, and therefore may work excessive hours without taking necessary breaks.

In case, online platform work is the worker's main source of income, he will be incentivised to accept as many tasks as possible, especially where pay is low, leading to excessive working hours.

In most jurisdictions, the application of working time regulations applies to online platform workers if there is an employment relationship. However, autonomous workers who can determine the organisation of their own working time are not necessarily excluded from being in an employed relationship, European Union (EU) Directive 2003/88/EC on the organisation of working time says. In fact, while the Directive does allow many exceptions in the terms of working time limits for autonomous workers, through an extensive interpretation of the rules, such Directive also applies to them (Article 17(1)(a)). Indeed, this is an element of protection for all workers irrespective of the nature of their contract or the existence of an employment relationship.

4.5 POLICY OPTIONS IN RELATION TO DIGITAL LABOUR PLATFORMS

As regards policy options in relation to digital labour platforms, several different options exist.[14]

One option is to apply/extend existing regulations to online platform work, possibly by a wide interpretation of the concept of employment relationship. This is, in essence, a 'baseline' or 'status quo' approach, followed in most EU Member States. In fact, there are numerous cases before labour courts concerning the recognition of the employment status of online platform workers.

In this regard, it should be noted that court judgments vary from country to country, with courts arriving at different conclusions with regard to workers involved with the same platform (such as Uber), or in the same sector. Thus, for example, the

13. Tolodi-Signes, A., *The 'gig-economy': Employee, self-employed or the need for a special employment regulation?*, 23 Transfer, 2017.
14. Choudar, S.P., *The architecture of digital labour platforms: Policy recommendations on platform design for worker well-being*, Geneva, ILO, 2018.

British Employment Appeal Tribunal judged in 2017 that Uber drivers are workers/employees and should enjoy statutory employment rights (Uber's appeal of this decision is pending); the Spanish labour inspectorate of Valencia community ruled in late 2017 classifying Deliveroo riders as employees and not self-employed as the platform claimed, whereas in April 2018, the Italian Labour Tribunal of Turin rejected the claim by delivery service couriers of Foodora that they should be treated as employees. It was after at the appeal level that it was recognised that free riders of delivery goods had the right to the same economic treatment as those employed in the logistic sector, and hence covered by the sectoral national agreement of that sector. The appeal tribunal recognised this only for the period during which the workers were providing services. Finally, California's lawmakers ruled, in September 2019, that Uber and Lyft drivers should be considered as employees.

Another approach for better dealing with such an issue is to devise a new category, somewhere between the employment relationship and self-employment, to capture digital platform workers. In the United States, for example, there has been a call for the introduction of a new 'independent worker' status. Advocates of that midway approach tend to call for legislative intervention to regulate relationships that do not easily fit into the employed/self-employed dichotomy. These independent workers would occupy a middle ground between the existing categories of employee and independent contractor; the latter are workers who provide goods and services to multiple businesses without the expectation of a lasting work relationship.[15] This approach considers that, based on a set of governing principles to guide the assignment of benefits and protections to independent workers, businesses would provide specific benefits and protections without fully assuming the legal costs and risks of being employers.

In other legal jurisdictions, such as the United Kingdom, with the recognition of a third category the law accepts the existence of a certain degree of subordination for such a 'median' group of workers by extending specific protections that are typically recognised for the employment relationship. However, workers in this middle group usually receive minimal protections, especially related to social security and rarely they can bargain collectively. As a matter of fact, large parts of labour law do not apply to this third category of workers.

Another option is to apply the existing regulations dealing with the employment relationship to everyone, including the self-employed. This approach would essentially, in relation at least to some benefits and protections, abolish the binary divide between employment and self-employment. In particular, some authors argue for the introduction of a minimum pay for all (e.g., in the form of minimum fees for the self-employed).

An additional approach is to introduce new, sector-specific regulatory regimes for online platform workers, since they show new and diverse manifestations vis-à-vis traditional categories of workers. In a good number of jurisdictions, there already exists a 'special labour law' for different professions, adapted to the specific features and

15. Ratti, L., *Online platforms and crowdwork in Europe: A two-step approach to expanding agency work provisions?*, 38, Comparative Labour Law and Policy Journal, 2017.

necessities of that profession. The same principle could be applied for online platform work. In this context, it has been proposed that these regulations should imply the following: (i) the workers' freedom to establish their own working schedules and hours, while employers should be allowed to set a maximum, and regulation should establish an overall maximum (regardless of whether the hours are worked for the same platform or others); (ii) the workers' freedom to work for several platforms; (iii) the workers' limited liability for damages, including damage involving clients and to the platform's reputation; and (iv) the introduction of minimum wage.

4.6 DIGITAL PLATFORMS AND FUNDAMENTAL PRINCIPLES AND RIGHTS AT WORK

The ILO Declaration on Fundamental Principles and Rights at work of 1998 calls all the ILO Member States to ratify and apply the eight core Conventions.[16] The gig economy prompts serious concerns about discrimination. Virtual work can indeed have positive effects on this issue. For instance, avoiding 'real' personal contact and anonymity on the net can contribute to reducing risks of discrimination, but crowdwork platforms, for instance, allow providers to restrict the geographical areas from where workers can undertake tasks online. This possibility may allow cutting out entire countries, regions or communities from access to work, without any guarantee that the limit is only imposed for objective grounds such as language. Discriminating practices can therefore definitely occur also in virtual work. Similar considerations are true also for work on-demand via apps. While some arguments exist that this kind of work may contribute to combat discrimination, the risk of discrimination is by no means ruled out in this respect. Both explicit and implicit bias of customers may play an important role in deciding whether to accept a worker for a particular job and, above all, when reviewing its performance. Since customers' reviews may be essential in preserving the possibility to accede to the app and to future jobs, a biased review could entail a major detrimental effect for workers' employment opportunities. Once, again, given that these working practices are still relatively novel, these risks may evade existing mechanisms and policies against discrimination and they call for action in ensuring coverage and effectiveness of these instruments also with regard to the gig economy.

In addition to these specific risks, as mentioned above, workers in the gig economy may face some problems with reference to Fundamental Principles and Rights at Work that affect non-standard workers in general. Particular difficulties and gaps have been reported in this respect, with regard to all forms of non-standard work and it is impossible to recap them here.[17] Some of these hardships are however particularly significant for workers in the gig economy, namely those related with self-employment and misclassification of employment status. The ILO supervisory

16. Tapiola, K., *The teeth of the ILO – The impact of the 1998 ILO Declaration on Fundamentals Principles and Rights at Work*, ILO, Geneva, Fundamental Principles and Rights at Work Branch (Fundamentals), 2018.
17. *See*, for non-standard forms of employment, Report for discussion at the Meeting of Experts on Non-Standard Forms of Employment (Geneva, 16-19 February), ILO, Geneva, 2015.

bodies have expressed their concern in various occasions on the fact that when self-employed persons are generally excluded from the application of employment and labour laws, they might find themselves also excluded from regulation protecting fundamental principles and rights at work. As a consequence, workers in self-employment or misclassified workers may find themselves excluded or limited in their right to freedom of association and to collective bargaining, also because they could find themselves in breach of regulation such as competition and antitrust law. Moreover, they could be not included in the scope of regulation against child labour and discrimination. Given that the risks of misclassification are some of the chief labour issues in the gig economy, the very same problems may concern these forms of work. This renders the question of employment status all the more significant in terms of workers protection as not only issues concerning minimum wages and employment benefits but also access to fundamental labour and human rights are at stake.

4.7 CONCLUSIONS

The fact that nine of the world's top twenty largest companies are now digital ones, compared to one in twenty just a decade ago, illustrates well the rise of online business and work opportunities. The digital economy has emerged as a major feature of the future of work. The existing rules and practices in many countries are ill-adapted to deal with this new economic reality. As the data and measurements of this digital phenomenon are still too scarce to inform evidence-based policymaking, our attention should focus on areas where regulatory needs are becoming more obvious, not least in reaction to court judgments that highlight ambiguities and gaps with regard to the employment status of platform workers, their social protection and labour rights, cross-border issues (notably in taxation field and dispute resolution) and consumer protection in a broad sense.

In this regard, it should be noted that at the European level, the European Parliament suggested that policymakers at national level should address the following regulatory aspects relating to platform work:[18]

- minimum earning requirements;
- information exchange with platforms on workers' income for tax declaration purposes;
- arbitration-mediation services needed to better protect platform workers;
- extended coverage of collective agreements beyond the employee category;
- clarification of employment status of platform workers and social security provisions;
- redefinition of liability regimes (for damage to third parties) and qualification requirements (such as for health care and electrical services);
- review of existing labour market legislation;

18. European Parliament, *The situation of workers in the collaborative economy*, In-depth-Analysis, October 2016, available at: http://www.europarl.europa.eu/RegData/etudes/IDAN/2016/587316/IPOL_IDA(2016)587316_EN.pdf.

- possibility of creating individual professional activity accounts, so that social benefits.

Moreover, according to the ILO,[19] several policy options have to be taken into account with a view to further regulating the digital platform work. These include:

- tackling employment misclassification;
- ensuring the freedom of association and collective bargaining rights for crowdworkers;
- applying the minimum wage based on the workers' location and ensuring transparency in payments and fees determined by the platform;
- establishing clear and concise contracts, with fair rules to govern non-payment, to enable workers to decline tasks, and to cover costs of lost work in case of technical problems;
- informing workers about their customers' identity, the purpose of the work and, where appropriate, the reasons why they receive unfavourable ratings;
- establishing codes of conduct for all platform users and a system of client review;
- ensuring that workers can contest non-payment, negative evaluations, qualification test outcomes, accusations of code of conduct violations and account closures;
- presenting clear task instructions that are validated prior to the posting of any work;
- enabling workers to view and export their work and reputation history at any time;
- allowing workers to keep working for a client outside the platform arrangement;
- ensuring that platform operators adequately respond to worker communications; and
- ensuring that psychologically stressful tasks are clearly marked.

At the same time, more attention should be given to the reform of the national social security systems. The reform should be adapted to cover 'workers in all forms of employment' regardless of the type of contract, to use 'technology to simplify contribution and benefit payments' and to strengthen tax-financed mechanisms of social protection.

19. *See* Berg, J., et al., *Digital labour platforms and the future of work: Towards decent work in the online world*, ILO, Geneva, 2018.

CHAPTER 5

The Division of Labor in the Digital Era

Michele Boldrin

The so-called "Digital Era" is nothing but one more step (in fact: thousands of steps) in a, so far, endless process that is only very partially understood and quite difficult to manage. It is therefore not surprising to observe a widespread fear of its effects whenever it accelerates along directions previously not predictable, as it has done during the last few decades. My aim is that of shedding a little light, from an economic and historical perspective, on this complex and essentially unpredictable process.

Allow me a rather unusual introduction: I will list, telegraphically, the main conclusions of my analysis, and I will do so in the form of predictions for the future. The terminology "predictions for the future" is meant to be partially sarcastic: economic predictions are notoriously wrong with probability one, especially when concerned with the long run. On the other hand, the empirical regularities and historical trends considered here seem so unusually clear—and persistent over very many centuries—to make it too difficult resisting the temptation of saying that—with the caveats I will add later—they are unlikely to stop and will probably become even more pronounced in the future decades. More than predictions, the following propositions should be taken as logical implications of historical processes already well under way:

(1) In the Digital Era the worldwide division of labor will continue increasing, probably at a faster pace than the one observed during the last thirty years. This trend is already apparent for the top decile of the world distribution of skills. It is likely to extend further, probably to the top quartile, as the composition of the high ladders of professional specialization are determined by the rhythm at which Artificial Intelligence (AI) improves its ability to handle dispersed information to reduce transaction costs.

(2) As a consequence of this ongoing process, the composition of the labor force will become progressively more heterogeneous and the market for highly

qualified workers even more global than it already is. The status and working conditions of professional elites will be determined by worldwide market conditions, and the national labor markets will become, in this respect, progressively irrelevant.

(3) Most likely various measures of income and wealth inequality will continue to worsen unless new and dramatically different regulatory policies, fostering competition and greatly reducing monopoly power, will be adopted. Because these processes are global, nothing less than a global approach is likely to work.

(4) Accumulation of a flexible and versatile human capital, through both formal education and learning on the job, will become an absolute precondition to navigate the labor market. The big, unresolved, issue is: will it be enough? In other words: as the Digital Era progresses, will it still be true that studying hard should suffice to acquire a decent job and a good salary? Or are we not, instead, facing the danger that a "cognitive divide" will split our socio-economic systems between those that can profitably handle AI and those that cannot?

The rest of the chapter develops along the following logical steps:

(1) For any given state of the technology, both conflict and cooperation are always feasible options: the choice of how much time and resources we dedicate to the first versus the second is, at the end, determined by expected profitability. The interaction between a given distribution of tools and the opportunities of choosing between conflict and cooperation determines, in turn, a distribution of labor skills and, hence, of the various forms in which human effort is realized.

(2) The frequency distribution of the various forms of human labor determines the shares of social surplus appropriated by different people (or social classes, if you like) while, in turn, it generates incentives for altering those shares. Being an "innovator" is a particular form in which human labor realizes itself: an innovator aims at changing the existing state of things in her favor. In doing so, she still faces a choice between conflict and cooperation and, again, which one is chosen depends, almost always, on the expected return to the innovator herself.

(3) As a matter of historical facts, cooperation (of which technological change is the most important form) tends, per se, to increase the division of labor, i.e., to create new and more specialized professional figures, thereby increasing the complexity of the economic system. On the contrary, conflict has, historically, reduced the complexity of the socio-economic system and set back, sometimes greatly, the division of labor.

(4) Fast forward to the last half century to notice the dramatic increase in the level of informational complexity of the world we live in. This is matched by a parallel increase in the "fragmentation and specialization" of labor and in the rapid dissolution of those forms of aggregation of homogeneous workers that

have been the central focus of much analysis in the social sciences since their inception. Note, finally, that the growing demand for handling the informational burden is the driving force behind what we call the Digital Economy and AI and it dominates—as of now, at least—the other.

5.1 TECHNOLOGY, COOPERATION, CONFLICT

The state of the technology—as embodied in knowledge, machinery and institutions—determines the set of possible economic activities as well as the frequency distribution of the various forms in which the division of labor is realized at any point in time. With the apparently anodyne expression "frequency distribution of the various forms in which the division of labor is realized," I refer to what in other literatures and contexts is often called "class structure" or "social class/groups." This choice of language is not to ignore or hide the conflicts of interest, among individuals and groups, that any given state of the technology and of the institutional framework in which it is implemented, determine. Quite the opposite: I aim at stressing the dynamic nature of such conflicts and their being inextricably linked to the existence of economic cooperation among individuals and social groups. I intentionally use the plural in "conflicts" and "groups" to stress that we are not facing a simple (binary) social structure but a multidimensional and evolving one.

Given a technology, we always face opportunities for both conflict and cooperation. As a matter of fact, they sustain each other because any fight over the distribution of output requires the production of the latter in the first place. Conflict and cooperation always operate in tandem, with changing weights.

Such interaction generates the drivers of further technological change that, in turn, alters the division of labor and the forms in which conflict and cooperation may take place. Economic theory is unable to provide a linear chain of causation going from one element to the other as this is unlikely to exist. We think of the dynamic interactions among technology, institutions, composition of the labor force, division of labor and innovative activity as a form of co-dependence. There is no egg coming before the chicken or vice versa but, instead, a coevolution of these various elements, similar to that taking place in an ecosystem.

Economic theory is most useful when applied to given historical circumstances. Consider, then, any point in time during the recorded history of humanity (say: year 0 CE) and look at it from the point of view of the existing technology and the division of labor. What do we observe? From our current perspective we are struck with the limited number of capital goods available, to which there correspond an equally limited number of labor skills. When the number of tools that humans may use to produce useful things is limited so are the corresponding human skills: this is a case of what the economists call "complementarity between human capital and physical capital." One shovel employs one man if and only if he knows how to use it. Knowing everything about electrical engines will not, in those circumstances, make you more apt at digging the ground than knowing nothing about them.

This means that, from a practical perspective, useful knowledge cannot be defined in the abstract (where any kind of knowledge is somehow useful) but only in relation to the tools currently in existence. The same applies to tools: if you parachute a PC in a city of year 0 CE it will be completely useless as the complementary skills are absent. Technology, tools, skills and the division of labor coevolve.

Productive tools and useful knowledge develop together in a kind of dialectical symbiosis. In fact, historical observation and common sense suggest that a certain type of human capital (a skill, for short) and a certain type of physical capital (a tool, for short) are always generated together and disappear together. One can hardly think of a tool without its corresponding skill and vice versa: developing a tool and learning how to use it always go hand in hand. Historical observations indicate that a combination of tools and skills (T&S, henceforth) disappears only when one or more other combinations of T&S are introduced that are capable of "replacing" them. The sense in which "replacing" should be understood will be clarified soon. Note, finally, that the process is cumulative and dependent upon initial conditions[1] as new combinations of T&S can be created only using the already existing combinations of T&S.

For our purpose, these simple observations have three important implications. First, they clarify the sense in which Adam Smith's famous dictum according to which "the division of labor is limited by the extent of the market" should be intended analytically. Second, it suggests that an increase in productivity requires the creation of both new machinery and new skills, thereby making an increasing specialization of labor a *conditio sine qua non* of economic progress. Third, it suggests that the level of the division of labor among "creators" and "replicators" and the degree of competition within and among these two groups may greatly affect the pace and directions of technological change. Let us consider these three points in turn.

The available technology (in the sense of pairs of mutually adapted T&S) determines the space of configurations over which the division of labor *may* range at any given point in time. The extent of the market determines which, among the available pairs of T&S, will be adopted in the given circumstances. Because this is relevant for our subsequent discussion, I will use this opportunity to define my terminology and related concepts more precisely.

I call any given list of tools and skills that need to be used together to produce some output of either goods or services an *activity*.[2] An activity is, in principle, replicable at any scale: if n units of tool A and m units of skill B are all it takes to produce Y units of a certain good, then it is obvious that 2Y units can be obtained from 2n units of A and 2m units of B. This is what economists call *constant returns to scale*, and it is the main pathway to a particularly unattractive type of economic growth: the one in which more goods are obtained simply by using more units of the same kind of

1. This is often termed "path dependence" in the technical literature. For an introduction (with valuable references), *see* the voice on Wikipedia, here https://en.wikipedia.org/wiki/Path_dependence.
2. Mathematically, this is represented as the combination of a pair of vectors of real numbers, the inputs and the outputs. The associated mathematical techniques are known as Activity Analysis, but I will avoid touching on its technical aspects. The interested reader can consult, as an introduction, the proceedings of a famous conference, edited by Tjalling C. Koopmans in 1951.

tools and skills. This increases the size of the economy but does not allow for any increase in the average standard of living: you get more output because you work more and use more tools. There is no innovation here, and your standard of living do not improve: you just become "fatter." Historical evidence strongly suggests that "fat economies/societies" first stagnate and then collapse,[3] something we should never forget in evaluating the perils that technological change may bring upon us. The alternative could be worse.[4]

A *technology*, or *technology set*, is defined as the collection of all the activities that are *feasible* at a certain point in time. Notice that, for an activity to be feasible, there must exist at least some units of the tools and the skills that are listed among its inputs. Creating new tools and skills is also an activity: you need tools and innovators both to make discoveries and to teach the skills associated to the new machinery. Those that first create a new combination of T&S from the existing ones I call *innovators*, while those that make copies of them, once they became available, I call *replicators*. Again, abundant historical evidence suggests that, always and everywhere, innovators are a small fraction of the total population, replicators the majority.

When you successfully introduce new tools and skills you get more output for the same amount of effort, hence your standard of living improves. Note, though, that this may be due to either production of additional new goods and services or appropriation of goods and services already produced by other people. We call the first innovation a *cooperative innovation* and the second a *conflictual innovation*; both of them are implemented through the use of different activities, i.e., combinations of tools and skills. When you introduce a new method of warfare that allows you to plunder other people's fields you are enriching yourself by impoverishing other. When you produce goods with less effort than before and exchange them with goods produced by other you enrich yourself and, possibly, the other.

In conclusion: it is always the technology set that determines which division of labor is possible, while the extent of the market plays a role only in certain specific, but nowadays frequent, circumstances. When a technology set contains different and competing activities capable of producing the same good (or a set of highly substitutable ones) the "extent of the market" plays a role in determining which level of the division of labor is actually observed. This is because different activities, competing in the market for the same good, will have different costs depending on how large potential demand is. Quite often activities with a high minimum size are more efficient than the rest, but they need a large enough market to be profitable because they require a large cost to be paid upfront. This observation will become crucial in section 5.4,

3. *See*, e.g., Diamond [2005] for a relatively recent survey of the theme.
4. The kind of fattening growth just described appears to be, almost invariably, the one that politicians advocate through subsidies and "demand driven" fiscal policies. When the stress is purely on increasing investment in the technologies already in place and increasing employment in the type of skills that already exist the result is (at best) "fattening" without any increase in the standards of living. While this type of technologically stagnant growth increases the power of unions and lobbying groups (if we always use the same skills and work in the same place, we may as well create a bargaining coalition) thereby improving their chances at capturing a larger fraction of national output, it will not produce long-run growth in income per capita.

when discussing the role of AI in reducing transaction costs, enlarging markets and, under certain circumstances, polarizing the income and wealth distributions.

With these concepts in place it is straightforward to address the second point. Go back to the example of the economy of year 0 CE and recall that the division of labor is quite limited: farmers (free or enslaved), sailors, traders, construction workers and soldiers define about 99% of the population. Above them we have a small number of intellectuals and of political or religious leaders controlling most wealth and power. Notice, further, that this extremely limited division of labor was hardly due to the small size of the markets, as they were not small at all. Trade took place across the whole Mediterranean Sea in the West and over enormous swaths of land in East Asia. In both cases tens of millions of people were exchanging goods and services using trade routes tens of thousands of kilometers long, and the organizations making such trade possible were capturing a large share of the social surplus. The constraint was first and foremost technological: using the available tools and skills, managing the information needed to coordinate trade was extremely costly and the most profitable activity available was controlling the trade, i.e., controlling political and military power.

Cooperation was profitable—within both the Chinese and the Roman empire the standard of life was higher than elsewhere and ever before—but conflict was even more profitable given the available technology set. This is a prototype case of path dependency: things being what they are, people will do what is more convenient to them, which is not necessarily “optimal” according to some ex-post or moral criterion. Which leads to the third point: both the Roman and the Chinese societies of the time—in fact, and as far as we know, any other society existing around the world at the time—had a distribution of innovators versus replicators that was particularly skewed toward the latter. Most individuals were obedient replicators and, among innovators, most of the efforts were focused on conquering, controlling, dominating, taxing and other forms of extracting surplus already produced by others. Traders, inventors and, in general, what we would call today economic entrepreneurs were rare indeed.

5.2 INNOVATION AND ITS DETERMINANTS

If we apply the same tools of analysis to other societies at other points in history, a number of interesting regularities arise. For our limited purpose, we note the following:

(1) Conflict over income and wealth distributions is unavoidable, and it takes place in the most varied forms among single individuals, families, clans, cities, states, social groups, classes, or even random bands of very heterogeneous individuals (e.g., pirates).

(2) When cultural, institutional and technological circumstances are aligned to favor cooperative innovations over conflictual ones we observe periods of growth in income per capita together with increasing inequality. On the

contrary, when conflict dominates and becomes widespread the standard of living collapses for almost everybody while inequality is somewhat reduced.[5]

(3) The division of labor *and* the extent of the market are co-determined by the available technology. For the second (market size) the collection and management of information (be it through political, bureaucratic and military means or through private and commercial ones) is always of crucial importance. Technological advances that reduce such transaction costs regularly create a pressure to increase the extent of the market and to deepen the division of labor.

(4) When innovative individuals introduce a new activity, this takes place through the creation of new tools and of their related skills, thereby increasing the division of labor. Interestingly, this is true for both cooperative and conflictual activities.[6] The opportunities for replicating the new tools and acquiring the new skills that go with them become, therefore, the key determinant of the speed at which income inequality will increase: when replication is relatively easy income inequality does not increase as fast as when replication is difficult.

This brings us to the next question: what are the incentives to innovate in one direction or another, and how do innovations impact on the division of labor, social structure, and income inequality? These are extremely difficult questions that economic and historical research has not yet been able to answer convincingly and probably never will. Nevertheless, we do know a few things that may help our understanding of what is going on today.

In our analysis we have introduced two kinds of binary classifications and two paramount causal rules. Innovations may be oriented toward either cooperation (production and exchange) or conflict (appropriation and extortion). People distribute themselves between innovators and replicators depending on the opportunities that the technological and institutional environment offers, which also determines how easy it is to replicate or innovate. Innovations always increase the division of labor but conflictual innovations, when implemented successfully, tend to reduce it and simplify (i.e., render more homogeneous) the distribution of skills. Finally, the size of the market and, hence, the amount of surplus an innovation may provide depend greatly on the reduction of transaction and informational costs the technological set allows for.

This makes for a lot of possible combinations, which are descriptively useful but would be analytically cumbersome if we intended to use this framework to build a

5. For a recent beautiful illustration of this long-observed but scarcely examined fact, *see* Scheidel [2017].
6. Documenting this apparently apodictic statement would take too long. I will limit myself to notice that new techniques of warfare usually require new, specialized fighters and tools (think of the medieval *chevalier* or of the contemporary terrorist) and that the same is true of new techniques to administer taxation, levy duties and so on. Unions require union members and union leaders, and the latter is a new skill, and so on. That once conflict becomes the dominant activity it often leads to destruction of cooperative tools and skills and to a "simplification" (at a much lower technological and economic level) of society does not contradict the observation that innovation, per se, tends to increase the division of labor.

deterministic theory of what has happened or will happen in human history. Fortunately, this is not the case; in fact, what I plan to do is to show that the "prediction problem" (i.e., developing a theory of "what causes what" in the interaction between technological change and changes in the labor market and in the distribution of income) is essentially unresolvable. No matter which way we cut it, we are invariably forced to face a "chicken and egg paradox," in the following sense.

Call *state of the world* the combination of technologies and institutions in place at a point in time. Social and legal institutions, after all, are nothing but a particular set of technologies aimed at managing human interactions, including economic ones: limited partnership, to name one, did not come from the gods but was invented by a sequence of innovations that various people undertook and the rest accepted and replicated. There is no effective or even meaningful separation between the set of things that common parlance labels as "institutions" or "norms" and the set of things that common parlance labels as "technologies." Because, as we already saw, a technology is essentially a collection of activities and these, in turns, are determined by the frequency distribution of capital tools and associated labor skills, it should become obvious that there is no "first cause."

Technological, institutional and professional structures coevolve, and this puts enormous constraints both in our ability to read where the world is going and in altering its course by means of well-targeted policy interventions. In fact, as an example, there is no meaningful sense in which we can advocate a policy intervention to favor, for example, this or the other institutional change expecting it will "cause" a certain desired kind of technical innovation. As another example: imposing this or the other regulation/restriction on the labor market or in the composition of the labor force may sometimes foster a desired change in the technology set (i.e., the prohibition of slavery induced labor saving innovations in the agricultural sector) while, some other times, it will yield a result opposite the one desired—i.e., increasing the rigidity of the organized labor market in the manufacturing sector induced a vast decentralization of production and the creation of a value chain system dispersed around the globe. Like the famous road to hell, unintended consequences pave the history of policy interventions driven by good intentions and simplistic economic thinking.

Before moving on to the next step in my analysis, I will take a brief detour to consider a now popular approach aimed at understanding technological change and its impact on growth and income inequality. This line of research restricts its attention to institutions, taking them as given and as the "causes" behind economic growth or the lack of it thereof. It is argued that we can distinguish among institutional arrangements that are "inclusive" versus those that are "extractive."[7] The first, basically, allows innovators to retain a "decent" share of the social surplus they generate while the second extract "too much" from them. Consequently, the first produces good outcomes (economic growth, democracy and a relatively egalitarian distribution of income) while the second set of institutions bring about bad outcomes (poverty and stagnation, income inequality and social conflict). There are many obvious examples, from one

7. The leading book pushing this line of analysis is Acemoglu and Robinson [2012].

side or the other, that could be used to question the empirical relevance of such a causal model, but here I will stick to the theoretical aspects as they may help us understanding the difficulties we encounter in modeling the impact of the Digital Era on the organization of labor.

Note first that the binary classification (inclusive versus extractive) is not defined *a priori* but after the fact: even the dictatorial systems of contemporary China or Pinochet's Chile could be inclusive, to the extent they may (as they did) produce economic growth that, eventually, may (in one case it did) lead to democracy and a less unequal distribution of income. The key point, though, is that institutions are never a datum from a historical point of view. The communal arrangements of Northern Italian cities in the late Middle Ages were not given but grew, organically, from different (in fact feudal and ecclesiastic) institutions as the technologies for craftsmanship and trade developed. There is no meaningful sense in which one can say "Venice grew rich through trade because it had a republican government" as Venetian trade and its republican (so to speak) form of government coevolved over many centuries. Similarly, one cannot say that German engineering and manufacturing powerhouse was "caused" by the democratic constitution imposed upon Germany after WWII because, in the same country, only fifty years earlier an even more powerful (relative to the rest of the world) manufacturing sector developed under completely different, in fact opposite, institutions.

The historical examples can continue forever because the internal logic of the argument is fraught: the boundary between "institutions" and "technologies" is, as already pointed out, totally ill defined. A given set of production activities requires another specific set of legal activities and organizational rules and the two cannot even be conceived in separation. This is a crucial point that I would like to be understood as it stresses that we cannot even think to manage the technological and behavioral changes brought about by the Digital Era in the absence of institutional and normative changes. Even property rights are highly dependent on the state of the technology and vice versa: eminent domain makes no sense absent a technology making public transportation, sewage, and other public utility networks feasible and useful.

Among other things, this set of theoretical and historical observations implies that innovations are always local and incremental and that their global impact is the outcome of a complex process of distributed diffusion and adaptation, which is, essentially, unpredictable. The PC did not bring about the World Wide Web overnight, even less everywhere; the latter did not make e-commerce and big-data collection and management immediately feasible and profitable; home robots managed from an app on the cell phone were not predictable outcomes of the first Motorola portable phone, and so on and so forth. A long and multidimensional sequence of other technological and institutional innovations took place during the process, unexpected complementarities emerged and legal frameworks were adapted. Pretending that the current configuration of our information and transaction-cost-reduction technology will be stable during the next decade and that we can design policy instruments leading it where we like is simply a bad mistake.

5.3 LABOR FRAGMENTATION VERSUS SOCIAL HOMOGENIZATION

Historical analysis supports the, admittedly vague, predictions of economic theory: cooperative innovations increase the division of labor which, almost always, benefits some groups of individuals more than other. This, in turn, leads to conflict (and conflictual innovations) as the people that are either gaining less or even losing from technological change react by trying to appropriate a larger share of the new pie. Given the current technological set people, either individually or in organized groups, will try to improve their standard of living, and this leads to a new technology or to a new institutional setting which may be more conflictual or more cooperative than the previous one. This defines a never ending game of winners and losers and, because the winners have apparently always been more than the losers, one may have the impression that technological change always plays against the "weak" and, as a consequence, it is always the same "social group" that remains on top.

These conclusions are so patently at odds with facts that I will not bother to discuss them: just compare the standard of living of the median citizen of Europe nowadays with that of the top 1 % of the United Kingdom (then the richest country in the world) in the middle of the nineteenth century. What I will focus upon, instead, is the idea that technological change always keeps the same people on top making social mobility difficult or even impossible. I intend to do this because—while this statement has not even remotely been true for the last few centuries—it may, in a sense I will clarify in section 5.4, become truer and trues in the future.

Before getting to that point let me go back to our four-fold partition: conflict versus cooperation, innovation versus replication, plus the issue of reducing transaction/information costs. Non-economists may find the latter reference obscure, hence, I will briefly clarify its relevance. A theoretical question often asked in economics[8] is the following: why do not we do everything through market transactions in which single individuals trade everything, including even the smallest contributions to the production and trading processes? Why do we have organizations such as cooperatives, partnerships, limited liability companies and so on that work under a command and control mechanism with a decision-maker on the top that gives orders, pays for services and take the residual risk? Why do we not contract out everything instead of hiring? Let me quote from Wikipedia,[9] which provides a good summary of the issue:

> there are ... transaction costs to using the market; the cost of obtaining a good or service via the market is actually more than just the price of the good. Other costs, including search and information costs, bargaining costs, keeping trade secrets, and policing and enforcement costs, can all potentially add to the cost of procuring something via the market. This suggests that firms will arise when they can arrange to produce what they need internally and somehow avoid these costs.

8. The standard initial reference on this topic is Ronald Coase [1937]. The literature on the topic is plain gigantic.
9. *See* Wikipedia https://en.wikipedia.org/wiki/The_Nature_of_the_Firm.

> There is a natural limit to what can be produced internally, however. ... The size of the firm is a result of finding an optimal balance between the competing tendencies of the costs outlined above.
>
> [Most relevant in this trade-off are the following elements:
>
> - Cost of information and coordination
> - Cost of transportation of components and final products
> - Bargaining power in the factor and output markets].

What I need the reader to notice here is that, basically, the lower information and transaction costs internal to the firm are, the larger will be the size of the firm while, on the opposite side, the lower those costs while trading on the market are, the smaller will be the size of the firm. Innovations may go either way, and there is nothing in either social theory, engineering or even in the psychological studies of innovative behavior capable of telling us when one or the other will dominate. As a matter of fact, we are facing a set of possible outcomes that is essentially unpredictable. Hence, let us see if our super-simplified framework of analysis may lead us somewhere near the Digital Era.

Innovators will capture a large share of the social surplus from their innovations, (call them competitive rents) and they can be very large: just think of the enormous rents accruing to Google because nobody has been able to invent a search algorithm better than theirs. Replicators will slowly reduce those rents to the extent that they can independently imitate the innovation and compete with the innovators. When this is either too difficult or legally impossible, replicators will have only the option of working for the innovator in her "firm." I understand this may sound like Mickey Mouse economics, but I invite the reader to think at the stylized story I am telling as if it replicated thousands of times in the economy. What we have is a relatively small number of innovators and a much larger number of replicators that may or may not succeed in competing with them by imitating and adopting their innovation or a variation of it.

When replication is feasible, and competition is established two consequences are likely: the price of the commodity drops and income inequality does not increase abnormally. These two consequences are related: competition reduces the mark-up that innovators can charge and this reduces both the market price of the good and the rents accruing to the innovator. When replication is either not feasible or very difficult the opposite happens: mark-ups remain high, rents increase, prices do not decrease equally fast and wealth inequality grows.

Consider now the second binary partition, the one between conflictual and cooperative innovations. In the first case, when replication and competition are implemented, the incentives to introduce new technologies for social conflict, i.e., for capturing part of the rents with means other than trading, are small. The opposite is true when there is little competition on the market and rents are high: in this case, taxing or expropriating them away with political innovations is much more attractive.

Finally, let us factor in the issue of transaction costs as briefly outlined above: technological and institutional innovations may either favor an increase in the size of the firms or create incentive for decentralizing production in smaller specialized units while retaining control of the overall process in the hands of the innovators. Also in this case, it is hard to establish an *a-priori* rule enabling us to make predictions: that, say, efficient car factories had to employ tens of thousands of homogenous workers in the 1950s-1980s period, while successful fashion companies may directly employ only a few hundreds nowadays is certainly a fact but hardly one about which we can theorize much.

To this large variety of possible combinations let us add a further, final, observation: when the technology favors the creation of large firms the structure of the labor market tends to simplify, and relatively homogenous socio-economic groups emerge. While the factory workers of the twentieth century may come immediately to mind, it is worth pointing out that a similar simplification of the labor market (and of social dichotomies) also characterized the Middle Age until the technologies for trading and city building did not begin to tear apart the feudal system.

The nineteenth and twentieth centuries' city, filled with commercial, professional and artisan activities, is probably the best known example of a very heterogenous labor force with a variety of professional skills and a very highly developed division of labor coordinated not within the firm (transaction and information cost would have been too high, given the available technology) but through markets. Just shopping for groceries would require visiting four or five specialized stores, and that number could increase substantially if personal services had to be added. Now compare that arrangement with, in order, supermarket, shopping malls, large megastores and online shopping. The trend is clear: as technological change allows for a cheaper management of information and a reduction in transportation and transaction costs, the size of the company increases, and the heterogeneity of the labor force decreases. Amazon is the iconic company seating, for the time being, at the pinnacle of this trajectory.

5.4 DOES THE DIGITAL ECONOMY IMPLY POLARIZATION?

What is the Digital Economy, then, if not yet another way of handling information and coordinating search? These is no doubt it is all that but, in fact, it is also something else, which is what makes the future much more uncertain than it would be otherwise. If all there was to the Digital Era were Amazon, Uber and Airbnb, one would not have to spend too much time in understanding the process. This is because in these and in many other standard examples, what technological change is doing is, simply, easing the searching and matching between buyers and sellers and allowing sellers to greatly reduce transaction costs by handling the distribution of goods and services at an unprecedented and highly efficient scale. But there is more, which we will now briefly consider.

The truly novel aspect of the Digital Era is the following: the reduction in the cost of information processing does not end at search and matching in the markets but extends, more and more, to tools handling and decision-making at the production level, i.e., to the internal operation of the firm. This is the true novelty we are facing, the long-run implications of which we find so hard to fully understand. One way of summarizing the problem is the following. While the AI empowering Uber or Amazon is relatively easy to model (reduction of search costs) the one powering robots, financial applications and medical machinery (just to give a few examples) seems to have a potential for disrupting the current modes of production unforeseeable only a couple of decades ago.

Innovation has always been labor saving: labor is scarce and costly, the incentive to save on it is always there. Ideally, any entrepreneur would like to run a business where machines did everything, and she could just dedicate her time to program them. But during the almost three centuries of the machine revolution (factories and plants) what technological progress did was to replace human effort and physical fatigue with the work of tools powered by non-animal energy. A lot of effort was put into making those sources of non-animal energy more and more efficient, i.e., less costly. This is an incomplete and imprecise description, but I trust it will suffice: human brains were still needed to handle the tools that allowed the replacement of brute human labor with skilled human labor. What the robotized machine does is to replace the human brain with a skilled (i.e., properly programmed) machine.

True: someone has to program the machine and someone has to write the code making AI work and someone must also collect the data (big data) that the AI program processes to behave smartly. Hence, in this sense, some human effort, somewhere, still plays a role. Hence, while the purely theoretical model fails to show a discontinuity—in the Digital Era we are, after all, just trying to replace human effort with some kind of machinery created by other humans—and the difference can still be classified as quantitative, one has the strong impression that it may become qualitative. A suitable metaphor is the one in which you replace workers at a lower step of the ladder with machines that are managed by technician at a higher step and then you replace the technicians with machines managed by engineer at a higher step and so on and so forth. You move up the ladder toward its ends, where a super-engineer is standing, with a smile on her face, programming everything below her.

The issue is: at which step of that ladder are we now and how fast will we move upward? The answer is: we do not know. An honest look at the world around us shows that we are still quite far from that last step where the super-engineer is standing. In our world billions of people are still working for a living using rather primitive tools; in the meanwhile, with the human time that technological progress is freeing we are inventing new jobs, new needs, new ways of making a living and feeling useful. How many psychologists were there fifty years ago and how many people would buy psychological therapy on the market? Incredibly fewer compared to today, not to speak of singers, artists, cooks, or travel guides, and so on and so forth. This is the optimistic view, and there is nothing in either history, engineering, economic theory or the neurosciences telling us that this may not be our future, one in which most of us earn a decent living and live a full life by providing the kind of creative services that AI will never be able to provide. Or, will it?

We do not know the answer and, even if globally the issue can still be placed in the remote future, it looks as incredibly actual in the most advanced countries. This brings our discussion to the last delicate point that is concerned with the degree of complexity of the dynamic interactions between innovators and replicators in the Digital Era. Innovative economic activities are characterized, today, by an increasing degree of complexity, which is, first and foremost, informational and computational. The structure of what is commonly called the "value chain" has become more organizationally fragmented or dispersed but also more informationally connected. As the network structure becomes denser and multidimensional, to know "who does what" and "who needs what" becomes progressively more demanding. Which also implies that, at any given point in time, a digital innovation taking place in some remote corner of the globe may impact, i.e., render obsolete, your skills here and now. This increasing degree of uncertainty needs to be handled by insurance mechanisms, either public or private, that we have not yet even started thinking about. If the reader had the impression that, in the last few lines, I am advocating the need for rethinking the whole structure of our welfare state, she got it right.

Increasing complexity and heterogeneity breeds increasing uncertainty and increasing connectivity means that remote perturbations may have quick effect at very long distances: if a bio-engineering innovation could allow Chilean wine makers to imitate the taste of Barolo (not such a far-fetched hypothesis as it may sound) a small event taking place on the other side of the globe would cause a major socio-economic crisis in Piedmont. There is no reasonable sense in which we can continue thinking of the frequency distribution of labor skills as stable over time: it may be so "on average," but it may change locally any time. This, as far as I know, is unprecedented.

There is a second, more delicate aspect that has to do with innovators and replicators. For a long time - in fact from the start of civilization until about half a century ago - most innovations were replicable and usable by most human beings with average cognitive abilities and education. Certainly, most people could not manage or build a nuclear reactor but most people, if properly trained, could work in it or in a number of advanced manufacturing plants. Advanced technology has never been for everyone, but it has always been exploitable by a large enough share of the population, if properly trained. I am not sure one can still say the same for the frontier technologies of the Digital Era.

A growing amount of evidence from advanced countries shows that—no matter how much one invests in formal education and no matter how well functioning the national education system is—a growing share of the population becomes, at best, a passive and incompetent user of the products of the digital technology. Furthermore, the extension of intellectual property protection is making it more difficult to replicate digital innovations thereby preventing competition from playing its role in reducing rents and redistributing the social gains of innovations to everyone through a price reduction. Finally, because of the reduction in information and transaction costs discussed above, the revenue size of the typical digital firm is rapidly becoming unusually large worldwide. A quick look at the surprising recent events surrounding the company TikTok will serve as a paradigmatic example of these claims.

I am not sure the gloom picture I just described will be realized, as the positive and countervailing possibilities described earlier may well dominate in the long run. Still, the building blocks of an unprecedented polarization in the labor market and in the distribution of income and wealth worldwide are in the picture and cannot be ignored.

5.5 CONCLUSION

There is not much to add, in the mode of a conclusion, to what I have already stated and summarized in the introduction. I have tried to illustrate the driving forces of technological innovations in the long run and concluded that, in the Digital Era, something new may be happening.

A graphic way of summarizing it is to say, rather brutally, that while, for many centuries, technical change has focused on replacing human muscles with mechanical tools and human intelligence, we have now entered a phase in which technical change aims at replacing human cognitive power with tools and AI and that the latter may not be replicable and manageable by most humans. This may be the source of a Digital Divide that, metaphorically, one is tempted to associate to the physical divide separating, more than a thousand years ago, those standing on a horse and branding a sword from those who could not do it. If this will bring about a similar polarization of society is hard to say: the complexity and human richness of our societies is such that any simplistic comparison to the early Middle Ages may be plainly absurd. Still, some of the elements are there, and it is not clear, as of now, which kind of policy actions may be undertaken to reduce the risk that such a divide will soon exist.

What is certain is that we will no longer face a stable class and income structure but a continuously changing frequency distribution of different forms of labor with an inner tendency to polarization along the cognitive divide. The traditional presumption, always realized so far, that technological change will create more and better jobs than those it eliminates is not as warranted as one would like it to be.

BIBLIOGRAPHY

Acemoglu, Daron and James Robinson [2012] *Why Nations Fail*, Crown Publishing Group, New York.

Coase, Ronals [1937] "The Nature of the Firm," *Economica*, 4(16): 386-405.

Diamond, Jareed [2005] *Collapse: How Societies Choose to Fail or Succeed*, Penguin Books, London and New York.

Koopmans, Tjalling C. [1951] *Activity Analysis of Production and Allocation*, Wiley, New York.

Scheidel, Walter [2017] *The Great Leveler: Violence and the History of Inequality from the Stone Age to the Twenty-First Century*, Princeton University Press, Princeton NJ.

CHAPTER 6

For a Human-Centred Approach to the Future of Work

Philip Jennings

'It was the winter of despair, it was the spring of hope' appeared in the opening lines of Charles Dickens novel *A Tale of Two Cities*, which was published 160 years ago. As the International Labour Organization (ILO) marks the centenary of its founding in 1919 those words echo again as we consider the current and future world of work. The anchor to the ILO Centenary celebrations is the publication today of the report of the ILO Global Commission on the Future of Work, titled *Work for a Brighter Future*. Chaired by Swedish Prime Minister Stefan Lofven and South African President Cyril Ramaphosa, the twenty-seven Commissioners over a fifteen-month period have produced a report which refers to the despair facing millions of workers and concludes that for the 'spring of hope' to materialise drastic and comprehensive policy changes are required.

The publication of the report is intended to trigger significant policy change. To avoid any risk of neglect, the Commission calls for every Member State of the ILO to get national tripartite talks underway to thrash out a national action plan on the implementation of the report's recommendations. The Commission has left no room for excuses with calls to action to governments, business and unions. This chapter intends to reflect the tone and content of the Global Commission's work whose recommendations are clear. There is no hiding behind the excuse of their not being a plan to ensure that people are not left behind.

6.1 THE URGENCY OF NOW

Martin Luther King said 'We are faced with the fact that tomorrow is today. We are confronted with the urgency of now'. There is nothing complacent in the Commission's message that it is not sending a reassuring message to the world. The report rejects business as usual. It calls for a change in the rules to deliver a reinvigorated social contract. It recognises that trade unions have a key role to play, that our ideas are part of the solution, that we are not legacy organisations and that we are key contributors to building a new social contract. The report sends a warning to the political and business world that unless we make readjustments required to bring about a reinvigorated social contract, then economic and social division will grow. The despair of economic insecurity brings with it the danger that this will further fuel the populist wave.

As the report states, 'The gap between the wealthy and everyone else is widening ... many of our societies are becoming more unequal ... millions of workers are disenfranchised, deprived of fundamental rights and unable to make their voices heard ... rising insecurity and uncertainty fuel isolationism and populism'.

The frustration with a world that seems to have turned its back on social and economic progress for workers is captured as follows: 'without decisive action we will be sleepwalking into a world that widens inequality, increases uncertainty and reinforces exclusion, with destructive political, social and economic repercussions'. The report sends a very clear and uncompromising message without social justice lasting peace and stability is endangered.

6.2 LABOUR IS NOT A COMMODITY

The starting point for future policy is a look into the past and the consensus that the ILO's Founding Constitution '[r]emains the most ambitious global social contract in history', and that as the remarkable 1944 Declaration of Philadelphia, which marked the post war direction of the ILO, stated 'Labour is not a commodity'. In doing so, the Commission is accepting that this characterises the world of labour today.

The intents of the Constitution and Declaration have lost none of their power in this changing world of work which is challenged by the disruption of technology, gender inequality, the ravages of climate change, the power of global business forces, a 'market rules' ideology, demographic change and underlying unfairness and inequality.

The Commission does not pull its punches. Labour has become a commodity, and the rights to pursue their material well being and spiritual development in conditions of freedom and dignity, economic insecurity and equal opportunity are not being adequately met today.

The Commission states 'that the absence of a social contract is to the detriment of all' and calls for a new approach 'that puts people and the work they do at the centre of public policy and business practice: a human centered agenda for the future of work'.

It takes a swipe at Big Tech and the new digital platform business models, which 'could create 19th century working practices and future generations of digital day labourers'.

The Commission has another vision which is aimed at 'Renewing the democratic underpinnings of our Labour markets and strengthening social dialogue, giving everyone a voice in changing shaping the changes underway and the quality of their working lives'. The 'Uberisation' business models, built on the fact that the denial of an employment relationship is the commodification of labour, was a point the Union Commissioners raised, and we welcome the Commission's observation that delivering a social contract 'means guaranteeing fundamental rights at work, ensuring that ALL workers are afforded adequate Labour protection and actively managing technology to ensure decent work'.

6.3 THE FRAMEWORK

The report recommendations identify three pillars of action: investing in people's capabilities, investing in the institutions of work and investing in decent and sustainable work. The agenda marks a change in direction and demands that the world of work become central of political decision-making on the future functioning of our economies. It realises that neither leaving matters to market forces nor a continuation of priority to shareholder returns, short termism and an absence of broader stakeholder presence in business decision-making will provide adequate solutions.

6.4 SO LET US SUMMARIZE SOME OF THE KEY POLICIES

Investing in people's capabilities calls for an entitlement to lifelong learning, to reconfigure the system to provide workers with the time and financial they need to learn, to introduce employment insurance to allow workers to take paid leave to engage in training and digital training possibilities to be anchored in access to universal quality education, delivered by well-trained and well-paid teachers.

It recognises that people have to be supported through transitions with the help of active labour market policies and that, in each sector of the economy, unions and employers should be negotiating transition agreements to provide for 'early intervention, counselling and financial support'. In the disruptive transitions ahead it underlines that 'collective bargaining plays a key role in building resilience and adaptation'.

The report underlines that we need a transformative agenda for gender equality and states that governments should guarantee universal social protection for all workers from birth to old age. Social protection must cover all workers including the self-employed. The report calls for continued protection for workers in all job circumstances.

6.5 UNIVERSAL LABOUR GUARANTEE FOR ALL

The report is clear that there has been a neglect of the institutions of work which it sees as 'the building blocks of just societies and includes laws, regulations, employment contracts, employers and worker organisations, collective agreements and Labour inspection'.

The Commission makes a welcome call to strengthen and revitalise institutions governing work which is considered a 'public good'.

The Commission recommends the establishment of a Universal Labour Guarantee (ULG) to apply to all workers whatever be their contractual arrangements or employment status. The ULG has to include fundamental rights and basic working conditions.

The ULG has to include fundamental rights and basic working conditions, which involves health and safety at work.

The Commission calls for more time sovereignty, the right to digitally disconnect, measures to provide workers with a guaranteed and predictable number of hours, work scruples to be negotiated and premium pay for those working inconvenient hours.

6.6 COLLECTIVE BARGAINING: THE CRITICAL COMPONENT

Collective representation through social dialogue is a public good that 'lies at the heart of democracy'. The core of the policy is the recognition that collective bargaining is a fundamental right and powerful tool for economic success and social equity.

The Commission recognises that the growth in income inequality can be addressed by investing in wage setting institutions 'where current policies have fallen short', and wage policies need to be 'revitalised, through appropriate statutory minimum and collectively bargained wages'. 'All workers must enjoy freedom of association' and the effective recognition of collective bargaining.

6.7 IT IS NOT JUST THE TECHNOLOGY

The report calls for business models to be aligned to a human centred agenda for the future of work. In effect it puts a question to old employers, and particularly to the new, to put their 'social contract' house in order, to build respect for fundamentals, build a social dialogue, recognise the right of workers to join unions and negotiate.

The Commission develops a digital social contract with several elements to put an end to gender bias in artificial intelligence (AI) where 'humans are in command', develops regulations to ensure data privacy, its use and algorithmic accountability, and welcomes attempts by authorities to examine business concentration consequences of Big Tech.

6.8 PLATFORM REGULATION

The Commission breaks new ground with the recommendation to develop an international governance system for digital labour platform that sets and requires platforms to respect minimum rights and protections and looks to the 2006 Maritime Convention as a model. It reaffirms that work is work and that the employment relationship is at the heart of our labour laws and protections. It calls time on those who seek to manipulate laws and misclassification workers.

6.9 JOBS FOR TOMORROW

The report ties its recommendations with the 2030 Sustainable Development Agenda and calls for all the key global institutions from the International Monetary Fund (IMF) and World Bank to recognise the leadership role of the ILO and to align their policies with a human centred agenda.

The report identifies the areas where there are rich job creating opportunities where the world needs to invest in care, mitigation of climate change, rural and agriculture, physical, digital and social infrastructures which includes 'high quality public services'.

Tens of millions of jobs stand to be created.

The report suggests urgent action to transform informal to formal work.

It calls for a change in the way businesses are run, it is time for workers on the board and an end to short termism. It says to governments to go beyond gross domestic product (GDP) in the measurement of economic progress to include unpaid work, to capture externalities of economic activities of environmental degradation and health-care costs, to include indicators of distributional and equity from household income, access to education, health and housing.

6.10 ILO AS NEEDED NOW

The report maps out an optimistic future for the ILO. It admits that the world of work is not prepared to deal with the new forces changing the world of work. They imply an absence of counteraction. The ILO should continue its standard setting role, bolster tripartisme, be the centre of policy to shape the future of work that we want, establish an innovation lab to examine how to apply new tools and create an expert monitoring group to analyse trends and contribute to policy development.

The call for transition agreements in economic sectors provides new opportunities for the ILO sector programme and time to invest also in cross-border dialogue and its promotion in supply chains.

In conclusion there are many constructive avenues to pursue. It is important that unions demand involvement in the elaboration of national action plans. There is much in this report to help people through the coming transformation. The workers groups also have the task to work in the governing body on the content of a centenary declaration for adoption at the centenary ILO in June.

About 160 years ago Dickens wrote in the same *A Tale of Two Cities*: 'It was the best of times, it was the worst of times, … it was the spring of hope, it was the winter of despair'. The Commission's report looks to create the best of times and a spring of hope.

Unions everywhere! Let us make it happen.

CHAPTER 7

Technological Change, Institutions, and the Labour Market

Luigi Salvati & Pasquale Tridico

Since its inception as an autonomous science, political economy has always been interested in the way technology affects economic systems. Since the era of the classical economists, it was soon clear that technological innovations could have disruptive effects on the supply side. By changing the technical conditions of production, some innovations - also thanks to the simultaneous presence of institutional elements, think of the movement of enclosures in England at the dawn of the Industrial Revolution - made it possible to obtain increase in production that were often unthinkable before their introduction. This, in turn, favoured the increase of that *surplus*, the object of all the theories of classical economists, which was at the basis of the capital accumulation process. In turn, the accumulation of capital, certainly in a non-mechanical, but still often decisive way, favoured further innovations. However, the same classical economists, well aware of the conflicting nature of an economic system based on the sharing of the surplus between different social classes, warned, not long after the Industrial Revolution, about the negative consequences that technological progress, in particular in the form of the introduction of machines in industrial plants and in agriculture, could have had for some layers of the population, above all for the working class.

The dual nature of technological progress (as an opportunity and as a potentially destabilizing factor) has accompanied the development of social sciences and, in particular, of political economy to date. Therefore, in an era of great technological changes and innovations that advance at extremely rapid rates, it becomes paramount to study how technology influences the relationships between social classes and the methods of production.

As stated by Brynjolfsson and McAfee (2011, 2014), we are currently facing a scenario of *exponential acceleration*, especially from the 2000s onward, with the development of the so-called digital revolution. This revolution is due especially to the progress in information and communications technology (ICT), made possible by the working of the so-called Moore's law. This famous law (Moore, 1965) notoriously states that the number of transistors in a dense integrated circuit roughly doubles about every two years: in other terms, overall processing power for computers doubles about every eighteen months (in an exponential or geometrical fashion).

However, ICT progress is not only a matter of processing power. In the last years, the expansion of the sector was mainly led by the creation of new immaterial goods, also made possible and fostered by the aforementioned increase in processing power and by the ubiquitous diffusion of portable devices, constantly connected to the internet. The exponential increase in the consumption and the production of these goods, i.e., *digital* goods, is a striking example of the effects that a change in technology can exert on the economic and social structure of societies.

Two almost unprecedented (at least on such a large-scale dimension) features characterize all these goods, like information, media, communication and social networks: non-rivalry in consumption and close-to-zero marginal costs of reproduction. In particular, user generated contents are essentially free for firms such as YouTube, Wikipedia, Facebook, Instagram and so on and so forth. Moreover, the goods 'produced' by digital firms are price-free for their users (think about free communication digital services as Skype or Whatsapp), who have experienced a surge in their utility as consumers.

These innovations can represent a great opportunity for growth and prosperity, but they may also bring with them negative effects. When new technologies are particularly profitable, they may also bring to an increase in inequalities between those who are skilled enough in the abilities that are necessary to take advantage of the new technological paradigm, on the one hand, and those who have skills that are more traditional and unskilled workers, on the other one.

In this scenario, inequalities also arise between countries; while some countries are thriving, by taking advantage of the possibilities offered by the new technologies, some seem unable to keep up with these innovations. Among the latter, Italy shows a particularly sluggish dynamics of productivity and economic growth, accompanied by an increase in income and wealth inequality.

In our survey, we shall concentrate on the following issues:

(1) Do ICT have an impact on labour productivity?
(2) Do ICT destroy employment? (i.e.: does a negative impact on employment levels exist?)
(3) Do ICT change labour forces' composition? If yes, in which way?
(4) By focusing on the case of Italy, in addition to the impact on employment levels or on labour forces' composition, which effects does technology exert on wages?
(5) Which future scenarios could emerge and what kind of policy implications can we draw?

7.1 THE IMPACT OF ICT PROGRESS ON LABOUR PRODUCTIVITY: DOES TECHNOLOGICAL PROGRESS DESTROY JOBS?

The impact of ICT progress on the dynamics of labour productivity is not immediate. Data shows that in the USA productivity growth started declining since 1973. This evidence brought some scholars to question the relevance of computer-based technological progress in explaining labour productivity growth. As Solow put it in a 1987 book review:[1] 'You can see the computer age everywhere but in the productivity statistics'. This statement would later become famous as the 'Solow paradox'. A representation of the dynamics of the GDP per hour worked in G7 countries can be found in Figure 7.1.

Figure 7.1 GDP per Hour Worked in G7 Countries – Constant Prices – Annual Growth

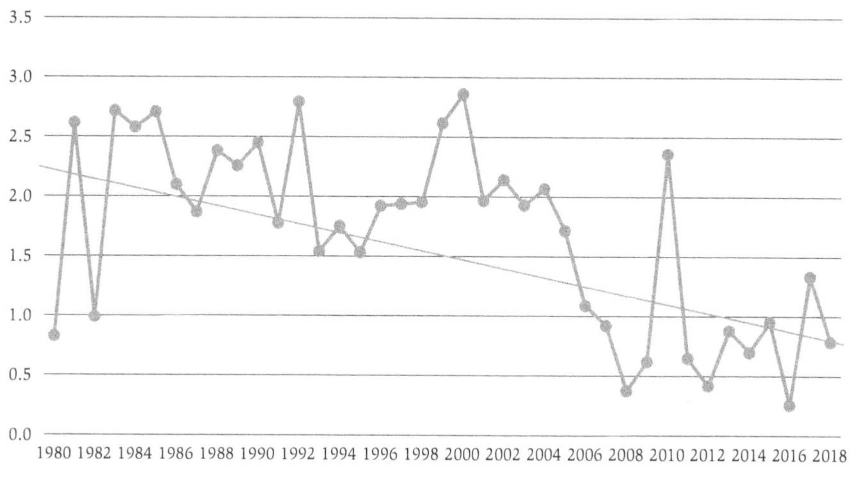

Source: OECD. Data extracted on 15 January 2020 17:00 from OECD.Stat.

However, since the middle 1990s, a boom in labour productivity began to take place, and it was steadily increasing until the 2007-2008 economic crisis. Brynjolfsson and McAfee (2014) suggest that the paradox might be explained by the temporal lag existing between the introduction of the new technology and the subsequent productivity increases, since, for any kind of technology, slow and sometimes painful organizational adjustments are needed (e.g., the introduction of electricity at the end of the nineteenth century).

Almost all the empirical research confirms a positive effect of ICT on labour productivity, an effect which, in general, is increasing in time.

1. Robert Solow, 'We'd Better Watch Out', *New York Times Book Review*, 12 July 1987, p. 36.

Of course, as expected, differences in estimates may arise when taking into account different levels of aggregation, historical periods or geographical areas.

For example, while sectoral and aggregates analysis suggest that ICT effects on labour productivity are wider in the United States (US) than in the European Union (EU), firm-level analysis tend to exclude the presence of such differences (Van Ark et al., 2003).

In the majority of these studies, the fundamental role of complementary investments arises, suggesting that technological progress, alone, cannot explain growth. Arrangements and new strategies have to be adopted in order to profit from new technologies. For example, changes have to be made in the organizational framework. Maybe more importantly, firms have to invest in high-skilled workers and into their training. A strand of literature has developed in order to explain the effect of these arrangements, known as 'complementary investments' (Davern & Kauffman, 2000; Ravichandran et al., 2005; Pilat, 2005; Mithas et al., 2011; Ceccobelli et al., 2012). This literature also confirms the validity of the suggestions of Brynjolfsson and McAfee: new technologies are a necessary, though not sufficient condition for an increase in labour productivity.

Figure 7.2 Correlation Between Internet Usage and Youth Unemployment

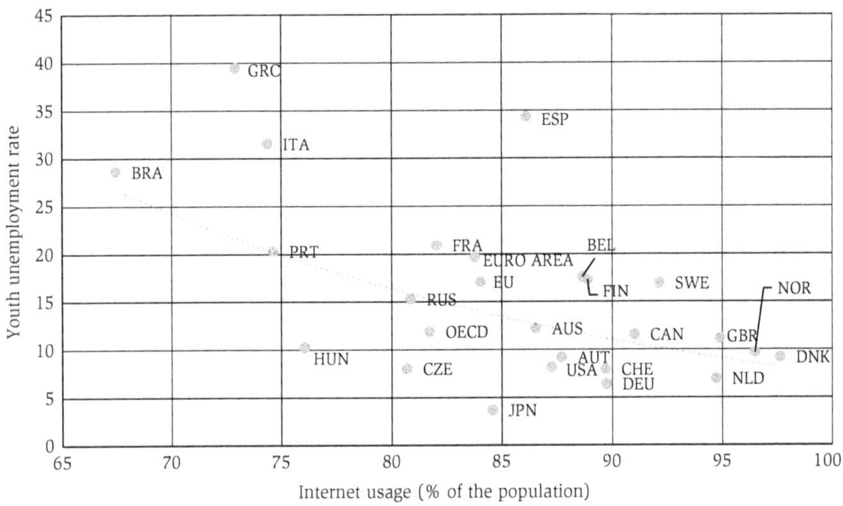

Source: WB International Telecommunication Union, World Telecommunication/ICT Development Report and database (for Internet usage) and International Labour Organization, ILOSTAT database. Data retrieved in December 2019.

Figure 7.2 shows the correlation between the rate of youth unemployment and Internet usage. The Internet usage variable is 'Individuals using the Internet (% of population)'; the youth unemployment rate variable is 'Unemployment, youth total (% of total labour force ages 15-24) (modelled ILO estimate)'. Reference year: 2018 (except Australia – AUS, Brazil – BRA,

Canada - CAN, Switzerland - CHE, Japan - JAP, OECD members - OECD and US. For these countries, the reference year for the Internet usage variable is 2017 - last available year in the dataset).

Figure 7.2 shows that the diffusion of the Internet is negatively correlated with youth unemployment. It suggests that employment opportunities for the young are easier to find in countries in which the use of new technologies is widespread in the population. On the other side, new technologies may also have a downside: the so-called technological unemployment.

The idea of 'technological unemployment', i.e., unemployment caused by the fact that machines are used instead of workers is not new. One of the founding fathers of political economy, David Ricardo, in his *Principles* notoriously stated that, 'The opinion entertained by the labouring class, that the employment of machinery is frequently detrimental to their interests, is not founded on prejudice and error, but is conformable to the correct principles of political economy' (Ricardo, 1817).

Also, John Maynard Keynes, in his 1930 pamphlet *Economic Possibilities for our Grandchildren*, seemed to accept the fact that technological unemployment exists, although he held a very optimistic vision about the future: 'We are being afflicted with a new disease of which some readers may not yet have heard the name, but of which they will hear a great deal in the years to come - namely, *technological unemployment*. This means unemployment due to our discovery of means of economising the use of labour outrunning the pace at which we can find new uses for labour. But this is only a temporary phase of maladjustment. All this means in the long run that mankind is solving its economic problem. I would predict that the standard of life in progressive countries one hundred years hence will be between four and eight times as high as it is to-day. There would be nothing surprising in this even in the light of our present knowledge. It would not be foolish to contemplate the possibility of a far greater progress still' (Keynes, 1930, emphasis added).

More recently, Leontief argued: 'Any worker who now performs his task by following specific instructions can, in principle, be replaced by a machine. That means that the role of humans as the most important factor of production is bound to diminish - in the same way that the role of horses in agricultural production was first diminished and then eliminated by the introduction of tractors' (Leontief, 1983).

Ricardo and Keynes had no idea of, and Leontief could simply imagine, the boost in technological progress brought about by the Internet revolution. However, if Ricardo's concern is well founded and Keynes' optimism is not, such an increase in our level of technological possibilities should be seen as a reason for pessimism about the future by the workers.

Figure 7.3 Difference Between Number of Employed and Total Labour Force (Difference Between Growth Rates)

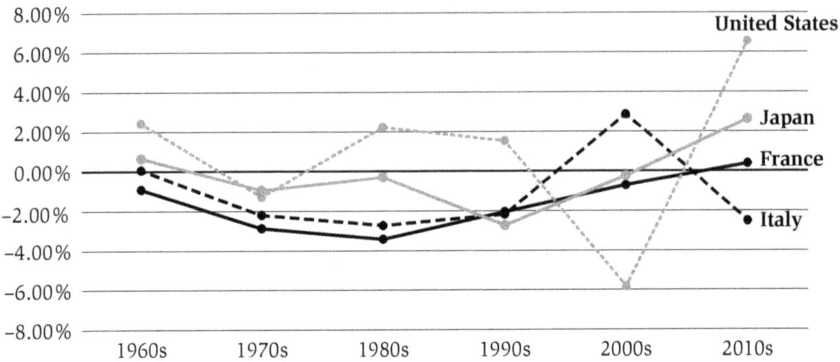

Source: Authors' elaboration on data from AMECO Database. Data retrieved on 16 January 2020.

The period 2010s represents 2010-2018. This graph depicts the dynamics of the difference between the growth rates of two aggregates: the number of employed and total labour force in the last six decades. Positive values represent a decade in which the growth in the number of employed has been greater than the increase in total labour force.

Certainly, it is early to fully evaluate the effects of technological innovations on employment dynamics (Figure 7.3 shows that in different countries and different decades, the results on whether growth in the number of employed people has kept up with the growth of the total labour force have been very heterogeneous). The observation, proposed by Brynjolfsson and McAfee, that in recent years the growth in the number of employees in the US has been lower than in the past, even in periods of sustained growth (the so-called jobless recovery), is supported by the available data (*see* Figure 7.4). Indeed, if we compare the growth in the number of people employed in the US in the decade 2000-2009 with that of each of the previous four decades, the result could appear as astonishing. Furthermore, as seen in the graph below, the growth in the number of employed workers in the first decade of the twenty-first century was well below the growth in the workforce.

Figure 7.4 US Job Growth by Decade, 1940s-2000s

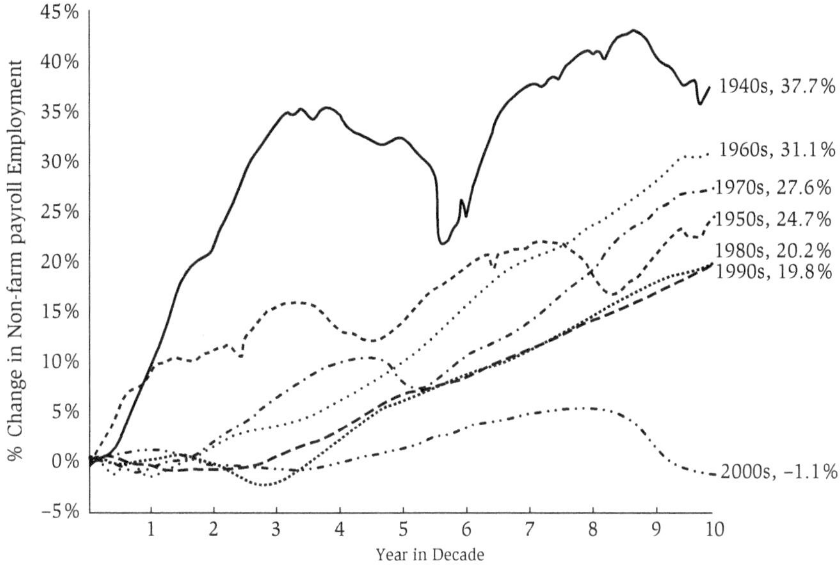

Source: Copyright: Andrew McAfee. Retrieved on 30 January 2020 from https://www.slideshare.net/mobile/amcafee/mc-afee-econ-data.

Before drawing excessively pessimistic conclusions, however, it is necessary to make some clarifications. For example, it should be stressed that the decade in question was characterized by a profound economic crisis, which had a serious impact on the US: the low growth in the number of employees cannot be attributed only to the systematic introduction of new technologies and a reversal in the trend can be observed in the second decade of the century. Furthermore, as shown in Figure 7.3, other countries, although technologically advanced, have not experienced the same dynamics (*see also* Graetz and Michaels, 2018, for a 'prudent' viewpoint).

This leads us, on the one hand, to give credit to Keynes' predictions: the imbalances created by the introduction of new technologies could be temporary and theoretically governable. On the other hand, however, it suggests that we look in another direction, that of the changes in the composition of employment. If it is true, in fact, that there are no elements suggesting a generalized destruction of jobs, it is also true that some types of workers, specialized in certain tasks, could be more affected than others (and in a non-transitory way) by the introduction of technologies that make them less useful for entrepreneurs. We deal with this issue in the next section.

7.2 DOES ICT CHANGE LABOUR FORCES' COMPOSITION? IF YES, IN WHICH WAY?

What we would like to understand, at this point, is the effect of ICT progress on the dynamics of employment.

Many studies have developed about the situation in the USA: while the theory of Skill Biased Technological Change (SBTC, based on skills & educational attainment) tries to explain inequality during the 1980s, the theory of Routine Biased Technological Change (based on tasks) focuses on job polarization in the 1990s and 2000s.

In particular, an important strand of economic literature has developed, starting with the paper by Autor and Handel (2003, QJE), based on the following idea: ICT can be seen as a substitute for workers employed in routine intensive jobs (matching medium wages jobs) and as a complement for workers employed in non-routine jobs (at the top or at the bottom of the wage distribution). More precisely, the authors argue that their model implies measurable changes in the composition of job tasks, on which they focus by using data for the period 1960-1998. They claim that computerization brings about a reduction in the labour input of routine manual and cognitive tasks, while non-routine cognitive tasks labour input is increased.

The authors also claim to be able to explain 60% of the demand shift in favour of college labour in the period 1970-1998. This means that, while the former will tend to be poorer, the latter will tend to be better paid because of their increased productivity (*see also* Autor et al., 2003; Autor et al., 2008; Autor et al., 2015; Acemoglu and Restrepo, 2017).

Boehm (2014), by conducting a study based on data regarding the US, confirms the same results. In particular, he shows that, since the late 1980s, the US labour market has been characterized by an increase in the share of low-skilled and high-skilled workers, at the expense of the share of so-called medium-skilled workers. In the same work, the author shows that real wages have remained substantially stable for workers with average wages and have increased for the extreme sides of the distribution, with lower increases for low-skilled workers and higher increases for high-skilled workers. This would suggest, in the opinion of the author, that medium-skilled workers are under strong pressure both from the point of view of job opportunities and of wage dynamics.

Jaimovich and Siu (2012) suggest that job polarization and jobless recoveries are strictly related. In their words 'First, essentially all employment loss in routine occupations occurs in economic downturns. Second, jobless recoveries in the aggregate can be accounted for by jobless recoveries in the routine occupations that are disappearing'.

We can summarize the phenomena described so far (polarization of jobs and wages) in a graph. In Figure 7.5, we see two U-shaped curves. The higher one depicts the rate of growth of wages, which we have seen to be particularly high for high-skilled workers. For low-skilled workers the wage growth rate is higher than that for medium-skilled workers, whose pays are characterized by the smallest increases. The lower curve, on the other hand, depicts the job growth rate. This rate is positive for low-skilled and high-skilled workers, while it is negative for medium-skilled workers.

Figure 7.5 The U-shaped Curves of Jobs and Wages Polarization

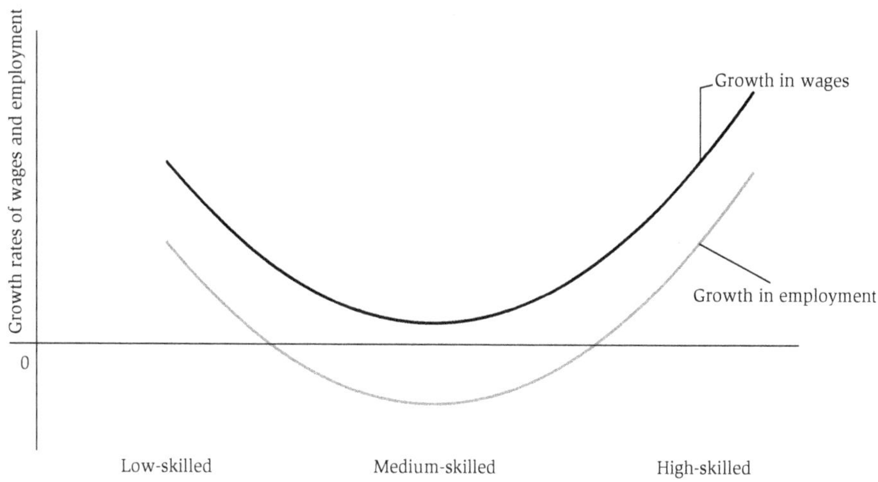

Source: Stylized depiction of the jobs and wages polarization suggested by the literature (*see* Autor et al., 2008; Boehm, 2014).

This graph depicts the phenomena suggested by the empirical literature on jobs and wages polarization. The higher curve represents the growth in wages for low-, medium- and high-skilled workers. The lowest values characterize medium-skilled workers, while the higher values represent the increase in wages for low-skilled workers (on the left) and high-skilled workers (on the right, with the highest growth rate). The lower curve represents the growth in employment for the same categories of workers. While low-skilled and medium-skilled workers are characterized by an increase in the number of jobs, medium-skilled workers are in the worst position, since their job opportunities are shrinking.

Many empirical studies tend to confirm this idea for the US: it can be demonstrated that among the less paid jobs there are especially non-routine manual jobs, whereas among the most paid jobs there are mainly non-routine cognitive jobs.

On the contrary, for the EU, there seems to be little evidence of wage polarization and of a polarizing effect of technology (*see* Michaels et al., 2014; Arntz, Gregory and Zierahn, 2016; Nedelkoska and Quintini, 2018; Hoftijzer and Gortazar, 2018 for studies showing no evidence; *see* Goos and Manning, 2007 and Goos et al., 2009 for the opposite conclusion). A pattern in which technology does not seem to have had a significant effect on wages and employment polarization can be observed in Italy, as we shall see in the next section.

7.3 THE EFFECT OF ICT PROGRESS ON EMPLOYMENT LEVELS, LABOUR FORCES' COMPOSITION AND WAGES: A FOCUS ON ITALY

Acemoglu and Autor (2011) have argued that Italy is among those few countries where, in addition to medium-paid jobs, also low-paid jobs are strongly declining. Anyway, Eurofound (2014) suggest that also in Italy, during the recent crisis, medium-paid jobs were the most affected.

Simonazzi and Barbieri (2016) also describe similar patterns. In addition, the authors underline that before the recent economic crisis, there was no evidence of wage polarization and, hence, of wage dynamics caused by SBTC. Moreover, Italy registered a substantially stable level of wage inequality since mid-1990s, not consistent with the existence of such a phenomenon.

This evidence could be explained by three hypotheses. The first one is that, especially before the 2000s, Italy was highly endowed with low-skilled labour and less endowed with high-skilled labour. Moreover, since the evidence on periods before the crisis show just a negligible impact of technology, not comparable to those observed in Anglo-Saxon countries, one could be tempted to look for the roots of these dynamics in the fact that Italy has been characterized by a low level of ICT investments. Finally, evidence is also compatible with the hypothesis that Italy shows very low skill-premia, that could bring to over-education and brain-drain phenomena. All these hypotheses tend to be confirmed by the available evidence.

The idea that Italy is particularly endowed with low-skilled workers seems confirmed by a recent report by the Organisation for Economic Co-operation and Development (OECD, 2017). In the paper, the fact that there is a very high concentration of low-skilled workers in the South is also underlined. Moreover, the report focuses on the fact that Italy is characterized by a relatively low percentage of tertiary educated workers (the share of 25-34 year-old people in Italy with a tertiary level education is 20%, while the OECD average is 30%), with an accordingly low number of new graduates entering the labour market.

But it is not only a problem of skilled labour supply. There is also a problem of demand for certain kinds of skills. Indeed, Italy in the last decades has been characterized by the pervasive phenomenon of brain-drain and graduates' outflows (Becker et al., 2004; Morano Foadi, 2006; ISTAT, 2018), both within the country (with graduate students from the South who often find a job in the North) and from Italy to other advanced economies.

With regard to the alleged low level of ICT investments in Italy, the hypothesis seems to be confirmed by some studies. For example, Hassan and Ottaviano (2013) underline that Italy has a very low level of ICT investment compared to countries such Germany and France. A very similar pattern is described by Schivardi and Schimtz (2018), who argue that the low level of ICT investment is to be blamed as one of the main factors causing stagnant productivity and slow growth in Italy. Also, OECD data show that between 2000 and 2010, ICT investment as percentage of total investment has lagged behind in Italy with respect to almost all OECD countries in which data are available (OECD, 2020).

Finally, Naticchioni et al. (2008 and 2010) confirm the existence of a general decline in the so-called educational wage premia in Italy in the period from 1993 to 2004. In particular, educational wage premia have generally decreased over time in the private sector and have remained basically stable in the public sector. They suggest that wage inequality in this country is not easy to interpret in terms of a skillbiased technical change and that the increase in the average level of education of the workforce might have been offset by a stable trend in the demand for skills.

Nowadays Italy is trying to combine the economic development with economic policy aimed at fostering technological change: the so-called Industria 4.0, a set of policies designed to incentivise firms to make investments in the sector of the modern technologies, is a step in this direction (*see also* section 7.5). These policies also go in the direction of increasing labour productivity, whose growth has been very sluggish since the 1990s, especially vis-à-vis its three leading trade partners (*see* Figure 7.6).

Figure 7.6 GDP per Hour Worked, USD, Constant Prices, 2015 PPPs

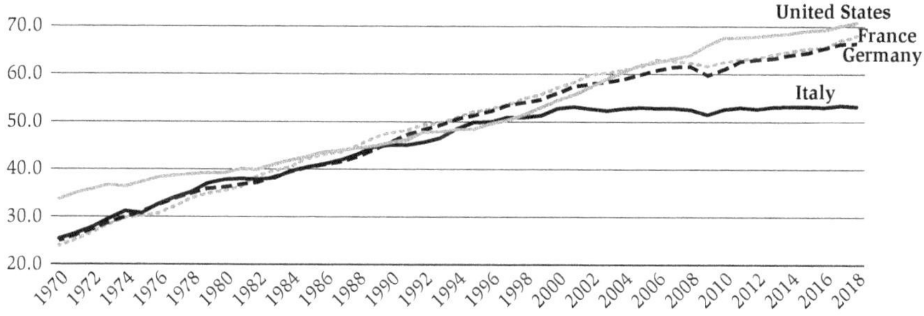

Source: OECD. Data extracted on 15 January 2020 from OECD.Stat.

However, this is not enough. Greater efforts have to be made in the field of public education and of direct public investment, both in the ICT and in the infrastructures sector. And, of course, the issue of the extremely low level of growth of the so-called Mezzogiorno (Southern Italy) has to be tackled, through policies aimed at increasing the living standards in those regions (an example of which is *Reddito di cittadinanza*, a sort of basic income provision, but more should be done in the field of the provision of services to the citizens). Moreover, the public sector should also provide for those infrastructural interventions that are absolutely needed to make private investments in the South profitable enough.

As regards the recent policies of the Italian Government to reduce the negative effects of technological changes on workers, some interventions have already been completed: in addition to the aforementioned *Reddito di cittadinanza*, the so-called dignity decree has been introduced, with the main objective of reducing the use of fixed-term contracts both by imposing stricter limits on the use of such contracts and incentivizing permanent ones. In 2019, protections for workers in the 'gig economy' were also increased, starting with the so-called riders.

Policies to help the workers to cope with the evolution of the labour market should go in two directions: the reduction of working hours (without decreasing pay) and the introduction of a law on minimum wages.

The aim of the first set of policies is to ensure that workers can work less, without suffering cuts in wages, and have a better balance between work and private life. At the same time, this would allow for new jobs to be created to replace workers who opt for shorter working hours, including through incentives for entrepreneurs. Such a policy would be consistent with what has been the development of the labour market in recent decades. In particular, as OECD data show,[2] in the most economically advanced countries we have seen an almost continuous reduction in the number of hours worked per worker (*see* Figure 7.7).

Figure 7.7 Yearly Working Hours in Nine Selected Countries

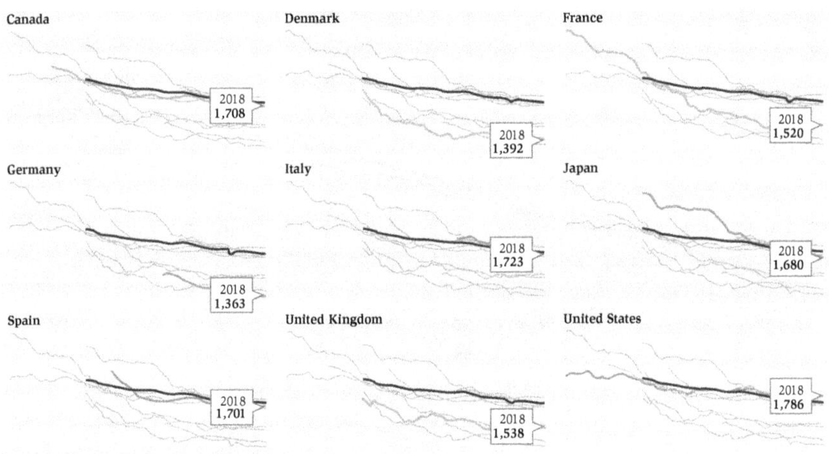

Source: OECD (2020), hours worked (indicator). doi: 10.1787/47be1c78-en (accessed 27 January 2020).

Reduction in yearly working hours in nine selected countries. The first year of the time series is 1950 for France (2,351 hours per week) and US (1,968 hours per week); 1961 for Canada (2,059 hours per week) 1970 for Denmark (1,845 hours per week), Japan (2,243 hours per week) and United Kingdom (1,779 hours per week); 1977 for Spain (2,036 hours per week); 1991 for Germany (1,554 hours per week); 1995 for Italy (1,856 hours per week). OECD average's first year is 1970 (1,945 hours per week), while the last one is 2018 (1,734 hours per week). The thick line is the OECD average.

The most striking example is given by France. In this country it has fallen from over forty-five hours per week for each worker in 1950, to around twenty-nine hours in 2018. For Italy, whose data have only been available since 1995, OECD data show a

2. Data retrieved from OECD.Stat, year 2018.

reduction from around thirty-six hours per week (1995) at thirty-three hours per week (2018). Furthermore, it is interesting to note that two of the countries where we work most in the EU (Italy and Greece, with thirty-three and thirty-eight hours per week, respectively) are also those characterized by the lower values of labour productivity (USD 53.3 and USD 36.4, respectively) and the employment rate (58.5% and 56.5%, respectively). Germany and Denmark, where we work between twenty-six and twenty-seven hours per week, on the contrary, show the highest ratio of GDP/hours worked (USD 66.4 and USD 73.4 per hour worked). Moreover, as shown in Figure 7.8, the countries with longer working hours are also the ones with the highest rates of unemployment.

Figure 7.8 Hours Worked Versus Unemployment Rate (2018)

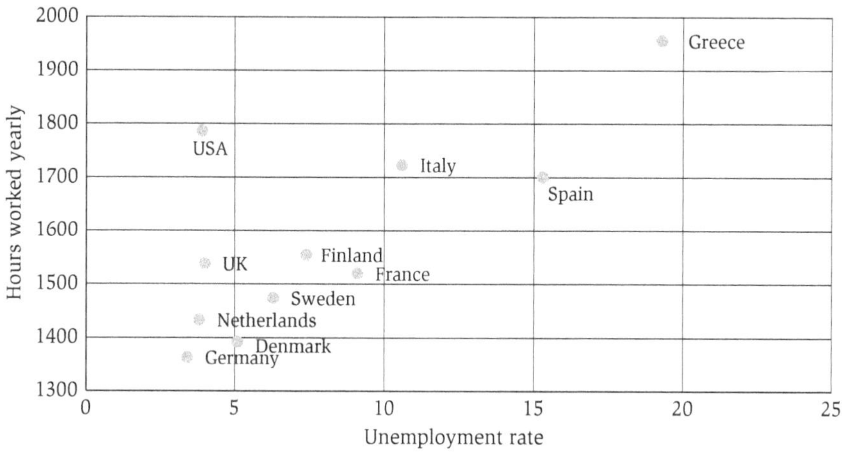

Source: Data extracted on 30 January 2020 14:11 UTC (GMT) from OECD.Stat. Unemployment rate values refer to the table 'Harmonised Unemployment Rate'; hours worked yearly refer to the table 'Average annual hours actually worked per worker'.

A law on the minimum wage, currently being examined by the Italian Senate, should aim to alleviate the suffering of the so-called working poor. Such a law should also address the issue of collective bargaining. In particular, it should aim to combat so-called pirate contracts, which allow small, unrepresentative trade unions to negotiate much lower wages than the average for a given sector.

Modern economies are going through a transition phase. In particular, what we are witnessing is a real structural change, a transition from a system in which manufacturing is the leading sector (characterized by strong investments in fixed capital) towards an economy in which services are the main economic sector (*see* the two graphs in Figure 7.9 for a depiction of the shrinking of manufacturing in many advanced economies). The services in which growth has been particularly sustained, however, are essentially characterized by a low content of capital and technology.

Furthermore, the greatest growth is concentrated in more mature sectors (food and accommodation, mainly). Consequently, it becomes fundamental to guide the transition towards strategic sectors – as is happening, precisely, with Industry 4.0. Paradoxically (at least if the dominant theory is taken into consideration), rigidities in the labour market can guide Italy towards productivity gains. Flexible and precarious work pushes companies to make labour-intensive investments (generally characterized by low productivity increases). Interventions such as the 'dignity decree' and the minimum wage go in the direction of creating rigidity against the use of competitiveness played on the decline in wages, pushing companies to make capital-intensive investments (Pariboni and Tridico, 2018).

Figure 7.9 Employment in the Manufacturing Sector as a Share of Total Employment

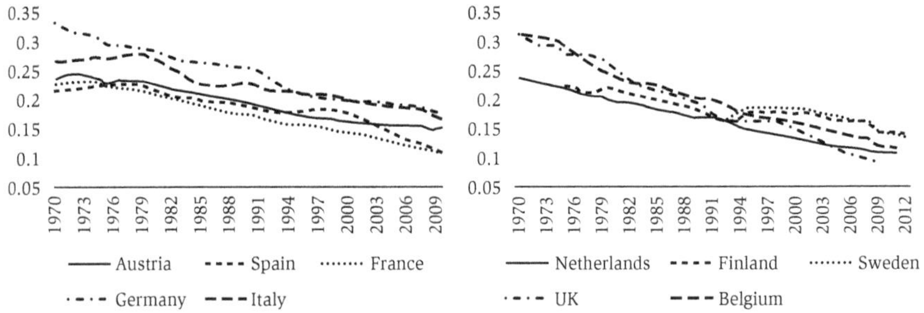

Source: OECD and EU Klems Project (*see* Pariboni and Tridico, 2018).
Employment in the manufacturing sector, share of total employment (1970-2012).

Figure 7.10 Value Added in the Manufacturing Sector as a Share of Total Value Added

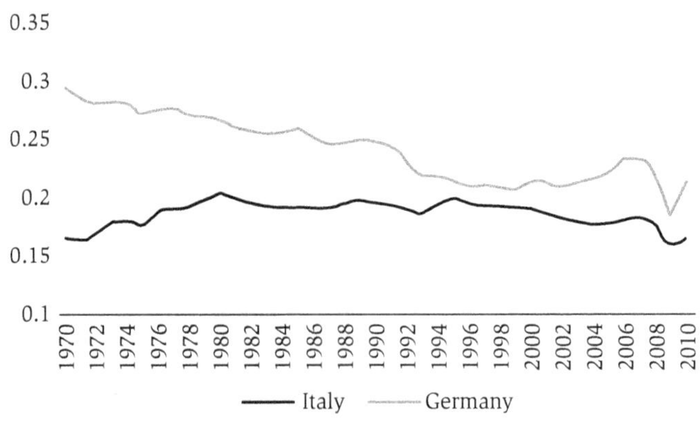

Source: EU Klems Project (*see* Pariboni and Tridico, 2018).
Manufacturing sector, share of total value added (1970-2010).

7.4 FUTURE SCENARIOS AND POLICY IMPLICATIONS

In order to face the increasing challenges posed by the powerful technological change we are experiencing, new policies have to be implemented. There are mainly four kinds of policies which are usually believed to be beneficial in achieving a more equilibrated growth:

(1) industrial policies;
(2) compensation of 'losers';
(3) higher taxation on 'winners'; and
(4) working hours reduction.

First of all, an *active industrial policy* aiming at taking advantage of recent technological developments, instead of passively accepting their consequences, is needed. This is the only way to try to steer the process and to avoid being overwhelmed by it. It is easy to describe the kind of industries we are going to find more frequently in the future.

Along what lines should such an intervention plan occur? Our age has been defined that of a 'Fourth Industrial Revolution', taking advantage of innovations in the fields of hardware, software, cloud computing, internet of things (IoT), and so on. The subset of innovations which can have a huge impact on the way firms will organize their activity has been called 'Industry 4.0'. This definition includes the so-called smart manufacturing (and 'smart factories'), lights-out manufacturing (or dark factories) and 'industrial internet of things' (IIoT). As defined by Davis et al. (2012), smart manufacturing is 'the dramatically intensified and pervasive application of networked information-based technologies throughout the manufacturing and supply chain enterprise'. The term 'lights-out manufacturing' encompasses a set of manufacturing processes where factories run fully autonomously, without any human intervention (or with a very small amount of it; it is also called 'dark factories' process: if humans are not required to work in the factories, lights are not required). The IoT is a system of interrelating computers or computing devices, objects, machines and people, characterized by the possibility of transferring data packages over a network without a direct human intervention. By extension, the application of the IoT technological paradigm to industries has generated what has been called the 'IIoT'.

What is the role of the public sector in the process of adapting the economic system to such a big change in the industrial paradigm? There is a quite wide consensus on the fact that governments should try to boost the readiness of their industrial system to take advantage of the new technologies by providing the right incentives. Things such as tax benefits in many different forms are widely accepted: very high rates of depreciation applied to innovative investments; contribution for the payment of interests on loans to invest in new capital goods; tax credit measures to increase the resort to innovative R&D processes; reduction of taxes on the incomes arising from the use of industrial patent rights, registered trademarks and new software; tax credit for training in the areas of Industry 4.0 and many other measures.

While, as we have just said, such measures are widely accepted, there is an animated international debate on the role of the public sector in fostering economic growth: should governments just focus on incentives? Or would their action be much more effective if they took direct intervention, for example by investing directly in new technologies and R&D projects? The main contribution in favour of a direct activity of governments is Mariana Mazzucato's book, *The Entrepreneurial State* (2013). She argues that in history entrepreneurial states have sparked investment in the private sector by making high-risk investments in new technologies. Moreover, she believes that the State still has a role to play in this dynamics, not only by encouraging or actively engaging in investments, but also by promoting a more inclusive process of economic growth, an objective that the private sector alone would not actively pursue. Atzeni and Carboni (2008) also argued that a strong intervention by the public sector in favour of ICT investments could be particularly effective both in boosting growth in Italy and in reducing the South-North growth and productivity divide.

In our opinion, Mazzucato has a point in underlining the importance of an inclusive growth and of the role of the State. All the innovations we have listed are potential threats to the levels of employment in the future. A growth which is guided only by the pursuit of higher rates of profit and by the reduction of workers is by definition non-inclusive. An active role of governments in trying to channel the innovation process in the direction of higher levels of employment and higher wages is of primary importance.

Industrial policies should also follow the direction of the so-called *green economy*. Faced with the continuous increase in the emission of greenhouse gases, governments are required to take action in order to reduce such emissions and try to slower the process of global warming. Moreover, more efficient and rational waste disposal and recycling techniques are necessary to thwart the rise of plastic pollution, which is threatening especially the oceans. These policies should also be implemented to solve the problem of the increasing scarcity of natural resources, and they should be accompanied by a transition to factories that make use, predominantly or exclusively, of renewable energies (such as hydroelectric, solar, tidal, wave and wind energy).

Of course, all of these policies are costly for the firms. As a consequence, a mix of subsidies, taxes and infrastructural interventions should be taken into consideration by the policymakers. At a cost for governments, too: especially in context, such as the EU, in which binding constraints limit the spending capacity of the public sector. And, on the background, the debate on whether the government should intervene directly or indirectly goes on. In addition, there is the problem of international competition with economic systems in which governments are less concerned about sustainability. Even in this case, a mix of coordinated policies has to be implemented, through international treaties, economic aid to developing economies and sanctions or disincentives for those countries unwilling to pursue a greener way of production.

At the same time, a greener economy should not bring with it a reduction in employment. In many cases, there seems to be a trade-off between environmental sustainability and employment. Firms are often in the position of placing governments and workers in front of a dilemma: are they ready to give up some employment in exchange for less pollution and more sustainability? These are the cases in which governments should take strong and resolute interventions in order to ensure both employment and respect for the environment.

What kind of employment should we pursue? In the last decades, policy-makers have pushed for a higher level of flexibility in the labour market. These policies, as suggested by the economists of the so-called Washington Consensus, should have generated higher employment and growth, by reducing the frictions in the labour market, and higher labour productivity, through incentives for workers. Actually, this did not happen and is not happening. Available data show that a higher labour market flexibility has not brought to higher growth, employment or productivity. As a matter of fact, these policies could have generated the opposite effect (Brancaccio et al., 2018; Vergeer and Kleinknecht, 2010 and 2014; Storm and Naastepad, 2007; on the Italian case: Jona-Lasinio and Vallanti, 2013; Fana et al., 2015).

There are many reasons behind the fact that deregulated labour markets, and, in particular, higher flexibility, tend to generate a downward pressure on labour productivity (*see* Pariboni and Tridico, 2019, for a review of the literature). Firms and workers will consider investments in training and education less profitable. Firms are unwilling to invest in the training of employees that will soon work for a competitor or in other sectors. At the same time, workers that are not sure of the fact that they will be keeping their job for a long time, would risk to see their effort in learning frustrated because of frequent changes in their job or sector (Salop, 1979; Shapiro and Stiglitz, 1984). Lucidi and Kleinknecht (2010) suggest that there are many channels through which a higher labour flexibility can hinder productivity growth. First, higher levels of flexibility bring to lower investment in capital-intensive techniques, as in the Schumpeterian Sylos-Labini approach (*see also* Dosi et al., 2017 and 2018). Moreover, as we have already said, short-term contracts are conducive to under-investment in training and to a more conflictual working environment. Finally, since short-term contracts generate a downward pressure on wages, this will probably bring to a reduction in aggregate demand (in particular in the so-called wage-led economies; *see* Rowthorn, 1981 and Bhaduri and Marglin, 1990). This, in turn, will damage labour productivity through the channel of the Kaldor-Verdoorn law (Verdoorn 1949; Kaldor 1978).

Another strand of policies is based on the compensation of *'losers'*. What do we mean by 'losers'? With this word we describe workers who are worse off because of technological progress (routine labourers with an obsolete skill endowment), especially among adults and elderly people.

A possible policy consists in the re-training of senior workers' skills. There is animated debate on the utility of such a policy of re-training. Heckman (2000), by arguing that re-training returns are decreasing in age and that, for this reason, they would be strongly inefficient, suggests a provocative alternative: it would be better – he says – to use economic resources to improve children skills instead of training old workers.

However, working is also a matter of human dignity and social cohesion, not only an economic investment and a conclusion like the one just drawn is too simplistic. If it is true that senior workers tend to show lower re-training returns, it does not mean that those workers should just be laid-off or left to their fate of being unproductive workers waiting for retirement.

Unemployment benefits and early retirements would be more suitable, thus allowing to focus the educational resources on the new generations, that show high relative returns in education.

Figure 7.11 Ratio Between Manager Compensation and Employee Mean Wages: Rich Countries

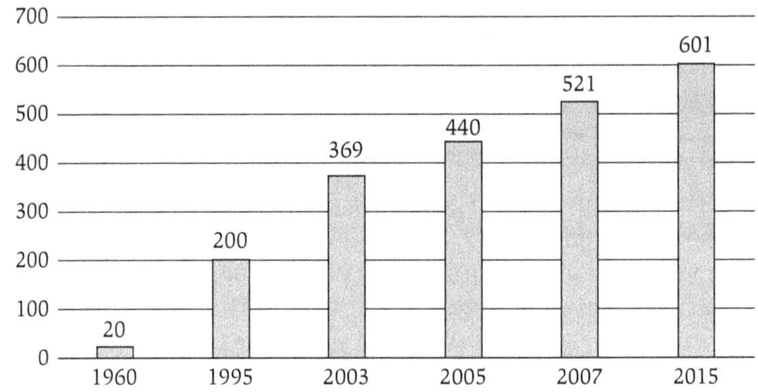

Source: ILO.

Figure 7.12 Labour Share in the G7 Economies: 1970s-2016

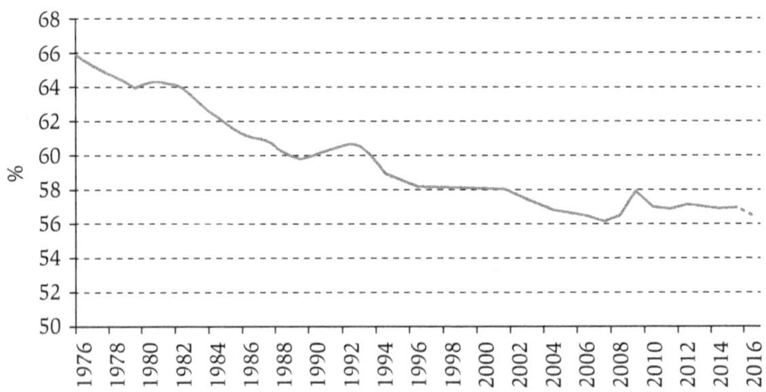

Source: AMECO Database.

Let us focus on the taxation of the 'winners' of the ICT revolution. As the Figures 7.11 and 7.12 show, in the last decades wealthy people have been increasing their wealth and compensations, while the middle class is in contraction and low-paid labourers are in expansion. As a consequence, overall inequality is growing, especially in advanced economies, and the labour share is falling. This is also a consequence of the so-called phenomenon of the 'decoupling' of productivity from labour earnings. As stated in a recent Economic Outlook (OECD, 2018) by the OECD, 'several OECD countries have been grappling not only with slow productivity growth but have also experienced a slowdown in real average wage growth relative to productivity growth, which has been reflected in a falling share of wages in GDP'.

Higher taxes for top incomes could contribute to the reduction of inequalities and could prevent social cohesion issues. Diamond and Saez (2011) and Piketty (2014) argue that optimal top income taxation could fairly exceed 70%. Note that in many countries income taxes until the 1970s were much higher than now, often above 50%. The reduction of taxation for higher incomes has influenced, along with the changes in the economic paradigm and in the labour market, the increase of inequality in advanced economies.

These data, coupled with the evidence showing that higher wages are often associated with higher growth rates (Hein and Vogel, 2007 and 2009; Onaran and Galanis, 2012; Lavoie and Stockhammer 2013) and that the increase in income inequality, alongside with financialization (Hein and Mundt, 2013), was one of the main factors to be blamed for the Great Recession (van Treeck and Sturn, 2012), show that, although it is not necessary to resort to the high levels of taxation cited above, a moderate redistribution of the tax burden could be both fair from an ethical and political point of view and conducive to growth. However, as we have seen for the efforts in environment-friendly policies, redistributive policies in a country could be offset by capital outflows and beggar-thy-neighbour strategies by other countries, willing to attract investments through favourable tax policies (fiscal competition) and deregulated labour markets.

Finally, let us focus on the reduction of working hours. While a higher flexibility in the labour market can be detrimental to productivity, some authors (Pencavel, 2014; Glaveski, 2018; Bassanini and Caroli, 2015; Messenger et al., 2007; Cette and Taddéi, 1993) have argued that shorter workweeks and workdays are a key to higher productivity. In addition, many leading firms (e.g., Microsoft Japan) have experimented four-day workweek without decreasing pay. As a result, firms report a boost in productivity, a higher level of satisfaction of their workers and higher efficiency. Other firms (such as Kellogg's, the US cereal manufacturer) operated six-hour working-day policies, with good results as well. Nowadays, even some national governments are willing to explore the possibilities offered by such arrangements of the workweek: it is not unlikely that this will be a relevant feature of the evolution of work in the future.

As we have seen in section 7.3, it seems that a reduction in working time (with unchanged wages) constitutes an adequate policy in face of the changes in the labour market of the last decades. It is necessary (and possible) to ensure that workers enjoy a greater balance between work and leisure. Such a policy could be implemented through the tax exemption of a part of the salary paid to the worker in the form of corporate welfare instruments.

The idea behind the policy is based on the fact that a reduction in working hours would result in a less than proportional loss in terms of product, since it would affect the least productive part of the working week (or day). Nevertheless, it would still be necessary to replace the hours previously worked by workers already hired with hours worked by newly hired workers. It could therefore be argued that such a policy could also lead to an increase in employment.

7.5 CONCLUDING REMARKS

In recent decades, computer technology has developed at an unprecedented pace. These developments can undoubtedly bring with them opportunities for growth and greater prosperity, but, at least in the short run, they can also generate negative consequences for some categories of workers. However, it is still too early to talk about generalized negative consequences on workers. Perhaps due to the lack of so-called complementary investments, it seems that the technological revolution has not yet affected all sectors and all countries in a uniform way. Yet, a particular category of workers, the so-called medium-skilled workers, seems to be the most penalized by new technologies.

In this scenario, Italy still seems substantially far from full participation in the new production methods made possible by the revolution in the ICT field. This is due to the low endowment of high-skilled labour compared to other countries, a low level of investment in ICT and a low level of skill-rewards. On the one hand, this delay has so far prevented the occurrence of job and wage polarization phenomena; on the other, however, it risks making the country fall behind in the modernization process. The Italian Government is implementing a mix of policies aimed, on the one hand, at favouring the adaptation process to Industry 4.0 and, on the other, at supporting those who could be penalized by these developments. Policies just implemented, such as minimum income (*Reddito di cittadinanza*), or reduction of labour flexibility such as the ones introduced by the 'Decreto dignità' go in the direction to push firms in human capital investment rather than exploit labour cost and flexibility as levers for competitiveness and to protect low-skilled workers. The current debate on minimum wage and working hours' reduction goes also in this direction.

As for the policy suggestions deriving from these considerations, they should go in three directions:

(1) industrial policies aimed at adapting productive systems to the innovations of Industry 4.0 including working hours reduction;
(2) support for the so-called losers of the ICT revolution;
(3) redistribution in favour of the most disadvantaged sections of the population.

As far as industrial policies are concerned, a debate is underway on the nature of these policies. Some authors believe that industrial policies should consist only of incentives, while others argue that the state should play an active role as an investor. Instead, there is an almost unanimous agreement that industrial policies must have the aim of accompanying economies on the 'green transition' path, which is now inevitable. Support for workers in difficulty should take the form of financial support for the unemployed and training for those whose skills are made obsolete by technological developments. A moderate redistribution of the tax burden – coordinated between the various countries to avoid phenomena of the 'beggar thy neigbour' type – would have the aim of supporting the policies mentioned above and of promoting a redistribution which, in countries characterized by wage-led regimes, would lead to an increase in growth rates. Finally, a gradual reduction in working hours (with unchanged wages) in particular in some selected productive segments (both from labour-intensive sectors and labour-saving sectors for opposite reasons), combined with work-family conciliation and forms of smart working, would be positive both for the workers' well-being, for productivity and employment.

REFERENCES

Acemoglu, D. & Autor, D. (2011). Skills, tasks and technologies: Implications for employment and earnings. In *Handbook of labor economics* (Vol. 4, pp. 1043-1171). Amsterdam: Elsevier.

Acemoglu, D. & Restrepo, P. (2017). Robots and jobs: Evidence from US labor markets. *NBER Working Paper* (w23285).

Arntz, M., Gregory, T. & Zierahn, U. (2016). The risk of automation for jobs in OECD countries. *OECD Social, Employment and Migration Working Papers* (No. 189).

Atzeni, G.E. & Carboni, O.A. (2008). The effects of grant policy on technology investment in Italy. *Journal of Policy Modeling*, 30(3), 381-399.

Autor, D.H., Dorn, D. & Hanson, G.H. (2015). Untangling trade and technology: Evidence from local labour markets. *The Economic Journal*, 125(584), 621-646.

Autor, D.H. & Handel, M.J. (2013). Putting tasks to the test: Human capital, job tasks, and wages. *Journal of labor Economics*, 31(S1), S59-S96.

Autor, D.H., Katz, L.F. & Kearney, M.S. (2008). Trends in US wage inequality: Revising the revisionists. *The Review of economics and statistics*, 90(2), 300-323.

Autor, D.H., Levy, F. & Murnane, R. (2003). The skill content of recent technological change: An empirical exploration. *Quarterly Journal of Economics*, 118(4), 1279-1333.

Bassanini, A. & Caroli, E. (2015). Is work bad for health? The role of constraint versus choice. *Annals of Economics and Statistics/Annales d'Économie et de Statistique*, (119/120), 13-37.

Becker, S.O., Ichino, A. & Peri, G. (2004). How large is the 'brain drain' from Italy?. *Giornale degli Economisti e Annali di Economia*, 63(1), 1-32.

Bhaduri, A. & Marglin, S. (1990). Unemployment and the real wage: The economic basis for contesting political ideologies. *Cambridge Journal of Economics*, 14(4), 375-393.

Boehm, M. (2014). Job polarisation and the decline of middle-class workers' wages. *VoxEU. org*, 8.

Brancaccio, E., Garbellini, N. & Giammetti, R. (2018). Structural labour market reforms, GDP growth and the functional distribution of income. *Structural Change and Economic Dynamics*, 44, 34-45.

Brynjolfsson, E. & McAfee, A. (2011). *Race against the machine: How the digital revolution is accelerating innovation, driving productivity, and irreversibly transforming employment and the economy*. Boston: Digital Frontier Press.

Brynjolfsson, E. & McAfee, A. (2014). *The second machine age: Work, progress, and prosperity in a time of brilliant technologies*. New York: WW Norton & Company.

Ceccobelli, M., Gitto, S. & Mancuso, P. (2012). ICT capital and labour productivity growth: A non-parametric analysis of 14 OECD countries. *Telecommunications Policy*, 36(4), 282-292.

Cette, G. & Taddéi, D. (1993). The economic effects of reducing and reorganizing working time. *Futures*, 25(5), 561-577.

Davern, M.J. & Kauffman, R.J. (2000). Discovering potential and realizing value from information technology investments. *Journal of Management Information Systems*, 16(4), 121-143.

Diamond, P. & Saez, E. (2011). The case for a progressive tax: From basic research to policy recommendations. *Journal of Economic Perspectives*, 25(4), 165-190.

Davis, J., Edgar, T., Porter, J., Bernaden, J. & Sarli, M. (2012). Smart manufacturing, manufacturing intelligence and demand-dynamic performance. *Computers & Chemical Engineering*, 47, 145-156.

Dosi, G., Pereira, M.C., Roventini, A. & Virgillito, M.E. (2017). When more flexibility yields more fragility: The microfoundations of Keynesian aggregate unemployment. *Journal of Economic Dynamics and Control*, 81, 162-186.

Dosi, G., Pereira, M.C., Roventini, A. & Virgillito, M.E. (2018). Causes and consequences of hysteresis: Aggregate demand, productivity, and employment. *Industrial and Corporate Change*, 27(6), 1015-1044.

Eurofound (2014). *Eurofound yearbook 2014: Living and working in Europe*. Annual report.

Fana, M., Guarascio, D. & Cirillo, V. (2015). *Labour market reforms in Italy: Evaluating the effects of the Jobs Act* (No. 2015/31). LEM Working Paper Series.

Glaveski, S. (2018). The Case for the 6-Hour Workday. *Harvard Business Review*.

Goos, M. & Manning, A. (2007), Lousy and lovely jobs: The rising polarization of work in Britain. *Review of Economics and Statistics*, 89(1), 118-133.

Goos, M., Manning, A. & Salomons, A. (2009), Job polarization in Europe, *American Economic Review: Papers & Proceedings*, 99(2), 58-63.

Graetz, G. & Michaels, G. (2018). Robots at work. *Review of Economics and Statistics*, 100(5), 753-768.

Heckman, J.J. (2000). Policies to foster human capital. *Research in Economics*, 54(1), 3-56.

Hoftijzer, M. & Gortazar, L. (2018). Skills and Europe's Labor Market: How Technological Change and Other Drivers of Skill Demand and Supply are Shaping Europe's Labor Market, https://doi.org/10.1596/29965.

Hassan, F. & Ottaviano, G. (2013). Productivity in Italy: The great unlearning. *VoxEU.org*, 30.

Hein, E. & Vogel, L. (2007). Distribution and growth reconsidered: Empirical results for six OECD countries. *Cambridge Journal of Economics*, 32(3), 479-511.

Hein, E. & Vogel, L. (2009). Distribution and growth in France and Germany: Single equation estimations and model simulations based on the Bhaduri/Marglin model. *Review of Political Economy*, 21(2), 245-272.

Hein, E. & Mundt, M. (2013). Financialization, the financial and economic crisis, and the requirements and potentials for wage-led recovery. In Lavoie, M. & Stockhammer, E., eds, *Wage-led Growth* (pp. 153-186). Palgrave Macmillan, London.

ISTAT (2018). *Mobilità interna e migrazioni internazionali della popolazione residente.* Report.

Jaimovich, N. & Siu, H.E. (2012). Job polarization and jobless recoveries. *Review of Economics and Statistics*. https://doi.org/10.1162/rest_a_00875.

Jona-Lasinio, C. & Vallanti, G. (2013). Reforms, labour market functioning and productivity dynamics: A sectoral analysis for Italy. *Government of the Italian Republic (Italy), Ministry of Economy and Finance, Department of the Treasury Working Paper*, (10).

Kaldor, N. (1978). *Further essays on economic theory*. Duckworth, London.

Keynes, J.M. (1930). *Economic Possibilities for our Grandchildren*. In *Essays in Persuasion* (pp. 358-373). New York: Harcourt Brace.

Lavoie, M. & Stockhammer, E. (2013). Wage-led growth: Concept, theories and policies. In Lavoie, M. & Stockhammer, E., eds, *Wage-led growth* (pp. 13-39). Palgrave Macmillan, London, 2013.

Leontief, W. (1983). Technological advance, economic growth, and the distribution of income. *Population and Development Review*, 9(3), 403-410.

Lucidi, F. & Kleinknecht, A. (2009). Little innovation, many jobs: An econometric analysis of the Italian labour productivity crisis. *Cambridge Journal of Economics*, 34(3), 525-546.

Mazzucato, M. (2015). *The entrepreneurial state: Debunking public vs. private sector myths*. London: Anthem Press.

Messenger, J.C., Lee, S. & McCann, D. (2007). *Working time around the world: Trends in working hours, laws, and policies in a global comparative perspective*. Abingdon: Routledge.

Michaels, G., Natraj, A. & Van Reenen, J. (2014). Has ICT polarized skill demand? Evidence from eleven countries over twenty-five years. *Review of Economics and Statistics*, 96(1), 60-77.

Mithas, S., Ramasubbu, N. & Sambamurthy, V. (2011). How information management capability influences firm performance. *MIS quarterly*, 35(1), 237.

Moore, G.E. (1965). Cramming more components onto integrated circuits. *Electronics*, 38(8), 114-117.

Morano Foadi, S. (2006). Key issues and causes of the Italian brain drain. *Innovation*, 19(2), 209-223.

Naticchioni, P., Ricci, A. & Rustichelli, E. (2008). Wage inequality, employment structure and skillbiased change in Italy. *Labour*, 22, 27-51.

Naticchioni, P., Ricci, A. & Rustichelli, E. (2010). Far away from a skill-biased change: Falling educational wage premia in Italy. *Applied Economics*, 42(26), 3383-3400.

Nedelkoska, L. & Quintini, G. (2018). Automation, skills use and training. *OECD Social, Employment and Migration Working Papers* (No. 202).

OECD (2017). OECD Skills Strategy Diagnostic Report. Italy. 2017.

OECD (2018). *OECD Economic Outlook*, Volume 2018 Issue 2, OECD Publishing, Paris, https://doi.org/10.1787/eco_outlook-v2018-2-en.

OECD (2020). ICT investment (indicator). doi: 10.1787/b23ec1da-en (Accessed on 13 January 2020).

Onaran, Ö. & Galanis, G. (2012). Is aggregate demand wage-led or profit-led. National and global effects. *ILO Conditions of Work and Employment Series* (31).

Pariboni, R. & Tridico, P. (2018). *Produttività, cambiamento strutturale e riforme sbagliate*, anno 10, n. 15, sem. 1. www.economiaepolitica.it.

Pariboni, R. & Tridico, P. (2019). Structural change, institutions and the dynamics of labor productivity in Europe. *Journal of Evolutionary Economics*, 1-26.

Pencavel, J. (2014). The productivity of working hours. *The Economic Journal*, 125(589), 2052-2076.

Piketty, T. (2014). Capital in the twenty-first century. *Harvard University Press*.

Pilat, D. (2005). The ICT productivity paradox. *OECD Economic Studies*, 2004(1), 37-65.

Ravichandran, T., Lertwongsatien, C. & Lertwongsatien, C. (2005). Effect of information systems resources and capabilities on firm performance: A resource-based perspective. *Journal of management information systems*, 21(4), 237-276.

Ricardo, D. (1817). *On the Principles of Political Economy and Taxation*. London: John Murray, Albemarle-Street.

Rowthorn, B. (1981). *Demand, real wages and economic growth*. Thames Papers in Political Economy | Autumn 1981 TP/PPE/81/3Salop, S.C. (Spring 1979). *Monopolistic competition with outside goods*. The Bell Journal of Economics, 10(1), 141-156.

Schivardi, F. & Schmitz, T. (2018). *The IT Revolution and Southern Europe's Two Lost Decades*. CEPR Discussion Paper No. DP12843.

Shapiro, C. & Stiglitz, J.E. (1984). Equilibrium unemployment as a worker discipline device. *The American Economic Review*, 74(3), 433-444.

Simonazzi, A. & Barbieri, T. (2016). The middle class in Italy: Reshuffling, erosion, polarisation. In Vaughan-Whitehead, D. ed., *Europe's Disappearing Middle Class*, Cheltenham: Edward Elgar Publishing Ltd., 360-395.

Storm, S. & Naastepad, C.W.M. (2007). *Why labour market regulation may pay off: Worker motivation, co-ordination and productivity growth*. International Labour Office, Economic and Labour Market Paper 2007/4 .

Van Ark, B., Inklaar, R. & McGuckin, R.H. (2003). ICT and productivity in Europe and the United States. Where do the differences come from? *CESifo Economic Studies*, 49(3), 295-318.

Van Treeck, T. & Sturn, S. (2012). *Income inequality as a cause of the Great Recession?: A survey of current debates*. ILO, Conditions of Work and Employment Branch.

Verdoorn, P.J. (1949). *Fattori che regolano lo sviluppo della produttività del lavoro*. L'industria.

Vergeer, R. & Kleinknecht, A. (2010). The impact of labor market deregulation on productivity: A panel data analysis of 19 OECD countries (1960-2004). *Journal of Post Keynesian Economics*, 33(2), 371-408.

Vergeer, R. & Kleinknecht, A. (2014). Do labour market reforms reduce labour productivity growth? A panel data analysis of 20 OECD countries (1960-2004). *International Labour Review*, 153(3), 365-393.

PART II The Challenges of Digitization to the Regulatory Categories of Labour Law

CHAPTER 8

Platform Capitalism and Labour Law

Adalberto Perulli

8.1 WORK THROUGH DIGITAL PLATFORMS: BETWEEN POIESIS AND DOMINATION OF TECHNOLOGY

The change in the organizational forms of post-Fordism has posed to the social sciences the problem of a new 'geography of power' that erodes the social dimension of the market, generates new inequalities and isolation of the subjects, disintermediates trade union representation, radically transforming the twentieth century idea of work, which 'is not a possession and no longer even has a fixed content. It becomes a point in a constantly changing network'.[1] In this scenario, which marks the definitive liberation from the Weberian model of social cohesion dominant in the twentieth century, the digital revolution breaks through, proposing, within an uncertain and changing social-economic framework, a new form of dialectic between labour and technology. The fundamental matter is to understand whether the capitalism of the digital age allows us to valorize the connection between the idea of *homo faber* and that of *technikòs ánthropos*, freeing work from the chains of the Fordist era, or whether the digital economy, with its forms of precarious, fragmented and de-spatialized work, re-propose the dominion of technology over the worker, reduced once again to an *animal laborans*.[2] We know - thanks to Heidegger - that technology is 'a way of revealing'. If technology is not a mere *instrumentum* in view of the goals set by the human being, but a 'pro-vocation' that does not reveal itself in a 'production' in the sense of *poiesis*, but it consists in the 'im-position' (*Ge-stell*) from which humans approach the world in a controlling and dominating way, we should wonder about the sense and the direction of the umpteenth change produced by technology on capitalist

1. R. Sennet, *The Culture of the New Capitalism*, London, Yale University Press, 2006.
2. On the distinction between *homo faber* and *animal laborans*, *see* H. Arendt, *The Human Condition*, Chicago, University of Chicago Press, 1958.

production on the one hand, and on the meaning of capitalist imposition on the other, in its original connection with human labour.[3]

The debate, within social sciences and also in labour law, seems to be polarized on two opposing views. According to a positive interpretation of the effects of digitization on the labour market, we are facing a new poietic mode, a frontier of society where the technology guided by the idea of collaboration and sharing will allow employees to free themselves from the subordinating dimension of technology,[4] with the formation of a multitude of 'collaborative prosumers', that is, producers and at the same time workers and consumers. In this optimistic vision, which seems to realize the utopia of the liberation of work through technology, prosumers are subjects capable of producing, consuming and exchanging goods and services with each other in a collaborative *commons* at increasingly reduced costs, thus favouring new forms of organization of economic life and overcoming the traditional model of the capitalist market.[5] The very nature of work undergoes an epochal change, and the old categories of the economic paradigm – producers and workers, sellers and consumers – disappear, while material needs are satisfied by a society characterized by almost zero marginal costs. The collaborative economy thus ends up upsetting both business activity and consumer attitudes, posing radical questions on the very essence of labour as we have known it to date, and therefore on the law that founds its *raison d'etre* on labour.

This optimistic vision of a democratic and sustainable technique is opposed by another one, which seems to re-propose the idea of technology as an imposition: in this perspective, platform capitalism actually unveils a new form of technological domination with the creation of app-driven subjects that perform on-demand services given and monitored by a super-ordinate provider within an oppressive re-edition of Taylorism. If this analysis were correct, far from realizing the dream of overcoming the market, the neocapitalism characterized by sharing economy would re-propose the usual logic of labour exploitation, going back to the conditions of the early twentieth century. Not surprisingly, concepts such as 'collaborative economy' or 'sharing economy', very popular at the beginning of the phenomenon, are progressively rejected: the platforms are based on a business model that has very little to do with the altruistic idea of sharing, while we have the prevalence of the dimension of the intermediation of work or, as established by the European Court of Justice (ECJ) in the Uber case, of the commercial service aimed at profit.[6]

3. M. Heidegger, *The Question Concerning Technology* (W. Lovitt, Trans.) The Question Concerning Technology: And Other Essays, New York, Harper & Row, 1977.
4. According to a tradition of thought that dates back to Aristotle, *Politics*, Book I, 4, 1253 b.
5. J. Rifkin, *The Zero Marginal Cost Society: The Internet of Things, the Collaborative Commons, and the Eclipse of Capitalism*, London, Palgrave Macmillan.
6. ECJ 20 December 2017, Case C-434/15, *Asociación Profesional Elite Taxi/Uber Systems SpainSL.*

8.2 THE NEW FORMS OF WORK MEDIATED BY PLATFORMS: BETWEEN SUBORDINATION AND AUTONOMY

Between the two narratives, the second undoubtedly appears to capture the real nature of the phenomenon of platforms and its repercussions on work, although the emphasis on the imposition of the technique, reproductive of a pure dependence, is not fully convincing. The phenomenon of platform work is, in fact, more articulated and complex: depending on whether the service is offered online or offline, depending on the professional level required to perform the service, depending on the contents of the contracts used, the platforms have different features and, consequently, the legal nature of the work relationships involved can change significantly, passing from forms of subordination to types of quasi-subordinate work up to genuinely independent relationships.

What is certain is that the technological platform is, speaking in general, a *capitalist enterprise*, an economic actor creating value thanks to economies of scale on the demand and supply side, according to a model – central to the network economy, or scale economies of demand – where many producers independent from the platform interact with a multitude of users.[7] Likewise, it is equally simplistic to think that the platform, as an employer, represents nothing other than a business model in which the immateriality and immediacy typical of the dimension of the infosphere lies on a hierarchical organization of work. Probably, as it happens in all the phases of innovation and change of production paradigms, in platform capitalism, technological devices of subordination and imposition (a) are supported by innovative forms of production that make the worker more autonomous in the performance of the service (b).

With regard to (a), the imposition is present in the interpretation that sees in the platforms the revival of the division of labour, no longer Marxianly linked to specific and exclusive activities, but to increasingly casual and precarious forms of activity, emblematically identified by the term 'Gig Economy'. In this perspective, just as in the *société salariale* of the twentieth century work was determined by technology; likewise, today, the digital revolution would reproduce the forms of traditional subordinate work, but dematerialized and outsourced. In the twentieth century the Taylor-Fordist factory, governed by the principles of the scientific organization of work, was based on prescriptive direction, which specifies not only what should be done, but also how it should be done and in how much time, with complete written instructions, describing in detail the task assigned to the worker, as well as the tools he/she will have to use. This model would be re-proposed in crowdworking, where the human labour provided by the cyber-proletariat is again reduced to simple, standardized and programmed movements. An example of this immense reconnection of work within a digital but neo-Tayloristic logic is the *Mechanical Turk* by Amazon, which in the name of the platform – the machine built in 1706 by Baron von Kempelen commissioned by Maria Theresa of Austria – reproduces the idea of the fake chess player automaton (actually

7. *See* P. Veltz, *La société hyper-industrielle. Le nouveau capitalisme productif*, Seuil, Paris, 2017.

manoeuvered by a master hidden in the mechanical body). This 'operational showcase' collects job advertisements for the performance of certain tasks - generally very simple, mechanical and repetitive - not automatically achievable by an artificial intelligence and therefore crowdsourced by anonymous clients to a not identified crowd of operators who, thanks to the help of a virtual platform on the internet, are confined in an indefinable condition between self-employment and enslavement. In particular, given the opportunity to earn by exploiting the downtime not occupied by other activities, users-providers, as formally autonomous, are forced to carry out their activities without any kind of protection in the event of illness or accident and without no social security coverage, accepting the rates recognized by the platform (generally under the parameters of a decent salary) to which they must grant a percentage of 10%, bearing unquestionable negative judgments by the clients, which may lead to the demotion of their position and reduce the future earning opportunities, exposing oneself to penalties and 'deactivations' in case of refusal to perform a job. Some analysis regarding the distinct but connected phenomenon of work on demand via app lead to similar conclusions, above all in the sectors of transport, cleaning, etc., through platforms such as Uber, Taskrabbit, Handy and so on, which also actively intervene in the preparation of standards of quality of service and in the selection of management and workforce.[8] It is significant that in the ECJ ruling on Uber, the Court underlines how the platform exercises a certain control over the quality of vehicles and their drivers, as well as over the behaviour of the latter, which can lead, if necessary, to their expulsion.[9]

With regard to (b), digitalization can be considered the vector of a real paradigm shift in the world of work, heralded by the advent in the company of methods of conception, production and collaboration that represent just as many methods of thinking, working and organizing.[10] In this new scenario, many elements of the phenomenology of work are decomposed: the *fil rouge* that in the legal tradition links the firm to the forms of imputation and responsibility of labour relations, is lost in a new nebula, where the production of wealth is independent from the ownership of the means of production, and focuses on the *control of information*,[11] without prejudice to the question of the legal nature of the social relations of production. The digitization of the economy therefore implies, first of all, a profound reconsideration of work, its organization, its social meaning and its legal regulation, which opens up new possibilities for expansion for forms of independent work.

8. *See* V. Di Stefano, *Introduction: Crowdsourcing, the Gig Economy and the Law, in Comparative Labor Law & Policy Journal*, 37, 2016, 1 ff.
9. ECJ 20 December 2017, Case C-434/15, *Asociación Profesional Elite Taxi/Uber Systems SpainSL*, 39.
10. *See* the so-called *Mettling Report*: B. Mettling, *Transformation numérique et vie au travail*, 2015, and, on this Report, V. Pontif, *Transformation numérique et vie au travail: les pistes du rapport Mettling*, in Rev. Dr. Trav., 2016, 185 ff.
11. A. Supiot, *Les voies d'une vraie réforme du droit du travail*, in *Au-delà de l'emploi*, nouvelle édition 2016, Flammarion, Paris, 2016, p. XLII.

In this perspective, some of the literature indicates the decline of subordinate work and the increase in self-employment as a peculiarity within the platforms.[12] It is self-employment rather than subordinate work that is a potential beneficiary of the exponential advantages made available by the new digital technology. Research conducted globally has revealed that independent platform-related businesses are growing rapidly in both the United States (US) and Europe, creating new opportunities and options for individuals seeking self-employment, with positive effects in terms of participation to the labour market, employment and productivity of both capital and labour. Macroeconomic benefits go along with microeconomic benefits for businesses and individuals, with a joint effect of *empowerment* for millions of workers and development for new economic activities that the traditional tools of hierarchical organization or, on the contrary, of *outsourcing*, are no longer able to stimulate.[13]

This vision of a platform capitalism that promotes self-employment as a reference to the new digital economy does not exclude, and indeed expressly admits, that the growing needs for protection and contractual and welfare protection, hitherto confined to subordinate work, are and will necessarily be pertaining also to independent work. Social security, access to forms of benefits for lack of activity/employment, insurance for illness and accidents at work, training, contractual protection tools in the context of a relationship often characterized by asymmetries of power – and therefore exposed to risks of abuse of economic dependence – are just as many issues on which labour law, understood in a broader and more comprehensive sense, is stimulated to rethink its function and its scope. However, it is not a matter of thinking about the tout-court extension of labour law protection techniques to self-employed workers, but rather of rethinking the principles of basic protection, applicable to labour 'without adjectives',[14] as well as imagining new ad hoc protections for these specific groups of economically dependent workers.[15]

In this perspective, rather than embracing, in an almost ideological way, a vision of platform work as *necessarily subordinate*, it is appropriate to make a more problematic and articulated assessment, careful to verify the links between technique and labour in a perspective open to new solicitations that the economic model proposes, also in terms of protection of social rights and of the individual, without using only the traditional regulatory framework and, above all, without losing sight of the new, extraordinary opportunities for growth offered by the 'second era of machines'.

12. *See* M. Sheeham, R. Ortlieb, A. McNamara, *Business Start-Up&Youth Self Employment*, in European Policy Brief No. 7, December 2016.
13. *The Future of Work. OECD Employment Outlook*, 2019, OECD Publishing, Paris, 146 ff.; *see also Independent Work: Choice, Necessity and the Gig Economy*, McKinsey Global Institute, October 2016.
14. The term 'work without adjectives' was used by Italian doctrine in the 1990s to indicate the need to free labour law from the notion of subordination, in order to embrace a broader vision of work, in the direction that will later be developed by the Supiot Report, from the various thesis on 'personal working relationships', and from the doctrine on economically dependent self-employment: *see* A. Perulli, *Economically Dependent/Quasi Subordinate (Parasubordinate) Employment: Legal, Social and Economic Aspects*, Brussels, EC, 2003.
15. *See* Manfred Weiss, *The main challenges for labour law*, in *Regulating the Platform Economy. International Perspectives on new forms of work*, Lourdes Mella Méndez (ed.), London, Routledge, 2020.

8.3 THE QUALIFICATION OF EMPLOYMENT RELATIONSHIPS: A PROBLEM OF 'INSTRUMENTAL' OR 'AXIOLOGICAL' RATIONALITY?

The irruption on the economic scene of actors, such as digital platforms, capable of disrupting the basic subjective references of labour law, exacerbate the problems of relationship qualification and propose new value issues, related to the consequences of qualification. The boundary between subordination and autonomy, which has always been uncertain and porous – despite the dogmatic rigor with which the *summa divisio* can be traced *in apicibus* – tends more and more to get blurred, and the materials contained in one as in the other neighbouring universe move, dragged along by the factors of production, to be recomposed by legislators focused on tracing, in this uncertain upheaval, a rational compass of regulation. The outcome of these processes concerns a paradigm shift in labour law also in the context of the classification/qualification of the cases concerning work relationships, in a logic that progressively departs from the rigidly binary setting of the categories of subordinate and independent work.

The problem posed by the impact of technological evolution on work relationships does not simply refer to the use of the legal technique of qualification, according to self-referential interpretative schemes. The challenge posed to qualification methods, raised by the profound changes in the organization of work and production, is not simply referable to the 'instrumental rationality' of the system (in the sense of adequacy of the means with respect to the goals), understood as the ability of the system itself to carry out in a 'correct' way the qualification of the relationship in terms of subordination or autonomy. The question that arises comes before qualification, and is of an axiological-teleological nature: it does not so much concern the validity of the traditional categories and related indicia, questioned to verify their suitability to solve the problems of qualification of employment relationships in the context of the platform capitalism, but it concerns *the rationality of the effects that qualification produces in regulatory terms*. It is therefore a problem of 'axiological rationality' of the system. This '*dark side*' of qualification is usually neglected by the labour law doctrine, engaged in sophisticated conceptual disputes, but very reluctant to go into the agone of the axiological perspective, which in some cases remains expressed by the reconstructive options operated in the interpretative stage. As a matter of fact, it is clear that the general categories of subordination and autonomy (and related indicia) present the dogmatic qualities in order to carry out the qualification of work relationships, adapting to any work process, from pony express to Foodora riders, from Uber drivers to call centre operators, from freelance journalists to platform workers in general, etc. The real problem that arises today is another: that is, whether the use of those categories, inserted in a systemic logic of *either/or* produce a rational and equitable qualification on the level of values and protection, regardless of the solution of the formal matter of qualification. A rational and equitable labour law system, based on values of social justice, must not be satisfied with having dogmatic categories (whatever they are) that are consolidated and capable of bringing social reality back into the rigid boxes of the typological system, but it must provide regulatory responses that avoid, in the operation of those qualification processes, the attribution of hyper-protection on the one hand, and little or no protection on the other, if the (in our case, digital) worker still expresses a need for social protection. If, hypothetically, the Foodora rider or the Uber drivers are formally qualified as self-employed (or possibly 'para-subordinate' workers) based on the current regulatory categories (because they are not subject to managerial power and free to accept or not the job), it is of little interest to observe the continuing validity of the normative categories, obviously capable of qualifying those relationships in one sense or another. Rather, we should be worrying that those riders or drivers, even if formally independent, may, in hypothesis, receive a salary that is totally inadequate compared to the service provided; they may remain excluded from the protections regarding health and safety at work; they are subject to an 'ad nutum' annulment on the part of the platform, perhaps with a simple notification or without even this minimum precaution, and they have no right to access trade union rights, as being independent contractors. If this happens it is because, evidently, the use of existing categories, in a labour market much more articulated and complex than that of the Fordist era, does not *produce rational results from an axiological point of view*: hence a new and worrying discrepancy between the 'case' and the 'legal effects' arises in an aggravated way, in the era of the digital economy affecting millions and millions of workers on a global scale.

The problem of a rational and equitable labour regulatory system is not solved with the production of formalistically correct qualifications, or with the avoidance/reduction of qualifying uncertainties, but with the achievement of equity and social justice in the regulation of relationships. That equity that a rigidly binary system, applied to a constantly evolving labour market, is no longer able to produce, fuelling increasingly less understandable and acceptable regulatory segmentations and fractures. The problem does not concern only continental legal culture, but affects all legal systems. As the comparative analysis shows, even in the US the disputes raised by digital workers have subjected the flexible qualification techniques developed overseas to unprecedented tensions, highlighting the inadequacy of those index, the randomness of judgments, the search for solutions based on to a 'remedial technique' often practiced by the courts.

8.3.1 The Option of Subordination 'At All Costs'

In view of the multiplication of intermediated work by on-demand platforms and the inadequacy of the binary qualification system, a first defensive reaction leads to an observation of social reality in such a way as to activate, at the level of legal qualification, the protections of standard subordinate work. In this perspective, a part of the doctrine, also of Anglo-Saxon matrix, tends to recognize in the phenomenon of the digital economy the umpteenth paradox of neo-liberal precariousness, in which the exploitation of work through platforms expresses the maximum potential for dehumanization and commodification of work.[16] Adopting this interpretative attitude, digital work tends to appear, depending on the operating modes of the platform, either as the extreme edge of the casualization of work, which is achieved through a micro-fragmentation of the activity that is performed under the payment of micro-wages, either as an unprecedented form of social Darwinism where work, in its most professional forms, is brought back to a sort of prize lottery, and paid only in favour of the winners, while the platform still holds the right of ownership over intellectual work.[17]

The unconditional response of this kind of analysis appeals to the usual protections administered by labour law, whose gateway, due to the persistent binary system that characterizes most legal systems, is represented by the qualification as an employee of the platform worker-user. The attack of labour law has therefore focused on the use of dogmatics through devices for expanding the case of subordination through the use of various techniques:

(a) the use of tests aimed at adapting, in the peculiar conditions of *crowdworking* and *on-demand work*, the protective ratio to the social vulnerability of the worker, such as the *control test* and the Anglo-Saxon *economic reality test*, or the criterion of the *service organisé* adopted by the French jurisprudence (*see infra*);
(b) the adoption of *presumptions* of subordinate work, as it happens in the State of California, and as it is proposed to generalize in an interpretative way on the basis of the provisions of International Labour Organization (ILO) Recommendation no. 198/2006;[18]
(c) a general tendency to consider as subordinate any service that can be said to have been 'organized' by the platform;[19]
(d) a *purposive* interpretation of subordination, in which the criteria of the democratic deficit and that of economic dependence are added, although this is not referable to any type of platform.[20] Pathways of redefinition of subordination in a broad sense are known in *common law* Countries, where formalistic approaches in terms of interpretation of the notion of employee are replaced by a principle of reality, adopted by the United Kingdom (UK) Supreme Court, and by a *purpositive* approach aimed at avoiding workers to be excluded from the protections of labour law, and that part of the doctrine would like to push towards a general presumption of *employee status*.[21]

16. *See* M. Freedland, *Le contrat de travail et les paradoxes de la précarité*, in Rev. Dr. Trav., 2016, pp. 289 ff.
17. W. Däubler, *Challenges to labour law*, in *L'idea di diritto del lavoro, oggi. In ricordo di Giorgio Ghezzi*, A. Perulli (ed.), Milan, Wolters Kluwer Cedam, 2016, p. 503.
18. *See* V. Di Stefano, *The Rise of the 'Just-in-Time Workforce: On Demand Work, Crowdwork and Labour Protection in the 'Gig Economy'*, Geneva, ILO, 2016, p. 22.
19. *See* A. Lyon-Caen, *Plateforme*, in Rev. Dr. Trav. 2016, p. 301.
20. G. Davidov, *Setting Labour Law's Coverage: Between Universalism and Selectivity, in Oxford Journal of Legal Studies*, vol. 34, Autumn 2014, 543-566.
21. G. Davidov, *A Purposive Approach to Labour Law*, Oxford University Press, 2016, pp. 116 s.

The generosity of these proposals, in addition to clashing with the difficulties of bringing the complex and variegated phenomenology of app-driven labour back into the categories of subordination, suffers the further problem deriving from the quality of the protections that can be granted in the event of a judicial requalification of operators as subordinate workers: qualification that can result in a Pyrrhus victory, at least in those systems in which the protective statute of the subordinate worker is effectively emptied thanks to the presence of 'zero hour' contracts, since the employer is not required to guarantee a minimum of paid working hours,[22] that is to say, the intermittent, discontinuous and random nature of the working activity constitutes an obstacle to access to social rights, such as maternity leave, holidays, and more generally, to the set of rights related to the status of worker in a relationship having a certain duration;[23] hence, the result of this strategy of appealing to subordination can result as; in terms of safeguards, very limited or even as a failure.

Obviously, this is not intended to deny *a priori* the attributability to subordination of a large part of the work through platforms. If, over the years, labour law has necessarily had to deal with a constantly evolving economic reality, adapting the notion of subordination to allow the protective *ratio* not to be excluded due to the progress that the technique itself ambiguously proposed, it is certainly possible that a portion of the cases attributable to the operating schemes of the platform economy can be correctly attributed to subordinate work. However, there are those who support the thesis that the activity performed in the context of the platform/collaborative economy is characterized by being immediately productive and a source of wealth without having to be framed and regimented in the contractual schemes of subordinate work;[24] actually – it is the lapidary judgment of a French jurist – *le salariat est l'anti-modèle du monde numerique.*[25] What is certain is that the platform workers constitute a heterogeneous group, with respect to which it is not reasonable to envisage uniform regulatory solutions.[26]

8.3.2 The 'Remedial' Perspective and the Modulation of Protection by Thresholds

A different perspective, which relativizes the question – generally considered fundamental – of the qualification of the employment relationship, is today cultivated by many as a ground for experimenting with work protection techniques conveyed both

22. A. Adams, M. Freedland, J. Prassl, *The Zero-Hours Contract: Regulating Casual Work, or Legitimating Precarity?, in Giornale di diritto del lavoro e di relazioni industriali*, 2015, 147, 529 ss.
23. V. Di Stefano, *The Rise of the 'Just-in-Time' Workforce: On Demand Work, Crowdwork and Labour Protection in the 'Gig Economy'*, *supra*, p. 8.
24. In the Italian doctrine this position is supported by G. Bronzini, *Economia della condivisione e lavoro autonomo: una prospettiva europea*, in A. Perulli, (ed.), Lavoro autonomo e capitalismo delle piattaforme, Milan, Wolters Kluwer Cedam, 2018, p. 1 ff.
25. T. Pasquier, *De l'arrêt FORMACAD aux travailleurs 'ubérisés'*, in Rev. Dr. Trav. 2017, p. 106.
26. For an analysis of the different ways in which a platform 'organizes' a particular market, *see*, in French doctrine, A. Fabre, *Plateformes numériques: gare au tropisme 'travailliste'!*, in Rev. Dr. Trav., 2017, pp. 166 ss.

by jurisprudence and, *de jure condendo*, by the legislator. The urgency of identifying adequate protection for platform workers must move towards a remedial approach that goes beyond traditional qualification schemes, enhancing the general principles of the legal system, in particular the constitutional ones relating to work and its protections. The same methodological perspective is adopted by those who emphasize the inadequacies of the binary qualification scheme, proposing the transition from a regulatory logic based on the idea of a *binary divide* among cases to a regulation by '*thresholds*' that cross the cases:[27] while the binary divide follows the principle according to which the regulatory disciplines of work relationships are distinguished by reason of the subordinate or independent nature of the contractual relationships, the 'threshold' instead indicates a space that exceeds the type-logical pattern of the ultimatum and defines a new 'topo-logical' regulatory criterion, where the determination of the divide gives way to a disciplinary space that relativizes, without completely eliminating them, the typological barriers, providing that combinatorial situation where the constitutional protections of work are delineated in areas that do not necessarily coincide with those designated by the standard type of subordinate employment relationship.

The remedial logic, or, if you prefer, the technique based on the modulation of the protections by thresholds, is used pragmatically in all the hypotheses in which the protections of labour law, far from remaining confined within the narrow scope of subordinate work (identified as such according to the convergent criteria of law or jurisprudence), are applied, in whole or in part, to intermediate situations between subordination and autonomy; and this trend of '*proliferation of intermediate categories*'[28] seems to respond to the demands of a constantly evolving production system, capable of creating hybrid professional figures, who act on the labour markets without a precise or fixed 'home' in the social-typical (even before legal-typical) categories of subordination or autonomy.

The issue was dealt with in methodologically different ways, but converging in the need to rethink the boundaries of labour law, its universalistic expansion, or its capacity – only apparently opposite – to selectively penetrate social areas lacking social consideration and relegated to a purely civil or commercial regulation. Consider, for example, the analysis of those who come to the point of considering the binary distinction between subordination and autonomy as being even 'false' – and in any case insufficient – suggesting to identify, in its place, a new 'family of contracts', with seven empirical types of work relationships (standard subordinate work, public work, liberal professions, freelancers, atypical jobs, trainees and voluntary work) characterized by a personal bond (*Personality of Work*), a broader concept of the *contract of employment* and such as to justify selective administration of protections also to self-employed workers, extended to the freedom of organization, trade union association and strike and the right to safety and social security.[29] Within a dogmatically

27. *See* A. Perulli, *Costanti e varianti in tema di subordinazione e autonomia*, in Lav. Dir., 2015, pp. 262 ss.
28. G. Davidov, *A Purposive Approach to Labour Law*, *supra* note 21, pp. 135 ss.
29. M. Freedland, N. Kountouris, *The Legal Construction of Personal Work Relations*, Oxford, Oxford University Press, 2011; M. Freedland, *The Personal Employment Contract*, Oxford, Oxford University Press, 2003; M. Freedland, *From the Contract of Employment to the Personal Work*

different perspective, but in part convergent *quoad effectum*, are those who theorized to address the issue of 'economically dependent' work from a legislative point of view (not only at national but also at European level), a concept that unites subordinate and (part of) the autonomous work, qualifying a 'supra-typical' category of work relationships whose inclusion in the regulatory framework of labour law is justified both in a selective logic (since it refers to a particular social group that expresses specific protection needs) and in a universalistic direction (as it expands the spectrum of action of labour law, or parts of it, to additional categories of workers).[30] Finally, the prospect of a selective extension of protections beyond subordination is promoted by the Organisation for Economic Co-operation and Development (OECD) Employment Outlook (2019): the imbalance of bargaining power among the parties and the existence of monopsonist labour markets are the main guilty party for the situation of vulnerability of self-employed workers. It is therefore proposed to act in a double direction: on the one hand, we can identify an area characterized by a 'genuine ambiguity' in the qualification of employment relationships (genuine in the sense that the related relationships are not attributable to the category of 'false self-employed persons'); in this 'gray' segment of the labour market, which should be reduced to a minimum in a logic of contrasting misclassification, a series of legal safeguards should be extended beyond standard employees, to guarantee independent workers fair pay, regulating working time, occupational safety and health, anti-discrimination, employment protection. On the other hand, the improvement of the conditions of self-employed workers should be implemented through social dialogue and collective bargaining, training programs and social protection schemes, also acting through exceptions to the prohibition of collective bargaining for genuine self-employed groups with strong bargaining power imbalance.

These proposals, which tend to redesign the criteria for the attribution and selection of labour protections, lead to critically rethink the opposition of subordination/autonomy in order to organize the passage from the *binary divide* to a new dimensional geometry of labour law; geometry that suggests, instead of the traditional opposition, a space of crossing, mobility and change of labour. It is a prospect that, far from reflecting purely formalistic or efficiency requirements of the qualification processes, must be grasped in the context of a new vision of the values of solidarity, equity and social justice that inform the regulatory objectives of the labour law system. A perspective that reconnects the ancient (but ultimately never completely lost) links that connect self-employed and subordinate work,[31] proving the relativity and myopia of the visions that place those work worlds on parallel lines and not on a

Nexus, *in Industrial Law Journal*, vol. 35, 2006, 1 ss.; M. Freedland, *Sur l'application du droit du travail et de l'emploi au-delà du contrat de travail*, in, Revue internationale du Travail, vol. 146, 2007; more recently *see* N. Countouris, V. De Stefano, *New Trade Union Strategies for New Forms of Employment*, ETUC, Brussels, 2019.

30. *See* A. Perulli, *Economically Dependent/Quasi-Subordinate (Parasubordinate) Employment: Legal, Social and Economic aspects*, EU, Bruxelles, 2002.

31. *See* B. Veneziani, *The evolution of the contract of employment*, in *The Making of Labour Law in Europe*, B. Hepple (ed.), London-New York, Mansell Publishing Limited, 1986, pp. 31 ff.; S. Deakin, *The Contract of Employment: A Study in Legal Evolution*, ESRC Centre for Business

continuum: hence, the alternativity promoted by the supporters of the 'ontological fracture' should give way to a legislative project based on the ability to identify an area in which the labour contracts enter into communication beyond the distinction between subordination and autonomy.

8.4 ARE DIGITAL PLATFORMS EMPLOYERS?

Platform capitalism questions the categories of the 'old' labour law, without denying its regulatory dimension: on the contrary, paradoxically, the digital revolution applied to production creates the conditions for a profound rethinking of the functions and 'figures' of labour law. First of all, as we have seen, the figure of subordination in its relationship with autonomy, understood not only as categories to measure the scope of traditional labour law, but also, in perspective, as categories to redefine regulatory links between technology, work and protection of people; second – and not necessarily in a specular way – the figure of the employer, the conditions of exercise of entrepreneurial powers, in particular the power of management and control, which are widely questioned by the digital modalities of platform capitalism; and finally, the legal figures of the organization of work, starting from place and time, up to the issues of quality and health/safety, called into question above all for the risks connected with the subdivision of work into micro-tasks as it occurs on many platforms, or the risks of overworking, or the risks related with the safety equipment of the platforms.

If technology, as a provocative im-position, constantly questions us about 'whether and how we explicitly commit ourselves to what the imposition itself unfolds its being', the first question posed by the use of technological platforms concerns the conditions of use of technology, to its being a threat or, on the contrary, 'that which saves', in the sense that 'what constitutes the being of the technique contains within itself the possible emergence of that which saves'.[32] The juridical projection of this awareness linked to the structural ambiguity of the technique mainly concerns the nature of the juridical relations involved, their identification and their treatment, the perimeter in which they move, in a scenario where what is questioned is actually the classic labour law paradigm, based on the exchange between a performance of subordinate work and remuneration, in the context of a community of work and within a circumscribed and identifiable company-employer.

In this perspective, it was opportunely observed that 'a significant portion of the supply conveyed by the network is projected well beyond the conceptual lines that define traditional work: the autonomy/subordination dichotomy, the discrete importance of hetero-direction, the relationship of legal power in production report'. The development of the collaborative economy, but even more the digitization of production, therefore contribute to the emergence of new forms of activity situated beyond the classic distinction between subordination and autonomy, in an indistinct archipelago

Research, University of Cambridge Working Paper No. 203, June 2001; A. Perulli, *Il lungo viaggio del lavoro autonomo dal diritto dei contratti al diritto del lavoro, e ritorno*, in *Lav. dir.*, 2017, p. 251 ff.

32. M. Heidegger, *The Question Concerning Technology*, Garland Publishing, New York City, 1977.

of activities that are not legally adjectivized. These are hybrid forms, which on the one hand benefit from spheres of freedom due to direct contact with the client, the consequent self-determination of times and the possibility of combining different forms of activity, but on the other hand, they suffer from situations of economic dependence over the platform, often undergoing ambiguous control and conditioning mechanisms, through general regulations or conditions of use that unilaterally establish the negotiation conditions (such as the setting of the price of the service, the control over the execution, the appreciation clauses of the service provided online, the deactivation of users). Deprived of protection as subordinates, these platform 'operators' do not benefit from the advantages of true independence on the market, ending up adding the drawbacks of both statuses.

But let us start with the basic defining elements of labour law: the category of the employer and that of the worker are both strongly put into question. The on-demand economy has seen the birth of economic activities based on the use of internet platforms that allow immediate *matching* between a user who requests a good or a service and another person who is able to provide it by sharing his/her assets and skills. Therefore, opportunistic and transient forms of activities proliferate, such as *digital corporations* and *crowdsourcing*, which replace the assignment of a worker to a workstation in the company with an *open call* on platforms. The latter, far from proposing themselves as employers, express a different organizational rationality, which does not concern so much - as in the classical labour law scheme - the organization of work for productive purposes, but the organization of 'markets' of services, which create relations among customers and workers.

Sometimes this organization gives rise to the stipulation of three distinct contracts: this is the case of sites that provide for a mediation contract between the site and the customer, a kind of consultancy (or selection) contract between the site and the worker and a contract for the provision of services between the worker and the client. In such a configuration, the platform selects independent workers without interfering in the execution of the provision of services, not even in the matter of compensation, which is paid directly by the customer to the worker, while the site makes its profit by asking the customer to pay a commission. This model, which seems to combine the legal framework of the contract and that of the administration, seems to exclude the possibility of identifying an employer within the platform.

More often, however, the intermediation of the platforms is less decomposed, and the operation is organized through the establishment of general conditions of sale for the customer, and the preparation of a contract for the provision of services between the site and the worker, where, in general, there is a clause stating that the worker delegates the site to collect the customer's payment and to pay him/her a sum after the withdrawal of a commission. Even in this case, the attribution of the employer figure to the digital platform seems to be excluded, as the scheme of the procurement contract prevails for the website managers.

The employer figure would seem to re-emerge, at least partially, in cases where the platform establishes the price of the service, or sets the contractual conditions for the bidder and the technical specifications or requirements of the offer. The first question to ask is therefore whether the platform, under these specific profiles, is an employer or whether, even in this case, the organization functions are ancillary to a primary intermediation function of a subject who – as Uber claims – provides a smartphone user with a '*user interface*', essentially a computer program, as part of a service offered by the worker.

Also in this case the answers appear strongly polarized.

According to a first vision, which was accredited by the ECJ in the Uber case, the platform is not limited to carrying out an intermediary function: arguing that the drivers whose services it coordinates are independent workers, Uber, which actually carries out an activity of production of services for profit, conceals a very different reality, where workers are subjected to a very penetrating management and control, so that the technological device of the platforms would be at the basis of a brutal commodification and dehumanization of work.[33]

In other analyses, more aware of the difficulties of tout-court identifying the legal traits of a traditional employer in the platform, a functional-typological vision is adopted, with the aim of selecting at least one prerogative among the various employer functions, exercised by platform, which makes it possible to at least partially attribute the employer's status to the platform.[34]

In this perspective, it is stated that, given that the platform often determines the price of the service, and this function typically pertains to the employer, under this specific profile the platform can be considered as an employer: not to all intents and purposes, but only in relation to the price determination function, with the consequence that, if the wage paid falls below the minimum wage, the platform will be responsible for the violation. Likewise, the platform may be called to respond as a 'functional' employer for the violation of the anti-discrimination legislation if, for example, in determining the price of the service, the platform systematically reduces the cost of female labour.

These functionalist views are not fully convincing. Generally appealing to the commodification and dehumanization of work that the crowdworking phenomenon determines does not seem sufficient, nor does it seem legally correct to break down, recompose and multiply the notion of employer on the basis of completely extrinsic indices, such as price fixing of the service, which is the prerogative of any strong contractor, employer or even client. This, as we will *see* (below), does not absolutely mean giving up identifying regulatory tools and strategies to moderate the negative social effects of platform capitalism, through more appropriate regulatory devices and, perhaps, more responsive to the same protection needs of the weak worker-contractor.

A completely opposite view to the one observed so far argues that the platform does not provide top to bottom services, but it acts as a technological 'enabler', putting

33. M. Freedland, *Le contrat de travail et les paradoxes de la précarité*, p. 295.
34. *See* J. Prassl, *The Concept of the Employer*, Oxford, Oxford University Press, 2015, who deems to identify the employer in the entity, or combination of entities 'playing a decisive role in the exercise of relational employing functions, and regulated or controlled as such in each particular domain of employment law'; *see also* J. Prassl, *Towards a Functional Concept of the Employer*, paper presented at *The Annual Conference of the European Centre of Expertise (ECE) in the Field of Labour Law, Employment and Labour Market Policies: The Personal Scope of Labour Law in Times of Atypical Employment and Digitalisation*, Frankfurt, April 2017.

the seeker directly in contact with those who offer and thus becoming a vehicle of reputation, trust, belonging. In this perspective, the platform can offer services of added value by designing the environment where interactions take place, without however influencing the actors who are enabled. Furthermore, the assets and skills that generate value for the platforms belong to the people and not to the platform, as, on the contrary, is the case in traditional companies; the same actors are interchangeable, presenting themselves in some cases as 'those who offer' and in others as 'those who seek'.

It appears evident that, according to this prospect, the platform does not perform any of the typical functions of the employer, not even that of fixing the price of the service (as is the case for some digital platforms), while the user-operator cannot be classified as subordinate worker, lacking the decisive element of control/direction of work. As if to say that, according to this regulatory provision, it is quite possible to provide a service through a platform, without the need to establish an employment relationship with an employer, and with the possibility for the worker to operate simultaneously for multiple platforms, in favour of a multitude of users.

It is therefore clear that where the platform does not exercise forms of *command and control* over the activity of the operator-user, the latter must be qualified as a self-employed worker. This brings us back to the heart of the qualifying problem related to how the legal subordination relationship that possibly connects the provider to the platform must be understood within the case involved. As a matter of fact, if the platform actually exercised a control/management power over the performance, we should not only attribute to the worker the nature of a subordinate worker, but we should also recognize the status of employer for the platform; in short, we should recognize that, in this case, the platform-enterprise – and the economic power on which it is based – continues to identify itself with an organization (and with a power of organization) of work, and not only as an entity that only organizes a market by providing IT systems that coordinate the performance of operating users.

8.5 MORE ON THE QUALIFICATION OF RELATIONSHIPS: THE EC POINT OF VIEW AND THE COMPARATIVE PERSPECTIVE

The issue was addressed by the European Commission under the so-called European Agenda on the collaborative economy, and placed in the context of a 'structural change', induced precisely by the collaborative economy, about the forms and methods of performing a service, often based on activities carried out outside a stable, regular and timed schedule.[35] As pointed out in the European Agenda on collaborative economy, in this context, the borders between independent workers and employees are more and more blurred, and there is an increase of fixed-term contracts, that is, the number of people that have more than one job, according to the Eurostat data. The rights guaranteed by the Social Chapter of the European Union are applied only to those subjects that may be defined as 'employees' under European Union (EU) case law.

35. COM (2016) 356 final.

According to the Court of Justice of the European Union, the essential feature of subordinate employment is that, for a certain period of time, a person performs services for and under the direction of another person, in return for remuneration. However, what application would this general – and very traditional – criterion identifying an employment relationship have with regard to, for example, workers that operate through a digital platform? According to the European Agenda, *for the criterion of subordination to be met, the worker must act under the direction of the collaborative platform, the latter determining the choice of the activity, remuneration and working conditions. In other words, the worker is not free to choose what services he/she will provide and how, e.g., as per the contractual relationship he/she established with the collaborative platform.*

In the EU Agenda, they do not explain what the 'direction' of the collaborative platform means, but we may assume, on the basis of the Commission's declarations, that the existence of the subordination, in this case, is not necessarily dependent on the actual exercise of management or supervision on a continuous basis. As a matter of fact, the services provided through digital platforms permanently seem to overcome the traditional notion of subordination as subjection of the employee to the employer's directional power, towards forms of 'organizational subordination'. In this perspective, the above-mentioned 'direction' – that according to the EU Agenda must anyway be present – may actually be achieved even in view of an IT platform that pre-defines the modalities and the conditions of work, thus realizing the 'direction' of the labour through the platform. Or, according to an even broader view of the concept of employee, when the worker is in a position of 'economic dependence' towards the platform based on a series of criteria such as the personality of the service, the relationship with a (or few) platforms, the lack of operational resources for the worker, etc.[36] It is not clear, however, whether, in this way, the European Commission really opens up to a broader notion of subordination, of an 'organizational' type, which will in any case have to be verified in the individual legal systems of the Member States on the basis of the criteria used by the National Courts.

8.6 THE NATIONAL JURISPRUDENCE: A COMPARATIVE ANALYSIS

If the existing legal categories do not allow offering these workers basic guarantees, there is a problem of 'axiological rationality' of the legal categories of positive law, and in this respect the binary view of subordination and autonomy built around the notion of hetero-direction (according to the command and control model) appears too narrow to meet these needs for substantive justice. It is therefore necessary to resort to the interpretative dimension. However, as we have seen, interpretation not always can provide adequate answers, thus posing a problem of 'axiological rationality' also in relation to hermeneutics, which, as we know, do not proceed by dogmas but use the

36. *See* M. Risak/T. Dullinger, *The Concept of 'Worker' in EU Law: Status Quo and Potential for Change*, European Trade Union Institute, 2018, Report 140, p. 46 f.

juridical categories in order to establish judgments that are consistent with the values of protection of the worker, in relation to the legal system.

As mentioned, jurisprudence is an important vector in the process of adapting the axiological rationality of labour law in the digital age.[37] The adaptation of the notion of subordination to the new organizational and production context and to the new ways of providing work is one of the major issues of doctrinal discussion. In this perspective, the 'purposive approach', practiced above all (but not only) in common law systems, has been valorized. However, even this approach is not free from criticalities and limits of use: interpreting the law at a higher level of abstraction (that of its *justification*) rather than that of the political compromise that produced it,[38] generates a series of problematic issues, of theoretical and practical nature, ranging from the increase in judicial subjectivism (aggravated by the different *pre-understanding* of the law that any judge can have) up to the risk of undue overcoming through jurisprudence of the meaning of the norm as derived from the sense of words used by the legislator. Moreover, this approach should (in theory) be used only in the face of a real uncertainty in understanding the law, providing a meaning that the normative statement can reasonably support from the semantic point of view, and not to fill gaps or 'failures' on the part of the legislator.[39] But even the correct operation of these intrinsic limits to the purposive approach are of uncertain application, given that the line between the most natural and ordinary meaning, and between an unnatural meaning and a new meaning are not clear: what can be understood by some as 'overriding clear words' may be described by another as 'a broad interpretation'. It is certain that in a legislative definition of positive law (such as, for example, in Italy, Article 2094 of the Italian Civil Code), which indicates the exercise of executive power by the employer as the main criterion of subordination, it is very difficult to be able to argue that the meaning of the normative statement is really uncertain, so as to be able to interpret it 'purposively', attributing a different normative content to the concept of subordination (arbitrarily replacing the legislative criterion with a different jurisprudential criterion).

The revision of the subordination indices, to adapt them to the new context, is another path that is now followed by jurisprudence. In California, the traditional *Borello* test, based on multifactorial indices, has been replaced by a simpler (and generous) ABC test, capable of significantly broadening the concept of subordinate work and, consequently, the scope of application of labour law, even at the expense of

37. *See* A. Perulli, *The legal and jurisprudential evolution of the notion of employee, in European Labour Law Journal*, 11(2), 2020, 117 ff.
38. *See* G. Davidov, *Setting Labour Law's Coverage: Between Universalism and Selectivity*, in *Lavoro autonomo e capitalismo delle piattaforme*, A. Perulli (ed.), Milan, Wolters Kluwer Cedam, 2018, p. 70, referring to H.M. Hart Jr., A.M. Saacks, *The Legal Process: Basic Problems in Making and Application of Law*, Cambridge, Tentative Edition 1958, 1200.
39. *See* K. Tokeley, *Interpretation of Legislation. Trends in Statutory Interpretation and the Judicial Process*, Victoria University of Wellington Law Review, 33, 2002, 969: 'First, the purposive approach should only be applied where there is uncertainty in the words of the statute. Secondly, it should only be used to employ a meaning that the words of the statute are reasonably capable of bearing. The courts should not use the purposive approach to make a law consistent with Parliamentary intent if Parliament has failed to effectively state that intent in the statute'.

an excessive simplification of the social-economic framework of reference. The risk, in this case, is that the regulatory system, by modifying the qualification processes to re-establish congruence and optimization, will provide an over-simplified representation of social reality, eventually modifying reality itself through the normative logic.

In France, for example, jurisprudence has played a decisive role in expanding the concept of subordinate worker through a redevelopment of the *lien de subordination juridique*. The maximum extension of this expansive trend was reached with the identification of subordination in the service performed within the framework of an 'organized service' where the employer unilaterally determines the conditions of execution of the service. This criterion, however, was soon downsized and, with the *Société Générale* ruling, it was downgraded to a mere index of subordination, reaffirming the principle according to which *the lien de subordination juridique* consists in the execution of the service under the authority of the employer, who has the power to issue orders and directives, to check the compliance and to sanction any non-conforming behaviours of the worker. However, precisely with reference to the cases of work through platforms, a part of the doctrine seems inclined to reactivate less orthodox interpretative paths, as happened in the past with the heretical judgment *Labanne* in 2000, in which the judges emphasized the economic dependence of a taxi driver able to self-determine the times and places of his activity, and as stated with the *Formacad* case, in which the Court of Cassation has requalified the activity of some professional trainers operating under a self-employment regime on the basis of a series of extrinsic indices of the absence of independence, such as the lack of personal clients, the presence of non-competition clauses, the continuity of the service, which, considered together, represent an approximation of the case towards being considered as pertaining to subordinate work rather than self-employed work. Faced with this need for axiological rationality in the qualification of labour relations, some interpretative guidelines get to employ the same legal categories with greater adherence to labour protection requirements, even at the cost of raising some doubts about the full compliance of the decision with the conceptual substrate of traditional subordination. This is the case of the French Court of Cassation, which has deemed as appropriate to classify the Take it Easy *livreurs* as subordinate employees, valuing two factual elements of the relationship which, according to the Court, would be indicative of a state of subordination: the geolocation that allows following in real time the position of the worker and the accounting of the number of kilometres covered by the courier, and the existence of a bonus/malus system similar to the disciplinary power. According to the ruling of the Court, from these two elements, we can infer the existence of a power of management and control of the execution of the characteristic performance of the '*lien de subordination*'.[40] The reasoning of the Court is very problematic. In fact, it is impossible to understand how from the elements considered (in particular a geolocation device) it is possible to deduce the existence of a directive power and a power of control, while other indices, such as the presence of an 'organized service', were not taken into consideration by the Court. However, it is precisely this critical nature of

40. Cour de cassation – Chambre sociale, Arrêt n°1737 du 28 novembre 2018 (17-20.079).

judicial reasoning that clearly demonstrates the willingness of jurisprudence to adapt, even at the cost of an extensive interpretation of traditional criteria, the concept of subordination to forms of work that do not present the traits of the accepted dogmatics but, nevertheless, require adequate social treatment.

The Australian Fair Work Commission moved in the same direction with a decision concerning a Foodora employment relationship.[41] In a regulatory context that is different from the French one, where the subordination is identified, the factual elements that are valued coincide with those of the case decided by the French Court de Cassation. The Decision has in fact recognized Foodora as having considerable capacity to control how the applicant performed the service, and it fixed the place of work and the start and finish times of each engagement or shift, and this was reflected by the metrics that were used in the batching system which ranked the work performance of, *inter alia*, the applicant. The operation of the batching system meant that in order to maintain a high ranking the applicant would be required to perform a certain number of deliveries during any particular engagement, to work a minimum number of shifts in a week, and work a number of Fridays, Saturdays or Sundays nights (paragraph 73). In essence, the level of control that might be exercised in employment situations by way of direct verbal or written instruction to an employee from the employer, was obtained by *Foodora* by virtue of the operation of the batching system: as a matter of practical reality, the applicant could not pick and choose when and where to work, or how fast or slow to make deliveries. Furthermore, the worker had a substantial investment in capital equipment that he used to perform his delivery work (paragraph 78). The consequence is that 'the correct characterization of the relationship between the applicant and the respondent is that of employee' (paragraph 102).

These cases demonstrate that interpretative techniques can move in the expansive direction of the notion of subordination if the system allows it in terms of coherence with existing normative categories. In truth, this capacity of the jurisprudence to apply the law by employing the lenses of the evolution of social relations in a flexible way has been questioned in a very clear way by a part of the doctrine, which has been found as one of the main elements of crisis of the current labour law.[42] Such criticism is right on target, but only in part, because – as we have seen – there is no lack of examples of an adaptive process, sometimes even at the cost of obvious hermeneutical forcing of the notion of subordination on the part of the courts. Rather, in my opinion, it is the national and supranational legislator who appears as being rather static, neglecting to intervene on the legal notion of subordination to adapt it to a new context. The case of Germany is emblematic of this legislative inertia. The European legislator is not exempt from this criticism: just think of the recent text of the European Parliament on the proposed Directive on transparent and predictable working conditions, in which one adheres strictly to the interpretation criteria of the ECJ case law in the qualification of working relationships with the consequence that domestic workers, on-call workers, intermittent workers, voucher workers, workers through platforms, etc. could fall within the scope of the Directive provided they meet these criteria.

41. FWC 6836 *Joshua Klooger v. Foodora Australia Pty Ltd* (U2018/2625).
42. *See* G. Davidov, *A Purposive Approach to Labour Law*, *supra* note 21.

Consequently, if the platform workers cannot be qualified as subordinate according to the traditional notion of an employee, which implies the subjection to the employer's power, they will not be able to benefit from the rights provided by the Directive.

In other words, if the legislator does not decide to consider structural, and probably irreversible, changes in the sphere of production and consequently in the new ways of working,[43] the adaptive task of jurisprudence is left to the case-by-case basis, to the sensitivity of individual courts and to the feasibility of an innovative interpretative approach due to the textual rigidity of the law (where it exists) or the fluidity of the defining framework, with little rational and unpredictable outcomes in the process of qualifying the working relationships of the platforms as subordinates or autonomous.[44] This is why it is important, in this scenario, to also consider - and above all - alternative routes in the legal treatment of platform workers, for example through the use of 'alternative' categories to traditional ones. An alternative to the qualification problems of the workers of the platforms as employees is offered by the intermediate categories, which although criticized in doctrine, sometimes offer satisfactory solutions to the request for protection of the platform workers. The London Labour Court has acknowledged Uber drivers the qualification of 'workers' (not employees), complying with the Employment Rights Act that guarantees to this intermediate category social legislation only in a small part (on matters such as Minimum Wage).

Mutatis mutandis, paths of redefinition of subordination in a broadening sense are also known in UK. Here, the formalist approach in interpreting the notion of 'employee' is replaced by a principle of reality, adopted by the UK Supreme Court and by a 'purposive approach', aimed at avoiding that workers are excluded from protection, which a part of the UK doctrine would like to push for the creation of a 'general presumption' of employee status. The UK jurisprudence moved in a similar perspective. On the one hand, by considering the public interest pursued by labour law legislation, the courts tend to interpret the concepts that determine the scope of labour law in an extensive way. On the other hand, the use of the *economic reality test* provides a more adequate representation of the social and economic reality of subordination. To this end, it is necessary to verify where the financial risks are allocated and if the worker is in the condition to make profit out of such allocation with the help of this qualification method of the contract. This *test* is not limited to assess who bears the risk of employment, but it considers other elements such as the ownership of the production equipment or the ways of payment, useful in determining whether the worker carries out an activity for his own, organizing work and thus assuming the risks or whether he/she is inserted in the business of someone else.

43. *See* F. Hendricks, *Regulating New Ways of Working: From the New 'Wow' to the New 'How', in European Labour Law Journal*, 9, 2018, 195 ff.; *see also* F. Hendricks, *From Digits to Robots: The Privacy-Autonomy Nexus in the New Labor Law Machinery, in Comparative Labor Law & Policy Journal*, 40(3), 2019, 365 ff.
44. Not surprisingly, the 2017 *Taylor report* points out that 'Government should replace the minimalistic approach to legislation with a clearer outline of the tests for employment status, setting out the key principles in primary legislation, and using secondary legislation and guidance to provide more detail'.

By its use and the adoption of other ways based on formal criteria (in particular, the mutuality of obligation test based on the continuity and stability of the contract),[45] the courts were able to qualify many casual workers, who are atypical and irregular and who would remain without any protection, as subordinate. Such test also revealed the economic weakness of those workers who are not subject to a control and who are considered autonomous workers on the basis of the control test. In this perspective, the economic reality test can be considered a jurisprudential forerunner of the legislative concept of worker through which, as we will see, a part of the protective legislation was extended beyond the borders of standard subordinate work.[46]

Differently, in Italy, where the legal notion of subordination (Article 2094 civil code), expresses a structural element of the labour relationship, namely the *heteronomy*, a more rigorous and restrictive interpretation of employee has evolved. Indeed, an orientation that has become more determined in affirming that the Article 2094 Italian Civil Code (c.c.) should be interpreted as referring to an employment relationship characterized by directives given by the entrepreneur *on the execution of the work.* As for the qualification, the directional power should be interpreted as referring to specific and precise orders, inherent to the intrinsic execution of work. Even the Constitutional Court seems to believe that the subordinate employment relationship is characterized by a power of the employer that is expressed in pervasive, punctual, continuous directives, while the forms of 'coordination' of the working activity, which in the Italian system are typically present in the case of coordinated and continuous autonomous collaborations (Article 409 n. 3 Italian Code of Civil Procedure (c.p.c.)), are compatible with the concept of self-employment.[47] Generic or programmatic directives, or indeterminate instructions, are not sufficient to establish the existence of subordinate employment – given their compatibility with independent work. This does not exclude, however, that there can be 'softened' forms of subordination due to the particular organization and type of work, like in the case of journalists, doctors, managers and so on. In such cases, subordination is identified by the 'continuous, loyal and diligent availability of the worker for the employer according to the instructions of the counterparty'. The Italian doctrine on this point observes that the existence of the directional power should not be judged in absolute terms but 'in relation to the specific nature of work'.[48]

45. The '*mutuality of obligation*' test tend to exclude large groups of casual workers from the employment rights: *see* N. Countouris, *Uses and misuse of mutuality of obligations*, in *The autonomy of labour law*, A. Blogg, C. Costello, ACL Davies, J. Prassl (eds), Oxford, Hart, 2015, p. 169.
46. *See* A. Perulli, *Subordinate, Autonomous and Economically Dependent Work: A Comparative Analysis of Selected European Countries*, in G. Casale (ed.), *The Employment Relationship. A Comparative Overview*, Oxford, Hart-ILO, 2011, pp. 137 ss.
47. Constitutional Court, n. 76/2015.
48. A. Perulli, *Il potere direttivo dell'imprenditore*, Giuffrè, Milano, 1991.

8.7 THE INTERMEDIATE CATEGORIES: INDEPENDENT BUT ECONOMICALLY DEPENDENT

The difficulties in the qualification of employment relationships, and the resulting search for a more congruent correspondence between norms and facts, are the palpable expression of the axiological crisis affecting labour law. The reasons for this unsatisfactory situation must be referred, first of all, to the rigid binary distinction between subordinate work and self-employment, which does not take into account (or fails to fully respond) to the evolutions of the vital world, in which the old and new types of work are intertwined in an osmotic way. Subordinate jobs made increasingly autonomous due to changes in organizational models, and the growing incidence of digital technological innovation and robotics go along with independent jobs characterized by (economic and social) dependence and/or organizational conditioning the client, as it is also formally acknowledged in the legal systems that recognize the so-called intermediate categories, such as para-subordination or economically dependent self-employment. Labour law, still focused on the drastic and clear alternative between subordination and autonomy, does not take into account the changes in economic and social reality which, on the one hand, significantly modify the traits of the historical referent (the subordinate worker), but on the other hand, and at the same time, they redefine the traits of self-employment, making it more and more a 'functional substitute' for subordination. The outcome of this process consists in leaving out of the field of protection a series of workers who, although genuinely independent, express social protection needs that are very similar, if not coinciding with those of subordinate work, to the extent that the reality in which social vulnerability, contractual weakness and dependence are concentrated no longer coincide exclusively with classical subordination.

The advent of digital platforms today, like the processes of outsourcing of production yesterday, create a general confusion and make it harder and harder to represent the labour market with the binary schemes of the Fordist era, in which social vulnerability and the related need for protection concerned exclusively subordinate work, while autonomous work, a legacy of the noble 'liberal arts', was left to the discipline of private or commercial law. This dichotomous regulatory scheme, which seems to cut social reality in half to apply the protections of labour law only to subordinate work, abandoning what is 'other' to the logic of private law, now appears unsuitable to meet the protection needs that the world of work, as a whole, expresses.

Today, the needs for labour protection (in its contractual, social security, trade union dimensions) are no longer attributable only to the typical figures of subordinate work, but also involve many types of self-employed work, and in particular those forms of independent activity that we define with the term 'self-employed' work, or 'economically dependent' self-employed work, or 'para-subordinate' work, according to the different reference contexts. Often these are workers who, although not falling within the notion of subordination due to the lack of one or more identification criteria, are still socially vulnerable workers like subordinate workers in the strict sense: for example the worker who uses for his activity a digital platform and is not qualified as a subordinate because he can choose whether, when and how much to work, or the independent collaborator who, due to the functional insertion in the client's organization, is hetero-organized in some executive modalities of the activity, without for this reason being formally subordinate.

Faced with these phenomena that call into question the axiological rationality of labour law, various solutions have been proposed, some simply aimed at broadening the scope of labour law to forms of work that are mostly considered the expression of a 'false' self-employment: in this perspective, the crisis of axiological rationality is overcome through a new qualifying instrumentation capable of guaranteeing the category of subordinate employment contracts a greater degree of congruence with the data of social reality. The techniques used for this purpose are many: they range from the legislative extension of the notion of subordinate worker, as in the French proposal of the *Groupe de recherche pour un autre Code du travail* (GR-PACT) which provides for the alternative criterion of 'dependence' or subjection to a de facto power to qualify the employment contract,[49] to more pragmatic solutions of recourse to 'purposive' interpretation, or to the introduction of innovative tests as in the Californian case (ABC test).

The limit of this approach consists in reaffirming the dichotomous scheme simply by expanding the notion of subordinate work, confining genuine self-employment to the logic of the market, and valorizing universalism at the expense of the need for selectivity. Moreover, it is by no means certain that this perspective is rationally pursued by legal systems, which almost routinely reproduce the existing schemes, thus re-proposing the crisis of regulatory rationality we are talking about. For example, the German legislator, which recently amended the civil code by introducing for the first time an express legal definition of an employment contract (section 611a BGB) has substantially confirmed the old identification criteria of a jurisprudential matrix, emphasizing the 'personal dependence' and the subjection to the executive power regarding the modalities of performance execution, times and places of the activity.[50]

As it has already been observed, the scepticism towards a forced and, above all, generalized attribution to subordination of the multiple relationships that animate the protean experience of the activity mediated by digital platforms, is by no means equivalent to denying the need for the protection of platform capitalism operators, otherwise abandoned to a brutal government of the market or, worse, reduced to commodities traded in the virtual space outside any regulatory framework. It is no coincidence that, in the uncertain search for solutions capable of responding to the challenges posed by the new model, it is even tempting to turn to protections that are completely external to labour law, although aimed at protecting the weak part of an intersubjective relationship of exchange, such as, for example, the legislation set up for consumer protection. In this perspective, the user-operator would result not so much as a (subordinate or autonomous) worker, but as a user of a technological service, and,

49. Article L.11-3: 'le salarié est une personne phisique qui exécute un travail sous le pouvoir de fait ou sous la dépendence d'autri', in *Proposition de code du travail*, Dalloz, 2017, sous l'égide du Groupe de recherche pour un autre Code du travail (GR-PACT).

50. *See* B. Waas, *The position of workers in the collaborative economy: A view on EU law*, in *European Employment Policies: Current Challenges*, R. Singer, T. Bazzani (eds), BWV, 2017, 114.

ultimately, a consumer of that product that the digital technology is able to provide him/her through the platform. This is certainly not a prospect to be discarded, especially considering the levels of protection achieved by this sector of the legal system, which thanks to the impulse of supranational law has been able to build effective systems for the protection of the weak contractor, providing specific guarantees with reference to the stipulation of distance contracts and their digital content.

It is certainly preferable, however, to remain in the field of regulatory experience which includes, in a broad sense, labour law, which in the course of its history has been able to express even differentiated regulatory rationalities, not renouncing, in the face of the challenges - or opportunities - introduced by technology, to carry out its traditional role of reconciliation of conflicting interests, in the direction of protecting the fundamental values of the person.

In this regard, the themes of the protection of economically dependent self-employed work are highlighted, as well as, more generally, the prospect of a reconfiguration of work and its protections beyond the traditional binary divide. In these hybrid cases, intermediate categories - where they exist - can be used to offer protection to these subjects operating in conditions of imperfect subordination: it is no coincidence that the London Labour Court has recognized Uber drivers as workers, a category wider than that of employees, which, pursuant to the Employment Rights Act, guarantees only part of the labour legislation (with particular reference to the subject of minimum wages, leave and maximum duration of work).

A possible solution, aimed at restoring axiological rationality to labour law in the digital age, therefore consists in valorizing, in addition to the traditional subordination/autonomy dichotomy, elements such as economic dependence capable of selectively extending protections to non-subordinate employment relationships, either through the creation of intermediate figures (as the English legislator did with the category of 'worker'), or through the pure and simple provision, within the existing categories, of reserved subjective paths, in view of the use of certain requirements.

8.8 THE INTERVENTION OF THE LAW: THE FRENCH AND ITALIAN CASES

In France, the Loi Travail, containing *nouvelles libertés et de nouvelles protections pour les entreprises et les actif*, has moved in this direction, where it provides rules applicable to 'self-employed workers who resort to one or more multiple platforms for electronic networking', excluding, vice versa, the application of the rules related to telework. In particular, the law establishes an unprecedented 'social responsibility of the platforms', so much that, if the platform determines the characteristics of the services provided or the good sold and it sets its price, the worker is guaranteed a series of rights that are not normally recognized for self-employed workers. These are social insurance in the event of accidents and professional diseases, a right to professional training and certification of skills, but also collective rights such as the right to organize trade unions, a sort of strike right understood as a particular instrument of protection against the retaliatory behaviour of the platform, and finally a very important social right, relating to unemployment benefits for workers who lose opportunities to operate on the professional market through technological platforms. This regulation demonstrates, on the one hand, that forced attributions to subordination are not necessary to guarantee an effective basis of protection for app-driven workers and that, conversely, it is not enough to have effective qualifying categories in identifying the case, but it is necessary to intervene upstream of the qualification with selective regulations to protect the self-employed worker of the platform, to limit the prerogatives, sometimes very invasive, of a strong contractor who must be required to comply with adequate 'social responsibility'.

The Taylor Report written for the British government is placed in a similar perspective. The Review, in reiterating the usefulness of intermediate categories such as that of *workers*, underlines how platforms provide workers with the freedom to decide whether to work and which job to do or refuse, but at the same time expose them to risks to their health and they force them to receive fees that are below the *National Minimum Wage*. Consequently, it is proposed to redefine the notion of 'worker' by employing the concept of 'dependent contractor', attributing to it a status capable of ensuring that 'those working in the gig economy are still able to enjoy maximum flexibility whilst also being able to earn the NMW'.

While the French law appears very timid, affirming only a 'social responsibility' of the platform if the latter determines the characteristics of the service provided or the good sold and sets its price (Article L. 7342-1 Code du Travail), as well as to establish some very minimal rights - shifting the centre of gravity of the discipline on the recognition of trade union rights, which is lacking in the Italian legislation - the Italian law appears more structured in terms of individual rights (law n. 128/2019). First of all, it is possible to consider the riders of the digital platforms as 'collaborators organized by the client', with application of the discipline of the subordinate employment relationship. If this classification is not possible, and the rider is qualified as independent, a minimum mandatory discipline is provided for, regarding the formal requirements of the contract, the prohibition of discrimination, the provision of a fair remuneration and - in any case - not lower than that of collective agreements, personal data protection rules, the right to be excluded from the platform in case of refusal of the offer, safety and social security protections, health and safety protections in the workplace. In this way, a minimum basis of rights is ensured, regardless of the need to force the qualification of the relationship as subordinate (or as hetero-organized by the client).

8.9 CONCLUSIONS

Therefore, the basic problem, on which to test the axiological rationality of the system, does not consist so much in correctly qualifying the platform worker as independent or para-subordinate on the basis of the existing indexes, but in attributing to him/her a protection that guarantees his/her work status elements of dignity and equity that are currently not recognized.

On closer inspection, the French model by no means involves an assimilation to subordinate work, but rather the extension of some protections ad hoc designed for this category of workers: as if the legislator had thought of a 'statute' of digital integration, to which, further protection elements can possibly be added, also on the basis of the existing legislation on the protection of weak contractors on the market. Think, for example, of the notion of 'economic violence', introduced into the French legal system with Articles 1142 and 1143 of the Code du Commerce, or the Italian law for the protection of non-entrepreneurial self-employment (Law 81/2017), which can be invoked for the fight against all forms of abuse of economic dependence carried out by a technological platform against an app-driven worker: such an abuse can appear, for example, in the determination of a fee that is inconsistent with the quality and quantity of the service, or in any case that is lower than comparable standards (as in the case of fees lower than the minimum established by law or by collective bargaining), or to forms of unjustified and unannounced withdrawal from the platform.

This perspective, which seems to have a broader scope than the short-term one represented by the judicial requalification of the relationships involved as standard employment relationships, tends to make the undifferentiated extension of labour law less urgent, whose grammar tends to become more universal and at the same time more articulated. Basically this was the philosophy that animated the Supiot report, based on the rewriting of the regulatory contents of labour law according to four concentric circles, three of which calibrated on 'labour market membership' and one of these on 'occupational activity', such as include both subordinate workers and independent workers, preparing for them a threshold of common protections in matters considered as being indifferent to the binary logic of qualification. The paradigm of 'employment' is thus replaced by a paradigm of the professional status of people, which is not defined by reason of the exercise of a specific profession or job, but it incorporates the different forms of work that each person is likely to perform during his/her existence. In this perspective, which a part of the doctrine openly refers to in order to provide a regulatory edge to the global phenomenon of uberization, the redefinition of the notion of subordinate worker takes place in ways that are external to the notion of subordination, or, better, it takes place through a generalized basic guarantee for work in all its forms and applications, and then through a modular structure that takes into account the different degrees of vulnerability that define the continuum that goes from subordination to autonomy.

The systems recognizing the intermediate categories - economically dependent self-employment - go in this direction, but have experienced contradictory situations. In these cases, alongside the employee in the strict sense, the legal systems recognize the existence of situations of imperfect subjection, or quasi-subordination, in the context of cases that are typologically qualifiable as self-employment. The economic doctrine qualifies these situations as quasi-markets or quasi-hierarchy, hybrid situations of long term contracts characterized by incompleteness, in which on the one hand the criteria of traditional subordination are not present in an exhaustive way and, on the other hand, the worker's independence is limited due to conditions of economic dependence, or subjection to coordination of long-term services. On the one hand, the partial extension of the field of labour law towards situations of non-subordination seems to constitute a positive and effective strategy, insofar as it achieves an extension of the protections to non-subordinate employment situations, although characterized by a situation of vulnerability of the worker. The economic dependence, together with indices that denote the lack of 'full' independence, such as not having a clientele, continuity of performance, or the presence of the client's coordination prerogatives, are factors that require social protection, in order not to leave these typologies to the pure and simple normative logic of private law (i.e., to say to the economic logic of the market).

However, these juridical forms of para-subordination or of 'economic dependency' open the way to forms of systematic abuse, such as 'false independent workers', very much spread in Germany, Italy and Spain; recently badly evoked by the Court of Justice to identify those workers - precisely 'false self-employed workers' - who are not prevented from exercising their collective rights without entering into conflict with European competition law.

A solution to these problems of possible fraud should not lead to the choice to eliminate these intermediate forms, but to a more attentive legislative formulation, which may limit the possible abuses and guarantee the quality of the economically dependent forms of self-employment, together with a broader apparatus for their protection. It is well known that a good part of the doctrine is opposed to this regulatory strategy, arguing that the existence of intermediate categories actually legitimizes companies to structure their work needs with contractual forms that offer the possibility of dissembling (or disguising) relationships of subordinate work for the sole purpose of reducing the economic and regulatory costs of employment.[51]

These criticisms are partly founded (the phenomena of abuse actually exist, as in all cases where a rule is circumvented), but tend to confuse the plans of genuine self-employed economically dependent with bogus self-employment. The two plans must remain distinct: otherwise it is clear that the 'intermediate' category is totally identified as a fictitious device, suitable only to qualify fraudulently paid employment in terms of a false autonomy. If, as the juridical method requires, it is admitted that the two sides of the discourse are different (one thing is pathology, that is bogus self-employment, the other is physiology, that is a truly autonomous work though characterized by elements of para-subordination/economic dependence) the provision of more or less extensive protections in favour of genuine but economically dependent self-employed workers can only be viewed in a positive sense, as a selective strategy of universalization of labour rights. However, the issue is very complex and has long been under the attention of the European Commission, which already in the 2006 *Green Paper on the modernization of labour law to address the challenges of the 21st century* drew the attention of Member States to the value of making the boundaries between subordinate work and self-employment clearer, but also to provide a series of basic safeguards for economically dependent self-employed work. The European Economic

51. *See*, from last, N. Countouris, V. De Stefano, *New trade union strategies for new forms of employment*, ETUC, Brussels, 2019, p. 59.

and Social Committee, appropriately distinguished the new self-employment trends[52] from the phenomena of abuse of the status of self-employed,[53] recognizing the positive aspects of a specific discipline for workers who are not subordinated in the strict sense (also for the purpose of strengthening the 'entrepreneurship' of these subjects);[54] after all, the phenomenon of abuse does not depend on the legal characteristics of the contractual type, but on the elusive behaviour of employers (as shown, for example, by the long dispute, including European, on fixed-term contracts).

From a strict legal point of view, these forms of labour are generally qualified as self-employment but the condition of economic dependence or quasi-subordination justifies the growing trend towards the creation (or the extension) of legal protection for such work relationships. The OECD, in its Employment Outlook 2019, after recognizing the existence of an 'genuine gray area' between subordination and autonomy which requires specific social protections, proposes to encourage collective bargaining in the context of economically dependent self-employment. The European trade union organizations themselves see a driving force in the development of industrial relations to improve the social conditions of self-employed workers (ETUC 2018). Even the European Commission is fully aware of the importance of its role in supporting the profound challenges that industrial relations are facing in this changing world of work, and relaunches the link between good economic performance, trustful labour relations and high social cohesion especially in atypical and self-employed employee (EC, Employment and Social Developments in Europe, Annual Review 2018).

In those States where this trend has not yet brought about legislative amendments, one can observe that in the public debate there is a request expressed by different parties for a greater protection than the one made possible by the traditional binary model,[55] while in systems that already recognize 'third' categories, their improvement is discussed both in terms of identifying the notion and in terms of quantity/quality of the protections.[56] This is the perspective strongly longed for the EU (at least starting from the 2006 Green Paper where the necessity to supply a set of protections to economically dependent autonomous workers was highlighted), and this is the perspective that we should promote today, in view of the necessity to protect hybrid forms of work relationships in the economy of the fourth industrial revolution.

52. The more sharp-eyed social scientists, coined the term 'second generation' self-employment to highlight its innovative specificity and the distance from the traditional forms of '*locatio operis*', cf. S. Bologna, *The Rise of the European Self-employed Workforce*, Mimesis International, 2018.
53. *See* EESC, INT/628 12 March 2013.
54. *See* EESC, SOC/344, 29 April 2010.
55. For example, for France, *see* the '*Antomattei-Sciberras*' 2008 Report given to the Ministry of Labour for the creation of a protective statute in favour of *economically dependent workers*.
56. For example, with reference to the United Kingdom, the 2017 *Taylor* report points out that 'government should introduce a new name to refer to the category of people who are eligible for "worker" rights but who are not employees. We recommend that the legislation refer to this group as "dependent contractors"'. The indication of the report, however, risks being more definitional than content, in order to reflect more on the rights attributable to independent contractors.

This brings us back to the starting point: technology is not just a tool, but a provocation and 'a way of revealing', and it is up to the human being to make - within the highest danger of technology - that which saves grow.

CHAPTER 9

Digitalization and Its Impacts of De-spatialization and De-temporalization of Work and De-territorialization of the Labour Market: Is It Time to Rethink a 'Sustainable' Labour Law?

Valentina Cagnin

9.1 INTRODUCTION

During the last decades, the employment relationship has changed a lot. Digitalization, and more generally, the Fourth Revolution, has had a huge impact on labour, labour relationships and the labour market. Such revolution has contributed to the progressive destruction, started two decades ago, of the pillars of labour law, in the name of flexibility and economic efficiency.

This is the reason why scholars define the destabilization of labour law as a change of paradigm[1] or as a genetic mutation,[2] or, again, as a law 'under fire'.[3]

Even its peculiar function of rebalancing the unbalanced contractual parties, through the protection of the worker as a weak contractor, is questioned, due to the huge increase in the so called non-standard forms of employment in the last few decades (temporary employment, part-time, on-call work, temporary agency work,

1. A. Perulli, Il contratto a tutele crescenti e la Naspi: un mutamento di 'paradigma' per il diritto del lavoro? In A. Perulli, L. Fiorillo (a cura di), Contratto a tutele crescenti e Naspi, Decreti Legislativi 4 marzo 2015, n. 22 e 23, Giappichelli, Torino, 2015; V. Cagnin, Diritto del Lavoro e Sviluppo Sostenibile, Cedam Wolters Kluwer, 2018.
2. V. Speziale, La mutazione genetica del diritto del lavoro, in Dir. Lav. Merc., 2016, 2.
3. A. Goldin, Some Defining Component of Labour Law Influx, Pompeu Fabra University, Barcelona, 2013.

crowd-work, etc.). This makes it difficult to define who can be considered a worker as the historical dichotomy of 'standard' (protected) and 'non-standard' forms of employment (less or not protected) is more and more bygone, given the atypical character of jobs in the post-industrial era. We are facing a new era of labour, in which the standard work relationship (the employee under the direction, power and control of the employer in the Fordist factory) is more and more abandoned in favour of other flexible forms of labour which require an urgent revision of the discipline, in order to solve problems such as the work relationship qualification, the need of social security protection, the remunerations and the guarantee of new social rights for digital workers (such as the right to disconnect).

This chapter aims thus to analyse the biggest consequences of digitalization on labour and the necessity to rethink labour law, suggesting a change of paradigm to face the challenges of the new era of labour, such as the reference to Sustainable Development as a value framework to rediscover the roots of labour law and the evaluation of basic standards and decent work.

9.2 DIGITALIZATION AND THE RESULTING TRANSFORMATIONS ON THE ORGANIZATION OF WORK: DE-SPATIALIZATION AND DE-TEMPORALIZATION OF WORK THROUGH WORKING PLATFORM AND SMART WORK

Digitalization can be considered as 'a true change of paradigm in the labour world, allowing enterprises the use of tools of conceptions, production and cooperation which correspond to different ways of thinking, working and organizing'.[4]

As a matter of fact, new technologies and the improvement of existing technologies have bent labour in the last decade: thanks to the combination of automation and digital revolution, the nature of jobs and work, and that of the labour market, has changed at a rapid rate, overcoming the typically Taylor Fordist ways of production and allowing forms of work that are now de-spatialized and de-temporalized, thanks to digital work and, especially, to crowd-working.

The terms 'crowd-working' and 'crowdsourcing of work' refer to work carried out through online platforms (such Amazon Mechanical Turk, Clickworker, Crowdflower, Microtask) which allow organizations or individuals to gain access via the Internet to an undefined and unknown group of other organizations or individuals, named 'gig-worker',[5] prepared to solve specific problems or supply specific services or products in exchange for payment.[6] Moreover, digital work is not limited to platforms, algorithms and gig economy but is also widespread and pervasive in both private and

4. V. Pontif, Transformation numérique et vie au travail: les pistes du rapport Mettling, in Rev. Dr. Trav., 2016, pp. 185 ff. (about the report of B. Mettling, Transformation numérique et vie au Travail, 2015).
5. The risks are that of a dehumanized perception of workers with a devaluation and disguising of work ('gigs', 'tasks', 'services', 'favours' or 'microbusinesses'), with an increasing trend towards casualization of work and informalization of the formal economy.
6. Green A., De Hoyos M., Barnes S-A., Baldauf B. and Behle H. (2013) CrowdEmploy: Crowdsourcing case studies. An empirical investigation into the impact of crowdsourcing on employability,

public sectors, with the use of personal computer and emails, entailing a true de-spatialization of work and production[7] (whereas, in the Fordist regime, work and production are always tied to a locality) and de-temporalization of work and require to rethink the concept of 'place of work' and 'working hour' (that probably no longer exists as we have known it in the industrial age).

Digitalization is thus changing the parties' contractual rights and obligations.[8] In order to face the work digitalization, in Italy, for example, we had a recent regulation on smart work (*lavoro agile*), according to which (Article 18, co. 1, L. 81/2017) the legislator 'promotes smart work as a way of execution of subordinate work, established by an agreement between the parties without precise limits of working hour and place of work, within or outside the enterprise, with the only limit of the maximum daily and weekly working hour deriving from law or collective bargaining'. Here the de-spatialization and de-temporalization of work allows a radical revolution of labour law in terms of change of the parties' contractual rights and obligations: smart work is not typically regulated by a law or a collective agreement but by a bilateral agreement, signed by the employer and the employee (which are considered as peers and not, like in the past, as the strong and the weak part of the work relationship). This agreement then defines not only the way of job execution but also the directional power of the employee (Article 19, co. 1) and his sanctioning power (Article 21). Such consensual definition demonstrates a new space for autonomy and freedom of the employee: elements of self-employed work and subordinate work are more and more promiscuous, mostly because of this general consideration of the individual autonomy of the worker (that was typically limited in the past due to his weakest position).

The change of the work relationship conditions and the contractual balance power of parties is raising issues, not only in Italy, with regard to the application of existing legal frameworks, blurring established lines between employee and self-employed worker (as well as consumer and provider from which the term 'prosumer' derives, or the professional and non-professional provision of services). This can result in uncertainty over applicable rules, especially when combined with regulatory fragmentation stemming from divergent regulatory approaches at national or local level.[9]

9.2.1 The Matter of Work Relationship Qualification and Social Rights Recognition

The irruption on the economic scene of actors like platform economies, which are able to disrupt the historical subjective references of labour law, raises some problems

European Commission Joint Research Centre, Institute for Prospective Technological Studies, JRC Technical Reports, EUR 26,351, Luxembourg, Publications Office of the European Union.

7. U. Beck, The Brave New World of Work, Polity Press, 2000.
8. Gottardi D., Da Frankenstein ad Asimov: letteratura 'predittiva', robotica e lavoro, in Labour & Law Issues, vol. 4, no. 2, 2018, p. 8.
9. European Commission, A European agenda for the collaborative economy, Brussels, 2.6.2016, COM(2016) 356 final.

concerning the labour relationship qualification and places new questions of values, linked to the consequences of qualification.

The historical dichotomy between employment and self-employment, typically used to qualify the labour relationship in most countries, has become needless in the digitalization era.

This is demonstrated by the new recent jurisprudence on the matter of qualification of the *gig-workers*, which are qualified as 'self-employed' but concretely treated as 'employees'. Judges, facing the workers claims to be considered as employees, in different well-known cases,[10] defined those workers as independent contractors, as employees, as workers or, again, as independent workers.[11] Those discrepancies realized by judges, mostly due to the necessity of evaluating the peculiarity of the job relationship case by case, raise two main (among others) questions: (1) Is then the very notion of 'worker' doomed to disappear, or will everyone be a digital worker, whatever the juridical qualification of the work relationship? (2) Which protections are recognized to these workers without a clear contract qualification?

With regard to the first question (1), platforms usually qualify workers as self-employed to avoid the application of labour laws or to unmask the constructions that make it difficult to identify the employer and therefore the related responsibilities in economic and regulatory terms: the inhabitants of the jungle of the platforms are able to negate their relationships without anyone being an employer or an employee.[12]

If we map all the important legislative news on this field of regulation, to monitor the legislative progresses on the field of qualification of these 'digital' workers, we can find some useful implications on the contractual status and on the consequent legislation protection for Industry 4.0 workers in the French Legislation.

10. Perulli A., Lavoro e tecnica al tempo di Uber, in RGL, 2017, 2, I, 195 ff; Ichino P., Subordinazione, autonomia e protezione del lavoro nella gig-economy, in RIDL, 2018, II, p. 294 ff; Treu T., Rimedi, tutele e fattispecie: riflessioni a partire dai lavori della gig economy, in LD, 2017, III/IV, 367 ff; LOI P., Il lavoro nella gig economy nella prospettiva del rischio, in RGL, 2017, II, 259 ff; Prassl J., Risal M., Sottosopra e al rovescio: le piattaforme di lavoro on demand come datori di lavoro, in RGL, 2017, II, 219 ff; De Stefano V., The Rise of the 'Just-in-Time Workforce': On-Demand Work, Crowdwork and Labour Protection in the 'Gig-Economy', in Comparative Labor Law and Policy Journal, 2016, XXXVII, pp. 471 ff; Biasi M., Dai pony express ai riders di Foodora. L'attualità del binomio subordinazione-autonomia (e del relativo metodo di indagine) quale alternativa all'affannosa ricerca di categorie, in Zilio Grandi G., Biasi M. (a cura di), Commentario breve allo statuto del lavoro autonomo e del lavoro agile, Wolters Kluwer, Milano, 2018, 67 ff.
11. The reference is to the cases of Employment Tribunals London, 28 October 2016; *Dewhurst v. CitySprint UK Ltd*, 5 January 2017; Trib. Regional do Trabaiho Behlo Orizonte, Brazil, 13 February 2017; Trib. Regional do Trabaiho San Paulo, 20 April 2017; Trub. Regional Brasil, 23 May 2017; Trib. Torino 7 May 2018; Trib. Milano 10 September 2018. For an analysis of this debate, *see* P. Tullini, La digitalizzazione del Lavoro, la produzione intelligente e il controllo tecnologico nell'impresa, in Ead. (a cura di), Web e lavoro. Profili evolutivi e di tutela, Giappichelli, 2017, pp. 3 ff; G. Valenduc, P. Vendramin, Digitalisation, between disruption and evolution, Transfer, 2017, vol, 23, no. 2, 121 ff; A. Perulli, (a cura di), Lavoro autonomo e categorie delle piattaforme, Cedam Wolters Kluwer, 2018; M. Biasi, Uno sguardo oltre confine: I 'nuovi lavori' della gig-economy. Potenzialità e limiti della comparazione, in Labour and Law Issues, vol. 4, no. 2, 2018; Del Conte M., Razzolini O., La gig economy alla prova del giudice: la difficile reinterpretazione della fattispecie e degli indiciategoriesi, in DLRI, 2018, p. 673.
12. A. Lyon-Caen, Plateforme, in Revue du Droit du Travail, 2016, p. 301.

In France, the Loi Travail,[13] recognizes some protection to the platform workers, referring to them in terms of *travailleurs indépendants recourant, pour l'exercice de leur activité professionnelle, à une ou plusieurs plateformes de mise en relation par voie électronique* (Article L. 7341-1 Loi Travail). According to this law, when the platform determines the characteristics of the service provided or the good sold and fixes its price, the platform has, with respect to the workers concerned, 'a social responsibility', guaranteeing a series of individual and collective rights to those workers, such as a social insurance, a right of learning, the right of collective bargaining and unemployment benefits, which usually concern only the employee (and not the self-employed).

In Italy, at the moment, the only important attempt on regulation for riders is the 'Charter of fundamental digital social rights in the urban context' (*Carta dei diritti fondamentali del Lavoro digitale nel contesto urbano*) promoted by the Municipality of Bologna, signed on 30 May 2018 by the Municipality, a local Riders Union, some platforms (Snam and Mymenu) and by the main territorial trade unions,[14] which fix some minimum standards for digital workers, regardless of the type of employment relationship.

With regard to the second question (2), in the majority of countries, the matter of qualification is still essential for the fruition of social rights. And these new digital workers need a special protection because, if, on one hand it is true that thanks to the new technologies workers may enjoy the freedom and the flexibility to choose their time and place of working and reduce commuting time resulting in a better overall work-life balance and higher productivity, on the other hand, they may also have certain drawbacks, such as a tendency to work longer hours and an overlap between paid work and personal life (which could lead to stress), nervous breakdown risk, hyper-connection (the worker sees his personal life invaded by the work), isolation of the worker due to not having contact with peers, decrease of productivity (if telework is not well planned or executed) and part of the savings generated for the company can mean expenses for the worker (in workspace, cost of supplies, etc.).[15]

This is why digital workers must be protected, not only with 'classic' rights (social security, remuneration, training, collective bargaining, etc.) but also with some 'new' rights, such as the right to disconnect.

Referring for example to remuneration, if we refer to crowd-work, compensation is often lower than minimum wages, workers must manage unpredictable income streams, and they work without the standard labour protections of an employment relationship.[16]

Then, due to the de-spatialization and de-temporalization of work, spheres of personal and professional life are subject to a process of cross-colonization, which raises the need of a disconnection from work.

13. Loi n. 2016-1088 relative au travail, à la modernisation du social dialogue et à la sécurisation des parcours professionels.
14. The main Italian trade unions are CGIL (Italian General Confederation of Labour), CISL (Italian Workers' Trade Unions Confederation) and UIL (Italian Labour Union).
15. ILO Report, Working anytime, anywhere: The effects on the world of work, 15 February 2017.
16. ILO Report, 20 September 2018, *Digital labour platforms and the future of work towards decent work in the online world.*

The new French Law (Loi Travail) recognizes for example the *droit à la déconnexion*, obliging the company to set up devices for regulating the use of digital tools, with a view to ensuring the respect of rest and leave periods as well as personal and family life, guaranteeing the full exercise by the employee of his right to disconnection (Article 55 Loi Travail).

In Italy this right has been mentioned (even if not sufficiently ruled) in the context of the smart work discipline (Article 19, co. 1), where the legislator provides that the agreement stipulated between the employee and the employer must identify (among the other aspects of the work relationship) 'the times of rest of the worker as well as technical and organizational measures necessary to ensure the worker disconnection from technological work tools'.

9.2.2 Some Very Recent Victories for Gig-Workers in France, UK and Italy

The matter of qualification is so important for such workers because their rights are strictly linked to the qualification they have: subordination remained the key to accessing the fundamental core of labour law protections (and the main object of the related litigation).

Aware that the speed of change means that laws are not up to date with circumstances (France is a pioneer on this field), scholars and judges must identify new tools, models and regulation techniques (or revise the existing ones) so as to ensure that workers affected by digitization have adequate social rights, especially in terms of adequate remuneration, insurance coverage and trade union freedom.

Contrary to the discontinuity in the judge's decisions already mentioned, in some very recent decisions, we can see a step forward for gig-workers in France, United Kingdom (UK) and Italy, which could suggest a stronger protection to those workers.

In France, for example, in November 2018, there has been a new important decision for riders.[17]

If, according to the previous decision of the Court of Appeal, there was not a subordination link between the worker and the company for food delivery *Take Eat Easy*, the Court of Cassation identified the existence of a link of subordination because 'it was clear that the application was equipped with a geo-location system allowing the real time follow-up by the company of the position of the courier and the counting of the total number of kilometers traveled by him/her and that the company had a power of sanction with regard to the courier'.[18] And thus, repeating the necessity to evaluate case by case, the existence of a directional, control and sanctioning power for *Take Eat Easy* suggests the existence of a situation of subordination for the worker.

In the same direction, in the UK, Uber (December 2018) lost right to classify UK drivers as self-employed: a landmark employment tribunal sentence[19] states that the

17. Arrêt n°1737 du 28 novembre 2018 (17-20.079) – Cour de Cassation – Chambre sociale.
18. Garbuio C., Il contributo della Cour de Cassation francese alla qualificazione dei lavoratori digitali: se la piattaforma esercita i poteri tipici del datore, esiste un lien de subordination, in corso di pubblicazione.
19. London Court of Appeal, 19 December 2018.

firm must also pay drivers national living wage and holiday pay. The sentence is not the end of the trial for Uber. The firm has taken the case to the employment appeal tribunal, and following its decision there could be further hearings in the Court of Appeal and then the Supreme Court, but this decision has a huge implication for gig economy as judges recognized important social rights in the field of remuneration to gig-workers.

More recently, in Italy, the Court of Appeal of Turin (11 January 2019) has accepted for a substantial part the appeal of five former riders of Foodora who demanded the recognition of the subordination of the employment relationship. In the first instance, last year,[20] the requests had been rejected in its entirety. Now, the judges sanctioned the applicants' right to have a sum calculated on the remuneration established for employees by the national collective contract establishing the right of the applicants to be given, in relation to the period in which they collaborated with Foodora, sums of money calculated 'on the basis of indirect and deferred direct remuneration established for employees of the fifth level of the collective transport logistics contract goods', deducting what was already perceived at the time.

What is more important is the fact that those riders have been recognized as ether-organized collaborators (a third category in the middle between self-employed and employee, which could correspond, in some way, to the English 'worker') ex Article 2 Legislative Decree 81/2015: such qualification allows such workers to gain the protection given to the employee, without the need to be qualified in that manner.

Those three recent decisions show both the awareness of judges to unmask the situation of subordination and the necessity to protect such workers, assuring them some basic social rights.

9.3 DIGITALIZATION AND THE DE-TERRITORIALIZATION OF THE LABOUR MARKET

The new global or spatially de-concentred methods of production lead to a de-territorialization of the labour market:[21] a sort of work realm that is stretched tight across the gap between what constitutes local and global.[22]

This new dimension of the labour market with no borders raises, first, a global competition among workers: crowd-work allows the enterprise to assign the execution of a job in outsourcing to a 'crowd' of workers which are potentially connected from every corner of the world and are at the same time supporters and protagonists of a real 'social' competition.[23]

Second, the lack of borders implies a disintermediation of the collective action and of the collective relationships: everything takes place on an individual level and this undermines the existence of a collective interest, as digitalization individualizes

20. Trib. Torino 7 May 2018.
21. Mundlak G., De-Territorializing Labour Law, Law & Ethics of Human Rights, 2009, vol. 3, no. 2.
22. U. Beck, An introduction to the Theory of Second Modernity and the Risk, Routledge, 2013, p. 112.
23. M. Rigaux, Droit du travail ou droit de la concurrence sociale? Essai sur un droit de l'égalité de l'homme au travail (re)mis en couse, Bruylant, Paris, 2009, pp. 8 ff.

work relationships. The union in the workplace is extremely fragmented in gig-works, not only because in many countries collective rights are recognized only to employees (and not to self-employed workers), but also because of the difficulty to create connections between work councils and trade unions, which should be strengthened in order to organize collective actions, negotiation and conflict to negotiate better wages and working conditions.

Lastly, international markets and competition on a global scale, based on cutting labour costs, make local initiatives ineffective and impel towards a global approach to workers' rights. Indeed, if the platforms act at supranational level, cooperation between trade unions at national and international level is critically needed in order to build a framework of workers' rights at global level.[24]

This problem is perceived both at the European level (the revision of European Union law in the framework of the European Social Pillar proposes to enlarge social protection to all workers, regardless of the type of employment relationship, including those in atypical and new forms of work) and at the international level: the ILO[25] proposes different approaches to include non-standard workers in the collective bargaining process; for instance, by recognizing them legally the right to organize or bargain collectively, facilitating the capacity of Unions to be considered representative in sectors employing a high proportion of non-standard workers, and promoting actions to organize and collectively represent workers in non-standard employment.

9.4 IS IT TIME TO RETHINK LABOUR LAW? A QUESTION THAT CAN NO LONGER BE POSTPONED

The digitalization's consequences on work and the labour market demonstrate the incapacity of a traditional labour law to adequate its regulatory and cognitive structures to a new economic, social and cultural context in a profound change.[26]

Starting from this assumption, the crisis of this field of regulation, which leads also to a general de-regulation because of economic and flexibility reasons, could be an occasion to find a new reference paradigm to define the founding values of a new 'sustainable' labour law.

If the whole evolution of labour law of the last century was based on the protection of the employee, intended as the weak part of the relationship to be protected, today the same notion of subordination is under discussion, and, at the same time, it is that of working hour and place.

It is thus time to rethink labour law, to switch from the industrial to the digital era, and this could possibly rediscover its historic values of universalism, community

24. Lassandari A., Problemi di rappresentanza e tutela collettiva dei lavoratori che utilizzano le tecnologie digitali, in RGL, 2017, 2, pp. 59-70.
25. ILO, Non-standard Employment Around the World Understanding challenges, shaping prospects.
26. R. Del Punta, Epistemologia breve del diritto del lavoro, in L. Nogler, L. Corazza (a cura di), Risistemare il diritto del lavoro. Liber amicorum Marcello Pedrazzoli, Franco Angeli, Milano, 2012, p. 330.

and solidarity, which have been in the last decades too often pushed aside in the name of competition, de-regulation and flexibility.

A way to act this re-modulation of labour law could be the adoption for the legislators and for judges of a new paradigm of reference for labour law: that of Sustainable Development.[27]

This paradigm is based on two main considerations: (1) the pillars of Sustainable Development (economic development, social development and environmental protection) are equally important, interdependent and mutually reinforcing; (2) intra- and inter-generational solidarity: development can be defined as sustainable when it 'meets the needs of the present without compromising the ability of future generations to meet their own needs'.[28]

If labour law assumed such paradigm as a polar star, as a torch, in the necessary re-modulation, there should be: (i) an adequate promotion of social rights, which should be considered as necessary for the whole general development and not erased or reduced by an economic ratio; (ii) a salvage of some labour law values such as equity, solidarity and fairness, in order to reduce the gap between insiders and outsiders and inequality among self-employed and employees or among distant workers.

These guidelines could lead the legislator to the elaboration of new 'sustainable' norms, more adapted to the new (digital) context and/or to a fair interpretation of the existing norms, generally reconsidering the importance of social rights as human rights and no longer as subsidiary social goods[29] that can be scarified if they are an obstacle to the economic growth.

Another necessary step for a re-modulation of labour law, which is in line with the application of a universality of rights and solidarity among workers proposed by Sustainable Development is the exiting from the *tropisme travailliste* that reduces labour law to a subordinate labour law, recalling, for example, the idea of *un droit de l'activité* proposed by Alain Supiot, based on the personal dimension of each work activity, speaking of a *tout-court* 'labour law' without any adjective limiting its application. An example to follow is the solution given by the French Legislation (Article 60 Loi Travail), which has given a reply focused on essential rights and protections, without the pretension to legally define digital work and abandoning the legal traditional and rigid categories.[30]

Then, the adoption of the Sustainable Development paradigm should lead to a revision of the conditions of access and the conditionality of social protections: what digital workers need is a sort of hard-core of basic protections, unrelated from the contractual qualification. Such social rights should rather be connected to their need for protections, which depend on every single case, as demonstrated by the recent case

27. V. Cagnin, Diritto del Lavoro e Sviluppo Sostenibile, Cedam Wolters Kluwer, 2018.
28. United Nations, Report of the World Commission on Environment and Development, 1987.
29. T. Novitz, Core labour standards conditionalities: A means by which to achieve sustainable development? In J. Fandez, C. Tan (eds), International Economic Law, Globalization and Developing Countries, Edward Elgar, Cheltenham, 2010, p. 237.
30. A. Jammaude, Uber, deliveroo: requalification des contrats ou denunciation d'une fraude à la loi, Semaine Sociale Lamy, 178, 4 September 2017, pp. 4 ff.

law. In this sense, Treu suggests the valorization of the basic standards of treatment,[31] which correspond to the notion of decent work given by the ILO: the evolution of the work and that of the labour market diversify the forms of work, and it is thus fundamental to find some fundamental rules and rights for the worker, whatever their legal qualification may be, protecting the dignity of anyone who is performing a service.

As a matter of fact, decent work is considered as a tool to reach a Sustainable Development and thus as a key application of this paradigm to labour law.

The adoption of the Sustainable Development as a new paradigm should thus be considered as the fundamental step of the post-modern era to adapt labour law to the new social, economic and digital context and thus to have its lost legitimacy back.

31. Treu, WP C.S.D.L.E. 'Massimo D'Antona'.IT – 371/2018, p. 8.

CHAPTER 10

Platform Work: A Call to Reconsider the Institutions of Social Law

Céline Wattecamps

10.1 INTRODUCTION

In recent years, more attention has been drawn to the emergence and development of 'platform work'.[1] This phenomenon, which came from the United States, has taken roots in Europe.[2] In some aspects, platform work shows us novelty, as its genuinely global dimension allowed by the use of the Internet.[3] However, main principles of the 'dominant'[4] business model of digital platforms 'organizing'[5] work, i.e., based on a

1. By 'platform work' I target both work mediated and performed online through digital platforms and work mediated online through digital platforms but performed physically.
2. The number of people working through digital platforms remains limited. The authors allow themselves to share this finding, which is based on available statistics, in most of the reports and articles related to gig economy. In general, they are talking about 2%-22% of adults who have already worked via digital platforms, depending on the definition or type of platform work envisaged, the time period considered, the frequency of work and the countries surveyed.
3. The 'digital turn' is often considered radically new or 'disruptive'. Rather these changes 'are rooted in a set of technological, economic and social trends that emerged during the two last decades of the 20th century'. They are deemed to be 'a mix of disruption and continuity' (G. VALENDUC & P. VENDRAMIN, 'Digitalisation, Between Disruption and Evolution', *Transfer: Eur. Rev. of Labour & Research*, May 2017, vol. 23, no. 2, p. 122).
4. This chapter does not include the scope of analysis of the increasing number of initiatives that aim to develop alternative business models, mainly in the form of workers' cooperatives.
5. At least in its primary sense: '*to make arrangements for something to happen*' (https://dictionary.cambridge.org/). Some authors use the term 'administer' (C. CODAGNONE, F. BIAGI & F. ABADIE, *The future of work in the 'sharing economy': Market efficiency and equitable opportunities or unfair precarisation?*, JRC101280, Publications Office of the European Union, Luxembourg, 2016, p. 17, https://ec.europa.eu/jrc). My belief is that the business model of digital platforms leads many of them to 'organize' platform work in the term's second sense either: '*to do or arrange something according to a particular system*' (https://dictionary.cambridge.org/). Indeed, digital platforms will inevitably embody certain political postures; they will determine the rules that

relationship where workers are self-employed contractors benefiting from a certain flexibility and where platforms are intermediaries that are not keen on taking up any other responsibility than providing a technological/logistical service, let us rather think of old forms of work. Platform work has even been compared to industrial homework and the 'putting out' system known since the Early Modern Europe, before the expansion of factories and legal regulation.[6]

The interview for a website dedicated to digital news of a 'juicer'[7] in Paris is an interesting starting point to put this statement into context. While talking about his job, which consists of collecting, recharging and serving electric scooters for the platforms *Lime* and *Bird*, a juicer explains that he spends long days and nights of work chasing electric scooters that have an empty battery. He has the status of 'auto-entrepreneur', and earns EUR 7-EUR 8 per scooter he manages to put to charge for five hours. Considering the fact that each juicer is supposed to receive four chargers, and taking into account the rate of minimum wage in France, one can claim it is not a good remuneration. However, apart from the eventually questionable status that is recognized to him, and the eventually unenviable working conditions that he describes, the most shocking assertion in his story is at the end of the article. He says he really fears the growing competition between juicers who are sometimes two or three on the same scooter, and he wonders whether they could ever come to blows.[8] The testimony of this worker has something quite terrifying because it brings us almost two centuries back in the past, when people had to fight physically for a few hours of work and a pittance. In a sense, this narrative takes us back to the violent reality of the 'sans-travail'.[9]

These old forms of work and that terrible reality preceded social struggles and first social legislation. They are what prevailed for many workers before 'social law'[10] came into existence. If these alienating experiences that one has sought to overcome through social law threaten to happen again today, one has to ask oneself a simple question: 'What is wrong with labour and social security law?' This chapter aims to highlight that platform work leads us to question the current institutions and categories of social law. It does not mean that I am advocating for a substantial change in these institutions and categories. Rather this chapter is about suggesting that in view of the emergence and development of platform work one should reflect on their relevance.

govern their strategic development and market mechanisms. Platforms control their fundamental architecture to keep control over all interactions (N. Srnicek, *Capitalisme de plateforme: l'hégémonie de l'économie numérique*, Montréal, Lux Editeur, 2018, pp. 51-53). They are not designed to be democratic (M.S. Silberman & L. Irani, 'Operating an Employer Reputation System: Lessons from Turkopticon, 2008-2015', *Comp. Labor Law & Pol. Journal*, 2016, vol. 2015, no. 3, p. 539). The ecosystem governance becomes an essential skill (M.W. Van Alstyne, G.G. Parker & S.P. Choudary, 'Pipelines, Platforms, and the New Rules of Strategy', *Harvard Business Rev.*, 2016, vol. 94, no. 4, p. 5).

6. M.W. Finkin, 'Beclouded Work, Beclouded Workers in Historical Perspective', *Comp. Labor Law & Pol. Journal*, 2016, vol. 37, no. 3, pp. 603-618.
7. This is how the digital platform *Lime* calls workers (https://help.li.me/hc/en-gb/categories/360002431994-Juicer-Help).
8. N. Lesage, '"On joue les rapaces": on a discuté avec un chargeur de trottinettes électriques Lime et Bird', 5 October 2018, https://www.numerama.com/.
9. P. Hamp, 'Le droit au travail', *Europe*, 1925, vol. 9, no. 35.
10. In this chapter 'social law' refers to 'labour and social security law'.

Nevertheless, I do not make or analyse any policy recommendation at this stage, because obviously the answers are not simple. As a theoretical framework, the conception of social law that *Supiot* develops in his essay *Critique du droit du travail*[11] will be used. In this perspective, I will start by explaining my understanding of *Supiot*'s approach. In the following sections, the intention is to make the useful links with platform work, which will lead us to apprehend this form of work in both an abstract and a concrete way. I will share in the concluding section my reading of the challenges that social law faces today.

10.2 SOCIAL LAW AS A PLACE OF HARMONIZATION BETWEEN THE TWO SIDES OF WORK

According to *Supiot*'s approach, social law allows to rehabilitate the person of the worker in a contractual relationship in which work is only a good, reduced to an exchange value. The workers see four elements reappear in the employment relationship thanks to social law: their physical safety, economic safety, collective identity and individual identity.[12]

Regarding safety at work, *Supiot* starts by reminding us that in the employment relationship, above all, what is at risk for the workers is their *physical safety*. The social law regulations must therefore first contribute to guarantee the physical integrity of workers. In this sense, they must prevent and compensate physical injuries that may result from work, but also ensure workers' safety in all aspects of their biological existence (including working time and rest periods).[13] *Supiot* then explains that workers must find through work the means to perpetuate their labour force, i.e., the means to live and support their families. The social law rules must also lead to ensure the workers' *economic safety* and thus concern both the labour income that should be guaranteed to the workers and the replacement income, which enables them to subsist even if they are no longer able to work.[14] *Supiot* also considers that a community of workers must exist through work. The legal recognition of institutions representing workers provided by the social law rules allow to express this *collective identity* according to *Supiot*. The workers as a community can enter the 'legal arena' to face the employer. Preventing, negotiating and resolving disputes are made possible, as well as

11. A. Supiot, *Critique du droit du travail*, Quadrige, Paris, PUF, 1994. In this essay, it seems to us that *Supiot* analyses labour law in a broad sense, which is why I use the term of social law.
12. 'Il faut donc revenir, pour comprendre quelque chose au droit du travail, à cette antinomie première entre patrimonialité du travail et suprapatrimonialité du corps humain, car c'est sur elle que le droit du travail s'est d'abord cristallisé par strates successives. L'analyse contractuelle appréhendant le travail comme un "bien", le droit du travail consiste en somme à remettre ce "bien" dans sa peau, à réinsérer la dimension corporelle, et donc extrapatrimoniale, du travail dans le jeu des catégories du droit des obligations, et à partir de là, à y réinsérer par cercles concentriques, tous les autres aspects de la personne du travailleur. Le droit du travail s'institue dans cette réapparition de valeurs non patrimoniales dans un échange marchand (...)' (*Ibid.*, p. 67).
13. *Ibid.*, pp. 68-74.
14. *Ibid.*, pp. 74-81.

developing rights uniformly recognized to all workers.[15] In *Supiot*'s vision, the identity while working is the ultimate step to reintroduce the worker's person into the employment relationship. It aims to recognize the personal dimension of work as such. Work is no longer seen as a commodity because it is per se the expression of the worker. The workers bring something of themselves, something of their professional conscience so that the work is well done. The recognition of workers' rights over their work, the rights to freedom of expression or to training and qualification are keys that contribute to affirm the *individual identity* of workers.[16]

In this way, *Supiot* highlights the fundamental functions of social law. The workers recover their personal status thanks to social law. However, and this is a very important element in the author's theoretical approach of social law, it does not remove the abstract nature of work. On the contrary, social law also fully enshrines this side of work, in particular through the institutions of employment contract and subordination. In its ideal version, social law would rather be a place of harmonization between the two sides of work: work as a commodity (in other words, the abstract nature of work, source of external and quantifiable wealth), and work as an expression of the human person (which is the concrete nature of work, source of internal non-quantifiable richness).[17] *Supiot* also notes that law incorporates an ever-increasing number of standards or concepts from technology or from the economic and social sciences.[18] Regarding the evolution of the institutions of social law, one could understand that it contributes to distracting it from its ideal and its fundamental functions. The tension between the fundamental functions of social law and its institutions is at the heart of the issue on regulating platform work.

This chapter mobilizes the conception of social law as developed by *Supiot* in his essay. It is a theoretical and ideal approach to social law, which I use to highlight certain realities and consequent limits or dysfunctions of the current institutions and categories of social law. There is, of course, a plurality of theoretical frameworks that could be used to study work organization and working conditions within the platform economy, and to question the human character of this form of work. In this respect, social law does not have a monopoly, nor does *Supiot*'s conception of social law.[19]

15. *Ibid.*, pp. 86-97.
16. *Ibid.*, pp. 98-106.
17. *Ibid.*, p. 256.
18. *Ibid.*, p. 184.
19. *Supiot* uses the notion of *sujet de droit* to designate the worker who has recovered his personal status thanks to social law. Despite its original dimension, I do no longer use this notion, as my understanding is that it may introduce confusion. Indeed, this term besides other related terms are linked to numerous legal or 'meta-legal' meanings. I refer here to Dorssemont's in-depth analysis of the concepts of *rechtssubjectiviteit*, *rechtsbekwaamheid* and *subjectieve rechten* in his thesis work (F. Dorssemont, *Rechtspositie en syndicale actievrijheid van representatieve werknemersorganisaties*, Brugge, Die Keure, 2002, pp. 245-328). On the one hand, from a legal point of view, the recognition of a legal personality to workers may seem obvious. On the other hand, meta-legal approaches to legal personality and its components open us to a horizon of reflection: does this quality contribute to alienating or emancipating workers?.

10.3 PLATFORM WORK AS A COMMODITY

First, the essential characteristics of platform work demonstrate its mercantile nature. Platform work is working in exchange for a compensation.

Work may be performed under an employment contract or as part of an independent contract, concluded with the platform and/or the users.[20] The tasks carried out can be of varied nature. However, the key element is the mobilization of a workforce, unlike the sale of goods, the rental of a property or a car, which are activities that do not present issues in social law comparable to the phenomenon of interest to us.[21] Similarly, registration of one's details on mainstream job search sites in order to search for permanent or temporary work with conventional companies offering traditional employment contracts is not platform work.[22] Moreover, this work - still performed by human beings[23] - is carried out in exchange for a compensation, or at least in the aim of making a profit.[24] One should not deny the professional nature of platform work. There is a persistent discourse on platform work being something related to small services provided for 'pin money', 'out of boredom' and/or by generosity.[25] Regardless of the reasons that motivate workers to engage in such activities, it is clear that the performance of tasks such as driving a car, cleaning flats, translating documents or performing secretarial work 'shall not be considered merely as an act of good neighbourly relations or a spare-time activity' just because they are performed through digital platforms.[26]

---

20. The question whether it constitutes a professional activity subject to self-employed or salaried workers social security system arises afterwards.
21. C. Codagnone, F. Biagi & F. Abadie, *The future of work in the 'sharing economy': Market efficiency and equitable opportunities or unfair precarisation?*, *supra*, p. 17.
22. U. Huws et al., *Work in the European gig economy: Research results from the UK, Sweden, Germany, Austria, the Netherlands, Switzerland and Italy*, FEPS, UNI Europa, University of Hertfordshire, 2017, p. 14, http://uhra.herts.ac.uk/.
23. 'Crowdwork is a type of work performed remotely on on-line platforms. It emerged in the second half of the 2000s with the growth of the internet and the need to have *human* input into a range of tasks needed for the smooth functioning of web-based industries'. J. Berg, 'Income Security in the On-demand Economy: Findings and Policy Lessons from a Survey of Crowdworkers', *Comp. Labor Law & Pol. Journal*, 2016, vol. 37, no. 3, p. 543.
24. In particular, situations in which work is performed without being exchanged for a compensation are excluded (C. Codagnone, F. Biagi & F. Abadie, *The future of work in the 'sharing economy': Market efficiency and equitable opportunities or unfair precarisation?*, *supra*, p. 17) as 'digital labor' and the issue of co-production of value by Internet users (Conseil National du Numérique, *Travail. Emploi. Numérique. Les nouvelles trajectoires*, 2016, pp. 47-48, https://cnnumerique.fr/, ref. to M.-A. Dujarier, *Le travail du consommateur: de MacDo à eBay: comment nous coproduisons ce que nous achetons*, Paris, La Découverte, 2014; D. Cardon & A. Casilli, *Qu'est-ce que le Digital Labor?*, Paris, Editions de l'INA, 2015).
25. C. Codagnone, F. Biagi & F. Abadie, *The future of work in the 'sharing economy': Market efficiency and equitable opportunities or unfair precarisation?*, *supra*, p. 53. *See also* J. Berg, 'Income Security in the On-Demand Economy: Findings and Policy Lessons from a Survey of Crowdworkers', *supra*, p. 565.
26. V. De Stefano & A. Aloisi, *European legal framework for 'digital labour platforms'*, JRC112243, Publications Office of the European Union, Luxembourg, 2018, p. 11, https://ec.europa.eu/jrc.

Second, there is no doubt about the mercantile nature of platform work when one looks at the business model of 'digital platforms of work'.[27]

Without closely analysing the business model of digital platforms as 'multi-sided markets',[28] it is useful to note some of its characteristics through their application to digital platforms of work. These platforms connect (also indirectly)[29] 'consumers of work', i.e., people who order tasks to be performed, with 'producers of work', people who are ready to perform them. They provide a digital infrastructure and sets governance conditions for these interactions.[30] As this is the case for all platforms, digital platforms of work must enable value-creating interactions between consumers and producers. In order to be efficient, these markets must then attract and retain users, and be able to orchestrate repeatable interactions between them.[31] Attracting consumers and producers of work will require platforms to set up specific pricing structures and strengthen network effects. It is therefore when digital platforms of work seek to attract the most consumers of work that they will increase the costs borne by the producers of work.[32] In order to retain users and stimulate operations and their repetition, platforms will seek to reduce transaction costs[33] and market failure (through standardizing consumer experience and manipulating information),[34] as well as building trust between users (through reputation systems requiring consumers to rate and/or review workers - most of the time).[35] In addition, to ensure market liquidity, some digital platforms of work will focus on algorithmic scheduling and management of work.[36]

It is often acknowledged that digital platforms of work provide workers with access to new income generation opportunities and remove barriers to market access. They give workers the ability to choose schedules and enable them to discover clients

27. In principle, a distinction should be made between platform owners and platform operators. In this chapter, I overlook this distinction and simply refer to 'digital platforms' or 'digital platforms of work'.
28. *See* V. Hatzopoulos, *The collaborative economy and EU law*, Oxford, Portland, Oregon, Hart Publishing, 2018, pp. 9 ff., refer to definition given by D. Evans & R. Schmalensee, *The Antitrust Analysis of Multi-Sided Platform Businesses*, Cambridge, MA, National Bureau of Economic Research, February 2013, p. 7, http://www.nber.org/, and the very rich literature on multi-sided markets and to pioneers: J.-C. Rochet & J. Tirole, 'Platform Competition in Two-Sided Markets', *J. Eur. Econ. Assoc.*, June 2003, vol. 1, no. 4, pp. 990-1029; J.-C. Rochet & J. Tirole, 'Two-Sided Markets: A Progress Report', *RAND J. Econ.*, September 2006, vol. 37, no. 3, pp. 645-667. For a more critical approach to these markets, *see* in particular N. Srnicek, *Capitalisme de plateforme*, *supra*; M.W. Van Alstyne, G.G. Parker & S.P. Choudary, 'Pipelines, Platforms, and the New Rules of Strategy', *supra*; G. Parker, M. Van Alstyne & S.P. Choudary, *Platform revolution: How networked markets are transforming the economy and how to make them work for you*, s. l., WW Norton & Company, 2016.
29. For example, digital platforms offering services of electric scooters.
30. S.P. Choudary, *The architecture of digital labour platforms: Policy recommendations on platform design for worker well-being*, Research Paper ILO Future of Work Research Paper Series, 2018, p. 1, https://www.ilo.org/.
31. *Ibid.*, pp. 2-4.
32. *Ibid.*, p. 3.
33. *Ibid.*, p. 4.
34. *Ibid.*, p. 5.
35. *Ibid.*, pp. 3-5.
36. *Ibid.*, p. 6.

and build new relationships. Platforms allow more efficient use of surplus assets. They offer workers technologies and tools that can improve their services, or increase their customer base. Digital platforms of work can also provide opportunities for workers who are difficultly engaged in regular employment, such as parents of young children or students. Flexibility of working hours and workplace is particularly sought by some workers. Categories of workers known as 'marginal' or 'in transition' can access these markets more easily. To some extent, digital platforms of work can thus be a tool to encourage entrepreneurship. Some platforms occasionally publish data showing positive results on these issues.[37]

However, the business model of digital platforms of work also forces them to create an efficient market that can increase the platform's market share. Therefore, if required to create an efficient market, digital platforms of work will make design choices that lead to 'workers exploitation', resulting in unfavourable working conditions for them.[38] Platforms would even contribute to 'pulverizing' the stable employment relationship.[39] In this respect, it is of course less costly to engage self-employed workers, who use their own equipment and bear all the costs associated with the activity (investment, maintenance, insurance and depreciation costs).[40] This particular model 'allows the management of a contingent workforce mobilized on a 'just-in-time' basis, thus responding to demand peaks and shifting the impact of fluctuations on the worker's shoulders'. The advantage of digital platforms of work would then essentially derive from their failure to comply with labour and social security law regulations.[41] It has already been specified that 'a severe commodification of work' characterizes platform work, due to the significant dehumanization and extreme flexibility of the employment relationship it implies,[42] a commodification that is rarely chanted by platforms.[43]

37. *Ibid.*, pp. 6-7.
38. *Ibid.*, p. 8. In his paper, the author proposes a framework for understanding worker exploitation within the platform economy, discussing five key elements: removal of free agency; reduced bargaining power and rights; domination; dependence; and fairness (*Ibid.*, pp. 9-30).
39. V. De Stefano & A. Aloisi, *European legal framework for 'digital labour platforms'*, *supra*, pp. 14-15.
40. N. Srnicek, *Capitalisme de plateforme*, *supra*, pp. 87-89.
41. V. De Stefano & A. Aloisi, *European legal framework for 'digital labour platforms'*, *supra*, pp. 14-15. *See also* N. Srnicek, *Capitalisme de plateforme*, *supra*, pp. 81-82.
42. V. De Stefano, 'The Rise of the "Just-in-Time Workforce": On-Demand Work, Crowd Work and Labour Protection in the "Gig-Economy"', *Comp. Labor Law & Pol. Journal*, 2016, vol. 37, no. 3, pp. 472, 476-480.
43. As an exception, however, *see* the words of the CEO of CrowdFlower: 'Before the Internet, it would be really difficult to find someone, sit them down for ten minutes and get them to work for you, and then fire them after those ten minutes. But with technology, you can actually find them, pay them the tiny amount of money, and then get rid of them when you don't need them anymore' (V. De Stefano, 'The Rise of the "Just-in-Time Workforce": On-Demand Work, Crowd Work and Labour Protection in the "Gig-Economy"', *supra*, p. 476). Such a compromising statement that goes beyond the usual platforms' rhetoric on encouraging entrepreneurship or peer-to-peer relationships is quite rare in terms of communication. *See* on this topic A.J. Ravenelle, 'Sharing Economy Workers: Selling, Not Sharing', *Cambridge J. Reg. Econ. Soc.*, July 2017, vol. 10, no. 2, pp. 281-295.

10.4 PLATFORM WORK AS THE EXPRESSION OF A HUMAN PERSON?

Although few in terms of number, studies provide useful data on platform work and, in particular, a worrying first insight into the working conditions within the platform economy.[44] These studies unanimously found that platform work offers flexibility and new opportunities of work and income, which workers are looking for. On the other hand, they also highlight several factors that demonstrate a reality of precarious work for platform workers.

Social isolation and various health problems are a primary concern.[45] Platform workers complain about the lack of human interaction at work (especially from management) due to the pre-eminence of technology. A subsequent feeling of alienation and voicelessness was described.[46] The absence of social contact has been highlighted in a study regarding online platforms workers. Workers explained that they appreciate the ability to work from home, enabling them to avoid long, uncomfortable and costly commutes on public transport and to keep control over the place of work (mostly working from home then). It also makes it possible for workers to combine this work with other forms of work such as studying, domestic work, caring and other activities or for people with disability to simply access work. However, a downside to working from home is social isolation. The loneliness of working without interpersonal contact was an important theme of the interviews with some workers.[47] In addition, both online and offline platform workers report a variety of health problems linked to their work, including physical health problems like eye strain, back, kidney, knee or hips problems, injuries resulting from traffic accidents, assaults, domestic accidents; and mental health problems as depression, stress, burn-out.[48]

---

44. I focused on these studies: J. Berg, 'Income Security in the On-Demand Economy: Findings and Policy Lessons from a Survey of Crowdworkers', *supra*; U. Huws et al., 'Work in the European Gig Economy', *supra*; A. Pesole et al., *Platform workers in Europe: Evidence from the COLLEEM survey*, JRC112157, Publications Office of the European Union, Luxembourg, 2018, https://ec.europa.eu/jrc; International Labour Organization, *Digital labour platforms and the future of work: Towards decent work in the online world*, Geneva, International Labour Office, 2018; A.J. Wood et al., 'Good Gig, Bad Gig: Autonomy and Algorithmic Control in the Global Gig Economy', *Work, Employment and Society*, February 2019, vol. 33, no. 1, pp. 56-75. The scope of these studies covers a variety of countries and (types of) platforms. Each study has its own definition of platform work, some of them concern both online and offline platform work others online platform work only. In this chapter, I summarize the main results of these studies regarding the working conditions within the platform economy, without systematically specifying the scope of the study that delivered them.
45. Except from the COLLEEM Survey results, suggesting 'a wide agreement that the conditions of platform work are safe'. Indeed, according to responses, platform work would allow most workers to perform tasks 'under safe environmental conditions'. However, there was 'a significant share of online platform workers who say that their work is stressful' (A. Pesole et al., *Platform workers in Europe: Evidence from the COLLEEM survey*, *supra*, p. 46.).
46. U. Huws et al., 'Work in the European Gig Economy', *supra*, p. 41.
47. A.J. Wood et al., 'Good Gig, Bad Gig', *supra*, p. 66. On people with poor health or disability enabling to access work, *see also* J. Berg, 'Income Security in the On-Demand Economy: Findings and Policy Lessons from a Survey of Crowdworkers', *supra*, p. 553; and for specific comments on women, *see* International Labour Organization, *Digital labour platforms and the future of work: Towards decent work in the online world*, *supra*, pp. 69-71.
48. U. Huws et al., 'Work in the European Gig Economy', *supra*, pp. 46-47.

Another important issue clarified by these studies concerns the loss of control over working hours. Of course, workers say they value the flexibility that allows platform work,[49] but a majority of them admit that they have to work intensively. Indeed, it is especially documented that many platform workers work during long and atypical hours,[50] although there are significant differences by categories of platform workers.[51] To earn a decent income, workers often have to work long hours. When they combine this work with another activity, working hours are often in the evening, at night, on weekends and on holidays. The study on online platform workers in some developing countries included several explicit testimonies in this regard. Some workers were talking about working up to seventy-eight hours a week, seven days a week, eighteen hours a day, nights, etc. Therefore, it seems possible for platform workers to value flexibility just as much that they suffer from it. The reason is that client expectations come first, even if it means working at night. There are many testimonies in this sense.[52] Moreover, the insufficiency of work within the platform economy is a reality that ultimately leaves little room to workers for freely choosing their working time.[53] Indeed, platform workers experience high levels of competition. In order to increase their earnings, they have to complete more tasks as quickly as possible, thus increasing work intensity. Furthermore, they have to minimize unpaid downtime[54] requiring workers to diversify tasks and work for several clients. Dealing with multiple clients' deadlines and requirements, of course, also results in increasing work intensity.[55]

Low pay is another major concern in platform work.[56] The very competitive environment within the platform economy has impact on income levels. It led workers to feel that they could easily be replaced, especially by workers living in another country who are assumed to be willing to work for less money.[57] A study shows that workers carrying out more skilled work earned more than those doing low-skilled

49. *Ibid.*, pp. 40-41; A. Pesole et al., *Platform workers in Europe: Evidence from the COLLEEM survey, supra*, pp. 43-45.
50. International Labour Organization, *Digital labour platforms and the future of work: Towards decent work in the online world, supra*, pp. 67-71.
51. A. Pesole et al., *Platform workers in Europe: Evidence from the COLLEEM survey, supra*, pp. 48-49.
52. A.J. Wood et al., 'Good Gig, Bad Gig', *supra*, pp. 67-68.
53. On insufficiency of work, *see* J. Berg, 'Income Security in the On-Demand Economy: Findings and Policy Lessons from a Survey of Crowdworkers', *supra*, pp. 561-562; International Labour Organization, *Digital labour platforms and the future of work: Towards decent work in the online world, supra*, pp. 61-67.
54. Regarding unpaid time spent waiting or bidding for work, *see also* U. Huws et al., 'Work in the European Gig Economy', *supra*, p. 43; J. Berg, 'Income Security in the On-Demand Economy: Findings and Policy Lessons from a Survey of Crowdworkers', *supra*, p. 557.
55. A.J. Wood et al., 'Good Gig, Bad Gig', *supra*, p. 65-66.
56. J. Berg, 'Income Security in the On-Demand Economy: Findings and Policy Lessons from a Survey of Crowdworkers', *supra*, pp. 557-559; Organisation internationale du Travail, *Digital labour platforms and the future of work: Towards decent work in the online world, supra*, pp. 49-59; A. Pesole et al., *Platform workers in Europe: Evidence from the COLLEEM survey, supra*, p. 51.
57. A.J. Wood et al., 'Good Gig, Bad Gig', *supra*, p. 68.

work. However, even among workers doing low-skilled work, massive income disparities were found. This suggests that other forms of worker power besides skills are also important in determining income. This other form of power is reputation. Work flowed to those workers who manage to maintain a strong reputation over a long period and are thus known by clients and highly ranked by platform algorithms. A lack of strong reputation would necessarily lead to low incomes,[58] in some cases below the national monthly minimum wages.[59] Workers who are in demand thanks to skills and reputation enjoyed several job quality advantages over others. For example, they can afford to save some of their income and pay for private health insurance.[60] Differences in pay, sometimes significant, were also reported across gender, and between regions as well as between developed and developing economies.[61] Low pay is deemed to be particularly worrying as many workers rely on the income from platform work to make ends meet. As a result, many of them are reported to live in a precarious financial situation.[62]

Beyond the amount of income that can be earned, it is also the unstable nature of this income that is considered as an issue within the platform economy. Platform workers have no formal job security. At any time, they can 'lose their job', i.e., they can have their contract terminated at any time without notice, and be replaced. This fear of being replaced was evident among a significant number of platform workers.[63] Studies report unilateral arbitrary deactivations, whereby platform workers suddenly found their registration with the platform suspended, often with no explanation or warning.[64] Financial insecurity and poor social protection coverage are also documented.[65]

In view of the results described above, it seems that workers' physical safety as well as economic security and collective identity are severely compromised within the platform economy. Regarding their individual identity, on the contrary, it could be argued that the possibilities of working in a flexible and autonomous way contribute to better asserting it in platform work than in other forms of salaried work. However, I feel that this first impression must be put into perspective. First, even if it has not been discussed much in this chapter, the control exercised by platforms, in the form of what some have called 'management by algorithms',[66] should not be underestimated. Second, I wonder whether the idea of working in a flexible and autonomous way really

58. *Ibid.*, p. 69.
59. *Ibid.* International Labour Organization, *Digital labour platforms and the future of work: Towards decent work in the online world, supra*, p. 50.
60. A.J. Wood et al., 'Good Gig, Bad Gig', *supra*, p. 69.
61. International Labour Organization, *Digital labour platforms and the future of work: Towards decent work in the online world, supra*, p. 52.
62. *Ibid.*, pp. 57-58.
63. A.J. Wood et al., 'Good Gig, Bad Gig', *supra*, p. 68.
64. U. Huws et al., 'Work in the European Gig Economy', *supra*, p. 42; International Labour Organization, *Digital labour platforms and the future of work: Towards decent work in the online world, supra*, pp. 72-78.
65. J. Berg, 'Income Security in the On-Demand Economy: Findings and Policy Lessons from a Survey of Crowdworkers', *supra*, pp. 562-563; International Labour Organization, *Digital labour platforms and the future of work: Towards decent work in the online world, supra*, pp. 59-61.
66. In particular, *see* A. Rosenblat, *Uberland: How algorithms are rewriting the rules of work*, Oakland, California, University of California Press, 2018.

is compatible with an environment where workers' physical safety is not guaranteed, that leads to ever longer working hours, does not offer any decent or qualitative remuneration, that is inherently precarious and contributes to workers' social isolation. Workers who benefit from those protections by other means may not encounter difficulties and may value more the flexibility and autonomy that platform work allows, but workers in situations of greater vulnerability, as there is undoubtedly in platform work, will simply not have the opportunity to take advantage of this flexibility and autonomy. *Supiot* considers the four above-mentioned elements, which allow the workers to recover their status of person, in a hierarchical way, physical security coming first and individual identity last. The author therefore suggests that workers cannot feel recognized in their individual identity without benefiting from guarantees regarding their physical and economic security and their collective identity. This conception allows us to approach critically the situation of platform workers, and in particular, the flexibility and autonomy so highly praised within the platform economy.

10.5 CONCLUSION

With reference to our understanding of *Supiot*'s theoretical and ideal conception of social law, I think that social law does not fulfil its functions regarding platform workers. Therefore, reconsidering the institutions of social law should be encouraged[67] in order to 'address the special need for protection of platform workers'.[68] This chapter highlighted that, although platform work is considered a commodity, physical and economic security, collective and individual identity are not guaranteed to platform workers. A reason can be found in the fact that many platform workers are deemed to be self-employed. In this respect, the institutions of social law related to the distinction between self-employed workers and employees, i.e., the definition of these concepts[69] or connected concepts such as this of employer,[70] should be questioned. They could be clarified or reviewed in order to provide platform workers with the protection they need. However, other institutions of social law are worth thinking about. As a complementary approach, strengthening the effectiveness of existing fundamental and specific protections should be given priority over developing new regulation.[71]

67. It must be mentioned that alternative initiatives to social law are interesting and can also contribute to the physical and economic security of platform workers, as well as their collective identity. However, I do not analyse them in the context of this chapter.
68. V. De Stefano & A. Aloisi, *European legal framework for 'digital labour platforms'*, *supra*, p. 54.
69. *Ibid.*
70. J. Prassl & M. Risak, 'Uber, Taskrabbit, and Co.: Platforms as Employers – Rethinking the Legal Analysis of Crowdwork', *Comp. Labor Law & Pol. Journal*, 2016, vol. 37, no. 3, pp. 619-652.
71. L. Ratti, 'Online Platforms and Crowdwork in Europe: A Two-Step Approach to Expanding Agency Work Provisions Barriers to Union Organizing', *Comp. Labor Law & Pol. Journal*, 2017, vol. 38, no. 3, pp. 477-512; V. De Stefano & A. Aloisi, 'Fundamental Labour Rights, Platform Work and Human-Rights Protection of Non-Standard Workers', in *Research Handbook on Labour, Business and Human Rights Law*, J. R. Bellace, S. Blank, Beryl ter Haar (eds), Cheltenham, Royaume-Uni, Edward Elgar Publishing Ltd., 2019, pp. 359-379.

In essence, a rethink on the institutions of social law requires thus to see the broader picture. There is evidence on the growth of atypical forms of employment.[72] In particular, the rise of on-demand work arrangements is observed, seen as the 'over-flexibilization' of the labour market to the disadvantage of workers. Indeed, the insecurity that originates from these arrangements is manifold.[73] Elaborating on this point, one should keep in mind that the growth of atypical forms of employment should also be seen as a voluntary or involuntary outcome of regulation. Of course, it is not only due to regulation but it can be attributed to other factors such as the impact of global trade, the decline of the manufacturing sector, the massive expansion of the service sector in industrialized countries, as well as technological innovation. Nevertheless, following the authors on this issue, I believe that regulatory practices also play an important role that should not be underestimated.[74]

72. International Labour Organization, *Non-standard employment around the world: understanding challenges, shaping prospects*, Geneva, International Labour Office, 2016: 'Although the latest economic recession and some recent legal changes forestalled the growth of non-standard employment in some countries, this chapter has shown that – globally – there are strong tendencies in favour of NSE, and towards a diversification of its forms. As numerous forces responsible for the rise of NSE – notably structural transformation, technological change, globalization and the evolving structure of the labour force – will not only persist but may intensify in the future, it is not unreasonable to expect that NSE will continue to proliferate. And it will continue posing, in an increasingly intensified manner, numerous challenges. In developed countries, these challenges are likely to be linked to the creation of new employment opportunities without falling into the traps of dualism and segmented labour markets, as well as responding to the consequences of the on-demand economy. In developing countries, the challenge will be to continue the push towards greater labour market formalization without forsaking standard jobs and their inclusiveness. In all countries, the key questions will be linked to ensuring that non-standard jobs constitute decent work' (pp. 105-106).
73. V. De Stefano & A. Aloisi, *European legal framework for 'digital labour platforms'*, *supra*, p. 32.
74. V. De Stefano & A. Aloisi, 'Fundamental Labour Rights, Platform Work and Human-Rights Protection of Non-Standard Workers', *supra*, p. 361.

Part III Digitalization in the Organization of Work and the Employment Relationship

CHAPTER 11
Challenges for Labour Law in the Era of Digitalization: With Special Reference to Germany

Manfred Weiss

11.1 INTRODUCTION

Digitalization of working patterns has many faces, it is not to be conceived as a uniform or homogeneous phenomenon. Many details are still rather unclear. In a similar way as globalization, also digitalization undoubtedly leads to a dramatic transformation of the world of work. Each of the different working patterns leads to different implications for labour law and industrial relations. Three types are most relevant in this context.

Already for several decades communication technologies made it possible that work does not have to be performed in the premises of the employer but can be executed anywhere. The labels used for this type of work are 'tele-work' or 'mobile work'.[1]

Another trend of this digital evolution is labelled 'Industry 4.0' which stands for the fourth industrial revolution.[2] The label is somehow misleading because this type of work refers not only to manufacturing but also in the same way to services. Collaborative robots become intelligent, which means able to adapt, communicate and interact. Smart robots communicate with each other and with humans on interlinking tasks. These cyber-physical systems are quickly widening, including various functions in production, logistics or office management.

1. For the problems arising in the context of telework, *see* the contributions in R. Blanpain (ed.), European Framework Agreements and Telework: Law and Practice, A European and Comparative Study, Bulletin of Comparative Labour Relations 2007, 62.
2. F. Almada-Lobo, The Industry 4.0 Revolution and the Future of Manufacturing Execution Systems (MES), Journal of Innovation Management 2016, 16-21.

The third important trend is the increasing platform economy[3] where a crowd-sourcer launches a call or competition on an online platform, gathers proposals from the crowd and evaluates the proposals to select the proposal deemed most suitable for the intended purpose. Here basically two types are to be distinguished: 'internal platforms' to which only the workforce of a specific company has access and 'external platforms' with open access for anybody meeting specific criteria. Among the 'external platforms' again two types are to be distinguished: 'work on demand via app' where the work is performed in a traditional way (transport, cleaning, etc.) and 'online crowd-work' where work is performed by a crowd-worker online. Again there has to be distinguished between platforms where relatively simple tasks are performed by unskilled or low skilled persons and complex platforms where highly skilled persons are confronted with complex tasks.

There is no doubt that at least to a certain extent human beings will be substituted by robots, thereby losing their jobs. The challenge will be to keep the number of these people as small as possible and to reskill those who are substituted in order to re-integrate them into the labour market. The even bigger challenge, however, will be whether and how the work in view of digitalization can be regulated in a way which will guarantee the traditional goals of labour law to protect the worker, to respect his or her dignity, in particular to guarantee his or her privacy as well as his or her physical, mental and psychic health.

11.2 EXAMPLES OF REGULATORY PROBLEMS AND POSSIBLE SOLUTIONS

The problem to be sketched in this short contribution is the impact these developments have on traditional labour law. How these challenges can be met is still rather uncertain. Adaptation will be needed. This is nothing new. Labour law quite often in the past had to be adapted to new situation in the world of work. Since the Fordist model, which originally was the point of reference to labour law, the world of work has seen many transformations. At least so far labour law always has succeeded to cope with them.

The purpose of this chapter is to briefly indicate the direction in which regulatory strategies might be developed.[4] Instead of discussing comprehensively all the problems which might be relevant in this context, simply a few examples are selected to illustrate where the direction of future regulation might go. To be as concrete as possible I refer - whenever possible - to developments in Germany which, of course, I know best.

3. For the different types of work in the platform economy, *see* V. De Stefano, Introduction: Crowdsourcing, the Gig-Economy and the Law, Comparative Labor Law & Policy Journal 2016, 461-470.
4. For a good overview on this debate, *see* W. Liebman, The Gig Economy, Crowdwork and New Forms of Work; Soziales Recht 2017, 221-238.

11.2.1 Workers' Participation in Introducing and Using Digital Tools

The first example is a very specific German one. In Germany works councils are to be elected in each workplace of at least five employees. The works council represents the interests of the workforce and acts as counterpart of the employer. It has different rights of participation ranging from a mere right of information and consultation up to a right of co-determination. Co-determination means that the employer cannot do anything without the works council's consent. In case of disagreement, each side has access to an arbitration committee which resolves the conflict.[5]

In our context it is of utmost importance that the works council has such a right of co-determination for 'the introduction and use of technological devises by which the behaviour or performance of the employees can be monitored' (section 87 paragraph 1 number 6 of the Act on Works Councils). It is totally irrelevant whether the employer intents to monitor the employees or not. Decisive is only the mere possibility. Almost all digital tools qualify for this right of co-determination. This means that digital devices only can be introduced in close cooperation with the works council. And the same refers to the matter how they are to be used. A consensus has to be reached with the works council. Thereby, the body of workers' representation has to be involved from the very beginning. As empirical studies on introduction of former technological innovations show, this helps to reduce the employees' fear of negative effects of the introduction and use of technological devices. This co-determination right, of course, only becomes relevant where a works council exists. As will be shown below, this by far is not the case in all digital contexts. It might not be problematic in traditional companies where Industry 4.0 is at stake. But it might be very difficult in the context of the platform economy.

11.2.2 Training

Due to the already indicated possibility of job loss and of de-skilling by digitalization and the need of reskilling people to regain job opportunities, vocational training will play a much bigger role than ever. Its content and its organization have to be fundamentally reconceptualized. This insight has led in Germany to a legislative response in December 2018 and to a National Strategy on Continued Vocational Education in June 2019. This strategy is a joint venture of government, trade unions, employers' associations and chambers of commerce.

Traditionally Germany has a well-established system of vocational training: the dual system of apprenticeship, consisting of practical training in the enterprise, synchronized with theoretical education in special schools for vocational training. This has been a success story, highly appreciated all over the world. In this system not only the teachers in these schools but also the persons responsible for the vocational training in the companies have to meet specific requirements by passing specific

5. For details, *see* M.Weiss / M. Schmidt, Labour Law and Industrial Relations in Germany, 4th ed., Kluwer 2008, 222-247.

exams. Apprenticeship in the context of the dual system of vocational training is only possible for a listed number of occupations recognized as professions by the Federal Government. Apprenticeship ends with an exam.[6]

However, as good as the dual system may be, it is no longer sufficient. It is based on the idea that this highly formalized apprenticeship provides the worker with the knowledge and skill he or she needs throughout his or her working life. Formerly passing the exam after the apprenticeship was more or less a guarantee for professional success. This, of course, is no longer the case in the era of digitalization where the cycles of technological innovation are faster and faster, leading to ever changing professional requirements. Further training is needed.

A short look on the empirical situation in Germany shows that that more than 50% of the companies in Germany in 2016 were engaged in measures of further training. At the same time only a very small part of the unskilled and semi-skilled employees participated in such training measures whereas among the skilled workers these were almost 50% and two-thirds of academics. In short this means that the more one is already skilled and educated, the better the chance to participate in programmes of further training. This, of course, is an alarming situation because the risk to be substituted by digitalization is most probably the highest for those who are unskilled or semi-skilled.

The Act on Improving the Chances for Skilling of December 2018 mainly obliges the employment agency to subsidize measures of further training in the context of an employment relationship. So far the subventions were only possible for unemployed persons if additional skills improve their employability. Now the subventions are extended to employees who finalized a formal apprenticeship if certain conditions are fulfilled. The law states expressly that the subvention is supposed to particularly help employees who do have jobs which might be substituted by technology or in another way affected by structural change to adapt and further develop their professional skills.

This subvention is only supposed to take place if the employer participates in the costs of the training. This does not apply for employees in companies below ten employees: there the employment agency bears all the costs. No matter how big the company is, the employment agency also bears all the costs if the employee is at least 45 years old or if the employee is disabled. Not only employees but also companies whose employees participate in subsidized training are to be subsidized, differentiated due to the company's size.

In addition the law obliges the employment agency to take utmost efforts in advising employees on the possibilities to participate in measures of further training and on the advantages such education provides.

Whether this law will significantly change the present situation may well be doubted. It mainly improves the position of already skilled workers. The situation of the unskilled and semi-skilled workers remains more or less the same.

Therefore, there is agreement in Germany among all actors that a more comprehensive participation has to be made possible. Law has to provide the framework for

6. For a short description of the system of apprenticeship, *see* M.Weiss / M. Schmidt, *supra*, 70/71.

such skilling opportunities. Workers must get the time and the resources to engage in continuous learning processes. Not only the Government but also the actors in collective bargaining as well as the actors in workers' participation schemes are confronted with this task. Joint efforts of all these actors are needed.

That is why in June 2019 the already mentioned National Strategy on Continued Vocational Education started. It is supposed to establish a comprehensive system of continued vocational training for all employees. Many questions have to be resolved in this context: whether there should be an individual right for all employees to participate in such training, what incentives for employees and employers should be envisaged, how the costs are to be shared between employees, employers and the state, how the responsibilities are to be shared between legislation and collective bargaining and last not least what should be the content of lifelong learning in view of the fact that due to the fast changing technological developments nobody knows what skills are required in the future. As you can see, a long list of questions to be answered. But as the report of the International Labour Organization (ILO) Global Commission on the Future of Work[7] as well as the Centenary Declaration of the ILO[8] tell us lifelong learning for all is the precondition for coping successfully with the challenges of digitalization.

The Global Commission's report contains many helpful recommendations. Particularly the idea of an entitlement to training during working hours is to be supported. One might even go further and recommend an individual right for training during working hours, of course without loss of remuneration.

The German Government presently is preparing a bill of a law combining short time work in times of down-swing or structural transformation of the economy with the obligation to train people in the remaining time between full time and short time. This pattern already turned out to be very successful during the financial crisis when trade unions and works councils together with the companies agreed to not dismiss workers but to rather reduce their working time and use the free time for training. This gave the German economy a very good head start after the crisis. Now this pattern is supposed to be regulated by law.

And as far as financing of continuous training is concerned, the establishment of an 'employment insurance', as suggested by the report, deserves strong support. Thereby, the costs for such a training scheme may be covered to a great extent by contributions of employers and employees together. The question, of course, remains, whether and how far such a training scheme which is not only in the interest of workers and employers but also for the society as a whole is to be subsidized by the system of taxation.

The biggest problem, however, is the content of continued training. So far training has been focussing on skills required for the different well-known professions. In the future it will no longer be possible to focus on such well-established skills. The new skills which are needed are unknown to a great extent. And they will quickly be replaced by others. Therefore, the report of the Global Commission is correct by

7. Global Commission on the Future of Work, Work for a Brighter Future, Geneva ILO 2019.
8. International Labour Conference, ILO Centenary Declaration for the Future of Work, adopted by the conference on its 108th session on 21 June 2019.

insisting that in the future the focus has to be much more on 'learning how to learn' in order to become able to adapt to new situations. This, of course, requires highly qualified teachers: an enormous challenge for all who are responsible for the educational system.

11.2.3 Classification

The question is whether the scope of labour law application has to be extended in view of all the changes, including platform work.

Already for quite a long time it has become evident that the demarcation line between employment and self-employment is very difficult to draw.[9] To an increasing extent there are persons labelled as being self-employed but in reality being employees. The problem of drawing a demarcation line between employment and self-employed will further increase in the era of digitalization. The degree of autonomy in performing work makes it more and more difficult to categorize the persons involved in such work, even if a closer look reveals that the autonomy is ambiguous because new mechanisms of more efficient control are in place. Many of those who participate in crowdsourcing certainly are not employees but rather self-employed.

The question is what to do with those who undoubtedly are self-employed and work alone without employees but are economically in a similar position as employees. They are not reached by labour law protection. They are not included in minimum wage schemes, health and safety arrangements or guarantees of decent working time, to just give some examples. Theoretically there are different possibilities to provide for them the necessary protection: the broadening of the notion of employee, the creation of a specific intermediate category or the extension of the scope of labour law to economically dependent self-employed (solo self-employed) and so on.

The broadening of the notion of employee is the pattern we can presently see in the many lawsuits all over the world determining the question whether Uber drivers are employees or self-employed. In many countries the notion of employee has been extended significantly. However, this strategy has limits. If the notion is extended too far, it would become meaningless. And it never will be possible to include all economically dependent employees.

The introduction of an intermediary category between employment and self-employment might be a solution.[10] However, as the examples in quite a few countries show, it only has provoked uncertainties and led to many controversies. It increases the complexity, thereby rather leading to more problems than less. Therefore, Italy recently has given up this approach.

A more radical possibility would be the inclusion of self-employed up to a certain wage level under the protective roof of labour law and social security law. As far as the inclusion into the social security system is concerned, some countries – as for example

9. *See*, for a comprehensive discussion of this problem, G. Davidov/B. Langille (eds), Boundaries and Frontiers of Labour Law, Oxford/Portland 2006.
10. Germany has such a pattern. For details, *see* B. Waas, Crowdwork in Germany, in B. Waas et al., Crowdwork a Comparative Perspective, Frankfurt 2017, 142-186 (160-162).

Austria – have followed this path already, and it seems to work quite well. Whether, however, such a strategy might work also for labour law may be doubted. It cannot be denied that many protective patterns are linked to the relationship between employer and employee in the employment relationship. The rules on protection against unfair dismissal might be a good example to illustrate what I mean. Therefore, a mere extension of labour law to self-employed might not be the right strategy.

Therefore, a change of paradigm might be more helpful. Instead of putting workers in different categories we should discuss the floor of rights all working people need, no matter what their status is. This is in line with the universal labour guarantee as suggested by the already mentioned ILO Commission on the Future of Work (and unfortunately no longer contained in the ILO centenary Declaration of June 2019). It focuses on protection of workers regardless of their contractual arrangement and of their employment status. The focus should be on the shape of the protective umbrella, not on the boxes where workers are put in. This, however, implies another problem: Who is responsible for providing the protection? The solution might be relatively easy in case of platform work. But it is certainly difficult for other self-employed workers.

11.2.4 Hours of Work

Digitalization will focus more on goals to be achieved in a certain time frame. Presence at the workplace is becoming less important. How and when within the given time frame work is to be performed is more or less left to the discretion of the worker. This 'autonomy' leads to the question whether traditional working time regulations still are appropriate to cope with this situation. Working time regulation so far was focusing mainly on daily and weekly maximum working time, on breaks and rest periods between the days and providing holidays and vacations. Step-by-step flexibility had been built in. Daily and weekly maximum working time could be exceeded to a certain extent if compensated by reduction of working time within a certain period. However, in spite of the flexibility element working time regulation still remains rather rigid.

In the digital world there is the danger that working time never ends. Workers may be supposed to remain online, to answer e-mails and phone calls also after normal working time as well as on holidays and vacations. And even if the workers are not asked by the employer to do so, they might do it voluntarily. This has far-reaching implications on health and safety of the workers as well as on their private life. Relaxation and rest, as it is supposed by traditional working time regulation, is no longer possible under these conditions. Self-exploitation is an ever-increasing danger. The eight-hour day, the big achievement of the labour movement in the early twentieth century is in danger to be abolished.

The question is, whether regulations are possible at all. The blocking of access to crowd-platforms for specific hours might not be very helpful; the crowd-workers might still continue working on their projects and put the results later on in the platform.

Nevertheless in Germany some companies have concluded with the works councils' agreements according to which the servers are disconnected after a certain time of the day and during the weekend and employees are not to be called. During vacations the account for the respective worker is to be blocked. Thereby, the employee enjoys a right to non-availability. The Government intends to establish a general right of non-availability. This plan, however, has not yet led to legislation. But there is a likelihood that it might be combined with the legislative amendment implied by the judgment of the CJEU[11] on documentation of working time. This amendment will be passed soon.

Such a right on non-availability shows the way into the right direction. It, however, only can be a first step. Not all employees are happy with such a regulation, some are afraid of the increased workload they are confronted with after the periods of disconnection.

Things are even more complicated when workers are involved in production or service processes with workers in other time zones. Then such disconnection might be counterproductive. In short and to make the point: the traditional working time regulation is no longer feasible. But an appropriate alternative is not yet in sight.

11.2.5 Data Protection

Digital devices allow collection and use as well as abuse of data to an extent never known before. This evidently is a big danger for employees' privacy.

In Germany in order to protect employees' privacy the judiciary has taken recourse to the values as expressed by the fundamental rights in the Constitution. Human dignity as the core value and the fundamental right to freely develop one's personality (Articles 1 and 2) were the main source for such a strategy.[12] In addition since the 1970s Germany had a law on data protection. This law has been amended in 2018 due to legislation of the European Union (EU). In May 2016 the EU passed the General Data Protection Regulation which became effective for the Member States in May 2018. This means it has to be applied without any Act of transformation.

However, there is an exception of the general European rule. According to Article 88 of the Regulation, 'Member States may, by law or by collective agreements, provide for more specific rules to ensure the protection of the rights and freedoms in respect of the processing of employees' personal data in the employment context'. The Article lists up examples for the purposes of such rules made by the Member States.

The German legislator has made use of this possibility by a law of 30 June 2017. It regulates that personal data of employees only may be processed if necessary for the creation, performance and termination of the employment relationship. This is in conformity with the case law developed by the German judiciary.

Further personal data may be processed if the employee agrees. This consent, however, has to be voluntary. Whether it is voluntary has to be evaluated in view of the dependency of the employee in an employment relationship and in view of all the circumstances in which the consent is given. There is a presumption of voluntary

11. CJEU Judgment of 14 May 2019, Case C-55/18, *Federación de Servicios de Comisiones Obreras (CCOO) v. Deutsche Bank*.
12. M. Weiss, The Interface Between Constitution and Labor Law in Germany, Comparative Labor Law & Policy Journal 2005, 181-198 (187-189).

consent if the interests of employer and employee are identical. The consent always has to be in written. This is a very complicated regulation, not easily to be handled. However, the aim is clear: only exceptionally the consent may be evaluated as being voluntary. In addition there is an obligation of the employer to inform the employee on all personal data to be processed on him or her.

In case the employer is violating the rules, the EU Regulation provides for fines up to EUR 20 million or 4% of the worldwide turn over. In this context it is important to know that the German law provides for a Data Commissioner to be established in all workplaces where at least ten employees permanently are occupied by processing digitally personal data of employees. Thereby, a control mechanism is established.

However, not only the workers' privacy is endangered. It also has to be made sure that business secrets are not endangered. This is further complicated by the fact that more and more often workers are supposed to use their own devices for professional purposes (smartphones, tablets, etc.). Thereby, not only business secrets are endangered, but also quite a few problems arise in the relationship between employers and workers. Can the employer dispose on the worker's private property? Can the employer prohibit that the worker's devices are also used by other people or that cloud services are used? And what about monitoring if business data and private data both are on such devices? Can the worker be obliged to report to the employer if his or her smart phone is lost or stolen? All these questions indicate that the policy of 'bring your own device' leads to a whole set of further unsolved problems.

11.2.6 Right to Home Office

Digitalization allows for many people to perform their work not in the premises of the employer but anywhere else. This allows employees to combine their work better with their private interests and to balance work and family life in case if work is performed at home. Therefore, it is not surprising that the coalition treaty of the present government in Germany promises 'to promote and facilitate mobile work by establishing a legal framework'. The Government presently prepares a bill on an employees' right to homework.

Empirical research shows that up to 30% of the employees in Germany might be interested in mobile work or home office. So far, however, only 12% are allowed to do it (most of the rotating between mobile work and work at the employer's premises). These are mainly highly skilled white-collar workers. But it should be mentioned that still about 60% of the jobs by their very nature do not qualify for home office.

There is already a right to home office for disabled people and in the Federal administration employers are supposed to offer home office for employees with obligations as care givers under certain conditions.

The idea of a general right to home office is, of course, to increase the employee's flexibility in planning his or her life. However, as empirical research shows, there is a whole set of risks: work and private life might no longer be separated (work-life-blending); self-exploitation is a real danger, leading to stress; individualization and isolation might become a problem; the team spirit of the workers' collective might get lost; the strength of trade unions and works councils might be affected, and finally it might be difficult to meet the requirements for protection of health and safety and of data protection. In short and to make the point: home office is ambiguous, and the intended freedom for the employee might turn out to be an illusion. Therefore, the issue is highly controversial, and it is uncertain whether the intended law will be enacted.

11.2.7 Collective Voice

In the first of the few examples presented here, the importance of works council's co-determination in Germany was stressed. The question, however, is whether such collective voice still can be organized in the era of digitalization. This might be particularly problematic in the platform economy.

In the course of segmentation and fragmentation of the workforce, divided in core groups and non-standard groups with significantly diverse interests collectivization has become more and more difficult. This trend has dramatically increased by the platform work. There is no more link between the acting individuals, they do not know each other and work in splendid isolation. The big question is whether and how this isolation can be overcome by patterns of collectivization, whether such collectivization can be embedded in existing structures of collective bargaining and workers participation or whether new specific structures are to be developed, as for example trade unions exclusively for platform workers.

From a merely legal point of view the problem might be that these workers – as explained – are by no means only employees in a traditional sense but to a significant part genuinely self-employed. According to the Court of Justice of the EU they cannot be included in collective agreements because of the competition rules contained in the Treaty of the Functioning of the EU.[13] This archaic and narrow-minded view of competition law which is based on a reality of the past, of course, would have to be overcome. Instead of discussing this any further I rather would like to focus on the practical problems. However, it at least should be kept in mind that according to ILO Convention 87 on freedom of association self-employed workers are fully covered.

The starting point has to be that collective voice only makes sense if it has a realistic chance to put significant pressure on the employers' side, more specifically on the digital platforms. Therefore, I think it would be preferable to use the strength of existing trade unions instead of relying on new associations exclusively composed of platform workers. An example of collective action by an existing trade union in this context is the protest by Deliveroo workers organized by the Independent Workers Union of Great Britain in London. This action by the way also shows the way on how to manage such collective action, namely by using social media.

Already for quite a while attempts by existing trade unions can be observed to overcome the workers anonymity and isolation in order to shape the basis for

13. CJEU Judgment of 4 December 2014, Case 413/13, *FNV Kunsten Informatie en Media v. Netherlands*.

collectivization. For example some years ago representatives of trade unions from Austria, Denmark, Germany and the United States of America as well as from the Service Employees International Union met in Frankfurt, Germany together with an international group of industrial relations experts to discuss possible strategies. This resulted in a joint declaration on platform-based work. Therein they explained 'the possibilities for a "co-operative turn" in labour-management relations in the "platform economy"'. And they identified platform providers as 'appropriate negotiating partners for platform-based workers seeking to improve their conditions of work'. In particular they insisted that 'all workers on the platform regardless of whether they are employees or independent contractors' are to be included in 'a platform's policies and information flows'.

The declaration contains a list of topics to be regulated (wages, social protection, etc.) and in particular a request for two strategies which might serve as a first step on this way to a 'cooperative turn': establishment of transparency and of a mechanism of dispute resolution.

To a great extent the whole operation of platforms remains in the dark. The declaration resumes that 'in short, the knowledge base required to make sound policy is missing'. Therefore, transparency is understood to be the indispensable precondition to develop a strategy for collective voice of platform workers.

As far as dispute resolution is concerned, the declaration proposes 'that platform operators work – with workers, clients, researchers, worker organizations, and other actors as appropriate – to develop transparent, accountable methods for resolving disputes between clients and workers, and, as needed, between workers'. In this context it may be of interest that in November 2017 the German Metalworkers' Union 'IG Metall' together with the German Crowdsourcing Association and eight important Crowd-working-Platforms has established an Ombuds-Office, composed of an equal number of platform representatives on the one side and representatives of 'IG Metall' and crowd-workers on the other side, chaired by a judge of the Frankfurt labour court. It mediates so far successfully conflicts between crowd-workers, platforms and clients and monitors the compliance with a code of conduct on which the participating platforms agreed as a form of voluntary self-regulation.

This code of conduct contains a whole set of principles to be respected by the platforms: (a) offering only lawful tasks, (b) information of the crowd-workers on the legal framework for their work, (c) fair wages, (d) user friendly and motivating working conditions, (e) respectful behaviour between platforms, clients and crowd-workers, (f) freedom of crowd-workers to accept or refuse offers without fear of negative consequences, (g) constructive feedback and open communication, (h) transparent procedure of acceptance of work results by the platform and (i) protection of personal data and privacy. All these principles are further described and explained in order to make them workable tools.

At the same time the 'IG-Metall' has established a platform where crowd-workers can communicate with each other and where the trade union can communicate with them. The idea is to, thereby, overcome the anonymity and isolation in order to create a collective consciousness a basis for collective organization and collective action. To further promote this goal the 'IG Metall' also conducts workshops with crowd-workers and platform representatives in regular intervals.

Such initiatives are an important first step in creating workers' voice in the platform economy.

It is not only important to create workers' voice as a countervailing power. It has to be kept in mind that the legislator may not be able to keep up with the technological changes. Legislation only can provide a relatively flexible framework. Solutions balancing the needs of the companies and the workers are also to be developed on a decentralized level. These solutions cannot be left unilaterally to the platforms but must be developed in cooperation with representative bodies of the workforce. In other words, the working conditions are to be shaped and monitored together with the workers' representatives. That is what basically is meant by 'cooperative turn'.

There are attempts to integrate platform workers in existing patterns of workers' participation as the works councils in Cologne, Germany and in Vienna, Austria for Foodora workers show, even if there still is the limitation that only workers are included who are employees in the traditional sense, a limitation which – as indicated – has to be overcome. And, of course, the existing systems of workers' participation have to be adapted to the specific needs of platform workers.

In short and to make the point: existing trade unions and workers representatives in the context of existing schemes of workers' participation are aware of the need to integrate platform workers in their activities and have started experiments on how to successfully meet this ambitious goal.

11.3 CONCLUSION

Digitalization is a very complex phenomenon, challenging labour law in many ways. This short contribution is meant to simply illustrate the need for adaptation to the new circumstances created by new technological developments. It also is meant to show that satisfying solutions are not yet in place but that efforts are made towards this goal. It finally is meant to demonstrate that, of course, the technological development has not yet come to its end but is continuing to provide further innovations in a speedy way which again will lead to new challenges for labour law. Therefore, the main and very ambitious task will be to help human beings to cope with all these changes by providing lifelong training opportunities as sketched above. And it will be necessary to regulate labour law in a way which makes sure that new technological developments cannot be used to exploit workers but instead allow workers to profit of them. Digitalization contains dangers as well as chances for the workforce. Labour law has to make sure that the chances can be realized.

CHAPTER 12

Artificial Intelligence: The Third Element of the Labour Relations

Michele Faioli

A new organisational model is being applied to work, overtaking the classic (and usually divisive) categories through which the phenomenon is analysed according to the Fordist theory (by way of example, organisation – subordination – powers – rights – obligations). Work entails important theoretical questions if it is linked to the most advanced technology (in Europe, in particular, Industry 4.0 and Gig Economy). If work has already been considered 'incomplete' (non-hyphenated word) because a feature of the employment contract under a market economy is its incompleteness, given that work-effort bargain and labour capacity cannot easily be specified ex ante, it should be expected to be all the more 'in-complete' in the future due to the peculiar legal relationship that will come to life among (i) the worker, (ii) the employer, and (iii) the machine endowed with artificial intelligence (intelligent machine). The hyphen between 'in' and 'complete' bears witness to such legal relationship. The intelligent machine can be considered as a third subject, as it is a 'third element' that takes part in the legal matters of the contractual pattern involving the employer and the worker. Therefore, beyond traditional scenarios in labour law, there are wider prospects. These prospects concern the impact of the intelligent machine on work organisation in the factory of the future. This is probably one of the reasons why labour regulation is changing and will change further. Law and collective bargaining provisions adapt to technology inasmuch as they are shaped by the latter; such provisions do not determine a separated system; labour regulation has instead built (and will build) the most important part of its logical and legal tools on technology. In the close future, the object of the employment contract will necessarily be complemented with the monitoring and regulatory action carried out by machines (third element) on those job tasks the worker will not be stripped of by the most advanced systems created by micro-electronics and computers and related to automation of industrial processes, logistics, transportation, data elaboration, accounting, quality and cost monitoring, medical interventions, biological and chemical processes, waste disposal, selection of materials, etc. My research sets out to provide some answers to the following questions: how is work in a company changing (or has it already changed) in view of the most recent and innovative technological developments, as well as of foreign investments betting on artificial intelligence? How will work labour-regulations change in Europe in the close future, taking into account that automated and smart technology develops at a fast pace in all productive sectors? To what extent and how should European Union (EU) labour regulations deal with the fact that intelligent machines (i.e., the third element of the employment contract), endowed with deep learning, will decide and monitor, patrol, indicate, define, workers' job tasks? Can we empower such intelligent machine with a sort of 'labour legal status'?

12.1 OUTLINING THE ISSUE: THE HIDDEN REVOLUTION – JOB TASKS, STAFF CLASSIFICATION, LAW AND COLLECTIVE BARGAINING IN ITALY

Litigation and bargaining (at individual or collective level) relating to Article 2103 in the Italian Civil Code have shown that rights stemming from staff classification systems and practices are among the most debated labour law issues. In other respects, those rights are also among the most relevant aspects of the recently adopted political strategy. In a comparative perspective, we can notice that, in other legal systems, neither literature nor legislative provisions – let alone case law – feature so abstract regulatory schemes as those referred to in Article 2103 of the Italian Civil Code and concerning the determination of job tasks. Taking a comparative look at such regulatory schemes, 'determination of job tasks' means definition of the contractual regulation in view of the accommodation of the contracting parties' competing interests. Whereas the interpretation, by Italian scholars and courts, of Article 2103 is based on the 'absence' of something (a gap to be filled with the judicial interpretation of the equivalence concept), the point of view adopted in the literature and case law of other comparable legal systems is based on the 'presence' of something (i.e., a procedure – set out by law or in a collective agreement – that allows for the accommodation of usually competing interests of the contracting parties). In this latter case, we can speak of completeness, whereas in the former case we should speak of incompleteness.

All of this provides food for thought in relation to the title of this chapter, which somehow represents an oxymoron: if work, intended as conduct, has already been considered 'incomplete' because 'an inherent feature of the employment contract under a market economy is its incompleteness [...] work-effort bargain and labour capacity cannot be accurately specified *ex ante*, the employer can expropriate the surplus from production *ex post*',[1] it should be expected to be all the more 'in-complete'

1. The choice of the title stems from the facts that will be described in this chapter concerning the relationship between intelligent machines and human work. The choice was confirmed when I read a recent essay by Deakin S., Zheng E., *Pricing Labour Capacity: The Unexpected Effects of Formalizing Employment Contracts in China*, in *Centre for Business Research*, University of

in the future due to the peculiar legal relationship that will come to life between the worker, the employer, and the machine endowed with artificial intelligence (intelligent machine).[2]

The hyphen between 'in' and 'complete' bears witness to such legal relationship. The *intelligent machine* can be considered as a *third subject*, as it is a '*third element*' that takes part in the legal matters of the contractual pattern involving the employer and the worker.

Therefore, beyond traditional scenarios, there are wider prospects that can be taken into account when focusing on job tasks.

These prospects concern the impact of the intelligent machine on work organisation in the factory of the future. This is probably one of the reasons why labour regulation is changing and will change further. Law and collective bargaining provisions adapt to technology inasmuch as they are shaped by the latter; such provisions do not determine a separated system; labour regulation has instead built (and will build) the most important part of its logical and legal tools on technology.[3] 'Technology' and 'intelligent machine' are used as synonyms in this chapter.

In the interpretation and application of Article 2103 of the Italian Civil Code, litigation and bargaining have triggered a *hidden revolution in labour law*. In the Italian legal system, the evolution of Article 2103 has separated the employment relationship

---

Cambridge Working Papers, 2016, No. 479. To define incomplete work, DEAKIN and ZHENG draw on COASE R.H., *The nature of the firm: Influence*, in Journal of Law, Economics & Organization, 1988, No. 4(1), pp. 33 ff. ('The incompleteness of the employment contract is a fundamental construct and practice of labour market institutions in advanced market economies, and is now becoming prevalent in emerging markets as wage labour becomes more common'). According to DEAKIN and ZHENG, the incompleteness of work stems from the fact that: (i) bargaining cannot *ex ante* specify work effort and labour capacity, here meaning job tasks and professional skills, and (ii) *ex post* the employer can take hold of the quantity of work performed by the worker, that exceeds the amount of work necessary to produce the livelihoods for the worker themselves. Cf. also DEAKIN S., *The Comparative Evolution of the Employment Relationship*, in DAVIDOV G., LANGILLE B. (eds), *Boundaries and Frontiers of Labour Law: Goals and Means in the Regulation of Work*, Hart Publishing, Oxford, 2006. *See also* my recent book FAIOLI M., *Mansioni e macchina intelligente*, Giappichelli, Torino, 2018.

2. The intelligent machine goes beyond the imitation of the human being. Cf. the reasoning by COWEN T., *Average Is Over*, Dutton, 2014 ('it does something other than imitate or try to imitate a man' – p. 144). Cf. also the remarks by the EXECUTIVE OFFICE OF THE PRESIDENT OF THE USA, *Artificial Intelligence, Automation, and the Economy*, December 2016, p. 8, in https://www.whitehouse.gov/blog/2016/10/12/administrations-report-future-artificial-intelligence, which underlines that 'Accelerating AI capabilities will enable automation of some tasks that have long required human labor. Rather than relying on closely-tailored rules explicitly crafted by programmers, modern AI programs can learn from patterns in whatever data they encounter and develop their own rules for how to interpret new information. This means that AI can solve problems and learn with very little human input. In addition, advances in robotics are expanding machines' abilities to interact with and shape the physical world. Combined, AI and robotics will give rise to smarter machines that can perform more sophisticated functions than ever before and erode some of the advantages that humans have exercised. This will permit automation of many tasks now performed by human workers and could change the shape of the labor market and human activity'.
3. In this regard, cf. the remarks by VARDARO G., Tecnica, tecnologia e ideologia della tecnica nel diritto del lavoro, in Politica del diritto, 1986, No. 1, pp. 75 ff. and by GIUGNI G., Il processo tecnologico e la contrattazione collettiva, in MOMIGLIANO F. (a cura di), Lavoratori e sindacati di fronte alle trasformazioni del processo produttivo, Feltrinelli, Milano, 1962, pp. 293 ff.

from the specific pattern of trade relationships; it can be said that the introduction of the single pay scale structure, as a prototype of staff classification, has led to the consolidation of the idea according to which job tasks and their evaluation must be related also to the worker's potential skills.

Work organisation has come to grips with, and has adapted on a case-by-case basis to, these theoretically unchangeable skills, also taking into account the continuous changes demanded by the market. All of this replaced the classic conception of trade relationships, which would instead have determined a remuneration level based on the utility actually provided by the worker to the employer.

Although my research starts from the legal framework recently reformed by Legislative Decree No. 81 dated 15 June 2015 (the so-called Jobs Act), it sets out to elaborate, on the one side, the outcomes of the above-mentioned hidden revolution (through the screening of business practices) and, on the other, to provide some answers to the following questions: how is work in a company changing (or has it already changed) in view of the most recent and innovative technological developments, as well as of foreign investments betting on artificial intelligence? How will work change in the close future, taking into account that automated and smart technology develops at a fast pace in all productive sectors? In legal terms, what about the role played by Article 2103 of the Italian Civil Code within business practices and (recent or older) organisational patterns? Are classification systems set forth by national collective bargaining agreements (NCBAs) adequate to provide a response to such transformation of work? Why, following the 1970 labour law reform, was the management of conflict on job tasks shifted from individual/collective bargaining (the natural scope of application of Article 2103) to court?

Having these questions in mind, I have drawn on the analysis of *legal fundamentals* and of the *social meaning of job tasks*, as well as on related concepts (grade, category, professionalism, unilateral change of the working activity to be performed, equivalence, the effects – in terms of pay – of unilateral changes, and the consensual modification of the working activity to be performed).

At this point it may turn out somehow useful for an initial comparison to sum up the schematisation of *the two legal regimes* (Article 2103 of the Italian Civil Code as amended by the Workers' Statute – hereinafter also 'pre-2015-reform regime' – and Article 2103 as amended by Article 2 of Legislative Decree No. 81/2015 – hereinafter also 'post-2015-reform regime'):

Subjective Position	*Pre-2015 Reform Regime (Following the 1970 Workers' Statute)*	*Post-2015 Reform Regime – Jobs Act*
Employer's unilateral power	The worker is assigned: (i) the job tasks that were assigned to them upon hiring; (ii) job tasks corresponding to the next category; and (iii) job tasks that are equivalent to the latest ones carried out by them, being entitled to the same pay level.	The worker is assigned: (i) the job tasks that were assigned to them upon hiring; (ii) job tasks relating to the next pay grade; and (iii) job tasks falling under the same grade and legal category of the latest ones carried out by them.
Employer's unilateral power (modification *in peius*)	Case law indications or specific cases envisaged by law (rules on collective dismissal and mobility)	The worker is assigned job tasks belonging to the previous pay grade - limitations as to: (i) same legal category/entitlement to the same pay grade; (ii) modifications to organisational patterns; (iii) other cases defined by collective bargaining; (iv) written form; and (v) entitlement to the same pay level.
Employer's unilateral power (modification *in melius*)	The worker is assigned higher-level job tasks, with entitlement to the corresponding pay level and to future promotion - three months.	The worker is assigned higher-level job tasks, with entitlement to the corresponding pay level and to future promotion - six months.
Amending agreement	Invalid	Valid under a specific form and in the framework of a determined procedure, Article 2113 I.C.C. and Article 76 of Legislative Decree No. 276 dated 10 September 2003, with modifications to job tasks, legal category, pay grade, and pay level - the worker's legal interests to be protected (employment, professionalism, and life)

Discussions on these issues have triggered an unprecedentedly passionate debate at personal, political and union, academic, and case law levels. Making reference by way of analogy, we can recall Article 18 of Law No. 300 dated 20 May 1970 (hereinafter, 'the Workers' Statute'), in view of the quantity and quality of available studies. It is therefore not surprising that so many scholars focusing on the individual and collective dimensions of law and on the organisational pattern within companies have dealt with this topic.

Drawing on such studies, my research work sets out to consider labour law in dynamic connection with work organisation within the firm, reinterpret the relationship between job tasks/professionalism and *the new technological or artificial intelligence systems* (organised/integrated economic activities).

This issue is particularly interesting, also due to its *methodological aspects*. An unprecedented transformation in terms of *technology and work organisation* is currently going on.

We are going *beyond the industrial revolution and Fordism*. A *new business model* is being applied to work, overtaking the classic (and usually divisive) categories through which the phenomenon is analysed according to the Fordist theory (by way of example, organisation - subordination - powers - rights - obligations). Work entails important theoretical questions if it is linked to the most advanced technology.[4] It is impossible to contrast the change in, or the adaptation of, corporate organisation, which is strongly affected by competition, international trade, spreading of smart models for HR management, smart technology and hi-tech systems, drone technology, and advanced research hubs. To sum up, that company is a '*smart factory*'.[5]

4. This argument has already been made by Vardaro G., *Tecnica, tecnologia ..., supra*, pp. 77 ff.; cf. the more recent study by Nogler L., *Tecnica e subordinazione nel tempo di vita*, in *Giornale di diritto del lavoro e di relazioni industriali*, 2015, No. 147, pp. 337 ff.
5. 'Smart factory', also 'factory of the future' in this text, refers to organised digital technology governing production and distribution systems as well as work. Sticking to the definition provided in the research by *MIT Technology Review*, *The Future of Work* (Business Report, 2015), the smart factory corresponds to what is connected to cyber-physical system (CPS) technology, information communication technologies (ICT), digital technology, and the integration of such elements into the physical systems that are in use and with which production is carried out, including work. Everything that is connected to Industry 4.0 can be considered as 'smart factory'. In this sense, Porsche represents the factory of the future inasmuch as it adopted a production model based on the 'fishbone diagram principle': according to it, the client can submit an order online, customising their car, and then go to the car dealer to finalise the purchase. The order, once registered, is managed by a central information system that allows for the synchronisation of all the actors (fish bones) involved in the delivery chain of the components in the line. For instance, in Corbetta (close to Milan) Magneti Marelli periodically receives production programmes through the Electronic Data Interchange (EDI); only five days prior to the assembly in Stuttgart, it receives, through the Value Added Network (VAN, a dedicated network), the green light to produce the sequence of items of the electronic instrument cluster that will be installed in Germany. Designs and bills of materials are available online on a platform of the group, to which all suppliers have free access. Therefore, Porsche is already leveraging on several digitalisation elements of production processes in a large and collaborative network: this process is currently evolving at a fast pace. The car manufacturer is going along this path starting from the benefits enjoyed by the so-called stakeholders (clients, suppliers of components, suppliers of machinery, collaborators, and internal management) and, based on them, it defines use cases. New technology allows for a continuous evolution of the productive model just described, with a view not only to efficiency but also to growth. For instance, client profiling makes it possible to understand which accessories are more interesting for the client. In this perspective, we can refer to the essay by Magnani M., *Organizzazione del lavoro e professionalità tra rapporti e mercato del lavoro*, in *Giornale di diritto del lavoro e di relazioni industriali*, 2004, No. 101, pp. 165 ff. More

The rupture in the Fordist paradigm, which – according to some scholars – has not been fully perceived yet,[6] is going to impact, with all its strength, also on those sectors that are more reluctant to experience changes. It should be noted that there is strong opposition by collective bargaining.

Unlike in the legal systems of other EU countries, in the *Italian legal system* regulation has focused on forms of flexibility to be applied when entering (types of contract) or leaving (remedies in case of dismissal) the labour market; however, regulation *has not dealt with forms of flexibility within the employment contract*, which include the worker's in-company *mobility*. The latter underlies the possibility to change (unilaterally or consensually) job tasks in relation to a specific classification system/pay scale structure.

The Italian case law has offered different interpretations of in-company mobility.

On the one side, we can observe the cases in which the court recognised the validity of the collective bargaining clause that, creating job positions that carry out tasks typical of a postal worker and of a counter operator, combines different interests (Judgment of the Court of Cassation No. 25033 dated 24 November 2006).[7] On the other hand, we can observe case law according to which the prohibition on modifying *in peius*, as per Article 2103 I.C.C., *entailed, before the 2015 reform*, that the worker cannot be assigned, even according to a formal equivalence criterion, job tasks being substantially inferior to those previously carried out. The court having jurisdiction on the substance shall actually ascertain whether the new job tasks comply with the employee's specific professional skills, ensuring the protection of the professional level they have acquired, as well as the implementation and improvement of their professional skills (Judgment of the Court of Cassation No. 4989 dated 4 March 2014).

12.2 THE NECESSARY UPDATES IN THE LABOUR LEGAL SYSTEMS: INDIVIDUAL AND COLLECTIVE PROCEDURES FOR IMPROVING WORKPLACE REGULATIONS

We can thus become aware of the existence of a problem underlying all the other issues, which has been outlined in case law: *can collective bargaining encounter limitations in this specific area of protection?* What kind of professionalism are we

recently, also NOGLER L., *Crescita economica e riforma della disciplina dei rapporti di lavoro*, in *Massimario di Giurisprudenza del Lavoro*, 2012, pp. 450 ff. has pointed to the decrease in the flexibility of job tasks and to the confusion engendered in the relationship between *jus variandi*, mobbing, and needs in terms of efficiency.

6. PERO L., *Come cambia il lavoro di fabbrica. Tecnologie, globalizzazione e intelligenza collettiva*, in *La società degli individui*, 2013, No. 46, pp. 30 ff. More recently, as to artificial intelligence and work organisation, cf. the report by the EXECUTIVE OFFICE OF THE PRESIDENT OF THE USA, *supra*, 2016.
7. According to this case law, it is possible to introduce fungibility-related collective bargaining clauses 'that, if specific de facto conditions are met, allow for horizontal mobility between the job tasks carried out and those ones for which the worker has initially been deemed suitable based on a potential professionalism criterion that takes into account what the worker can do, although they are not currently doing it'. This is to make it possible to 'enhance the potential professionalism of all the workers in that specific grade'. In this regard, cf. OCCHINO A., *La clausola collettiva di fungibilità tra mansioni contrattualmente, ma non legalmente, equivalenti è valida per esigenze aziendali temporanee*, in *Rivista Italiana di Diritto del Lavoro*, 2007, No. 2, pp. 336 ff.

seeking protection for before the court in the case of the worker with a specific job task, compared with the one who is tasked with mail delivery, if professional mobility has been confirmed in the collective bargaining contract, including in the firm-level one?

The questions referred to in the previous paragraph show that *Article 2103 of the Italian Civil Code*, before the 2015 reform, *was definitely inadequate with regard to the rupture in the Fordist paradigm*. In many respects, *the same provision was inadequate also with regard to Fordism*.[8] Unlike other legal systems, in the Italian one it has not been possible to introduce a firm-level procedure, to be authorised by law, that allows the employer, in cooperation with employee representatives, to take measures (also with divesture if justified by objective reasons) that have a substantial impact on individual positions. The choice made by some legal systems (in particular, France and Germany) is underpinned by the idea that the worker's mobility does not fall under civil law, nor is it an issue to be fully regulated through NCBAs. It should rather be dealt with *at firm level, in compliance with a specific procedure involving agents authorised to exercise rights and powers in the interest of the working community*. In more proactive terms, the NCBA, which is tasked by the legislator with setting out and periodically updating classification systems, is supposed to establish the procedure (taking into account the sector, firm size, and other specificities) as well as to monitor compliance within the firm through the use of paritarian institutes. In a corporate context, instead, economic, individual, and collective interests appear to be intertwined, balanced, and reconciled in the procedure involving the employer and workers' representatives.

Following the 2015 reform, the Italian regime has been modified, bearing in mind the scenarios that had long been 'envisioned' (cf. the report prepared by the National Economic and Labour Council – *Consiglio Nazionale dell'Economia e del Lavoro*, CNEL[9] – in 1985 and the Agreement on Productivity signed in November 2012).

It was clear why the court has been asked by the parties to an individual employment contract to interpret the concept of equivalence of job tasks and why trade

8. Liso F., La mobilità del lavoratore in azienda: il quadro legale, Franco Angeli, Milano, 1982, p. 71.
9. Liso F., Brevi osservazioni sulla revisione della disciplina delle mansioni contenuta nel decreto legislativo n. 81/2015 e su alcune recenti tendenze di politica legislativa in materia di rapporto di lavoro, in WP C.S.D.L.E. 'Massimo D'Antona'.IT, 2015, No. 257; as to the 'expected' reforms of Art. 2103 I.C.C., cf. also the CNEL report Osservazioni e proposte sulla revisione della legislazione sul rapporto di lavoro, Assembly No. 206 held on 4 June 1985 (Speakers G. Giugni – L. Mengoni, President P. Boni), which outlines that 'Article 13 of Law No. 300/1970 ..., in its practical application, has turned out to excessively bind workers to the job tasks assigned upon hiring. Two major problems arise: the definition of the criterion of equivalence of job tasks, taken as a limitation on jus variandi, and the prohibition on demotion, which in the wording of para. 2 is formulated in absolute terms. Case law contribution to the solution of the first problem has been inadequate due to the court's structural difficulty in exercising control powers in this area. The best solution would be to modify the provision that tasks collective bargaining with defining in concrete terms the equivalence relationship, e.g. by referring to pre-set indices and/or case-by-case assessment procedures. As to the right to arrange differing agreements, ... para. 2 should be amended without prejudice to the collective bargaining agreements that envisage the possibility of temporarily assigning a worker lower-level job tasks (e.g. in the framework of professional development processes through turnover at the workplace) and, in relation to individual agreements, by replacing invalidity with voidableness as per Article 2113 I.C.C., with the related exceptions listed in the last paragraph ... '.

unions and employers' organisations have partly refrained from regulating the phenomenon, failing to adapt classification systems to the new organisational and technological structures. Under the previous regime (1970-2015), the court was asked to interpret the concept of equivalence of job tasks and create significant consequences on corporate organisation. This is why the worker's professionalism has been identified as a limitation on the exercise, by the employer, of managerial powers and of the right to modify the work conditions without employees' consent (*jus variandi*).

In the aftermath of the 2015 reform, given the new functions that the law assigns the collective bargaining, the professionalism of the worker will not be less protected. Further, in the aftermath of the 2015 reform, the professionalism of the worker will be likely to receive more protection by means of the collective bargaining in relation to the internal (corporate) market or the external (inter-company) market. The new functions and scope of collective bargaining in the framework of the 2015 amended Article 2103 I.C.C. are related to each and every corporate context.

The focus is on the collective bargaining and firm-level unilateral regulation that have set rules on job tasks, and in particular, the clauses defining modalities of internal flexibility concerning the pay scale structure, job tasks, versatility, and wage are outlined (small and medium enterprises (SMEs) and European, Asian, and United States multinationals, emphasising the impact of corporations, private equity funds, and foreign direct investments on work organisation and job tasks).

My recent analysis demonstrates that there exists a *certain ability of collective bargaining* (or of firm-level internal regulations) to *anticipate needs* and to *tackle problems*, even beyond applicable legislation.[10]

12.3 INTELLIGENT MACHINES AS THE 'THIRD ELEMENT' OF THE LABOUR RELATIONS

But *this is not enough*. In the close future, the object of the employment contract will necessarily be complemented with the monitoring and regulatory action carried out by *intelligent machines, or here also 'robots'*, on those job tasks the worker will not be stripped of by the most advanced systems created by micro-electronics and computers and related to automation of industrial processes, logistics, transportation, data elaboration, accounting, quality and cost monitoring, medical interventions, biological and chemical processes, waste disposal, selection of materials, etc.

We will access that '*deep learning software*' technological phase through which the machine is enabled to make sense of the language, create connections, and interact as human beings usually do. In this sense, today workers can still 'avoid' that some activities are carried out by machines because the former decide what the latter can or cannot do; in the close future, instead, intelligent machines, which are endowed with deep learning, will decide whether and to what extent they will 'strip' workers of their job tasks.

10. *See also* FAIOLI M., *supra*, 2018.

The technological development process appears to be irreversible. Ever-more advanced research and the fact that costs are becoming day by day more affordable, also by SMEs, show that the process has already been marked out.[11]

It is a process that goes beyond Post-Fordism. It is *the machine that teaches itself what to do, how to do it, and which outcome(s) should be achieved, coordinating human beings, too.*[12] The evolution of the object of the employment contract will be determined by the relationship between, on the one hand, the job tasks still performed by human beings and, on the other, those ones human beings have been stripped of by automated and computerised machines that monitor/manage processes in their entirety.

All of this will lead to *the reorganisation of classification systems or pay scale structures*, as well as of hierarchies (more or less pyramidal in nature) and the procedures for the assignment of tasks and roles. Workers will be required to carry out more flexible tasks featuring the already known phenomena of job enrichment (determinable job tasks) and job enlargement (modified job tasks). The replacement of workers in those tasks will also be determined by organisational models applied at firm level for the production or provision of the service, including in subcontracting chains (drive system of management - DSM, scientific management - SM, lean production - LP, quality-focused involvement - QFI, teamwork production systems - TPS, modular production - MP, and acceluction).[13] Such *organisational models will impact on the object of the employment contract*; as a consequence, they will be translated into specific contents of job tasks, in addition to affecting working time management, pay, staff training, etc.

The incidence on the employment contract means: (i) integration of work organisation with the firm-level technological model; (ii) integration between technological procedures and HR management; and (iii) integration between workers' training and job tasks. If we focus on these three items, we can see that the company premises are defined by technological, automated, and computerised innovations. This vision translates into the fact that *a shift is taking place from the (geographically identifiable) production unit to the global supply chain*, in which several, virtually

11. To substantiate this concept, suffice it to observe on a regular basis the websites of the largest academic research hubs and the programmes currently under development. For example, cf. http://tech.cornell.edu/research; for a useful summary of this issue, cf. Simonite T., *Teaching Machines to Understand Us*, in *MIT Technology Review*, August 2015. Cf. also Shah M., *How Do Artificial Neural Networks Learn?*, in *Futurism*, in https://futurism.com/how-do-artificial-neural-networks-learn/.
12. The terms 'machine', 'automation', 'technology', etc., which will be used in the following pages, can be referred to Post-Fordism. In this regard, as to sociological and economic profiles, cf. the classics by Aglietta M., *A Theory of Capitalist Regulation*, Verso Book, London, 1979; Amin A., *Post-Fordism: Models, Fantasies and Phantoms of Transition*, in Amin A. (ed.), *Post-Fordism: A Reader*, Wiley-Blackwell, Oxford, 1994; Jessop B., *The Transition to Post-Fordism and the Schumpeterian Workfare State*, in Burrows R., Loader B. (eds), *London Towards a Post-Fordist Welfare State?*, Routledge, London, 1994; and Jessop B., *The Future of the Capitalist State*, Wiley-Blackwell, Cambridge, 2002. For a broader debate on the relationship between human beings and things, between anthropotechnics and nature, cf. also Esposito R., *Le persone e le cose*, Einaudi, Torino, 2014.
13. *See also* Faioli M., *supra*, 2018.

unlimited, production units – which are based on one of the organisational models referred to above – are connected. In this way, the wall-to-wall dimension of the company unit at global level is enlarged, and a new relationship with clients, suppliers, markets, etc. is established.

12.4 CONCLUSIONS: THE 'LABOUR-ROBOT LAW' CHALLENGES AND SCENARIOS

Within such a complex framework, a worker (or group of workers) with specific job tasks and covered by a specific employment contract, including a specific classification system stemming from national collective bargaining, is concerned by a wealth of automated and computerised technology innovations, which impact on them as an individual and require specific knowledge (through the replacement of workers by machines, as said above) and probably coordination with other workers (in the same workplace or somewhere else).

This does not hold true only for the most advanced types of professionalism. Instead, the opposite is true, based on the close observation of some significant companies in sectors deemed to be strategic for the Italian economy. *Such technological evolution also determines the transformation of job tasks and classification systems.* This demonstrates that *the classification systems envisaged in NCBAs are outdated.* Almost all the NCBAs have regulated (and continue to regulate in their renewed versions) staff classification systems, taking into account mere operational activities that are simple, repetitive, and classifiable.

Consequently, job tasks, too, were/are intended as tasks – inseparable basic units – that are assigned to the worker in the framework of a specific business organisation. It follows that the job task is still considered as a combination of phases, operations, and elementary movements.[14] Those classification systems are not based on models aimed at the coordination, management, and monitoring of results from the combination involving the worker, the working team, and automated technology, the latter being responsible for stripping workers of their assignments, functions, and activities, shortly of their job tasks.

It follows from the above that there exists a new setting of job tasks in an industrial world that changes owing to bio-inspired automation, artificial intelligence, and the most technologically advanced organisational models (the so-called CO-BOT). Such legal setting is shaped by this technology.[15]

---

14. If we read once more the classics in relation to this issue, we get the impression that, as early as during the Italian economic boom, there were some doubts on this vision. We can feel the change already in Giugni G., *Mansioni e qualifica nel rapporto di lavoro*, Jovene, Napoli, 1963.
15. To define some technological innovations that will impact on the organisational model of the factory of the future, cf. House of Deputies (*Camera dei Deputati*), Commissione X, *Indagine conoscitiva su 'Industria 4.0'*, 30 June 2016.

Inasmuch as the provision in force prior to the 2015 reform was inadequate with regard to the evolving reality,[16] the theory of job tasks does no longer properly tackle the issues raised by technology.[17]

A *(new) theory of job tasks* must, instead, shift to the idea that – through a specific procedure – rights, too, can be balanced against situations that may affect the exercise of the right to work.

The (new) theory should deal with the entitlement itself: *could workers' representatives in the company be deemed to be entitled to enjoy those rights?* If so, could the exercise of that entitlement be proceduralised? The (new) theory should acknowledge the existing limitations on the exercise of the power of divesture in the framework of collective bargaining.

From this perspective, *the goal of my research* is to propose a methodology aimed at outlining a *theory of job tasks in a changing industrial world under pressure from the intelligent machine,* which teaches itself, 'coordinates' the working activities of human beings, and strips workers of their job tasks.[18]

Over time, the picture will become more complex as company-related events will be measured, thus generating huge quantities of archived data (big data); such data will furthermore be analysed by systems aimed at supporting decision making and based on artificial intelligence technology (cognitive systems). It should be added that there will be the possibility to communicate such data with real-time remote control from one end of the world to the other; as a result, employers' powers, business networks, and even the notion of 'employer' will be reshaped.[19]

This is a *new theory of job tasks,* here also defined *'Labour Robot Law',* in the factory managed by *artificial intelligence* (third element of the employment contract): the relationship between the intelligent machine, representing *a sort of third element of the contract,* and the employer's powers should be more precisely investigated.

Such *third element is key* to understand the *legal issues relating to the compatibility between job tasks, staff classification, and the most innovative organisational models* (acceluction, lean production, team working, etc.), which are included into the organisational processes that are directly coordinated by machines endowed with artificial intelligence.

16. Cf. the commentary by Pisani C., *La modificazione delle mansioni,* Franco Angeli, Milano, 1996, p. 98.
17. In this perspective, cf. the observations on the first twenty years of enforcement of Art. 2103 I.C.C. with regard to staff classification in De Luca Tamajo R. – Bianchi D'Urso F., *La mobilità professionale dei lavoratori,* in *Lavoro e Diritto,* 1990, pp. 233 ff.
18. Cf. Faioli M., *supra,* 2018; cf. also Manyika J. et al., *Harnessing Automation for a Future That Works,* in *MGI Report,* 2017, in http://www.mckinsey.com/global-themes/digital-disruption/harnessing-automation-for-a-future-that-works.
19. Cf. the synthesis report by the House of Deputies, Commissione X, *Indagine conoscitiva su 'Industria 4.0',* 30 June 2016, in www.camera.it, and the 2019 investigations on artificial intelligence of the Italian Government in https://www.mise.gov.it/index.php/it/intelligenza-artificiale-call.

We have at least *two forthcoming scenarios*. The first is related to the short-middle term. The second may occur somewhere in the longer term. Both scenarios are based on the idea that legislation is just one of the regulatory instruments: we should have and promote a *balanced mix of law, collective bargaining norms, market and technology* in order to determine better outputs than just black letter law can offer.

First, regulating artificial intelligence or robots at workplace level does not mean regulating artificial intelligence/robots themselves or having them as the target of regulatory intervention (at least until a legal capacity of artificial intelligence/robots is defined by law).

Regulating artificial intelligence or robots at workplace level implies that *collective bargaining, within a frame that should be fixed by law, pursues the aim to allow a fair interaction between workers and robots*.

Hence, *labour robotics regulation* is a more accurate term to indicate an *academic field* we are proposing in this investigation: *such regulation is aimed at influencing the behaviour of workers in the context of robotics application and developments at firm level*.

The *second scenario* is more complex to explain, but very useful for the conclusions. In the case, somewhere, in the longer term, artificial intelligent would be considered as legal subject acting at firm/plants level, labour regulation should build part of logical and legal tools on advanced technology, robots, smart factory, etc. The dilemma is that regulators can neither intervene too early, nor too late.[20] EU/States labour regulations should deal with the fact that intelligent machines will improve its own ability to decide, and monitor, patrol, indicate, organise, and define workers' job tasks.

If we empower such intelligent machine with a sort of 'labour legal status', we should also empower collective bargaining for facing intelligent machines because we need a *context-specificity* regulatory approach. Robots, which differ in many features, must be addressed at concrete levels in their own contexts. Collective bargaining, at firm level, is therefore the best way to regulate such phenomenon. Regulation must be dynamic, cyclic, interactive, and a means to involve unions and employers.

Empowering such collective bargaining will determine that not the technology, but rather *the adverse effects at firm level* of artificial intelligence should be regulated by unions and employer, within a general legal frame and by means of procedures. The law could be inadequate to cope with robots' adverse effects at firm level, while collective bargaining could more precisely regulate such adverse effects, and, consequently, *vary in time and place* and be more or less flexible, in relation to the firm and the production, the research in technology and the application at firm level.

20. Collingridge D., *The Social Control of Technology*, St Martin's Press, 1980.

This proposal is based on the fact that 'while legal regimes can be adapted to accommodate such substantive challenges, regulators must also be aware of fundamental but rather invisible challenges at a deeper level of the law. Robotics also challenge assumptions underlying regulatory frameworks as a whole, such as the distinction between things and humans ... This requires careful reflection on *what regulation aims to achieve*, when society slowly but inexorably changes shape through fundamental socio-technical changes'.[21]

21. Leenes R., et al., *Regulatory challenges of robotics: Some guidelines for addressing legal and ethical issues*, Law, Innovation and Technology, 2017, No. 9(1), pp. 1 ff.

CHAPTER 13

Regulating the Employment Relationship in the Organization 4.0: Between Social Justice and Economic Efficiency

Iacopo Senatori

13.1 INTRODUCTION

The rising role of digital technologies in production processes naturally poses the crucial question of who will benefit most from the implementation of new organizational models in the workplaces: the company, in terms of increased efficiency, or the workers, who may face a growth of the quality of their jobs?[1] However, from a labor law perspective a second question, even more demanding and ambitious, can be envisaged: what can the law, and regulation more broadly, do to ensure that both the terms of the alternative can be pursued without frustrating each other?

This question is inherent in the very nature of labor law. Labor law has always combined the purpose of protecting and empowering workers,[2] as the vulnerable parties of the employment relationship, with the function of legitimizing the employer's authority. While vesting the workers with rights aimed at safeguarding their basic

1. E. Ales, Protecting Work in the Digital Transformation: Rethinking the Typological Approach in the Intrinsically Triangular Relationship Perspective, in E. Ales, et al. (eds.), *Working in Digital and Smart Organizations. Legal, Economic and Organizational Perspectives on the Digitalization of Labour Relations*, Palgrave Macmillan, Cham, 2018, 11; V. De Stefano, "Negotiating the Algorithm": Automation, Artificial Intelligence and Labour Protection (May 16, 2018), in *Comparative Labor Law & Policy Journal*, 2020, 41, 1, available at SSRN: https://ssrn.com/abstract=3178233 or http://dx.doi.org/10.2139/ssrn.3178233, who correctly emphasizes the crucial issue of employment quality.
2. The literature on the topic is too broad to provide an exhaustive set of citations. With a view to bringing together samples of the most significant recent and classical contributions, *see* G. Davidov, *A Purposive Approach to Labour Law*, OUP, Oxford, 2016, and O. Kahn Freund, *Labour and the Law*, Stevens & Sons, London, 1972.

personal interests and goods within the employment relationship, labor law grants the conditions for the exercise of the employer's prerogatives on the work performance in the framework of a lawful pursuit of an economic activity, with a view to maintaining the prerequisites of a fair competition.[3] Compromise between social justice and economic efficiency is therefore a recurring theme in labor law, although the practical balance of the two factors is historically uneven and subject to periodical changes, as a result of the alternate pressure of manifold forces. The advent of digital technologies is surely one of the turning points capable of altering the established equilibrium.

The potential (and the problems) brought about by the phenomenon commonly referred to as the "digital transformation" of employment relations have already been investigated by an extensive body of legal literature. Nevertheless, two issues still await to be fully brought into the debate. On the one hand, the abovementioned literature so far has been more focused on the implications of the new technologies for the new forms of work (like on-demand work) and the material scope of labor law than on the changes that may affect the core area of subordinate employment. On the other hand, digitization is certainly one of the topics whose full understanding demands opening a dialogue with other disciplinary domains (like, in the case at stake, organization theory, sociology, labor economics). Nonetheless, as it is often the case when dealing with such kind of topics, legal research is prone to the risk of neglecting or underestimating the complexities that lay behind the explanations and the theoretical constructions elaborated by those complementary domains, and tends to adhere almost mechanically to mainstream representations.[4]

The relationship between the implementation of new technologies at the workplace and the legal characterization of subordinate employment, as well as the question whether and to what extent the former can influence the latter, are indeed some of the issues that require a sound and substantive understanding of the underlying phenomena, before one ventures into the elaboration of new interpretative and regulatory solutions. Subordination, in legal terms, is a formal and conventional representation of a given reality. Conversely, the "forms of subordination" that go hand in hand with changes in work organization are part of the manifold factual outcomes of a new reality. A reality that is shaped by factors such as artificial intelligence, automation, algorithmic management, robotization and other evocative concepts that the law must understand and assimilate, if it aims at intervening on their relationship with the employment contract in a meaningful way.

For the reason just explained above, this chapter will firstly attempt to conceptualize the main constitutive features of the digital transformation and the way they may affect the subordinate employment relationship, drawing from the elaboration of the sociological and organizational literature.

3. M.G. Garofalo, Un profilo ideologico del diritto del lavoro, in *Giornale di Diritto del Lavoro e di Relazioni Industriali*, 1999, 1, 9.
4. T. Fabbri, Le relazioni di lavoro come questione interdisciplinare: implicazioni per la ricerca e la didattica, in F. Basenghi, L.E. Golzio (eds.), *Regole, politiche e metodo. L'eredità di Marco Biagi nelle relazioni di lavoro di oggi*, Giappichelli, Turin, 2013, 126.

The implementation of digital technologies in production processes and work organization is probably at a too early stage to say if it will be best handled, in juridical terms, by a comprehensive paradigm shift or a simple adaptation of the established legal categories. This chapter will adopt a narrower perspective, and will try to shed light on the following questions: (1) what is the normative justification for regulating the introduction of digital technologies in work organization; (2) what does it mean to pursue a win-win outcome in this peculiar context, in the light of the characterization of the interests of the parties involved; (3) what regulatory arrangements should be practically put into place to ensure that changes in work organization will positively affect the substantive elements of subordination, mitigating its most burdensome and distasteful features, and protecting workers from the risk of an impairment of the terms and conditions of employment.

The introduction of automation and digital work devices in workplaces is capable of altering the established human-to-human relationships, given the groundbreaking role of mediation that machines are almost set to play.[5] As such, it can affect the functional elements of subordination in different ways, encompassing several intertwined legal institutions that supervise over the coordination of each individual work performance with the wider organization. To name but a few, one can mention in this regard the contents of the obligation to work and the exercise of managerial powers, for instance as long as timing, monitoring and assessment of the work performance are concerned. As this chapter aims at a preliminary understanding of such an intricate phenomenon, it will consider all the above elements together. This will necessarily entail a certain degree of approximation, but it is not the purpose of this analysis to reach conclusive findings. Rather, the objective is to set up a general interpretative setting that could be taken as a reference to develop further sectoral investigations.

After reviewing the conceptual coordinates of the digital transformation, and following a brief discussion of its linkages with the work organization and the theoretical foundations of the employment contract, the chapter will look deeper into the employer's perspective. This approach is justified by the observation that changes in the production process are normally decided and planned by the company, in the light of an economic goal. Therefore, the overview of the reasons and the conditions that drive the managerial actions represents an appropriate preparatory step in the study of the employment effects of the digital transformation. In this regard a two-stage analysis is envisaged. First, it is necessary to understand in what fashion and to what extent an innovation of the organizational design entails a change in the assumptions and expectations of the company about the meaning of an efficient and productive integration of the work performance into the new workplace patterns. In the second stage, the analysis will move to ascertain whether such new assumptions and expectations on the employer's side have a correspondence in the legal schemes that administer the employment relationship, and whether this correspondence can affect the contents of the mutual rights and obligations of the parties.

5. The "third element," as M. Faioli puts it in *Mansioni e macchina intelligente*, Giappichelli, Turin, 2018.

The chapter will then shift to the perspective of the worker. The objective is twofold. First, to find how the workers' interests (concerning, for instance, the remuneration of the work performance, the preservation and enhancement of the professional skillset, the wellbeing and the employability) are influenced and reshaped by the changes made in the workplace to achieve an efficient functioning of the organization in the new technological environment. Second, to infer from those findings some propositions about the arrangements and regulatory tools (e.g., new rights or new ways to exercise the established rights) that may be set out to ensure that the terms and conditions of the employment contract adequately reflect (and take care of) the actual workers' interests, consistently with the idea of maintaining a fair balance between the mutual positions of the parties.

To conclude, the chapter will briefly address the question of what regulatory sources and techniques can best serve the purpose of accompanying the digital transformation of employment relations towards a win-win outcome.

13.2 DIGITIZATION, THE ORGANIZATION 4.0 AND THE EMPLOYMENT CONTRACT

The "digital transformation" is an umbrella-concept that brings together a wide array of technological and organizational patterns.[6] Drawing from organization theory, it can be described as the aggregate of a set of "abilitative technologies" that have the potential of simplifying existing production practices or putting in place new ones.[7]

Its main distinctive features are the enhanced practicability of remote communications among the factors of the production process and the subsequent possibility to collect and elaborate data and information from those communications on a large scale and on an intensified speed, to use them in the next stages of the process.[8] In a nutshell, it represents a step forward in the enduring quest of economic undertakings to increase their efficiency and productivity.

According to a persuasive statement, technology can be portrayed as a social system, conceptually distinguished from both the organizational system and the regulatory system.[9] Those systems can interact on diversified patterns, but still maintain a mutual separation. Such a construction leads to the assertion that the role of technology in society is neutral and should be construed under a non-deterministic approach. Referring to an "impact" of technology on employment relations is therefore

6. Or "a multifaceted topic with large implications for labour markets, the world of work and society at large," in the words of the European Social Partners Framework Agreement on Digitalization signed in June 2020.
7. A. Gasparre, Digitalizzazione e cambiamento organizzativo, in A. Salento (ed.), *Industria 4.0: Oltre il determinismo tecnologico*, TAO Digital Library, Bologna, 2018, 53.
8. T. Fabbri, Digital Work: An Organizational Perspective, in E. Ales, et al. (eds.), *Working in Digital and Smart Organizations. Legal, Economic and Organizational Perspectives on the Digitalization of Labour Relations*, Palgrave Macmillan, Cham, 2018, 29.
9. S. Deakin, C. Markou, The Law-Technology Cycle and the Future of Work, in *Giornale di Diritto del lavoro e di Relazioni industriali*, 2018, 2, 445.

inaccurate, strictly speaking, as there is no univocal effect attached to the implementation of any technological innovation.[10]

The introduction of new technologies can produce diverging impacts, depending on the specific organizational environment in which those technologies are meant to operate. The design of an organizational environment, in turn, depends on peculiar managerial strategies that represent the outcome of case-specific choices.

As a result of this logical sequence, the implementation of new technologies can entail different effects that can be appreciated on two distinct levels.

In the workplace as a whole, remote communication and managerial practices based on the use of algorithms and "big data" processing can on the one hand enable a pervasive monitoring of the work procedures, the mechanical dictation of stringent and frequent directives and an analytical and sophisticated assessment of the work performance (as it may be the case with the wearable technologies used in the "digital sweatshops" of the logistic sector[11]). Conversely, they can promote the establishment of horizontal relationships, the replacement of punctual instructions with the definition of general objectives and the following assessment based on the degree to which such objectives have been achieved by the workers. Thus, artificial intelligence can enhance the decision-making ability of workers as well as obliterate and replace it. Again, this confirms that automation can enable a strict centralization and a wide decentralization of managerial power at once.

At a narrower level, the effects of a certain organizational design can impact unevenly on the individual employment conditions. For instance, the provision of an extensive decision-making power to an employee may be offset by the production and collection of broad and detailed information about his or her performance, supported by the use of big data technologies. As it has been maintained, "many of the same communication technologies and the inexpensive computing power that make horizontal collaboration easier also permit much more computer-aided monitoring of work and communication, thereby creating environments with more control and less behavioral discretion than in the past."[12] The outcome of automation at work may thus be contradictory, and in any case it cannot be mechanically brought back to a one-fits-all pattern.[13]

10. A. Salento, Industria 4.0 e determinismo tecnologico, in A. Salento (ed.), *Industria 4.0: Oltre il determinismo tecnologico*, TAO Digital Library, Bologna, 2018, 6.
11. L. Tirabeni, Technology, Power, and the Organization: Wearable Technologies and Their Implications for the Performance, in T. Addabbo, et al. (eds.), *Performance Appraisal in Modern Employment Relations: An Interdisciplinary Approach*, Palgrave Macmillan, Cham, 2019, 61; B. Cattero, M. D'Onofrio, Organizing and Collective Bargaining in the Digitized "Tertiary Factories" of Amazon: A Comparison Between Germany and Italy, in E. Ales, et al. (eds.), *Working in Digital and Smart Organizations. Legal, Economic and Organizational Perspectives on the Digitalization of Labour Relations*, Palgrave Macmillan, Cham, 2018, 141.
12. J. Pfeffer, You're Still the Same: Why Theories of Power Hold Over Time and Across Contexts, in *Academy of Management Perspectives*, 2013, 17, 4, 269, quoted by T. Fabbri, Digital Work: An Organizational Perspective, in E. Ales, et al. (eds.), *Working in Digital and Smart Organizations. Legal, Economic and Organizational Perspectives on the Digitalization of Labour Relations*, Palgrave Macmillan, Cham, 2018, 34.
13. "As with the introduction of any other technological innovation in the economy in the past, there is some ambivalence over the potential consequences for work and employment of the ...

Following this line of reasoning, it appears clear that the proper focus of a legal analysis on the relationship between the technological transformation and the employment contract is not technology in itself, but rather the organization that implements such technologies. In other words, the ambivalent and subjective character of the company's organizational choices represents both the justification and the subject of regulation.

It represents the justification, because the rationale that drives a given regulatory arrangement does not necessarily have to align with the economic motivations that lay behind the different managerial strategies. Regulation, both in its autonomous/contractual and heteronomous/legal characterizations, embodies the authority of societal forces and the balance between the diverging interests expressed by those forces, as opposed to the atomistic stances of individual economic entities.

Organizational choices also represent the subject of regulation. In fact, while regulation lays down the foundations of managerial power, likewise it can and must set the limits to its exercise.[14] This is a crucial function that puts regulators permanently on the verge between the protection of fundamental social and personal rights and the preservation of the drivers of innovation, in such a way that the latter are not hampered but rather driven towards the improvement of universal wellbeing.[15]

The arguments presented above set the stage for a critical review of the assumptions formulated by a sector of labor law scholarship, that draw a rather radical linkage between the digital transformation and the very nature of the employment contract. Starting from the circumstance that the new technologies entrust some jobs (those not put at risk of disruption by the advent of artificial intelligence) with a remarkable degree of autonomy and responsibility in the organization and the execution of the work performance, some authors infer that the automation and digitization bear the potential of shifting the foundations of the employment contract away from the established exchange schemes based on an ontological conflict of interests, towards cooperative or semi-associative models.[16]

Again, organization theory provides for some elements of knowledge that suggest a more cautious approach to the matter. First of all, in organizational terms the general and a-technical concept of autonomy can be broken down into two more specific categories: autonomy in a strict sense and discretion. While the former implies that the

technologies": *see* E. Fernandez-Macia, Game-Changing Technologies for European Manufacturing, in M. Neufind, J. O'Reilly, F. Ranft (eds.), *Work in the Digital Age. Challenges of the Fourth Industrial Revolution*, Rowman & Littlefield, London—New York, 2018, 133, 139.

14. V. De Stefano, "Negotiating the Algorithm": Automation, Artificial Intelligence and Labour Protection (May 16, 2018), in *Comparative Labor Law & Policy Journal*, 2020, 41, 1, available at SSRN: https://ssrn.com/abstract=3178233 or http://dx.doi.org/10.2139/ssrn.3178233.
15. In the words of a fashionable philosopher, "The danger is that if we invest too much in developing AI and too little in developing human consciousness, the very sophisticated artificial intelligence of computers might only serve to empower the natural stupidity of humans": *see* Y.N. Harari, *21 Lessons for the 21st Century*, Jonathan Cape, London, 2018, 70.
16. B. Caruso, Strategie di flessibilità funzionale e di tutela dopo il Jobs Act: fordismo, post fordismo e industria 4.0, in *Giornale di Diritto del lavoro e di Relazioni industriali*, 2018, 1, 81, 105. For a divergent view, *see* M. Barbera, Impresa, lavoro e non lavoro nell'economia digitale, fra differenziazione e universalismo delle tutele, in *Giornale di Diritto del lavoro e di Relazioni industriali*, 2018, 2, 403.

worker is vested with the power to create new rules in the production process, discretion entails a (more circumscribed) capacity to choose among a closed set of rules predetermined by a coordinating authority (like for instance the choice of work patterns).[17] Thus, if on the one hand the tasks embedded into digital and automated (and therefore formalized to a certain degree) work procedures are almost incompatible with the idea of autonomy in the strict sense, the use of artificial intelligence in production processes can lead to a degree of explicit formalization so high as to reduce even the exercise of discretion to very low margins.[18] Against this background, there are very little, and certainly not granted, chances to find a correspondence between the ways work is performed in digital and automated workplaces and the definition of autonomy that is accepted in labor law, i.e., the freedom from the managerial power to direct the work performance.

The theoretical assumptions about the autonomy brought to the workers by digitization should also be tested against the practices of "flexible standardization" of production processes that the new technologies can enhance, as sociological and organizational studies explain. Such practices mean that, in cases where a worker's autonomous initiative generates innovative solutions to the unexpected problems and errors that may arise in the production process, digital technologies make it possible to formalize and incorporate those solutions in the organization *a posteriori*,[19] in line with the "continuous learning" pattern that characterizes the artificial intelligence.

In other words, even when a real autonomy is exercised in the employment relationship, its persistence may be short, and its outcomes may not constitute a mutual asset of the workers and the organization but may instead be swiftly appropriated by the latter.

Furthermore, the level at which decision-making is exercised is also relevant to assess the effective degree of freedom that digitization may grant to the workers in the context of the employment relationship, and whether such degree is high enough to justify a revision of the ontology of the employment contract.

In this regard, organization theory distinguishes among three levels of decision-making as long as the application of technologies in workplace practices is concerned. The first level is called "design" and has to do with the choice of the goals and functions that a given technology is meant to pursue in a specific organization. The second level is defined as "adoption" and is addressed to the identification of the sectors and stages of activity in which a technological equipment will be used within that organization. The third level is known as "use" and concerns the decisions that each agent can take while actually applying a technological device in the production process.[20] While the first and the second levels, i.e., those where the strategic directives are defined, are

17. B. Maggi, Digitalizzazione e regolazione dei processi di lavoro, in A. Salento (ed.), *Industria 4.0: Oltre il determinismo tecnologico*, TAO Digital Library, Bologna, 2018, 41.
18. G. Masino, Industria 4.0 tra passato e futuro, in A. Salento (ed.), *Industria 4.0: Oltre il determinismo tecnologico*, TAO Digital Library, Bologna, 2018, 23.
19. A. Salento, Industria 4.0, imprese, lavoro. Problemi interpretativi e prospettive, in *Rivista Giuridica del Lavoro e della Previdenza Sociale*, 2017, 2, 175.
20. G. Masino, Industria 4.0 tra passato e futuro, in A. Salento (ed.), *Industria 4.0: Oltre il determinismo tecnologico*, TAO Digital Library, Bologna, 2018, 23.

exclusive prerogatives of executives and managers (or even of political decision-makers), workers can enjoy some involvement only at the third and lowest level.

This means that, except in cases where strong codetermination institutions are in place that allow workers or their representatives to have a say on the most strategic issues,[21] workers' "autonomy" can hardly justify any pledge for a reframing of the employment contract into cooperative schemes, not to speak of the associative ones. In fact, even in those cases where the new organizational patterns bring about a significant power to self-determination of workers, such power is mostly functional to a goal that is planned by higher levels.

In broader terms, it seems that the material effects of automation and digitization of the employment relationship cannot be generalized, as they depend on the peculiar choices and arrangements made by each organization. In any case, while the benefits that may come for the workers need a further investigation, there is a risk of overestimating the breadth of the changes that such phenomena can impress on the legal foundations of the employment contract.

A second argument in favor of a marked shift towards a conceptualization of the employment contract as a cooperative scheme lies in the circumstance that the performance of a work activity in a digital environment often does not just imply the mechanical application of a set of technical skills, but involves more broadly the personal attitudes, knowledge and capabilities of the workers. As such, it has the potential of enriching the structure of the employment contract, making it a gateway to the worker's self-fulfillment.[22] This is an appealing and partly shareable view. However, it should be pointed out that while the enhancement of personal capabilities is a crucial factor, that regulation can't overlook if it has to drive effectively the digital transformation of work towards win-win outcomes, this is more a matter of regulatory goals and techniques (how to promote the development of capabilities at work) than a new constitutive element of the employment relationship.[23] Above all, it would be dangerous to bring self-fulfillment into the exchange scheme of the employment contract, as if it was a special reward factor for highly skilled digital occupations. In fact, on the one hand self-fulfillment is (or rather should be) an ordinary effect of any work (and human) activity and not a compensation per se. Furthermore, self-fulfillment is an immaterial good; hence it is—unlike other such goods, like for instance health—difficult to quantify and to fit into a contractual scheme.

To conclude and summarize this part, one element should be remarked. Despite the ambivalences brought about by the digital transformation of work, power issues and conflict of interest remain inherent elements of the employment contract. As a consequence, any regulation addressing the sphere of managerial decisions and

---

21. In this sense, S. Paba, G. Solinas, In Favour of Machines (But Not Forgetting the Workers): Some Considerations on the Fourth Industrial Revolution, in E. Ales, et al. (eds.), *Working in Digital and Smart Organizations. Legal, Economic and Organizational Perspectives on the Digitalization of Labour Relations*, Palgrave Macmillan, Cham, 2018, 39.
22. B. Caruso, Strategie di flessibilità funzionale e di tutela dopo il Jobs Act: fordismo, post fordismo e industria 4.0, in *Giornale di Diritto del lavoro e di Relazioni industriali*, 2018, 1, 81.
23. For a summary of the debate on the relationship between the capability approach and labor law, *see* B. Langille (ed.), *The Capability Approach to Labour Law*, OUP, Oxford, 2019.

practices cannot refrain from taking into account the power imbalances between the parties. An imbalance that may even be sharpened by other innovative features of digitization, like for instance the risk of occupational displacement (and replaceability) that stems from the possible failures that workers may meet in their continuous adaptation to technological change,[24] and the fragmentation of the collective sphere of representation which represents the by-product of the distinctive value increasingly attached to each individual or team performance, especially in high-skilled work environments.

13.3 THE CONTENTS OF THE EMPLOYMENT CONTRACT IN THE DIGITAL WORKPLACE FROM THE EMPLOYER'S PERSPECTIVE

As it was maintained in the previous section, the organizational innovations linked with the digital transformation are basically addressed to increase the efficiency and the productivity of an undertaking. Hence the same goals also lay in the background of those changes in the production models that closely affect the employment relationship. Changes of this latter kind operate on three main grounds: the content of the obligation to work, the surveillance on the work performance and the chronological and topographical coordinates of the integration between the work performance and the organization.

As far as the contents of the obligation to work are concerned, the utility that digitalized organizations expect from an increasing number of jobs can be described in terms of professional versatility. The concept of versatility is probably better suited to capture an array of nuanced situations, that more commonly used concepts like flexibility or adaptability do not evoke as much clearly. The point for a worker dealing with automation and artificial intelligence, in fact, is not only his or her readiness to swap flexibly from one task to another or to adapt his or her skillset to the requirements of a changing environment.[25] The evolution of job contents (at least of those not immediately threatened of being replaced by machines) in the digital transformation unfolds along the double track of enrichment and enlargement. On the one hand, the performance of these jobs requires the accumulation and the application of a set of sophisticated and specialized skills and the shift of a certain amount of responsibilities from the management to the worker. On the other hand, the spectrum of the specific tasks embedded in each job tends to increase under the pressure of technologies, leading to the growth of "polyvalent" or "multi-tasking" jobs and to the corresponding need to update the job classification criteria. Against such background, the role of soft skills (such as adaptability, problem solving, intra-team communication), once relegated to a secondary place, seems to become particularly relevant, so that the

24. This is probably the issue which has received the highest consideration in the current debate, at least at the policy level; *see* European Commission—Directorate-General for Communication Networks, Content and Technology, *Report of the High on The Impact of the Digital Transformation on EU Labour Markets*, Brussels, April 2019.
25. L. Corazza, Industria 4.0: lavoro e non lavoro di fronte alla quarta rivoluzione industriale, in *Economia & Lavoro*, 2017, 2, 15.

common distinction between the core work obligation and the ancillary duties may gradually lose its significance.

These developments are reflected also in the assessment of the work performance. Not only the new paradigm makes it possible to assess the performance on manifold grounds, in line with the evolution of the job contents, but these grounds also tend to become less objective and predictable. The simple compliance with working time schedules and professional diligence standards is being replaced by other criteria. In fact, for a performance to qualify as productive and effectively integrated in the production process, the focus will be increasingly placed on the actual accomplishment of specific individual or team results, and more attention will be paid on the evaluation of the proficient use of a worker's competences and skills.[26]

In all, it seems clear from the above that in response to the pressures exerted by digital-driven organizational changes, the contents of the obligation to work become more complex and broader than in the past, and their boundaries can result at times blurred and difficult to circumscribe for the workers.

Surveillance is probably one of the most extensively analyzed aspects of the digital transformation of employment, also from a labor law perspective.[27] As it is well known, the use of digital devices in the work performance opens serious problems with regard to the separation between work and private life. In fact, digital and remote work and communication tools make it technically possible for the employer to intrude pervasively into the worker's personal sphere, and have access to information that either pertain exclusively to the individual or have only an indirect connection with (and are often not relevant to) the work performance, like opinions, feelings and states of mind. Nevertheless, also keeping the focus restricted on matters that have a straight functional correlation with the organization of the production process, it seems possible to argue that the digital transformation allows for an unprecedentedly broad and pervasive control over the work performance, making it possible, for instance, to track until the smallest detail the number of tasks executed in a given time unit or the pace kept. Furthermore, such breadth and pervasiveness are not unintended side-effects but are indeed fully inherent to the goals of the organization in terms of efficiency and productivity.

Surveillance on the work performance can take different shapes. The most evident one consists in the continuous remote monitoring, operated by means of digital working tools that put the worker in a condition that may be defined as "hyper-subordination." The paramount example is represented by wearable technologies that, while providing instructions to the worker with a view to maximizing the efficiency of

26. Y. Curzi, T. Fabbri, B. Pistoresi, Performance Appraisal Criteria and Innovative Work Behaviour: The Mediating Role of Employees' Appraisal Satisfaction, in T. Addabbo, et al. (eds.), *Performance Appraisal in Modern Employment Relations. An Interdisciplinary Approach*, Palgrave Macmillan, Cham, 2019, 11.
27. *See*, for instance, L.F. Eisenstadt, Employer or Big Brother? Data Analytics and Incursions into Workers' Personal Lives, in T. Addabbo, et al. (eds.), *Performance Appraisal in Modern Employment Relations. An Interdisciplinary Approach*, Palgrave Macmillan, Cham, 2019, 165; F. Hendrickx, Privacy 4.0 at Work: Regulating Employment, Technology, and Automation, in *Comparative Labor Law & Policy Journal*, 2020, 41, 1.

his/her performance, at the same time are capable of tracking and measuring his/her actions and motions, and in some cases also the related biological parameters. As it has been well explained, wearable technologies are the expression of "a Neo-Taylorist trend where working bodies are continuously regulated through the imposition of productivity standards, time-motion measurement, transmission and analysis of data and systems of punishment and rewards."[28]

Surveillance can also present itself in a more subtle and nuanced fashion. This is the case with those organizational patterns mentioned above, that on the one hand enlarge the scope of discretional choices enjoyed by the worker, but on the other hand surround it with a tight web of formalized procedures that make it possible to exert a rigorous coordination and control over the worker's behavior. Under such "hyper-standardization" patterns, the apparent autonomy granted to the worker (for instance, as long as the definition of the schedule and even the place of work are concerned) is offset by "standardized work procedures, which predetermine work behaviors and make them traceable, and can make control over work and subordination even stronger."[29]

At a third level, even workers that actually enjoy some degree of discretion and are free from a pervasive monitoring during the execution of their work performance may be subject to "people analytics" practices that bring control back into the hands of the company. In fact, such practices (and the devices on which they rely) allow the management to elaborate *a posteriori* the data created by the same workers during the performance of their tasks, and that make it possible to base managerial decisions (e.g., performance assessment or even disciplinary measures) on such elaboration.[30]

The changes embracing the chronological and topographical coordinates of the work performance have also attracted a considerable attention from scholars. As it has been maintained, "one of the effects that digitalization of business is likely to produce is the dematerialization of the workplace, pushing workers outside the undertaking or the establishment as physical places while keeping them attached to the company as economic and legal entity."[31] Unlike the factors considered above, this innovation does not respond to an affirmative requirement of the organization but to a negative one. In other words, it does not operate by means of an integration or an enhancement of the elements of the employment contract (the contents of the obligation, the surveillance power) but rather by a removal of some of such elements.

---

28. L. Tirabeni, Technology, Power, and the Organization: Wearable Technologies and Their Implications for the Performance, in T. Addabbo, et al. (eds.), *Performance Appraisal in Modern Employment Relations. An Interdisciplinary Approach*, Palgrave Macmillan, Cham, 2019, 61.
29. T. Fabbri, Digital Work: An Organizational Perspective, in E. Ales, et al. (eds.), *Working in Digital and Smart Organizations. Legal, Economic and Organizational Perspectives on the Digitalization of Labour Relations*, Palgrave Macmillan, Cham, 2018, 33.
30. E. Dagnino, People Analytics: lavoro e tutele al tempo del management tramite big data, in *Labour and Law Issues*, 2017, 1, I.1. M. Otto, "Workforce Analytics" v Fundamental Rights Protection in the EU in the Age of Big Data, in *Comparative Labour Law & Policy Journal*, 2020, 40, 3.
31. E. Ales, Protecting Work in the Digital Transformation: Rethinking the Typological Approach in the Intrinsically Triangular Relationship Perspective, in E. Ales, et al. (eds.), *Working in Digital and Smart Organizations. Legal, Economic and Organizational Perspectives on the Digitalization of Labour Relations*, Palgrave Macmillan, Cham, 2018, 13.

As it is well known, the existence of a workplace and work schedule were once considered as the fundamental conditions for a meaningful integration of the work performance with the organization and, as a result, they also represented the basic indicators of a subordinate employment relationship. In the digital organization they can easily be replaced (in an increasing number of cases) by other means of coordination, such as remote control, and by innovative metrics of work linked to achievement-based or data-based assessment procedures. Therefore, in the employer's perspective, softening the role of "old-fashioned" coordination tools like workplace and working time can even turn out to be a means to reduce costs.

13.4 THE IMPACT OF ORGANIZATIONAL CHOICES ON THE WORKER'S SPHERE: INTERESTS AND EMPLOYMENT CONDITIONS

The previous section described the factors that push towards an evolution of the key elements of the employment relationship from the perspective of the employer, or, to put it differently, from the perspective of the utility that the production process expects from a workers' performance.

It has already been pointed out (actually it represents the basic assumption of this chapter) that such evolution can affect the working conditions and the workers' interests for better and for worse.

This section will investigate which employment conditions and employment-related interests are actually implicated in the described process, and which arrangements may possibly be set out to provide for a meaningful protection of the worker in automated and digitized workplaces.

13.4.1 The Work Obligation

The first issue to be examined concerns the contents of the worker's contractual obligations and the related employer's prerogatives.

As it has been pointed out above, a typical feature of the work performance in the organization 4.0 is the enlargement of its boundaries, paired with the increased vagueness of its constitutive elements and aims. While polyvalent tasks and a certain degree of openness of work obligations are not inherently incompatible with the general scheme of the employment contract, a problem may arise if such characteristics end up to place an indefinite and arbitrary power in the hands of the employer, who may take advantage of such situation by shifting to the worker the risk for the failure to meet the organization's goals. Hence, the paramount interests of the worker in such circumstance are the transparency and the predictability of the terms and conditions attached to his/her specific work arrangements, like for instance being previously aware of the degree of discretion or autonomy attached to the job.

The said substantive requirements may be translated into legal terms as a worker's "entitlement to coordination." Such worker's prerogative may assume two different shapes. The first one is represented by the prior formalization of the organizational rules that the worker shall abide by, as regards both the targets to be achieved and the scope of the decision-making enjoyed in the execution of the work performance. One example of this kind may be drawn from Article 4, paragraph 2 of the recent Directive (EU) 2019/1152 of the European Parliament and of the Council, of June 20, 2019, *on transparent and predictable working conditions in the European Union* (hereinafter TPWCD). This provision includes among the "essential aspects of the employment relationship," that form the object of the obligation to provide information resting on the employer, "the principle that the worker is employed at various places or is free to determine his or her place of work," if no fixed or main place of work has been assigned (Article 4(2)b), and, in case the work pattern is mostly unpredictable, "(i) the principle that the work schedule is variable, the number of guaranteed paid hours and the remuneration for work performed in addition to those guaranteed hours; (ii) the reference hours and days within which the worker may be required to work; (iii) the minimum notice period to which the worker is entitled before the start of a work assignment and, where applicable, the deadline for cancellation (...)."

Another example is provided by the Italian legislation on "agile work" (*lavoro agile*), namely at Articles 18 and 19 of the Law n. 81 of 2017.[32] While granting the possibility to carry out this (subordinate) work performance without strict constraints as long as workplace and work schedule are concerned, the recalled provisions require the parties to the employment contract to determine in a specific individual agreement the rules on the organization of the performance, which can be based on phases, cycles and can goals *in lieu* of the common mechanical and top-down forms of direction, and the modalities and conditions for the exercise of the managerial power to direct, control and discipline the worker.

As an alternative to the prior formalization of the organizational rules, the "entitlement to coordination" may be construed as a right to continuous feedback. Under this kind of arrangement, the worker may infer by way of induction the rules that conform his/her performance, drawing from the feedback received from the employer. This may represent an equivalent means to reach the same goal, namely the transparency and predictability of the employment terms and conditions, especially in cases where the nature of the job forbids a detailed predetermination of those rules. However, for such a system to work properly and effectively it should not be limited to the mere fulfillment of a formal documentary obligation. It would be the employer's responsibility to provide a clear, detailed, consistent and intelligible feedback, at regular and frequent deadlines, and explain and discuss the outcomes of the worker's performance whenever needed.

Closely linked to the demarcation of the contents and the breadth of the work obligation stands the issue of performance assessment. Inherent in the scheme of the employment contract is the worker's legitimate interest to the transparency of the factors and the procedures that preside over managerial decisions, with a view to

32. For a comprehensive analysis, *see* C. Spinelli, *Tecnologie digitali e lavoro agile*, Cacucci, Bari, 2018.

reviewing and, if necessary, challenging them. This interest, indeed, does not encompass only the decisions that are strictly functional to a qualitative evaluation, but also those concerning other aspects of the employment relationship, like for instance the assignment of tasks. The problem of holding the employer accountable for such decisions is twofold. On the one hand, if the organizational constraints are low and the job is provided with a certain degree of discretion or autonomy, it may result difficult to bring back the decision to a clear-cut and objective reason; hence the exercise of managerial prerogatives may drift towards arbitrariness. In particular, it may remain unclear whether the real responsibility for the situation that justifies the decision (e.g., the failure to meet a target) lies in the performance per se or in the organizational conditions in which the work has been performed.[33] On the other hand, in cases where managerial decisions are mediated by remote communication devices and artificial intelligence, and/or enhanced by abilitative technologies that allow for an analytical and accurate scrutiny of data and information, it may be difficult to identify the real source of the decision, and especially to bring it back to a human rather than an artificial entity.

Regulatory arrangements aimed at meaningfully tackle these problems should impose on the employer a duty to disclose previously the assessment criteria and the elements on which the decision will be grounded, particularly as long as the causal correspondence between the achievement of any performance target and the related evaluation is concerned.

In this regard, proportionality should be reaffirmed as the guiding principle of managerial decision-making. Following this requirement, it should be possible for the worker to trace back the logical process followed by the employer and scrutinize the consistency between its outcome and the declared preconditions. In the case of decisions/assessments based on digital data analysis and algorithmic elaboration, then, the nature of the collected data and the modalities and conditions that authorize their collection and processing should be defined and declared in advance, and the worker should be entitled to review the related procedures and challenge their outcomes.[34]

33. E. Ales, Is Performance Appraisal Compatible with the Employment Relationship? A Conclusive Plea in Favour of an Achievement-Oriented Approach to Work Organisation, in T. Addabbo, et al. (eds.), *Performance Appraisal in Modern Employment Relations. An Interdisciplinary Approach*, Palgrave Macmillan, Cham, 2019, 2555, stresses the necessary distinction between the personal achievements of a worker and the "achievement of the work organization as a whole, to be understood as the outcome of the undertaking, as such falling within the sole responsibility of the employer/entrepreneur." As the Author maintains, "The possibility to make expectations legally binding lays in employers/entrepreneurs hands, depending upon the way in which they shape the work organization."
34. For an analysis of the problems posed by of automated decision-making technologies, with a particular focus on the EU Regulation No. 2016/679 (GDPR), its flaws and interpretative ambiguities, *see* V. De Stefano, "Negotiating the Algorithm": Automation, Artificial Intelligence and Labour Protection (May 16, 2018), in *Comparative Labor Law & Policy Journal*, 2020, 41, 1, available at SSRN: https://ssrn.com/abstract=3178233 or http://dx.doi.org/10.2139/ssrn.3178233.

Another typical worker's interest that may interact (or collide) with the new characterization of the work obligation is the fair compensation of the work performance. As it has been recalled above, the digital organization triggers the development of "working by objectives" patterns that require the worker to spend in the job a remarkable amount of his/her personal (cognitive and/or physical) skills, abilities and attitudes. Following the narrative that illustrates this changing pattern as a shift from the task to the person, one may reasonably argue that the entity of the goods transferred by the worker in compliance with his/her obligations has become more onerous than in the average pre-digital paradigm. The risk entailed in this phenomenon is that such increased burden is not translated into an equivalent adjustment of the economic conditions of employment, but is entirely charged on the worker, altering the balance between the quality and quantity of the work done and the economic value attached to it. This may happen, for instance, if wage-setting mechanisms in place in a company make wage raises totally conditional upon the effective achievement of a given target.

A fair application of the proportionality principle requires that at least a share of the increased value generated by the job performance be compensated unconditionally. The underlying assumption is that the value of a work performance is represented, both in qualitative and in quantitative terms, not only by the achievement in itself, but also by the higher professional and personal contents inherent in the job.

Finally, in an organizational environment characterized by a continuous pressure for innovation and by the fast evolution of the technological equipment, workers have an interest to keep at pace with changes that have implications for the execution of their performance, their career opportunities and, in the worst cases, the preservation their job. This interest can find a response in the update of the workers' professional, educational and vocational skills.[35] Such operation should be considered in two complementary dimensions: within the employment relationship and towards the external market.

In the first case, the continuous update of professional skills can be interpreted, in the perspective of the employee, as a duty as well as a right that can be claimed against the employer. In a context in which the contents of the work obligation become more complex and volatile, training represents a precondition for the worker to be in the condition of fulfilling the demands of the company. The employer's position can hence be qualified as a duty to cooperate to the accomplishment of the counterpart's obligation.

An example of this kind (in spite of its very mild normative contents) can be found in Article 2103 of the Italian Civil Code, as amended by Article 3 of the Legislative Decree n. 81/15. The provision, that sets out the rules on the assignment of tasks and job rotation, stipulates that any assignment to a new job must be accompanied by the fulfillment of the "training duty," although only "when necessary" and without any sanction in case of non-execution.

35. A. Bianco, The Reskilling Imperative for the Digital Economy, in *Economia & Lavoro*, 2018, 29, 3.

The second case involves the worker's interest to remain employable in case his/her job is displaced. The case may be particularly problematic since high automation is often coupled with high specialization: in other words, as long as each company or workplace develops its own customized technological environment, encouraging the development of a set of professional skills consistent with the requirements of that specific environment, the workers may find it increasingly difficult to use such skills in other companies. In this regard, policymakers have discussed the establishment of "Digital Skills Personal Learning Accounts." The *Report of the High on The Impact of the Digital Transformation on EU Labour Markets*, prepared for the European Commission and released in April 2019, defines such accounts as a mechanism "which allows workers to acquire relevant skills throughout their careers in order to stay relevant in rapidly transforming, digital labour markets. The accounts would belong to the worker and would be portable from job to job."[36]

Measures of such kind certainly go in the right direction, but they overlook an important element, i.e., the accountability of companies in ensuring an adequate support to occupational transitions. Once it is assumed, as it was mentioned in the previous sections of this chapter, that entrepreneurial choices trigger and drive the organizational innovations that may negatively affect the occupational position of the worker in the labor market, it should come as a result that the social costs of such choices should not be entirely charged on the State and the public sector, but should instead be shared by the companies.

For the same reason, the provision of Article 13 of the TPWCD on "Mandatory Training" does not seem fully convincing. This norm, that applies to the cases in which the law or collective agreements require the employer to provide training to a worker, appropriately stipulates that "such training shall be provided to the worker free of cost, shall count as working time and, where possible, shall take place during working hours." However, the said entitlement is limited to the training contents necessary "to carry out the work for which [the worker] is employed." In this way, the Directive enhances the (questionable, for what has just been said) principle according to which training activities that are functional to a direct interest of the production process deserve a better protection and a stronger commitment by the employer than the training activities generally aimed at reinforcing the position of the worker in the labor market.

13.4.2 Health, Safety and Wellbeing

It is generally acknowledged that automation and digitization can positively affect the wellbeing of workers. On the one hand, these factors may alleviate the most burdensome, repetitive and dangerous aspects of certain jobs, that can increasingly be taken over by machines. On the other hand, they can contribute to enrich the contents of the jobs and the degree of satisfaction attached to them, to unleash the personal attitudes

36. European Commission——Directorate-General for Communication Networks, Content and Technology, *Report of the High on The Impact of the Digital Transformation on EU Labour Markets*, Brussels, April 2019, 33.

of the workers, and to provide them with the freedom to organize their professional activities consistent with the objectives and needs of their private lives.
However, nothing of the above happens as a mechanical effect. In fact, under certain circumstances the shift of responsibilities from the employer to the worker that characterizes the digital production processes, as long as time management and achievement-based assessments are concerned, may lead to a work intensification, and in the end result in a deterioration of worker's wellbeing. This is typical, for instance, of the "always-on" work patterns.[37] As a sector of organization theory explains, "If time and space discretion is what characterizes digital work, then we might expect that at least some employees would perceive and experience that additional (time and space) discretion as an additional stressful burden."[38]

Regulatory arrangements aimed at protecting the health of workers and promoting their wellbeing in digital workplaces should hence be focused on the control of working time. A recent ruling of the Court of Justice of the European Union (CJEU), in the case C-55/18 (*CCOO*),[39] has reaffirmed the crucial function played by working time measurement for the sake of an effective protection and enforcement of the health and safety of workers, in line with the aims of the Directive n. 2003/88. The Court found that, if the maximum working hours thresholds are the legal machinery designed to protect the health and safety of workers, the lack of "An obligation to have recourse to an instrument that enables the objective and reliable determination of the number of hours worked each day and each week is not capable of guaranteeing (...) the effectiveness of the rights conferred by Article 31(2) of the Charter and by this directive, since it deprives both employers and workers of the possibility of verifying whether those rights are complied with and is therefore liable to compromise the objective of that directive, which is to ensure better protection of the safety and health of workers."[40]

In the same sense operates the "right to disconnect" elaborated, in different modalities, by the French and Italian legislations (in the latter case applicable only to "agile work" arrangements). Indeed, the implementation of this right in the context of digitally-enhanced forms of work that grant the workers the freedom to self-organize their working time, like in the just mentioned Italian case of "agile work" (in which, however, maximum daily and working hours thresholds remain applicable) does not necessarily need that an instrument for the measurement of working hours be put in place. To be precise, the circumstance may be even considered at odds with the principle of self-organization, also considering that the abovementioned CJEU ruling expressly confirmed the exemption granted by Article 17, paragraph 1 of Directive n.

37. R. Krause, "Always-on": The Collapse of the Work-Life Separation in Recent Developments, Deficits and Counter-Strategies, in E. Ales, et al. (eds.), *Working in Digital and Smart Organizations. Legal, Economic and Organizational Perspectives on the Digitalization of Labour Relations*, Palgrave Macmillan, Cham, 2018, 223.
38. T. Fabbri, Digital Work: An Organizational Perspective, in E. Ales, et al. (eds.), *Working in Digital and Smart Organizations. Legal, Economic and Organizational Perspectives on the Digitalization of Labour Relations*, Palgrave Macmillan, Cham, 2018, 37.
39. CJEU C-55/18 of 14 May 2019, *Federación de Servicios de Comisiones Obreras (CCOO)*, ECLI:EU:C:2019:402.
40. *Ibid.*, 50.

2003/88 to the cases in which "on account of the specific characteristics of the activity concerned, the duration of the working time is not measured and/or predetermined *or can be determined by the workers themselves*"[41] (emphasis added).

Nevertheless, while the applicability of this exemption to the Italian "agile work" needs to be further investigated in the light of the real degree of worker's self-determination permitted by the legislation in force, it must be stressed that the Court also reaffirmed that the general principles of health and safety protection have a universal scope. Against such background, time measurement may in practice represent a reasonable tool to protect the health and safety of flexible or agile workers, as an element of broader disconnection arrangements that may provide for the automatic and remote-operated disconnection of the worker once the maximum time thresholds are met.[42]

Another consideration that may be inferred from the *CCOO* doctrine concerns the possibility granted by sophisticated distance-control devices to analytically measure the timing of the work performance with a view to maximizing its productivity. The Court has made it clear that measurement devices should be conceived as a means to protect the health and safety of workers under the terms of the Working Time Directive. As a result, one may argue that "hyper-metrics" systems based on the oppressive timing of the performance, as they betray the function of measurement devices as the Court understood it, contravene the purpose and the rationale of European Union working time legislation.

13.5 CONCLUSION: THE ELEMENTS OF A WIN-WIN REGULATORY APPROACH TO WORK RELATIONS IN THE ORGANIZATION 4.0

It is a widespread view that subordination as a contractual scheme is no longer capable of fulfilling, on the workers' side, the protective function traditionally attached to the employment contract. If this remark may be correct as long as the (formal) criteria for the classification of an employment relationship and the consequent (mis)allocation of protections among the different forms of work is concerned, it seems possible to argue that the (substantive) mechanisms set in force under the subordinate employment contract to protect the interests of the workers are still valid.

As this chapter has attempted to demonstrate, those mechanisms only need an update, to re-align with the actual interests of the workers as the changing technological and organizational paradigms are reshaping them. Along such a pathway, the premises of a win-win regulation could be set.

For this purpose, it is necessary first of all to reaffirm the accountability of employers for the consequences of technological changes on employment conditions, on the grounds that those changes are closely related with managerial decisions and with the dominant role played by entrepreneurs in the organization. Hence, the digital transformation should not be conceived as an opportunity to shift towards the workers

41. *Ibid.*, 63.
42. M. Peruzzi, Sicurezza e agilità: quale tutela per lo smart worker?, in *Diritto della Sicurezza sul Lavoro*, 2017, 1, 1.

the responsibilities and the risks normally attached to the exercise of an economic activity.

Several interpretations have been proposed to update the conceptual premises of the employer's accountability: to name but a few, one can mention the shift from the concept of workplace to the concept of "work environment," as to boost an effective approach to health and safety issues in "dematerialized" organizations;[43] the possibility to bring back to the employers' sphere any fact involving the worker that presents a connection with a managerial decision, for instance as long as the work-life divide is concerned, so that if any "personal activity has some tangible connection to the employer's goals, it can become job-related such that employer liability may attach";[44] the circumstance that the digital business exposes the worker to the social risks typically attached to an employment relationship.[45]

On the other hand, the digital transformation opens up an array of opportunities for a real improvement of working conditions. Hence, any approach aimed at tackling the problems raised by the new phenomena with a merely defensive attitude may prove to be shortsighted. The conceptual framework of decent work and human rights protection, that is frequently advocated in this context, makes a crucial point but should represent an intermediate objective of regulation rather than its final goal. It should be possible, in the pursuit of a win-win approach, increase the quality of work going beyond the established standards.

This is one of the circumstances in which the guiding principle of regulation should be to grant workers a real freedom of choice in respect of the opportunities offered by digitization and automation: a freedom that may in turn lead to replace the general workplace regulations with customized individual arrangements, once the fundamental rights are safeguarded. This requires that, in cases where a managerial decision does not threaten the fundamental rights of workers, but conversely bears the potential to bring them an added value (for instance as it opens up opportunity for a professional advancement or for a better work-life balance), specific provisions should be in force (either of a substantive or of a procedural nature) to ensure that the individual agreement that accompanies such decision is the outcome of a genuine negotiation, or at least has been accepted by the worker in the context of a free appreciation of his/her interests.

In this field, a mixed regulatory technique based on the combination of imperative and responsive rules could be experimented. Rules of the first kind should aim at guaranteeing the fundamental rights of the workers, so that those rights are not hindered by the managerial decisions aimed at optimizing the operations of digital

43. E. Ales, Protecting Work in the Digital Transformation: Rethinking the Typological Approach in the Intrinsically Triangular Relationship Perspective, in E. Ales, et al. (eds.), *Working in Digital and Smart Organizations. Legal, Economic and Organizational Perspectives on the Digitalization of Labour Relations*, Palgrave Macmillan, Cham, 2018, 11.
44. L.F. Eisenstadt, Employer or Big Brother? Data Analytics and Incursions into Workers' Personal Lives, in T. Addabbo, et al. (eds.), *Performance Appraisal in Modern Employment Relations. An Interdisciplinary Approach, Palgrave Macmillan*, Cham, 2019, 165, 181.
45. P. Loi, Subordinazione e autonomia nel lavoro tramite piattaforma attraverso la prospettiva del rischio, in G. Zilio Grandi, M. Biasi (eds.), *Commentario breve allo statuto del lavoro autonomo e del lavoro agile*, Wolters Kluwer-Cedam, Milano, 2018, 113.

organizations (in other words, as the capability approach would put it, to safeguard the worker's "freedom as nondomination"[46]). Rules of the second kind should instead aim at unleashing the workers' "positive freedom" potentially embedded in the new workplace patterns.

A paramount role among the agents of regulation could be played by industrial relations practices, like the involvement of employees in the company's strategic and operational decisions and collective bargaining.[47] In particular, it is undeniable that collective bargaining has a crucial regulatory potential, as it could bring the necessary degree of normative flexibility in a context where, at the same time, the equality of power conditions is theoretically guaranteed.[48] However, it should not be overlooked that, in practice, often the trade unions might lack the strength to impose their conditions at the bargaining table, and thus a supportive intervention by the law may be required.

46. R. Del Punta, Is the Capability Theory an Adequate Normative Theory for Labour Law?, in B. Langille (ed.), *The Capability Approach to Labour Law*, OUP, Oxford, 2019, 83.
47. As other contributions in this book deal with into detail. In the same direction goes the initiative of the European Social Partners that signed in June 2020 a Framework Agreement on Digitalization. The Agreement is focused on four target-topics: "Digital Skills and Securing Employment," "Modalities of connecting and disconnecting," "Artificial Intelligence (AI) and guaranteeing the human in control principle," "Respect of human dignity and surveillance."
48. N. Contouris, V. De Stefano, *New Trade Union Strategies for New Forms of Employment*, ETUC, Brussels, 2019.

CHAPTER 14

The Impact of Digitalisation on Individual Labour Relations: Working Time as an Outdated Concept?

Iva Bjelinski Radić

14.1 INTRODUCTION

Digital revolution is characterised by the widespread use of digital technologies in the various aspects of human activity, whereby it tends to profoundly transform our society in economic, social and political sense. In the recent academic literature the possible impacts of digitalisation on the world of work are widely debated. In relation thereto different authors emphasise various key drivers with the potential to transform work and employment. Eurofound,[1] for example, identifies three vectors of change, namely automation of work,[2] digitalisation of processes[3] and coordination by platforms.[4]

On the basis of the literature review in this area, I believe that numerous implications of digitalisation on the world of work can roughly be divided into three basic categories. The first category refers to the impact of digitalisation on labour market. In that respect some of the most significant macroeconomic trends affecting

1. *See* the detailed discussion in Eurofound (2018), *Automation, digitalisation and platforms: Implications for work and employment*, Publications Office of the European Union, Luxembourg.
2. Automation of work implies the replacement of the human labour input by (digitally enabled) machine input for some types of tasks within production and distribution processes.
3. Digitalisation of processes is the use of sensors and rendering devices to translate (parts of) the physical production process into digital information and vice versa, and thus taking advantage of the greatly enhanced possibilities of processing, storage and communication of digital information.
4. Coordination by platforms implies the use of digital networks to coordinate economic transactions in an algorithmic way.

modern labour markets include especially job destruction and job losses, creation of new jobs, demand for new skills, labour market polarisation and emergence of the new forms of employment.[5]

The second category encompasses the effects of digitalisation on labour relations, both individual and collective. Namely, digitalisation affects labour relations in traditional businesses and industries, because it significantly changes the organisation of work. On the other hand, digital technologies also played the key role in enabling emergence of the platform work as a new form of economic activity. The emergence of platform work has led to uncertainties surrounding the employment relationship of platform workers and specific challenges with regard to their working conditions.[6]

Finally, the third category includes the impact of digitalisation on the social security systems. This implies new challenges for the existing social security systems arising from the changes in the concept of work as a consequence of digitalisation.[7]

The limited scope of this chapter does not allow the detailed analysis of all three proposed categories of implications of digitalisation on the world of work. Therefore, the central topic of this chapter is the impact of digitalisation on individual labour relations in traditional businesses and industries. As already mentioned, new forms of work organisation which have originated as a result of digitalisation may pose new challenges to the regulation and protection of workers. Hence, it is necessary to identify the main features of the new way of work organisation, as well as the main labour law issues arising therefrom.

This chapter is organised into four sections. After this introduction, in the second section the impact of digitalisation on individual labour relations is shortly described. The third section focuses on the specific working time issues arising in the digital era. Concluding remarks are provided in the fourth section.

5. *See*, for example, the following studies: (i) C.B. Frey and M.A. Osborne, *The future of employment: How susceptible are jobs to computerization?*, 2013, https://www.oxfordmartin.ox.ac.uk/downloads/academic/The_Future_of_Employment.pdf (accessed 8 November 2019); (ii) European Commission, *Employment and social developments in Europe, Annual review 2016*, 2016, Publications Office of the European Union, Luxembourg, https://ec.europa.eu/social/main.jsp?langId=en&catId=89&newsId=2704&furtherNews=yes& (accessed 8 November 2019); (iii) C. Degryse, *Digitalisation of the economy and its impacts on labour market*, working paper 2016.02, ETUI aisbl, Brussels, 2016, https://www.etui.org/Publications2/Working-Papers/Digitalisation-of-the-economy-and-its-impact-on-labour-markets (accessed 8 November 2019).
6. Further on the topic of platform work, *see*, for example, in: (i) J. Prassl, *Humans as a service: The promise and perils of work in the gig-economy*, Oxford: Oxford University Press, 2018; (ii) V. De Stefano, *The Rise of the 'Just-in-Time Workforce': On-Demand Work, Crowdwork, and Labor Protection in the 'Gig Economy'*, Comparative Labor Law & Policy Journal, vol. 37, no. 3, 2016; (iii) J. Prassl and M. Risak, *Uber, Taskrabbit, and co.: Platforms as employers? Rethinking the legal analysis of crowdwork*, Comparative Labor Law & Policy Journal, vol. 37, no. 3, 2016.
7. *See* more in P. Schoukens and A. Barrio, *The changing concept of work: When does typical work become atypical?*, European Labour Law Journal, vol. 8, no. 4, 2017, pp. 306-332.

14.2 THE IMPACT OF DIGITALISATION ON INDIVIDUAL LABOUR RELATIONS IN TRADITIONAL BUSINESSES AND INDUSTRIES

Widespread use of digital technologies in traditional businesses and industries significantly changes the organisation of work. Namely, digitalisation allows growing flexibility in respect of certain elements which form the content of an individual labour relationship. The mentioned flexibility manifests itself primarily as a change of the traditional notions of workplace and working time. Namely, flexible work organisation enabled by information and communication technologies (hereinafter: ICT) implies that physical workplace is becoming notably less important than before. Effective performance of work tasks is no longer bound by certain location.

In its well-known study on the new forms of employment Eurofound identified so-called ICT-based mobile work as a new work pattern supported by modern technologies.[8] According to Eurofound, ICT-based mobile work refers to work arrangements carried out at least partly, but regularly, outside the 'main office', be that the employer's premises or a customised home office, using ICT for online connection to shared company computer systems. Work takes place wherever and at any time it suits the work activities, business schedule and lifestyle of the worker, not necessarily at a specific place but also 'on the road'.[9] In the literature this work pattern is often referred to as 'smart work' or 'agile work'.[10]

Eurofound notes this is in fact a variation of teleworking. However, in contrast to traditional teleworking, ICT-based mobile workers do not work in another fixed location, but more flexibly, in various places or even on the road.[11] Ales suggests that in this case digitalisation of business produces the dematerialisation of the workplace.[12]

It should be pointed out that so-called dematerialisation of the workplace directly influences intensity of subordination of the employee to the employer, which is one of the key elements of an employment relationship.[13] Namely, now the employer and the employee are physically separated, therefore the employee enjoys a higher degree of autonomy compared with the traditional work organisation. The employer can no

8. Eurofound (2015), *New forms of employment*, Publications Office of the European Union, Luxembourg.
9. *Ibid.*, p. 72. According to the Eurofound's study it can be concluded that ICT-based mobile work it is not based on the new type of the employment contract, but it represents a new manner of work performance. Namely, Eurofound points out that such work is generally conducted on the basis of standard employment contracts, in most cases related to full-time positions of indefinite duration.
10. For example, *see* E. Ales, 'Protecting work in the digital transformation: Rethinking the typological approach in the intrinsically triangular relationship perspective', in E. Ales, et al. (eds), *Working in digital and smart organizations*, Cham: Palgrave Macmillan, 2018, p. 13.
11. Eurofound (2015), p. 73.
12. Ales claims that dematerialisation of the workplace pushes workers outside the undertaking or the establishment as physical places, while keeping them attached to the company as economic and legal entity. *See* more in Ales, pp. 13-17.
13. In Croatian labour law subordination can be inferred from Art. 7 of the Labour Act, which stipulates the fundamental obligations and rights arising from the employment relationship. Namely, Art. 7 sets out that the employee shall perform the work according to the instructions of the employer in line with the nature and type of work, whereby the employer shall be entitled

longer personally and continuously monitor quality and quantity of the performed work.[14] Some authors warn that physical separation which occurred due to digitalisation can have ambivalent consequences. This means that the employer may decide to exercise more or less control compared with the traditional work organisation.[15]

Taking into account the above-mentioned issues, it should be emphasised that further research is needed in order to determine whether the existing regulatory framework supports the changed reality of work organisation. Digitalisation allows working methods free from rigid respect of the place of work. Therefore, positive aspects of such flexibility should be encouraged, whereby the adequate regulation should be aimed at protecting health and safety of workers in the new work environment.

14.3 WORKING TIME ISSUES IN THE DIGITAL ERA

Apart from the changes regarding the workplace discussed in the previous chapter, digitalisation significantly affects working time organisation in traditional businesses and industries. The times during which work tasks are performed are becoming more flexible if workers can work on journeys, or from home.[16] In relation to that, in the recent literature the topic of blurring boundaries between work and private life is widely discussed. Some authors even describe the situation as the collapse of the work-life separation.[17]

As a starting point of the analysis of the working time issues arising with respect to ICT-based mobile workers, the specific features of the working time of such workers should be outlined. The recent studies demonstrate that a substantially higher share of ICT-based mobile workers enjoy a significant degree of working time autonomy than

---

to determine the place and manner of performance of work. Apart from subordination, other key elements of the employment relationship include voluntariness, personal work performance and remuneration.

See more in I. Grgurev, 'The Concept of Employee: The Position of Croatia', in B. Waas, et al. (eds), *Restatement of Labour Law in Europe Vol I: The Concept of Employee*, Oxford: Hart Publishing, 2017, pp. 59-83.

14. Eurofound observes that the companies introducing ICT-based mobile work either pay their staff based on results rather than working hours, or have technically advanced monitoring, such as systems that capture whether a worker is logged on to the company network and how long they work on each task. *See* Eurofound (2015), p. 77.
15. Ales, for example, explains that digitalisation enables the employer to enhance control on work performance by using IT-supported remote control devices. On the other hand, the employer may decide to reduce the intensity of control and to evaluate the performed work according to the results. *See* more in Ales, pp. 14-15.
16. European Economic and Social Committee (2017), *Impact of digitalisation and the on-demand economy on labour markets and the consequences for employment and industrial relation*, https://www.eesc.europa.eu/en/our-work/publications-other-work/publications/impact-digitalization-and-demand-economy-labour-markets-and-consequences-employment-and-industrial-relations (accessed 26 October 2019), p. 38.
17. For example, *see* R. Krause: '"Always-on": The collapse of the work-life separation in recent developments, Deficits and counter-strategies', in E. Ales, et al. (eds), *Working in digital and smart organizations*, Cham: Palgrave Macmillan, 2018.

their office-based counterparts. Namely, such workers usually have a wide discretion in relation to organisation of their working time.[18]

Moreover, the available evidence suggest that the above-mentioned type of work has the effect on both the duration and the organisation of working time. With respect to work duration, it seems that ICT-based mobile workers tend to work longer than those workers who always work at the employer's premises. In connection thereto, an important question arises whether such work is a substitute for regular work at the employer's premises, or a supplement to it. Eurofound and the International Labour Organisation (hereinafter: ILO) warn that the distinction between substitutional and supplemental working hours becomes blurred when it comes to ICT-based mobile work. The conclusion is reached that working outside the employer's premises using ICT appears to supplement normal working time to some extent, although this may or may not be required by the employer. Moreover, such supplemental work is often informal and unpaid.[19]

With respect to the organisation of working time the studies demonstrate that ICT-based mobile workers are more likely to work in the evenings and on weekends than 'office workers'.[20]

14.3.1 The Additional Work Beyond Regular Working Time

In light of the above-mentioned characteristics of the working time of ICT-based mobile workers, an immediate challenge arises for labour law. If there is supplemental work taking place beyond regular working time, whereby it may or may not be required by the employer, an important question is how to legally qualify such work. We start from the hypothesis that such additional work shall be regarded as working time within the meaning of the European Union law (hereinafter: EU law), as well as the Croatian national labour law.

The question of classification of such additional work is especially important if we take into account the main purpose of the existing limitations of working hours – being an occupational health and safety mechanism, as well as a factor enabling workers to achieve work-life balance. Therefore, there is a realistic danger that the described work extensions could have detrimental effect on workers' physical and mental health and ability to organise their free time.[21]

18. Eurofound and the International Labour Office (2017), *Working anytime, anywhere: The effects on the world of work*, Publication Office of the European Union, Luxembourg, and the International Labour Office, Geneva, p. 25.
19. *Ibid.*, pp. 21-25.
20. *Ibid.*
21. For example, *see* the recent ILO study demonstrating negative consequences of working time which exceeds forty-eight hours per week: International Labour Office (2012), *Working Time, Health and Safety: A Research Synthesis Paper*, Conditions of Work and Employment Series No. 31, International Labour Office, Geneva, pp. 16-19.

14.3.1.1 The Existing Regulatory Framework

On the EU level the most important source of secondary legislation regulating the working time matter is the Directive 2003/88/EC concerning certain aspects of the organisation of working time (hereinafter: WTD). The WTD lays down minimum requirements with regard to the organisation of working time, with the aim of ensuring a better level of health and safety protection for workers.[22] Concerning the concept of working time, it is important to notice that WTD adopts a binary conception, whereby there are only two mutually exclusive categories 'working time' and 'rest periods'.

Article 2(1) of the WTD defines working time as 'any period during which the worker is working, at the employer's disposal and carrying out his activity or duties, in accordance with national laws and/or practice'. This definition implies that working time has three elements, being any period: (i) during which the worker is working; (ii) at the employer's disposal and (iii) carrying out his activities or duties in accordance with the national law and/or practice.[23] On the other hand, rest period is negatively defined as 'any period which is not working time'. Defining the precise scope of the notion of working time is crucial for application of the rights guaranteed by WTD, i.e., maximum weekly working time and reference periods, daily and weekly rest breaks and rest periods, etc.

It should be pointed out that the Court of Justice (hereinafter: the Court) ruled that all three elements of the working time definition provided in Article 2(1) of the WTD have to be cumulatively met, whereby it has interpreted the third element in a very broad sense.[24] Namely, in its famous cases *Simap*[25] and *Jaeger,*[26] the Court made a distinction between on-call time and standby time. Both cases concerned the question of whether the whole or part of the time spent by doctors 'on-call' should be regarded as 'working time' or 'rest period' for the purposes of WTD. In *Jaeger* the Court decided that on-call time, where the worker is required to be physically present at a place specified by his employer, must be regarded in its totality working time, even where the person concerned is permitted to rest at his place of work during the periods when his services are not required.[27] As opposed to that, standby time is the time during which the workers are not obliged to remain waiting in the place designated by the employer, but only to be reachable at any time by the employer (so that they may be called upon to perform their professional tasks). According to the case law of the Court, standby time is not considered working time but rather a rest period. In those circumstances, only time linked to actual performance of work will be regarded as working time within

22. *See* more on the background, purpose, scope of the WTD, as well as the limits and entitlements guaranteed by the WTD, in C. Barnard, *EU employment law*, 4th edition Oxford: Oxford University Press, 2012, pp. 533-559.
23. Similarly, in Barnard, p. 547.
24. *See* more in J. Kenner, *Re-evaluating the concept of working time: An analysis of recent case law*, Industrial Relations Journal, vol. 35, no. 6, 2004, pp. 593-594.
25. Court of Justice of the European Union, Judgment of 3 October 2000, *Simap*, C-303/98, ECLI:EU:C:2000:528.
26. Court of Justice of the European Union, Judgment of 9 September 2003, *Jaeger*, C-151/02, ECLI:EU:C:2003:437.
27. *Jaeger*, para. 71.

the meaning of WTD.[28] One can therefore conclude that the distinctive element between on-call time and standby time is the spatial criterion.[29]

The Croatian Labour Act[30] basically follows the working time concept established in the EU law and differentiates between working time and standby time. According to the Article 60 of the Labour Act, working time is defined as a period during which a worker is obliged to carry out tasks defined by the employer or available to carry out his duties, in accordance with the employer's instructions, at his workplace or another place determined by the employer.

On the other hand, standby time shall not be regarded as working time. It implies a period during which a worker is not working, but must be available and ready for possible call-in to work, should a need arise, whereby the worker is neither located at his workplace nor at another place determined by the employer. Because the quality of free time may be potentially compromised while on standby, the worker is entitled to standby pay.[31] The standby period, as well as standby pay, shall be regulated by the employment contract or collective agreement. Similar as the EU *acquis*, Croatian labour law considers the period during which the worker is actually performing work upon the employer's request as working time, regardless of whether the work is performed at the place determined by the employer or the place selected by the worker.[32]

14.3.1.2 Working Time or Not?

In the situation of performance of work by using ICT beyond the regular working times, which appears to be the reality for ICT-based mobile workers,[33] the most important question from the labour law perspective is whether such supplemental work constitutes working time or not. We can imagine an ICT-based mobile worker responding to a business e-mail in the evening at home, or arranging a meeting with the client for the next day using his or her mobile phone, or preparing a written report for his or her boss. Some authors warn that modern results-oriented 'working culture' makes the situation far more complex. Namely, there is a clear trend of delimited work, whereby the workers themselves might also have internal motives to work more, either because

28. The Court argued that the workers who are obliged to be on standby may pursue their own interests and stay in their families/social environment, therefore they can manage their time with fewer constraints than the workers who are required to be physically present at a place specified by his employer (on-call time). *See Simap*, para. 50.
29. However, the Court has recently modified it approach ruling that standby time which a worker spends at home with the duty to respond to calls from his employer within 8 minutes, very significantly restricting the opportunities for other activities, must be regarded as 'working time'. *See* Court of Justice of the European Union, Judgment of 21 February 2018, *Matzak*, C-518/15, ECLI:EU:C:2018:82, paras 63-66.
30. Labour Act (*Zakon o radu*), Official Gazette Nos 94/2014 and 127/2017.
31. I. Grgurev and I. Vukorepa, 'Working time in Croatia: Critical analysis of legal framework', in T. Geiser and R. Müller (eds), *Arbeitszeiten in Europa (Working Time in Europe)*, Zürich/St. Gallen: Dike Verlag AG, 2015, p. 133.
32. Article 60 of the Labour Act.
33. *See* above under section 14.3.

they feel such behaviour is expected from them or because they do not perceive it as 'real work'.[34]

Regardless of the reasons for such additional work, it should be assessed whether it fits into the existing legal framework. Therefore, the analysis encompasses the three criteria listed in the working time definition in the Article 2(1) of the WTD. With respect to the third criterion, i.e., the need for the worker to be carrying out his activities or duties, one can conclude that it is definitely met. Namely, a worker who performs the described supplemental work using ICTs is without any doubt actively working. Furthermore, I am of the opinion that in these situations it is irrelevant whether a worker performs such work at the workplace or outside the office (e.g., at home or in a coffee shop). Namely, the absence of the fixed workplace is an integral part of being an ICT-based mobile worker,[35] therefore a place of work cannot be reduced to the physical presence in the employer's premises.

However, it might be problematic to determine whether the second criterion is satisfied, which requires the worker to be at the disposal of the employer. According to Advocate General Bot, this criterion implies an ongoing relationship in which the worker is subordinate to the employer. In legal terms, it is a situation characterised by the fact that the worker is subject to the instructions and organisational power of his employer, irrespective of where that worker is.[36] As already stated in the paragraph 3, the available evidence demonstrate that such supplemental work may or may not be required by the employer. Moreover, it is often informal and unpaid. Hence, it appears that the decisive factor in classification as working time or rest period should be the question whether the work is performed within the employer's sphere of influence. The real problem is a practical one. Namely, it might be very difficult to assess whether a worker is working beyond regular working time exclusively on his or her own initiative (e.g., constantly checking e-mails on his or her mobile phone or contacting clients late in the evening) or there was at least indirect initiative or tacit approval by the employer. In these specific circumstances it is unrealistic to expect that the employer would always (or even usually) explicitly order such supplemental work. Therefore, a broader context of the employer's behaviour should be taken into account in order to prove the existence of the employer's authority, for example, whether the employer accepted the results of work knowing it was completed late at night beyond regular working time.

Consequently, one can conclude that such additional work beyond regular working time shall be regarded as working time within the meaning of the EU law, as well as the Croatian national labour law, in all situations when the work is carried out under at least indirect or implicit control of the employer. This implies application of WTD provisions on delimitation of maximum weekly working time and the entitlements to rest periods.[37] In relation thereto, Krause emphasises the specific problem concerning very short interruptions of the rest periods (e.g., checking e-mails in five

34. For the discussion on the reasons behind this phenomenon *see* Krause, pp. 237-239.
35. *See* above under section 14.2.
36. Advocate General Bot, 2015, Opinion in Case *Tyco*, C-266/14, ECLI:EU:C:2015:391, paras 39-41.
37. Articles 3-6 of the WTD.

minutes), which pursuant to the existing law causes the consequence that the eleven-hour rest period starts again.[38]

It should also be pointed out that legal regulation of organisation of working time in Croatia is even more rigid compared to the provisions of WTD, whereby very complex and unclear provisions of the Labour Act do not provide the necessary level of flexibility.[39] Apart from the employer's duty to enable minimum rest periods, qualification of such work as working time in Croatian law implies an obligation to pay overtime work, as well as to comply with formal requirements related to overtime work.[40] Therefore, it is to be expected that effective enforcement of the existing working time regulations might be very challenging in case of the ICT-based mobile work. However, in my opinion such fear does not alter the legal nature of the additional work in question. It is up to the employer to put in place the necessary monitoring procedures to ensure compliance with the existing regulation. On the other hand, the difficulties in enforcement might accelerate discussion on the need of adjusting the rigid working time legislation to the changed reality of work performance.

14.3.2 Permanent Availability of ICT-Based Mobile Workers

Apart from the issue discussed in the previous chapter, another specific feature of ICT-based mobile work undermines an application of the existing working time legal framework to those workers. Namely, there is an issue of permanent availability of such workers. Risak notes that, as a direct consequence of digitalisation, an increasing number of workers are more or less permanently on standby being provided smartphones by their employers.[41] Although there is a broad spectrum between different kinds of availability,[42] a few general observations regarding permanent availability should be made from a working time perspective.

First, in my view a simplified definition of (permanent) availability covers the times when the worker is not actually working but, explicitly or implicitly,[43] required to be available via ICTs. Second, in a situation when there are only two mutually exclusive categories in the WTD and Croatian Labour Act, such periods have to be qualified as rest periods. Namely, due to the fact that the worker here is not obliged to

38. Krause, p. 235.
39. For an overview of the main provisions of the Labour Act regarding organisation of working time, rest periods and leave, *see* Grgurev and Vukorepa, pp. 131-136.
40. According to Art. 65 of the Labour Act, overtime work is allowed only in the case of *force majeure*, an extraordinary increase of the scope of work and in other similar cases of a pressing need, whereby it must be ordered in form of a written request before overtime work begins. There is a weekly limit of working time including overtime work (50 hours per week), as well as yearly maximum of 180 hours (or 250 hours if stipulated in a collective agreement).
41. M. Risak, *The scope of working time directive: Perspectives and challenges*, Working Paper, Annual Conference of the European Centre of Expertise in the field of Labour Law, Employment and Labour Market Policies, 2017, p. 8.
42. For the discussion, *see* Krause, pp. 235-237.
43. Krause explains that in situations with a lack of clear contractual arrangements, the features of ICTs promote the existence of grey areas of implicit expectations of both employer and worker that the worker is available to be contacted by the employer or by other person. Krause, p. 237.

remain waiting in the place designated by the employer, but only to be reachable by the employer, the situation falls under the category of standby time.[44]

Taking into account the real factual situation of being permanently available, one can claim that the existing working time legislation clearly fails to appropriately regulate permanent availability of ICT-based mobile workers. It is indeed questionable whether the spatial criterion as a distinctive element between on-call time and standby time is still a good choice when it comes to ICT-based mobile workers. Namely, as the absence of the fixed workplace determined by the employer is an integral part of being an ICT-based mobile worker, it is problematic to link the legal qualification of worker's availability period with the physical location of such worker. Hence, there are already some ideas in the recent legal literature to introduce a 'third time' as a new category between working time and rest periods.[45]

Moreover, although the worker on standby is clearly not working, the fact that availability via ICTs in now virtually permanent calls for the approach to the standby time from a new angle. An original court's argument in *Simap* for qualifying standby time as rest period implied that the workers who are obliged to be on standby may pursue their own interests and stay in their families or social environment, therefore they can manage their time with fewer constraints than the workers who are required to be physically present at a place specified by the employer (on-call time). One can argue this is not the case anymore when it comes to permanent availability via ICTs. In my view, permanent character of availability seriously undermines health and safety objective of the WTD and might also have detrimental consequences for family and social life of the worker. Therefore, a legislative action aimed at regulating and limiting availability of workers via ICTs shall be considered.[46]

14.4 CONCLUSION

The analysis provided in this chapter demonstrates that the widespread use of digital technologies in traditional businesses and industries allows growing flexibility in respect of workplace and working time.

From a working time perspective, ineffective enforcement of the existing regulations and/or inadequate regulation were identified as the main issues for the ICT-based mobile workers. The first problem refers to the additional work beyond regular working time using the ICTs. Although such work can in many cases be qualified as working time, effective enforcement of the existing working time regulations might be very challenging.

44. *See* above under section 14.3.1.1.
45. *See* Krause, pp. 241-242. Moreover, Risak notes that in this context the interruptions of rest periods are problematic, since workers with smartphones are regularly contacted by text-messages or e-mail. On the other hand, WTD explicitly states that daily rest periods have to be uninterrupted. *See* Risak, p. 8.
46. In that respect, it is worth mentioning that in 2017 the French legislator introduced a 'right to disconnection', intended as a response to the so-called always-on work culture that has led to a surge in usually unpaid overtime, and in some cases burnout https://www.bbc.com/news/world-europe-38479439 (accessed 29 October 2019).

On the other hand, permanent availability of modern workers does not seem to fit easily into the existing mutually exclusive categories, namely working time and rest periods. In light of the idea of working time regulation as primarily health and safety mechanism, further research is needed in order to determine the most appropriate measures aimed at adjusting working time legislation to the changed reality of work performance.

Part IV Institutional Aspects of Regulation: Between European Sources and Collective Bargaining

CHAPTER 15

Adapting Labor Law to "Digital" Work: Between Scholarly Interpretation, Case Law and Legislative Intervention

Edoardo Ales

15.1 INTRODUCTION

Labor Law, European Union (EU) included, has made the *undertaking* and the *establishment*, as physical and material, hetero-determined and hetero-organized aggregations of a certain number of workers, decisive for the definition of its subjective and objective scope of application, i.e., the entitlement to individual and collective rights.[1] In such a perspective, one can wonder whether the "dematerialization" of the workplace as a consequence of "digitalization" is likely to make such a selective criterion unfit to the purpose. It does not seem to be the case since one can look at both the *undertaking* and the *establishment* also as *juridical perimeters* of the "work community" relevant for Labor Law. In the same way, the notion of *integration into an alien organization* can still be relevant and effective if one emphasizes the *immaterial aspect* of organization, to be understood as *organizational function*.

Nevertheless, as any organizational change, the "digitalization" of the employment relationship is likely to confront Labor Law with some serious *adaptation problems* just as far as its scope of application, i.e., the entitlement to individual and collective rights are concerned.

The aim of this chapter is to address some of the issues that have stimulated the most scholarly and judicial reflection, investigating whether Labor Law can be adapted

1. *See*, for instance, the scope of application of dismissal law or of workers representatives' regulations.

by way of judicial or scholarly interpretation or if a legislative intervention at EU level is needed.

15.2 EMPLOYMENT STATUS

The changes that "digitalization" may produce in the way work is performed risk to reduce significantly the scope of application of Labor Law if it keeps on referring to *subordination* in the traditional meaning of *hetero-direction*.

In fact, making the exercise of managerial prerogatives in terms of "command and control" more difficult if not impossible, "digitalization" is likely to accelerate the process, already underway, of *"autonomization" of subordination*. By "autonomization," we mean that subordination is not necessarily characterized anymore by *hetero-direction*, as it "substantiates in the issuing of detailed orders referred to the specific activity performed, other than general guidelines, in a continuous and mandatory direction as well as a constant control, in an impingement apt to demean worker's autonomy."[2]

Within the "autonomized" subordination perspective, what is at stake is the "achievement of an individual or collective goal, designed by the employer that, although contributing to the accomplishment of the mission of the organization as a whole, does not coincide with it. Therefore, unlike autonomous work, the 'autonomized' worker does not bear the entrepreneurial risk, which is borne by the organizer as somebody profiting or enduring the losses of the relevant organization."[3]

Typifying "autonomized" subordination is everything but easy. It entails the proposal of an alternative to hetero-direction as qualifying condition of entitlement to Labor Law protection. As already proposed, "the most reasonable solution would be to deprive hetero-direction of the exclusivity as condition of entitlement, advocating rather for its substitution, in case of 'autonomized' work, with the notion of (immaterial) integration within the organization (as function) in the view of contributing to the accomplishment of the mission as designed by the organizer, who bears its risk."[4]

By consequence, "autonomized" work will remain in the boundaries of subordination that, at turn, shall be re-interpreted in the view of the *immaterial integration* within the *organization as function*, moving from *hetero-direction* towards *hetero-organization*, in cases in which the object of the employment contract substantiates in the performance/provision of a *result-oriented/service-like* activity.[5]

Therefore, if one sees *hetero-organization* as the main feature of "autonomized" subordination, the contract of employment could apply to "digital" work even if performed outside *hetero-direction* as typical of "strict" subordination, in which the employer molds the performance of the worker through continuous "command and control." What remains of subordination and justifies the application of its protective

2. Corte costituzionale, April 15, 2015, n. 76.
3. Ales E., *Subordination at Risk (of "Autonomisation"): Evidences and Solutions from Three European Countries*, in *ILLeJ*, 12(1), 2019, 66.
4. *Ibid.*, 67.
5. Menegatti E., *The Evolving Concept of "Worker" in EU law*, in *ILLeJ*, 12(1), 2019, 71.

statute is the fact the employer unilaterally decides the forms of coordination, limiting worker's self-organization capacity, although profiting from his or her autonomy in performing/providing in a *result-oriented/service-like* perspective.[6]

On the other hand, "autonomized" subordination does not seem to be compatible with the possibility of the worker to refuse/renounce at will to perform the tasks (provide the service) agreed upon as the latter play a substantive role in the achievement of the organizational goals as unilaterally defined by the entrepreneur/employer. Recently regulating riders' activity,[7] the Italian legislator has shared such a view by qualifying them self-employed whose work relationship cannot be terminated in case of refusal of an assignment proposed by the principal. On the contrary, quite surprisingly, the *Corte di cassazione*,[8] referring to a dispute occurred before the entry into force of the just mentioned legislation although decided after it, has concluded in favor of *hetero-organization* of riders, probably because this allows recognizing them (at least part of) the same protective statute attached to subordination.

Adopting a hybrid solution, the Italian legislator has intervened on riders' working conditions, in particular on remuneration, prohibiting it to be defined with reference to the assignment (piecework) if not so provided by collective agreements signed by comparatively most representative trade unions and employers organizations. In case of lack of collective regulation, riders shall be entitled to an hourly remuneration set taking into account the rates of pay provided by collective agreements signed by comparatively most representative trade unions and employers organizations that apply to similar branches.

One can doubt whether such a hybrid solution is compatible with EU Competition Law as interpreted by the Court of Justice with reference to the regulation of self-employed remuneration by collective agreements, unless one looks at riders as false self-employed in the meaning of *FNV*.[9] However, the fact that they can refuse at will the assignment proposed by the principal seems to exclude riders from being service providers in a situation comparable to that of workers who performed the same activity as an employer's employed workers, as required by the Court so that a collective agreement does not fall within the scope of application of Article 101(1) TFEU. This conclusion seems to be confirmed by the Court in Yodel, in which the independence of a courier has not be deemed to be fictitious, among the others because of his "absolute right not to accept the tasks assigned to him. In addition, he may himself set a binding limit on the number of tasks which he is prepared to perform."[10]

To conclude on this point, an interpretative tool such as "autonomized" subordination can help in including "digital" work in the realm of employment if the way in

6. Ales E., Is Performance Appraisal Compatible with the Employment Relationship? A Conclusive Plea in Favour of an Achievement-Oriented Approach to Work Organisation, in Addabbo T., et al. (eds.), *Performance Appraisal in Modern Employment Relations. An Interdisciplinary Approach*, London, 2019, pp. 255-262.
7. Decree-law September 3, 2019, n. 101, converted into Act November 2, 2019, n. 128, which has introduced Arts. 47-*bis* and ff. into Legislative Decree n. 81 of 2015.
8. Corte di cassazione, January 24, 2020, n. 1663.
9. CJEU, December 4, 2014, C-413/13, *FNV*, para. 42.
10. CJEU, 22 April 2020, C-692/19, *Yodel*, para. 40.

which is it performed corresponds to the idea of hetero-organization, thus limiting the self-determination of the worker to the extent that he or she is not allowed to refuse at will the assignment. Somebody who can refuse an assignment and who, on top of that, is protected against the termination of the relationship on the ground of that refusal cannot be looked at as a subordinate (though "autonomized"/hetero-organized) worker and looks more like a self-employed.

15.3 WORKING TIME IN THE HEALTH AND SAFETY PERSPECTIVE

As it should have been made clear in the above, "autonomized" subordination is triggered by an entrepreneurial choice and entails a substantive change in the way in which the employer can exercise his or her managerial prerogatives. Among the others, renouncing to "command and control" is likely to make *working time*, its measurement and its respect as contractual duties' discharge criterion unfit to the purpose. However, as shown by a paramount case recently decided by the Court of Justice on overtime, remaining within the legal boundaries of the employment relationship, employees can still be interested in a "traditional" (and even more stringent) arrangement of working conditions.[11]

In *CCOO*, the Court has been asked by the Spanish *Audiencia Nacional* whether Directive 2003/88/EC,[12] read in conjunction with Directive 89/391/EC[13] and Article 31(2) of the EU Charter of Fundamental Rights, must be interpreted as precluding a law that[14] "does not require employers to set up a *system enabling the duration of time worked each day by each worker to be measured*."[15]

Answering the question, the Court stressed the necessity of interpreting EU secondary law (Directives 2003/88/EC and 89/391/EC) "having regard to the importance of the fundamental right of every worker to a limitation on the maximum number of working hours and to daily and weekly rest periods" (Article 31(2) CFREU).[16]

In such a perspective, on the one hand, the Court admits that Directive 2003/88/EC, within the framework of partial harmonization, does not establish the *specific arrangements* by which the Member States must ensure the implementation of the rights that it lays down, leaving them, in their discretion, to take the *measures necessary* to that effect.[17] On the other hand, the Court emphasizes the need that "workers actually benefit from the minimum daily and weekly rest periods and the limitation on the duration of average weekly working time."[18]

On top of that, the Court recalls that the worker must be regarded as the "weaker party in the employment relationship" and that it is therefore "necessary to prevent the

11. CJEU, May 14, 2019, C-55/18, *CCOO*.
12. Articles 3, 5, 6, 16 and 22.
13. Article 4(1), Article 11(3) and Article 16(3).
14. According to the interpretation given to it by national case law.
15. *CCOO*, para. 29.
16. Ales E., *Article 31 CFREU:—Fair and Just Working Conditions*, in E. Ales, et al. (eds.) *International and European Labour Law*, Baden-Baden: Nomos—Hart—Beck, 2018, 1207.
17. *CCOO*, para. 41.
18. *CCOO*, para. 42.

employer from being in a position to impose a restriction of his rights on him."[19] Moreover, "on account of that position of weakness, a worker may be dissuaded from explicitly claiming his rights vis-à-vis his employer where, in particular, doing so may expose him to measures taken by the employer likely to affect the employment relationship in a manner detrimental to that worker."[20]

Therefore, according to the Court, in the absence of a *system enabling working time to be measured*, "it is not possible to determine objectively and reliably either the number of hours worked by the worker and when that work was done, or the number of hours worked beyond normal working hours, as overtime."[21] To the Court, "it appears to be excessively difficult, if not impossible in practice, for workers to ensure compliance with the rights conferred on them by Article 31(2) of the Charter and by Directive 2003/88/EC, with a view to actually benefiting from the limitation on weekly working time and minimum daily and weekly rest periods provided for by that Directive.[22]

Furthermore, in the view of the Court, a "national law which does not provide for an obligation to have recourse to an instrument that enables the objective and reliable determination of the number of hours worked each day and each week (...) *deprives both employers and workers of the possibility of verifying whether those rights are complied with and is therefore liable to compromise the objective of that directive, which is to ensure better protection of the safety and health of workers.*"[23]

Moreover, according to the Court, "such a system is necessary in order to enable worker representatives, who have a specific responsibility in respect of the protection of the safety and health of workers, to exercise their right, laid down in Article 11(3) of (the) directive, to ask the employer to take appropriate measures and to submit proposals to it."[24]

By consequence, "in order to ensure the effectiveness of those rights provided for in Directive 2003/88 and of the fundamental right enshrined in Article 31(2) of the Charter, the Member States *must require employers to set up an objective, reliable and accessible system enabling the duration of time worked each day by each worker to be measured.*"[25]

By so deciding, the Court seems to be in danger of dealing a fatal blow to "digitalization" (and smart work) or at least to their positioning within the boundaries of ("autonomized") subordination, pushing them outside it in the realm of self-employment.

However, reading carefully *CCOO*, one can find right there a solution offered by the Court itself when it argues that it is for the Member States, in the exercise of their discretion in that regard, to determine, the specific arrangements for implementing such a system. It applies, "in particular [to] the form that it must take, having regard,

19. *CCOO*, para. 44.
20. *CCOO*, para. 45.
21. *CCOO*, para. 47.
22. *CCOO*, para. 48.
23. *CCOO*, para. 50.
24. *CCOO*, para. 62.
25. *CCOO*, para. 60.

as necessary, to the particular characteristics of each sector of activity concerned, or the specific characteristics of certain undertakings concerning, inter alia, their size."

This, above all, "without prejudice to Article 17(1) of Directive 2003/88, which permits Member States, while having due regard for the general principles of the protection of the safety and health of workers, to derogate, inter alia, from Articles 3-6 of [the] directive, when, *on account of the specific characteristics of the activity concerned, the duration of the working time is not measured and/or predetermined or can be determined by the workers themselves*."[26]

Indeed, Article 17(1) Directive 2003/88/EC allows Member States to derogate daily rest, breaks, weekly rest period and annual leave provisions while guaranteeing, by different although equivalent means, health and safety. For digital workers, such goal can be achieved by recognizing them the right to disconnection, if they work online, or the self-determination of their working time, if they perform off-line.

Contrary to "autonomized" subordination as interpretative solution, the duty "*to set up an objective, reliable and accessible system enabling the duration of time worked each day by each worker to be measured*" can be derogated only by way of a legislative intervention providing for *alternative measures* aimed to guarantee the fundamental right to healthy and safe working conditions.

15.4 THE TRANSNATIONAL NATURE OF "DIGITAL" WORK

A further element that is likely to put Labor Law under pressure is that one of the (potential and probable) transnational nature of "digital" work, above all if performed through a platform.[27] This may cause difficulties in relation to the applicable legislation if the principle of territoriality keep on applying to Labor Law.

Unfortunately, although with all good intentions, the Court of Justice has recently provided a clear indication in this direction. In *Erzberger*,[28] the Court has been called to decide on one of the groundbreaking suits brought against the German codetermination model,[29] because it does not recognize the right to vote and stand for elections of *Aufsichtsräte* to workers employed in subsidiaries located outside Germany of an undertaking to which that system applies. Furthermore, if a member of an *Aufsichtsrat* moves (or is transferred) to such subsidiary he or she will lose his or her membership.

The *Kammergericht Berlin* has doubted whether it is "compatible with Article 18 TFEU … and Article 45 TFEU … for a Member State to grant the right to vote and to stand as a candidate for election as the workers' representatives in the supervisory

26. *CCOO*, para. 63.
27. According to the convincing definition of the Italian legislator, platforms are "programme and IT procedures used by the principal, that regardless of their place of establishment, are instrumental to the activity …, fixing its remuneration and defining the modality of execution of the performance." (Art. 47-*bis* (2) Legislative Decree n. 81 of 2015).
28. CJEU, July 18, 2017, C-566/15, *Erzberger*.
29. Krause R., *Zur Bedeutung des Unionsrechts für die unternehmerische Mitbestimmung*, in *AG*, 2012, 485.

body of a company only to those workers who are employed in establishments of the company or in affiliated companies that are within the national territory."[30]

In this respect, the Court notes that Treaty rules governing free movement of persons does not apply to activities, "which have no factor linking them with any of the situations governed by EU law." According to the Court, the fact that the subsidiary is controlled by a parent company established in a Member State other than that in which the subsidiary is established is not relevant in order to establish a link between the workers of that subsidiary with either of the situations contemplated by Article 45 TFEU.[31] Convincingly, freedom of movement is not at stake for those workers.

Less persuasive sounds the reasoning of the Court with reference to those workers of the group employed in Germany who leave that employment in order to be employed in a subsidiary belonging to the same group established in another Member State. After having confirmed that Article 45 TFEU "precludes any national measure which is capable of hindering or rendering less attractive the exercise by Union nationals of the fundamental freedoms guaranteed by that article," the Court makes a rather peculiar reference to its case law that excludes the neutrality, in terms of applicable social security system, of free movement of workers. This in the sense that "given the disparities between the Member States' social security schemes and legislation, such a move may be more or less advantageous for the person concerned in that regard."[32]

Without any further explanation, the Court extends this reasoning to the "conditions of employment" the worker enjoyed in the Member State of origin under the national legislation of the latter State,[33] forgetting the link that exists between the mother company and the subsidiary, above all in terms of *Aufsichtsrat*'s decision-making power on the destiny of the subsidiaries located abroad. The same qualification of the codetermination system as *condition of employment* does not seem to be entirely convincing, as that system refers more to the "representation and collective defence of interests, including co-determination" (Article 153(1)(f) TFEU) than to the position of the workers in the employment relationship with the subsidiary.

According to the Court, "in the absence of harmonisation or coordination measures at Union level in the field concerned (codetermination), the Member States remain, in principle, free to set the criteria for defining the scope of application of their legislation, to the extent that those criteria are objective and non-discriminatory."[34] Quite surprisingly, the Court offers no reflection on the "objective and non-discriminatory nature" of the "location abroad criterion" used by the German legislator, thus apodictically supporting the territoriality principle of Labor Law.[35] In fact, in the view of the Court, "EU law does not ... prevent a Member State from providing that

30. *Erzberger*, para. 21. Kammergericht Berlin October 16, 2015, 14 W 89/15 and, in the light of *Erzberger*, Kammergericht Berlin November 2, 2017, 14 W 89/15.
31. *Erzberger*, para. 28.
32. *Erzberger*, para. 34.
33. *Erzberger*, para. 35.
34. *Erzberger*, para. 36.
35. *Erzberger*, para. 38.

the legislation it has adopted be applicable only to workers employed by establishments located in its national territory." In the same way, "it is open to another Member State to rely on a different *linking factor* for the purposes of the application of its own national legislation."[36] Such a solution is justified by the fact that "the field of representation and collective defence of the interests of workers in the management or supervisory bodies of a company established under national law, ... to date, has not been harmonized or even coordinated at Union level ... ."[37]

The fact that "workers who, after having been granted a mandate as representative, during their period of employment in an establishment located in Germany, to the supervisory board of a German company, leave Germany in order to be employed by a company established in the territory of another Member State" are required "to give up the exercise of their mandate in Germany *is merely the consequence of the Federal Republic of Germany's legitimate choice to limit the application of its national legislation in the field of participation to workers employed by an establishment located in German territory.*"[38]

In absence of harmonization or coordination provisions at EU level, insisting on the physical location of the establishment as "objective and non-discriminatory criterion," the Court, as well as the national legislator, is likely to legitimize any organizational choice in favor of a *delocalization* of the ("digital") worker abroad, i.e., outside the territorial scope of application of national Labor Law. Depriving of any relevance the *immaterial link* represented by the belonging to the same group of undertaking means, as unintended consequence, to jeopardize the very possibility for delocalized ("digital") workers to invoke the law of the country of origin of their "real" employer and to favor the establishment of fictitious employers (platforms) in their country of establishment. The potential and actual negative impact on their "conditions of employment" is evident.

What would be desirable is an EU law intervention based on Article 153(1)(b) and (f), derogating, in case of work relationships with transnational elements, to the principle of territoriality of Labor Law, emphasizing any immaterial link to more favorable legislation on "working conditions" and "representation and collective defence of interests, including co-determination."

15.5 COLLECTIVE RIGHTS OF "DIGITAL" WORKERS

"Representation and collective defence of interests," to be understood in broad terms of the combination of workers, as spontaneous product of communication triggered by their *physical coexistence* and, in any case, by their *reciprocal interaction*, are further elements of Labor Law at risk to be problematized by "digitalization." Indeed, the *organizational fragmentation* (to the extreme of *isolation*) that can be one of the most relevant negative consequences of the "digitalization" is likely to jeopardize them.

36. *Erzberger*, para. 37.
37. *Ibid.*
38. *Erzberger*, para. 40.

On the other hand, even the combination "promoted" by the legislator through the recognition of the right of the workers to establish representative bodies within the undertaking risks to be put into discussion by the just criticized application of the *principle of territoriality*, as endorsed by the Court of Justice in *Erzberger*. The position of the Court is even more worrying if one considers the absence of any reference in its reasoning to the *transnational dimension* of the case that should have suggested taking a stance in relation to the role the European Works Councils Directive could have played in answering to the legitimate doubts of the referring judge. The fact that in *Erzberger* codetermination rights were at stake instead of information and consultation referred to in the EWC Directive does not constitute as such a sufficient ground of exclusion of the latter in the perspective of emphasizing the relevance the same EU Legislator has recognized to the *transnational dimension* of workers' representation.

The *organizational fragmentation* together with the application of the *principle of territoriality*, without any consideration of the *transnational dimension* of the employment relationship, is likely to have a chilling effect on the combination of "digital" workers, in the guise of both the spontaneous exercise of "freedom of association" and the "representation and collective defence of interest" within the undertaking.

In itself, the issue of workers' isolation is not new to the employment relationship, as made clear by the European Social Partners in the *Framework agreement on telework*, signed in 2002. According to it, "[t]he employer ensures that measures are taken preventing the teleworker from being isolated from the rest of the working community in the company, such as giving him/her the opportunity to meet with colleagues on a regular basis and access to company information" (paragraph 9(3)).

However, the duty of the employer to connect workers among each other is even more relevant for "digital" work, above all if performed through platform, since what is at risk is the same existence of the "*working community.*" Being aware of the differences between telework and "digital" work – in the sense that the latter does not require the worker to operate necessarily from a fix workstation, it could be a priority for the European Social Partner to review the 2002 Framework agreement in order to extend it to "digital" work and recognize such a duty to connect as well as a corresponding right of the worker to have a "*working community.*"

The European Social Dialogue would be an effective tool of intervention in facilitating "digital" workers' combination in the perspective of "freedom of association," as well known excluded from the competences of the EU Legislator (Article 153(5) TFEU).[39] On the other hand, a legislative intervention under the "representation and collective defence of interests" competence (Article 153(2)(f)) shall, in any case, be preceded by the activation of the European Social Partners (Article 154 TFEU), thus offering them the opportunity to recognize the duty/right to connection through "contractual relations, including agreements" (Article 155 TFEU).

39. Ales E., *Article 153 TFEU*, in E. Ales, et al. (eds.) *International and European Labour Law*, Baden-Baden: Nomos—Hart—Beck, 2018, 155.

On the other hand, workers' combination is not only something desirable in itself.[40] Making combination impossible is likely to make workers' *representation* impossible as well. Indeed, without the establishment of the employers' duty to connect and the workers' right to be connected among each other, the same opening remarks on the *undertaking* and the *establishment* as *juridical perimeters* of the "working community" and on the *immaterial aspect* of organization, to be understood as *organizational function*, will lose much of their sense.

The fact that combination is made so difficult or even impossible by the just mentioned factors should encourage to endorse the already proposed interpretation of the workers' right to be represented as a duty of the employer to have representation bodies established within the undertaking.[41] Indeed, this could constitute a viable solution in the view of guaranteeing a voice to "digital" workers as individuals as well as "working community," entitled to fundamental rights such as information and consultation (Article 27 CFREU). In a kind of virtuous circle, "representation and collective defence of interests" imposed by the Legislator can make combination, even as exercise of "freedom of association," possible and easier, at least for "digital" workers established within the EU. This is even more conceivable now that the Court of Justice has deemed the exercise of works councils' codetermination rights as falling within the scope of the fundamental right to collective bargaining.[42]

Moreover, the reference to the "appropriate level," at which the workers have the right to be informed, consulted and therefore represented, can constitute an important argument in order to reduce the impact of the principle of territoriality, by inducing the EU Legislator to focus on the undertaking or the establishment as (immaterial) *juridical perimeters* of the "working community." This is the only reference that seems to make sense in the "digital factory" perspective.

15.6 CONCLUSION: A BRIGHT FUTURE FOR "DIGITAL" WORKERS?

In its recent Communication "A strong Social Europe for just transitions,"[43] the European Commission has announced the adoption of "a new *Digital Services Act*," to be presented during the second semester of 2020, that "will upgrade [the] liability and safety rules for digital platforms, services and products, and complete [the] Digital Single Market." This could be a terrific chance –to regulate, alongside the technical and competition aspects, the Labor Law issues as highlighted in the above and shared by the same Commission when it comes to "employment status, working conditions and

40. *See* European Pillar of Social Rights, point 8. Ales E, *The European Pillar of Social Rights: An Ambitious "Soft-Law Guide" to Efficient Employment and Social Outcomes*, in R. Singer, T. Bazzani (eds.), *European Employment Policies: Current Challenges, Berliner Juristische Universitätsschriften*, Band 76, Berlin: BWV, 2017, 43.
41. Ales E., *Introduction: Workers' Involvement*, in E. Ales, et al. (eds.) *International and European Labour Law*, Baden-Baden: Nomos—Hart—Beck, 2018, 1534.
42. CJEU, April 4, 2019, C-699/17, *Allianz Vorsorgekasse*, 55.
43. European Commission, January 14, 2020, COM(2020) 14 final.

access to social protection of platform workers, access to collective representation and bargaining, as well as cross-border aspects of platform work."[44]

This can provide with some more effectiveness the *Platform Work Summit* the Commission has also announced in order "to discuss priority issues and possible solutions" for "digital" work. Without a legislative intervention or a strong action by the European Social Partners, also envisaged by the Commission,[45] the future of platform workers, as far as their fundamental right to "fair and just working conditions" (Article 31 CFREU) is concerned, does not seem to be particularly bright.

44. European Commission, 9.
45. *Ibid.*

CHAPTER 16

Platforms, Unions and Workers: Is Collective Bargaining Possible?

Alberto Pizzoferrato

16.1 PROTECTING THE VALUES OF DECENT WORK AND WORKERS' DIGNITY

Working through a digital platform has been designed to bring the supply and demand sides closer to each other and encourage users to use the service by reducing the costs for both companies that already work in the market and digital operators who want to enter new markets.

For companies that already work in the market, the platform is mainly a way to reduce the transaction costs; for operators who want to enter new markets, the purpose is to find staff *just in time,* to hire as independent contractors to meet the clients' requirements in a flexible way, depending on the level of demand on a case-by-case basis (delivery boys are a case in point), without mutual obligations, so that on one side workers are free not to answer calls made through the app, on the other side the company is free not to accept the service offered by a provider.

So the problem with companies already in the market is about adapting the protection system to the specific working method, but the context is the classic employer/employee relationship. For new companies, instead, the model is that of freelance work though intensely monitored and controlled by the company, so the worker still has wide power to organise the time and place where the service must be provided, so that the problem of social protection becomes remarkably more serious.

So, what have the main European legislators done to address such social issues that take inspiration from the fundamental values of *decent work* and *worker's dignity*?

First and foremost, as far as we know, no European national legislator has taken steps to lay down specific laws on such form of work. This is still governed by the general principles of 'abuse of the status of self-employed persons' and '*indisponibilità del tipo legale*' (non-availability of contractual legal type) as well as the European Union (EU) rules on free movement of workers, free provision of services and free competition. Article 101 TFEU establishes that companies cannot enter into agreements to prevent, restrict or distort competition. This includes agreements with trade unions in the interest of freelancers, given that they are really working on a freelance basis, in compliance with the national law, they do not work under the direction of an employer, which mainly means being free to choose the time, place and content of work, and not undertaking any business or financial risk, and given that they are not part of the manufacturing process of an employer during the term of the agreement as if they were one single business.[1]

After all, the EU has only recently dealt with *platform workers* in Directive of the European Parliament and of the Council on transparent and predictable working conditions in the European Union (Directive (EU) 2019/1152 of 20 June 2019). This, moreover, merely recognises the possibility that *platform workers* may fall within the scope of the Directive but only if they meet specific criteria and can therefore be defined as bogus freelancers, abusing the status of self-employment (Article 1, paragraph 2: 'This Directive lays down minimum rights that apply to every worker in the Union who has either an employment contract or employment relationship as defined by the law, or collective agreements or practice in force in each Member State with consideration to the case-law of the Court of Justice').[2] Therefore, the qualification of platform workers as *self-employed* is still on hold, because the provider is not obliged to perform the service, since platform workers are free to choose whether to answer a call or not; at least until the case will be better understood and could give reason to all the factual and organisational aspects of the job.

16.2 EU COMPETITIVE LAW INAPPLICABLE TO FALSE EMPLOYED AND DEPENDENT SELF-EMPLOYED

According to most platforms' terms and conditions, the platform business model is to operate powerful software applications ('apps') designed to match consumers who need a task done with entrepreneurs in search of their next 'gig'. Upon closer

1. Cf. Court of Justice, 4 December 2014, C-413/13, *FNV Kunsten Informatie en Media*, para. 36.
2. Recital 8 of the Directive states: 'In its case law, the Court of Justice of the European Union (Court of Justice) has established criteria for determining the status of a worker. The interpretation of the Court of Justice of those criteria should be taken into account in the implementation of this Directive. Provided that they fulfil those criteria, domestic workers, on-demand workers, intermittent workers, voucher based-workers, platform workers, trainees and apprentices could fall within the scope of this Directive. Genuinely self-employed persons should not fall within the scope of this Directive since they do not fulfil those criteria. The abuse of the status of self-employed persons, as defined in national law, either at national level or in cross-border situations, is a form of falsely declared work that is frequently associated with undeclared work. Bogus self-employment occurs when a person is declared to be self-employed while fulfilling the conditions characteristic of an employment relationship, in order to avoid certain legal or fiscal obligations. Such persons should fall within the scope of this Directive. The determination of the existence of an employment relationship should be guided by the facts relating to the actual performance of the work and not by the parties' description of the relationship'.

inspection, however, it quickly emerges that platforms offer much more than mere matchmaking services. They are in the business of *Digital Work Intermediation*.

This is the *Platform Paradox:* platform economy operators present themselves as marketplaces even though in reality they often act like traditional employers. Instead of passive matchmaking, platforms rely on rating systems and algorithmic control to ensure that each aspect of the worker's task is completed in compliance with company policy and customer instructions.

This Paradox plays a crucial role for purposes of EU law: in recent litigation, Uber suggested that its platform was an 'information society service' for purposes of the EU's electronic commerce directive. In Case C-434/15 *Asóciacion Profesional Elite Taxi v. Uber Systems Spain SL,* both Advocate General Szpunar and the Grand Chamber of the Court of Justice disagreed: given the tight control exercised over individual drivers, the company offered 'more than an intermediation service': indeed, the platform's 'intermediation service simultaneously offers urban transportation services' through its app.

While the context of the decision was not within the field of labour law, it is nonetheless an important precedent for present purposes: save where otherwise provided by Union Law, Member States retain domestic regulatory authority over platform operations. The judicial acknowledgment of tight platform control could also play an important role in litigation over disguised self-employment.

By the way, the question of antitrust limits to collective bargaining has continuously accompanied the collective initiatives aimed at bettering the conditions of self-employed and platform workers. In late 2014 the Court of Justice of the European Union (CJEU) issued a key judgment on this matter in Case C-413/13, *FNV Kunsten Informatie en Media*. The Dutch Union FNV had negotiated a collective agreement in favour of both employed and self-employed substitute orchestra players, also regarding their compensation. The Dutch antitrust authority had issued an opinion under which a collective bargaining agreement negotiated in favour of self-employed workers would not be excluded from antitrust law. The collective agreement of the orchestra player was then terminated, and the relevant employers' association refused to negotiate a new agreement. FNV started judicial proceedings to claim the legitimacy of such collective agreements, which led to a referral to the CJEU.

The Court of Justice held that collective bargaining agreements in favour of self-employed persons could not have immunity from competition law such as the one granted to collective bargaining in favour of employees under its 1999 *Albany* judgment. It also ruled, nonetheless, that both employees and the 'false-employed' are allowed to bargain collectively over their compensation under EU law.

It is essential, however, to clarify the meaning of 'false self-employed' workers in this context. The CJEU referred to the 'false self-employed' as those 'service providers in a situation comparable to that of employees'. The judgment also stated that 'the term "employee" for the purpose of EU law must itself be defined according to objective criteria that characterise the employment relationship' and recalled that under the CJEU's case law, 'the essential feature of that relationship is that for a certain period of time one person performs services for and under the direction of another person in return for which he receives remuneration'.

Reference to the 'direction' criterion may be misread as limiting the right to bargain collectively only to workers in an employment relationship defined under a strict test of control and subordination. If the notion of 'false self-employment' were to be construed accordingly, the exemption would apply only to blatant cases of employment misclassification, leaving outside the protection of collective labour rights multitudes of workers defined as self-employed workers under national legislations, including in countries like Austria, Germany, Italy and Spain where the law has long allowed some categories of self-employed persons to bargain collectively.

This notion of direction is based on independence from the market, as it focuses on the genuine financial and business autonomy of a subject rather than on the employment tests of control and subordination in the execution of work. Indeed, this is a more appropriate notion, suited to encompass workers that are dependent on their principals even if they do not qualify as employees under national laws. The need to look beyond these strict criteria is confirmed by a subsequent paragraph of *FNV Kunsten* where the Court states:

> the status of 'worker' within the meaning of EU law is not affected by the fact that a person has been hired as a self-employed person under national law, for tax, administrative or organisational reasons, as long as that person acts under the direction of the employer as regards, in particular, freedom to choose the time, place and content of the work, does not share in the employer's commercial risks, and, for the duration of that relationship, forms an integral part of that employer's undertaking, so forming an economic unit with that undertaking.

Arguably, these two paragraphs refer not only to the situation of workers formally classified as 'employees' according to the law of the respective Member States, but also to many workers that national laws may consider as self-employed. This is particularly relevant for many platform workers who are (correctly or wrongly) classified as self-employed workers.

The Court's approach still falls short of a real valorisation of freedom of association and collective bargaining as fundamental and human rights. It is clear that the CJEU's approach remains in many ways anchored to its earlier *Albany* decision. That judgment treated the recognition of collective bargaining of employees as an exception to the general antitrust principles, an approach arguably followed also by *FNV Kunsten. Albany*, however, was decided when collective bargaining was not yet recognised as a fundamental right under Article 28 of the Charter of Fundamental Rights of the EU, and a decade before the same Charter acquired the same legal values of the Treaties in 2009.

Importantly, given the relevance that the Treaty of Lisbon also assigns to the European Convention on Human Rights (ECHR), the *Albany* 'exception-to-rule' approach does not seem compatible with the case law of the Court of Strasbourg that treats the right to collective bargaining as an essential element of freedom of association under Article 11 of the ECHR and the importance assigned by this latter Court to the opinions of the International Labour Organization (ILO) supervisory bodies when the Court determines the scope of the ECHR protection of collective right. This is all the more relevant since the Court of Strasbourg also recognises the freedom of association of self-employed as protected under the Convention, and since the Charter of Fundamental Rights of the EU, in Article 52(3) also provides that 'In so far as this Charter contains rights which correspond to rights guaranteed by the Convention for the Protection of Human Rights and Fundamental Freedoms, the meaning and scope of those rights shall be the same as those laid down by the said Convention'.

In light of what has been argued above, only self-employed individuals that do not provide 'labour', but provide services by means of an independent business organisation that they actually own and manage, and whose relevance in the provision of the service in terms of capital and work of other persons is considerably superior to the relevance of the individual's personal work, should be restricted in the enjoyment of the right to bargain collectively. We would suggest that a similar approach also ought to be adopted in respect of collectively set professional standards and tariffs, at least in respect of those self-employed professionals that provide services in a predominantly personal capacity and are not operating a business in their own account.

However, this seems to be an inevitable conclusion if the recognition of collective rights as fundamental and human rights must be given significance, as well as the spread of non-independent workers who do not meet entirely traditional strict control and subordination tests accompanied by a consequent expansion of collective protection of those workers.

16.3 EMPLOYMENT, SELF-EMPLOYMENT AND WORK: THE ITALIAN LAWSUIT OF FOODORA RIDERS

Crowdworking, working on-demand or just in time, working for a collaborative economy, all foreshadow application scenarios that are difficult to trace back to the traditional role of the 'employee' and undermine the historical dualism between employee and self-employed, recalling the need for a third intermediate qualifying category, such as the one adopted in the Anglo-Saxon system (i.e., worker). Such a third category, experimented in the past by the Italian legal system (project work) and still nowadays applied albeit marginally (voucher-based work), should be re-conceived and implemented, assuming the role of reference case for situations of economic dependence that do not match the definition of subordinate work but that anyway require a minimal standard of social protection. This case is frequently recurring in the work brokered by the digital platforms, where contractual freedom in the assumption of tasks and social protection needs to come from the broad availability of the services provided thanks to the unfinished supply basin available and the penetrating capacity for control and coordination the contractor has access to, which directs, monitors and solicits the activity carried out via the app and through text or voice messaging systems.

On the other hand, the non-applicability to platform workers of any minimum standard of treatment, neither in terms of relationship nor in terms of social security, is not compatible with the principle of 'protection of work in all its forms and applications' set forth by Article 35 of the Italian Constitution. Regardless of the way the relationship is qualified, it is clear that these workers must be guaranteed the application of a minimum standard of pay, the right to holidays granted by the Constitution and the EU, accident and pension insurance, and exemption from the antitrust regulations, therefore the right of association and strike. '*The point is, however, that we need to find ways to operate this extension of the protections – at least the constitutional, essential, minimum ones – without interfering with the typical flexibility that is an essential feature of this form of work organization, not only in the interest of the company, but also in the interest of the worker.*'[3]

The work of Foodora and Deliveroo riders, Uber drivers, Pimlico plumbers and electricians in the USA or in Great Britain, for instance, cannot be considered effectively autonomous and independent but, at the same time, cannot even be regarded as subordinate, unless one pays the price of forcing an interpretation, with the effect of generating differing and conflicting jurisprudential outcomes, fuelling applicative uncertainty and unpredictable protection responses.

An emblematic Italian case is that of Foodora riders.

At the beginning of 2018, a group of Foodora riders filed a claim against the company before the Turin Labour Court[4] pleading for the recognition of the subordinated nature of the employment relationship between the parties and the subsequent provision of the minimum salary and contributions. The Tribunal, in reconstructing the case, found out that the workers were free to apply or not to a specific delivery run, depending on their availability and life needs. They had therefore freedom of choice to cover or not the different time slots of each shift. There was no obligation to perform work, just as, conversely, the employer was not obliged to accept it. Consequently, in the opinion of the Turin judge, '*if the employer cannot demand from the worker the performance of said work, he cannot consequently exercise the management and organisational power*'. Since the Court has not, in this case, found the core trait of the subordinate employment relationship, that is, being subject to the management and organisational power of the employer, the Tribunal of Turin ruled that the work relationship could not be qualified as subordinate employment and therefore rejected every economic request of the applicants.

The issue was even more complex since, without prejudice to the original act of workers' freedom, and only once the workers had guaranteed the availability to accept and perform certain shifts, the company carried out an incisive control and monitoring of the activities, and punished behaviour that did not comply with the instructions given. More specifically the workers, once the manager had confirmed their shift through a special smartphone application, had to reach, by the shift start time, one of the three default departure city zones, activate the application by logging in with their credentials, start the geo-localisation, receive an order notification by the app indicating the restaurant address, go to the restaurant with their own bicycle, take the products, check out the order and communicate by the appropriate app command that the check had been successfully carried out. Then, after placing the food in the box, the

3. *See* P. Ichino, *Subordinazione, autonomia e protezione del lavoro nella gig-economy*, in *RIDL*, 2018, II, p. 294.
4. Torino Tribunal Judgment No. 778 of 7/5/2018, in *ADL* 2018, n. 4-5, pp. 1220 ss., with case note of M. Biasi, *Il Tribunale di Torino e la qualificazione dei riders di Foodora*.

rider had to deliver it to the customer address provided by the app. Finally, the rider had to confirm through the app that the order had been regularly delivered. The entire process had to be carried out within thirty minutes from the food pick-up, otherwise the rider would be charged a EUR 15 penalty.

During the activity described above the riders were remotely monitored and received reminder calls in case of delays or deviations from optimal road routes. Furthermore, the riders could revoke their availability only before the shift started, through a special application option (swap). In this case, the system provided for a warning, the worker was immediately excluded from the possibility of opting for other shifts, was excluded from the corporate chat and was subject to penalties in the best workers ratings. The same sanctions (exclusion from corporate chat, exclusion from work shifts, penalties in merit scores) were also applied to other behaviours not appreciated by the company, even simple complaints or criticism by the riders about management and distribution of orders. Therefore, while it is true that there are different subjective reasons that lead the workers to accept delivery assignments (paid EUR 5.60 per hour, including tax and social security contributions), and if it is true that workers willingly accept those methods of organisation and management of work, nevertheless it is clear that the organisation of work performance is almost completely in the hands of the company and reduces every space of organisational autonomy on the side of the worker.

For these reasons the aforementioned decision was overhauled by the Court of Appeal of Turin,[5] and then confirmed by the recent ruling of the Supreme Court n. 1663/2020.[6] The Supreme Court reasonable affirmed that the existence of such a pervasive control and monitoring over the worker's activity represents an unambiguous flag of hetero-organised work requirement set by Article 2 of Law Decree No. 81/2015 together with the requirements of personality and continuity of the performance. As such, it justifies the application of statutory discipline of employment, even in the absence of the hetero-direction criterion required for the qualification of employee. This judgment makes it more difficult for delivery platforms to sustain a business model in Italy so highly reliant on independent contractors. Nevertheless, it was argued by Doctrine[7] that the Supreme Court decision does not seriously affect the digital market operators because it is only applicable to conflicts arisen before the entry into force of Chapter V-*bis* (Article 1, Law Decree No. 101/2019), that has given a new regulation of digital platform workers which substitutes the reference to subordinate discipline generally provided by Article 2 Law Decree No. 81. However, an opposite interpretation of the matter[8] keeps both provisions applicable to platform workers, depending on the continuity of performing their job and on the existence or not of a derogating collective agreement which could limit the application of subordinate

5. Torino Court of Appeal Judgment No. 26 of 2/4/2019.
6. Cassazione Judgment No. 1663 of 1/24/2020.
7. F. Carinci, *L'art. 2 d.lgs. n. 81/2015 ad un primo vaglio della Suprema Corte: Cass. 24 gennaio 2020, n. 1663*, in WP C.S.D.L.E. 'Massimo D'Antona'.IT – 414/2020, pp. 13 e ss.
8. A. Perulli, *Il diritto del lavoro 'oltre la subordinazione': le collaborazioni etero-organizzate e le tutele minime per i riders autonomi*, in WP C.S.D.L.E. 'Massimo D'Antona'.IT – 410/2020, pp. 59 ss.

legislative provisions in full or in part, while respecting the minimum standards offered to platform workers by the Chapter V-*bis* (pay, health insurance, prohibition of discrimination, personal data protection). The jurisprudence has not yet coped with this problem which is left to future implementation of collective practices and case law.

16.4 RISE AND DECLINE OF THE UMBRELLA COMPANIES

Two different, parallel experiences have been developed to give effective answers to the platform workers' need for protection during these years, since there is no legislation yet that introduces a third type of financially dependent freelance work.

The first one is *umbrella companies*, companies that bring together platform workers and act as intermediaries with the principal, such as service cooperatives. Such companies, which merely try to recruit people online and are service platforms themselves, play a double role: on one hand, they provide their members (platform workers) with sickness, maternity, disability and retirement insurance coverage, so that they can skip through many, complicated bureaucratic formalities, which are carried out by the company; on the other hand, they pay benefits to platform workers who have their own clients from funds that keep them afloat when they are not paid by the principal, and, in return, they pay a fee to the company.

It is a simple mechanism: the umbrella company hires platform workers on a job-on-call basis and makes them available on the principal's digital platform, collects the payments and fulfils all the administrative formalities involved in the employment contract. In this way, the employer/employee contract is a device to provide workers with wide insurance coverage, without the employer (i.e., the umbrella company) having any direct interest in their work or in cutting down transaction costs. Quite the opposite: it is the worker, not the employer, who, under the employer/employee contract, tries to cut down transaction costs, which he would otherwise have to pay for himself to collect the payments from users, while the employer's purpose is to take care of such payments.

The employment contract that is used for this purpose is therefore a simulation: in fact, the alleged employer is not a creditor in this respect; and the alleged outsourced labour that the umbrella company might enter into with the user, who it is not paid by, would be a simulation too, as it would be paid by the worker, who, under the bogus employment contract, is in fact looking for a service provider to manage the flow of his payments, for an opportunity to have insurance coverage for disability, retirement and industrial accidents, and to have access to a welfare fund to earn money on a permanent basis despite fluctuations in work or payments, for whatever reason.

To overcome the trick of the fake employer/employee contract, a bill of law, No. 2934 dated 5 October 2017, has been put forward in Italy at the initiative of Pietro Ichino, involving a new type of agreement (*contratto di assistenza e protezione mutualistica*) (social protection and assistance contract), whereby the company collects the payments through the digital platform and then pays them out to the workers, net of a service fee, the amount of which is set forth in the agreement, and pays contributions for national insurance, pension schemes and insurance against workplace accidents and occupational diseases. Moreover, umbrella companies may also act as trade unions for their employees and can negotiate with the main digital platforms to establish a minimum wage, regardless of the number of deliveries or jobs, they can help the workers with the payment of their work equipment (smartphone, bicycle, personal protection equipment, etc.), establish the minimum hourly shifts (e.g., three hours), even if a technical problem prevented the worker from finishing the shift, and provide specific safety training (the most famous case is the agreement between Smart and Deliveroo in Belgium in 2017).

The mechanism offered by umbrella companies mainly works for those workers whose job is broken up into a multitude of short- or very short-term jobs, working for multiple digital platforms, but it is hardly applicable to gig workers who mainly, if not solely, work for one digital platform only. In this case, the contractual power of the platform is stronger and leaves no room for other social associations or partners to step in. That is why in the last year such experience has started to be replaced by a new form of trade unions, consisting of workers' associations and traditional trade union federations, which have developed new methods to approach and aggregate digital work.

16.5 THE FIRST EXAMPLES OF PLATFORM WORKERS COLLECTIVE AGREEMENTS

The traditional trade unions (such as Ig Metall and Cgil) are developing new ways to find crowd workers online, on dedicated websites, on Facebook and apps that meet the workers' actual needs (e.g., WorkIt, an app designed to assist the staff at Walmart: it is an application for Android and iOS smartphones that gives workers real-time information on their rights, through a chatbot powered by IBM's Watson AI system, which can automatically answer the workers' enquiries). They are doing this by attempting to extend the workers' rights to information and participation in the digital world and, above all, by trying out new forms of 'in advance' bargaining systems that may give trade unions a chance to be involved in the development of the so-called workforce analytics throughout the recruiting process, the development of the career, the monitoring and fining of the workers.

Therefore, in the long run, trade unions should try to 'negotiate the algorithm', that is, manage to influence, through bargaining, the inputs given to the algorithm to establish the timing, professional qualifications, attendance, workload, corporate organisation, minimum quality ratings and so on.

Right now, the trade union has to promote negotiation, in a local either national or multinational scale, in the light of Hilfr Agreement of 1 August 2018, which represents the world's first collective agreement between platform company and trade union in Denmark. The agreement involves about 450 workers of Hilfr, a website platform providing cleaning services for around 1,700 customers across Denmark, and presents these key points: (i) minimum pay of EUR 19 per hour; (ii) contribution to private pension scheme; (iii) holiday pay contribution; (iv) sick pay; (v) welfare supplement. The agreement content is not thrilling and does not seem to be an enhanced tool for driving the social negative impacts for platform-based workers and to face the new forms of workers exploitation coming from the disintermediation of the services. In any case, it is a good starting point to build up a contractual practice that leads to a full recognition of trade union and to push through a collective and consensual approach in managing human resources timing and tasks. It has also shown the way for other following agreements signed in 2019 (e.g., Hermes and GMB, a delivery company providing courier services in the UK).

It is clear that the normative environment is uncertain and unstable: a lack of clarity as regards platform workers' legal status; wage rates which can be far below legal minimum levels once all expenses and time are factored in; and rating mechanisms which exercise significant control over platform workers' daily efforts. And that is not all. Three potential obstacles to ensuring collective voices can be found in the platform economy: operator resistance, from downright refusals to engage with worker representatives through to more subtle suggestions that collective bargaining is fundamentally ill-suited to platform-based work; workforce dispersal, as platform workers often find themselves working on individual schedules and scattered around a city - or in the case of online platform work, even the entire world; and different demands towards collective organisation from a workforce that could be highly heterogeneous across different platforms and personal needs.

In the absence of a defined place of work or regular work patterns, it appears difficult to find a way for organisers to connect with individuals. Most countries grant union organisers paid time off for their work and protect them against employer reprisals, as employers and legislators recognise the value of having a clear voice to represent workers' concerns. On-demand economy workers, on the other hand, must attempt to organise colleagues using their own time and resources, and can easily be deactivated from their platform in retaliation.

The platform economy workforce is not just geographically dispersed: it is also highly heterogeneous in its potential demands towards collective organisation. The interests and needs of students occasionally dipping into the platform economy might differ substantially from a worker seeking to make a full-time living, paying a mortgage and sustaining dependants: the former will primarily be interested in benefits which are most relevant 'in the moment' - whether it be the provision of safety equipment such as helmets for bicycle couriers, insurance when actually on the job, or assistance with the acquisition and maintenance of their vehicles and tools. For the latter group, on the other hand, long-term benefits such as holiday pay, pension contributions and income protection in case of illness might play a more important role. Finally, workers on comparatively well-paid click work tasks such as design work might be able to pay union subscriptions at regular rates, whereas the cost of union membership, particularly early on when few if any tangible benefits are available, can be prohibitive or at least act as a strong deterrent for those struggling at the very bottom of the wage distribution.

A related point arises from the often one-sided nature of ratings: while consumers can rate workers, the opposite is not always the case - or even if a rating is collected, it is not always made available to workers. Unscrupulous platform users can take advantage of this information asymmetry, for example, by refusing to pay for already completed tasks on quality grounds. The collection and diffusion of feedback about such users is the only way of tackling this problem.

None of these obstacles are in fact insurmountable, and they have been already solved during the past industrial revolution. The inherent flexibility and reflexivity of collective bargaining presents a unique opportunity to ensure fair working conditions for all workers in the platform economy, including dependent self-employed, given that collective agreements are not unlawful cartels under EU law.

16.6 SUGGESTIONS FOR THE COLLECTIVE BARGAINING TO COME

Topics such as hours, wages and holiday arrangements shall play a significant role, but it is also important to keep in mind the specificities of platform-based work, and try to carry out contractual actions tailored on the digital environment.

First of all the topic of ratings. Given the central role ratings play in shaping platform workers' daily experiences, collective bargaining over the operation of rating systems should play a central role. Potential aspects include the factors by which ratings are compiled (such as consumer feedback, compliance with policies, and the role of algorithmic monitoring) and their relative weighting in determining overall scores and/or task assignment. Platforms may also develop a system which allows workers to challenge ratings, for example when a low rating was given by a consumer in retaliation for a worker's refusal to bend the rules or worse (such as taking an extra passenger in a taxi, or work which far exceeds task descriptions). Collective agreements could also impose on the employer the portability of ratings: workers should be free to export their rating from a platform and take it to another operator.

Second, the topic of participation rights. As Prof. Weiss teaches us: '*the idea of workers' participation can be spread everywhere. The positive effects of the system of employee involvement in management's decision making are well documented by many empirical studies. To just mention a few of them: it leads to a change of focus from shareholder value to stakeholder value and tends to promote sustainability instead of short term effects at the stock markets. It has a big advantage compared to unilateral decision-making by the mere fact that management, who has to justify towards workers' representatives what it wants to do and why it wants to do it, tends to prepare the decisions much more carefully than it would be the case without this obligation. This leads evidently to better decision-making. The consciousness that workers' representatives are involved in management's decision making and that workers' interests are taken into account tends to increase the employees' motivation and thereby the company's productivity. Last but not least, the permanent dialogue between management and workers' representatives leads to mutual trust, changes the attitudes of both sides and absorbs unnecessary conflicts.*'[9] No doubt that it is an impervious route, but it may be followed to rebalance the powers and the asymmetries of the parties.

9. M. Weiss, Workers Representation, Paper submitted for 17th Modena international seminar in commemoration of Prof. Marco Biagi, 18-19 March 2019.

Third, the topic of pay arrangements. In addition to baseline collective bargaining over wages, platform-based work raises additional challenges in relation to payment calculation and regularity. In this context, a collective agreement could play an important role in ensuring pay transparency, for example, by setting out agreed mechanisms for the resolution of disputes between consumers and workers, or liability for incidental costs and equipment. Collective bargaining could also tackle regular payment mechanisms to ensure that workers have easy access to their platform income: the variability and unpredictability of certain operators' pay modalities is frequently subject to workers' complaints. Collective bargaining could also guarantee discounted legal services or insurance and roadside assistance to platform workers.

Fourth, the topics of public/private social insurance and conflict resolution. Regardless of employment classification, platform-based workers should have access to social security protections - including unemployment insurance, disability insurance, health insurance, pension, maternity protection, and compensation in the event of work related illness or injury. Contributions to relevant accounts should be shared - as appropriate by national context - between workers, platforms, clients, and the State, and should be prorated, portable and, if nationally appropriate, mandatory. The room for collective bargaining should be defined by the national legislator (in Italy the above-mentioned bill of law, No. 2934 dated 5 October 2017 provides for a mandatory withholding on hourly wages to a particular public social security scheme). In the absence of a specific legislative regulation for platform-based workers, collective bargaining should propose a private funding insurance covering the principal farm risks over workers health and safety (sick, injury, maternity and paternity). Closely linked to pay transparency is the question of conflict resolution between all parties involved in platform economy transactions. Disputes frequently arise, for example, between consumers and platform workers, whether it is a challenge to a particular route taken, the speed of a delivery, or the quality of online work. A collective agreement should set out clear procedures for the resolution of such conflicts, including, for example, the evidence admissible in disputes, and workers' rights to explain their position and if appropriate be accompanied to a disciplinary hearing.

Last, but not least, the topic of deactivation. In the context of online platforms with global reach, traditional models of dismissal protections (including, for example, an appeal deactivation hearing lead to an independent panel formed in a bilateral way, representatives of the company and trade union representatives), might not always be suitable (particularly to genuine autonomous workers whose protection for contract termination because of low feedback ratings is limited to vexatious or abusive clauses). Platform collective agreements should therefore include both clear criteria and an easily accessible process for deactivation, including for example a system of escalating warnings, a clear explanation of reasons, and the worker's right to make written or oral defences before the deactivation. And this disclosure (informative and comparing tools) should be at worker's disposal in all kinds of deactivation (by low rating or by cancellation rate - number of cancelled trips divided by the total number of accepted trips - or by acceptance rate - number of accepted trips divided by the total number of assigned trips). The deactivation procedure should also include explicit protection against retaliation, for example, for organisers or whistle blowers. '*Collective actors should have a guaranteed access to all information on technical procedures and company database, for example when it comes to matching algorithm parameters, deactivation thresholds, acceptance, cancellation and earning rates; asymmetries in information between labour and management produce inefficient social outcomes and must be overcome.*'[10]

This, of course, is only a list of general items. Specific industries and sectors will require implementation for particular issues. By the way, the advantage of collective bargaining lays on the flexibility and adaptive solutions it may offer to meet both workers' needs and business operation requirements in a specific production environment.

16.7 LABOUR, EVEN IN A DIGITAL ENVIRONMENT, IS NOT A COMMODITY

Given that the case of platform workers usually does not fit into the setting of employment relation, that EU competition law cannot prevent from collectively contracting for dependent self-employed, that EU and most national legislators have been insensitive to this new form of services, failing to provide specific provisions on social security and minimum working standards, it becomes evident that the only way of providing answers to gig workers is through collective bargaining at a company stage.

If unilateral codes of conduct, general company or organisations statements, devoted union representatives are generally good practices to reduce power imbalances in the digital labour market, they fall short of providing a minimum floor of rights to platform financially dependent workers. Hence, a specialised collective bargaining becomes necessary to guarantee decent work conditions. The purpose is not to harm gig economy or to remove flexibility in labour supply. It is, instead, to rebalance the existing asymmetry of information between contracting parties, and, in a certain sense, to implement a reallocation of company profits, as to improve life conditions for digital gig workers.

Let me conclude with the Frankfurt Paper declaration: '*"Labor is not a commodity". This is a philosophical principle that asserts the fundamental and universal dignity of human beings, regardless of the indifference with which they may be treated in any given social, political, or economic context. This principle has clear implications for policy, including centrally the protection of the right of workers to organize. This principle – and its policy implications – is just as crucial to a decent society in the "information age" as it was in the industrial era. We believe that information technology, shaped wisely, holds great promise for expanding access to good work.*'

10. G. Birgillito, M. Birgillito, *Algorithms and ratings: tools to manage labour relations. Proposals to renegotiate labour conditions for platform drivers*, in LLI, 2018, Vol. 4, No. 2, 2018, p. 41.

CHAPTER 17

The Labour Market and the Digital Revolution: Focus on Some Effects, Legislative Implications and the Role of Collective Bargaining

Marcella Miracolini

17.1 THE LABOUR MARKET AT THE TIME OF THE DIGITAL REVOLUTION: THE TRANSFORMATIONS ON EVOLUTIONARY DYNAMICS

In the last years, in Italy as in other European countries, external influences have been crucial throughout the ongoing transformation of labour law, which has undergone a phase of epochal change regarding all of the 'components of its historical model'[1] stemming from a deregulation process as well as a great change in the scientific paradigm. The subject's sensitivity to the external influences has resulted in a transformation, which has inevitably also affected the system of industrial relations, ultimately challenging the role and the dynamics of collective bargaining.[2] The work paradigm of the twentieth century appeared inadequate and insufficient to face all the challenges that had been emerging. Due to this, a new balance was sought.[3]

These changes are linked to the economic and financial crisis, as well as to a series of other equally disorderly factors, such as the effects of globalisation, low levels

1. A. PERULLI, *L'idea del diritto del lavoro, oggi*, in *Lav. dir.*, 2016, 1, p. 17.
2. T. TREU, *Le istituzioni del lavoro nell'Europa della crisi*, in *Giorn. dir. lav. rel. ind.*, 2013, 4, pp. 597 ff.; M. CARRIERI, T. TREU (edited by), *Verso nuove relazioni industriali*, Il Mulino, 2013.
3. D. GOTTARDI, *La crisi, il diritto del lavoro e le relazioni sindacali: una panoramica con tante ombre e poche luci*, in *Ec. e Soc. Reg.*, 2014, 1, pp. 7 ff.

of productivity, the definite overcoming of Fordism and also post-Fordism and phenomena related to the digital revolution.

Nevertheless, the introduction and the spread of new technologies in the labour market triggered a double development: on the one hand, it led to the spread of modern business models (variously defined: sharing economy, on-demand economy, etc.) and of new forms of work in the context of the so-called digital platforms. On the other hand, it resulted in the digitalisation of the industry as well as the beginning of a so-called Fourth (or New) Industrial Revolution.[4]

This series of quick technological transformations has revolutionised - and still revolutionises - the planning, production and distribution of systems of production and of products within companies; and finally, it has had different types of consequences for the labour market.[5]

The current goal is not to analyse the innovative profiles that new forms of work, developed on the web, have acquired, especially with regard to the digital platforms.[6] Rather, it is sought to briefly examine only some effects of the impact that the process of digitalisation has had upon traditional relationships and their management into industries, focusing mainly on job polarisation effect. They have resulted from the strong interaction between the work performance and the technologies applied to the existing productive processes, which, for instance, could be explained in terms of substitution or complementarity.

The impact of the innovations upon the traditional industry is not, indeed, less 'disruptive', thus imposing an equally engaging investigation, also through the lenses of collective bargaining and taking into account the role of involved sources.

With regard to the analyses of the cause-and-effect relations related to the emergence of information and communication technologies,[7] some phenomena are still hard to evaluate as, for instance, the impact on occupational levels and the risk of the so-called technological unemployment resulting from a shift of job profiles and duties. The comparison between the cyber-optimistic approach and the

4. German scholars first introduced the term *Industrie 4.0* to talk about the digitalisation and automation of production process resulting from introduction of new generation of technologies. H. Kagermann, W.D. Lukas, W. Wahlster, *Industrie 4.0: Mit dem Internet dei Dinge aufdem Weg zur 4. Industriellen Revolution*, VDI Nachtrichten, 2011.
5. *Inter alia*, L. Fiorillo, *Un diritto del lavoro per il lavoro che cambia: primi spunti di riflessione*, in *WP CSDLE 'Massimo D'Antona'.IT*, 2018, n. 368; A. Cipriani, A. Gramolati, G. Mari (edited by), *Il lavoro 4.0 – La quarta rivoluzione industriale e le trasformazioni delle attività lavorative*, Firenze University Press, 2018, 307; E. Signorini, *Il diritto del lavoro nell'economia digitale*, Giappichelli, 2018.
6. The following are just some of the contributions of the doctrine: A. Donini, *Il lavoro su piattaforma digitale 'prende forma' tra autonomia e subordinazione. Nuove regole per nuovi lavori?*, in *Dir. rel. ind.*, 2016, I, pp. 164 ff.; the monothematic volume P. Loi, V. Speziale (edited by), *Come cambia il diritto del lavoro nell'economia delle piattaforme*, *Riv. giur. lav. prev. soc.*, 2017, 2; T. Treu, *Rimedi e fattispecie a confronto con i lavori della Gig economy*, in *WP CSDLE 'Massimo D'Antona'*, 2017, n. 136.
7. Degryse identifies four areas of impacts of digitalisation: job creation, job change, job destruction, job shift. C. Degryse, *Digitalisation of the economy and its impact on labour markets*, in *Working Paper ETUI*, Bruxel, 2016, in https://www.etui.org.

pessimistic/disruptive perspectives, of those who fear an end of work,[8] cannot be easily appreciated, considering the multiple causes involved in transformations of the market and the contemporaneity of the phenomenon.

On the contrary, other effects are more evident and have inevitable implications on the labour discipline. It is called to evaluate the categories of its traditional model and renew itself, in order to enable the new productive method in *Industry 4.0*, without losing sight of the importance of the person, pursuing a better conciliation of life and work times (work-life balance).[9] This is the case of the growing space-time flexibility of working methods, resulting for instance from the increasing use of *smart working*, which was introduced by the collective bargaining, also at the company level, even before being fully regulated pursuant to Law no. 81/2017.[10]

17.2 THE EFFECT OF 'JOB POLARISATION' BETWEEN THE RIGIDITY OF THE SYSTEM AND NEW NEEDS

The digital revolution undertaken in productive companies has determined – amongst the effects causing an inner flexibilisation of the job market[11] – the *job polarisation* effect, which results in a change of the occupational job structure. This change is accompanied by a similar result, which is more or less evident and empirically confirmed, concerning salary levels, but mostly by the contents of the duties and the job profiles required. So, it leads to the need to rethink the contractual framework systems and the notion of professionalism.[12]

The phenomenon, which dates back to the 1990s but has nowadays gained a wider scope, concerns allocative dynamics and refers to the outcome of the increase in highly specialised jobs (higher professional levels, characterised by cognitive and interactive tasks) as well as in those that, conversely, are poorly specialised. Briefly, this trend has caused a decline in the middle class of workers who are in charge of intermediate and routine duties.[13] Empirical research, which has been carried out also

---

8. The expression was originally coined by J. Rifklin, *The end of work: the decline of the global labor force and the dawn of the post-market era*, Putnam Publishing Group, 1995.
9. *See* L. Fiorillo, A. Perulli, *Il jobs act del lavoro autonomo e del lavoro agile*, Giappichelli, 2017; M. Tiraboschi, *Il lavoro agile tra legge e contrattazione collettiva: la tortuosa via italiana verso la modernizzazione del diritto del lavoro*, in *Dir. rel. ind.*, 2017, pp. 933 ff.; G. Zilio Grandi, M. Biasi (edited by), *Commentario breve allo statuto del lavoro autonomo e del lavoro agile*, Cedam, 2018.
10. They are some examples of company agreements preceding the law: Supplementary Agreement of General Motors Powertrain – Europe Srl, 6 March 2015 (with Fim-CISL, Fiom-CGIL, Uilm-UIL); Agreement of Siemens Spa, 6 June 2017 (with Fim-CISL, Fiom-CGIL, Uilm-UIL), that had started the experimentation since 2011.
11. It was noted that in case of gig economy the external flexibility is involved; on the contrary, in case of *Industry 4.0* an internal flexibility is relevant. M. Faioli, *Jobs 'App', Gig economy e sindacato*, *supra*, p. 295.
12. L. Fiorillo, *Un diritto del lavoro per il lavoro che cambia: primi spunti di riflessione*, *supra*, pp. 3 ff.
13. D. H. Autor, F. Levy, R. Murnane, *The skill content of recent technological change: An empirical exploration*, in *Quarterly Journal of Economics*, 2003, 118, pp. 1279 ff. The Authors, from the so-called *Skill-Biased Technological Change* hypothesis, have developed a model based on the relation between the introduction of new technologies and the workers' tasks, updating the

in European countries,[14] has roughly confirmed the transversal existence of the polarisation effect, although its rhythm and intensity differs amongst countries. Finally, in Italy, the data on occupational variations showed a trend which is absolutely consistent with the model.[15]

The result is a primary need to adapt to the skills required. It consists of flexibility of competencies and professionalism that could avoid segregation effects and facilitate occupational transitions, thus reducing the likelihood of *mismatch* between requested skills and offers (in terms of *over-education* as a *skill-training*). In this regard, continuous training interventions and forms of requalification contribute to avoiding the professional marginalisation of weaker and more exposed segments of the labour market. Nevertheless, this is not enough: the effect challenges the standardised classifications of job profiles, as well as the notion of professionalism, which are both to be re-interpreted.

The mass production of the twentieth century developed a Taylorist work organisation. It was transposed by classification systems and frameworks of national collective agreements, which were able to indicate, in a rigid and sufficiently detailed manner, duties, schedules, shifts as well as related wages.

The breakdown and fragmentation of duties,[16] listed also according to the workers' tasks and qualifications,[17] allowed the evaluation of skills in relation to objective tasks, thus defining the substantial position of the worker within the organisation (so-called *objective qualification*),[18] rather than assessing their personal competencies. This facilitated the identification of the task performed and, at the same time, the determination of the salary levels. In this way, 'security' was defined by certainty and stability.

Within the overall transformations of the labour market, professionalisms take on a multiplicity of forms and boundaries becoming less and less defined, more blurred

model as *Routine-biased technical change*. D. Acemoglu, D. Autor, *Skill, tasks and technologies: Implications for employment and earnings*, in *Handbook of Labor Economics*, 2011, 4B, pp. 1043 ff.

14. As M. Goos, A. Manning, A. Salomons, *Job polarization in Europe*, in *American Economic Review: Papers & Proceedings*, 2009, 99, pp. 58 ff.
15. At the date of the conference the following data were available. The phenomenon at national level has just evidenced by this study Senato della Repubblica, XI Commissione lavoro, previdenza sociale, *Impatto sul mercato del lavoro della Quarta Rivoluzione Industriale*, 2017, at https://www.senato.it. The most recent data available are those of annual report of CNEL, in CNEL, *XX Rapporto mercato del lavoro e contrattazione collettiva (2017-2018)*, at https://www.cnel.it/Documenti/Rapporti, 2019; which confirm also those one of OECD, *How technology and globalisation are transforming the labour market*, in OECD, Employment Outlook, 2017.
16. M. Brollo, *Mansioni e qualifiche dei lavoratori*, in *Dig. disc. priv. Sez. comm.*, IX, Utet, 1991, pp. 243 ff.; G. Giugni, *Mansioni e qualifica nel rapporto di lavoro*, Jovene, 1963; G. Suppiej, *Mansioni del lavoratore*, in U. Prosperetti (directed by), *Commentario allo statuto dei lavoratori*, 1975, I, pp. 357 ff.
17. About the concept of qualification – *inter alia* – M. Napoli, in Aa. Vv., *Rapporti economici*, in G. Branca (edited by), *Commentario Costituzione*, Zanichelli, 1979, pp. 30 ff.
18. The classification of workers is considered independent of their abstract professional abilities, A. Garilli, *Categorie dei lavoratori (in generale)*, in *Dig. disc. priv. Sez. comm.*, III, Utet, 1988, pp. 44 ff.

and therefore uncertain. This brought inevitable consequences undermining the current system stability.

First, it resulted in the emergence of – and this is quite intuitive – the demand for new and additional skills and knowledge, to be applied to both old and new work contexts. It also introduces the need for increasingly transversal skills,[19] and workers are asked to find jobs in which their duties are not limited to the sole application of their already acquired 'professional knowledge'. On the contrary, they are required to develop a dynamic competence in relation to flexible organisational models of the companies. Second, the speed with which the models of production and of organising work are not consistent with the static nature of fixed frameworks.

In these terms, updating the contractual framework systems and rethinking the concept of professionalism appear to be the following logical steps. The old ones seem to be too rigid and unable to encompass the many facets of the activities performed and of the skills required, and too static because innovation runs faster than stabilisation times.

With regard to the doctrinal and jurisprudential debate, prior to the amendment of the Article 2103 of the Civil Code with the Legislative Decree n. 81/2015, both in its 1942 version and later in that one of Article 13 of the Workers' Statute, some guidelines aimed to statically interpret the notion of professionalism while tightening the possibility of a professionally flexible use of the worker's performance.[20] This approach was relevant in the positions regarding the interpretation of the concept of 'equivalence' in the case of the exercise of the horizontal *ius variandi* pursuant to Article 2103 of the Civil Code.[21]

The judgment had identified some limits on the employer power, to preserve the accumulated experience of worker, removing the protection to collective autonomy.[22]

A conservative or 'static' protection of professionalism was implemented. This was rooted in the professional patrimony acquired by the worker and identifiable with his know-how, that is with the wealth of acquired knowledge and the practical abilities entrenched in the profession exercised and pertaining to the experience matured in the company. This, therefore, defines an objective type of professionalism (which is to be differentiated from that of a subjective type).[23]

19. Work organisations, not least in order to prevent the danger of a technological unemployment, have to invent new jobs, and it must review the organisational procedures, M. Brollo, *La disciplina delle mansioni dopo il Jobs Act*, in *Arg. dir. lav.*, 2015, 6, p. 1156.
20. M. Brollo, *Mansioni e qualifiche dei lavoratori*, *supra*, p. 244.
21. The worker individual personality was identified through the job he did, representing a specific quantity and quality of level, M. Del Conte, *Mansioni (Nuova disciplina delle)*, in *Dig. disc. priv. Sez. comm.*, X Agg., 2016, p. 523.
22. There are countless cases. From most ancient to most recent for instance: Cass. 15 June 1983, n. 4106 in *Giust. civ.*, 1984, II, 233; Cass. 8 February 1985, n. 1038, in *Riv. it. dir. lav.*, 1985, II, 714; Cass. 23 January 1988, n. 539 in *Mass. giur. lav.*, 1988, 290; Cass. 20 September 1990, n. 9584, in *Nuov. giur. lav.*, 1990, 894; Cass. 12 January 2006, n. 425, in *Riv. it. dir. lav.*, 2006, II, 381; Cass. 8 June 2009, n. 13173, in *Mass. giur. lav.*, 2009, 757; Cass. 12 January 2012, n. 250, in *Guida lav.*, 2012, 7, 43; Cass. 3 February 2015, n. 1916, in *Giust. civ. mass.*, 2015.
23. About a 'static' view of professionality, see M. Persiani, *Prime osservazioni sulla nuova disciplina delle mansioni e del trasferimento del lavoratore*, in *Dir. lav.*, 1971, I, pp. 13 ff.

The perspective has already started to change long before; in 2006 the Supreme Court of Cassation tried to unveil a new phase, by moving the balance point towards to a more functional flexibility.[24] But the time was not ripe; the benchmark still remained the historical worker expertise. Only the emergence of the New Industrial Revolution with its effects has ultimately determined a re-need to understand professionalism in a dynamic and evolutionary sense.

This constitutes the central dimension of the capability which implies that the worker's background is not tied to a single workplace but is more generally expendable in the job market. Furthermore, it ensures the worker's integration within new organisational systems, also thanks to a continuous training which complies with the principle of lifelong learning,[25] consisting of multiple and differentiated work experiences, with the prospect of transitioning between jobs in the course of their lives.

The protection of the professionalism of the worker, therefore, hinges upon its dynamic interpretation; not an immobility of tasks, but a ductility of them, thanks also to contractual profiles less rigid. For this reason, it is deemed necessary to update the contractual framework systems as well as the way of understanding some traditional categories. This does not only mean adapting them through the recognition of new professional figures but rather rethinking the structure itself.

From a legislative point of view, the changed perspective appears to have been taken into consideration by the legislator of the Jobs Act, through the application of a potential strategic role of collective bargaining. With regard to Article 2103 of the Civil Code, with the amendment of the Legislative Decree no. 81/2015 (Article 3, paragraph 1)[26] the classification level was chosen as the safest parameter of that represented by gained professionalism, and collective bargaining was called to operate as a source of integration of the legislative previsions.

It follows that collective agreements acquire an in-company regulation function. Indeed, by equating the tasks within the same contractual level, collective agreements could offer an *ex-ante* estimate of the equivalence parameter which is useful to assess the legitimacy of the exercise of employer's *ius variandi*.

De facto, this means that the social partners are to assess – from the moment of the classification – an equivalence that may have essential results on the working life of the individual; and so, it is up to them to take into account the new prospects.[27]

---

24. Cass., U.S., 24 November 2006, n. 25033 in *Foro it.*, 2007, I, 786 and in *Riv. giur. lav.*, 2007, II, 193.
25. M. Weiss, *Digitalizzazione: sfide e prospettive per il diritto del lavoro*, in *Dir. rel. ind.*, 2016, 3, p. 654. An essential condition for workers and companies, which wants to remain competitive in the market, is to consider the educational element exercised continually on the job. F. Seghezzi, *Lavoro e relazioni industriali nell'Industry 4.0, supra*, p. 183.
26. About the revised Article 2103 c.c., *see inter alia* A. Bellavista, *Il nuovo art. 2103 nel Jobs Act*, in *www.dirittisocialiecittadinanza.org*, 23 February 2015; A. Garilli, *La nuova disciplina delle mansioni tra flessibilità organizzativa e tutela del prestatore di lavoro*, in *Dir. lav. rel. ind.*, 2016, 1, pp. 129 ff.; E. Gramano, *La riforma della disciplina dello* jus variandi, in G. Zilio Grandi, M. Biasi (edited by), *Commentario breve alla riforma Jobs Act*, Cedam, 2016, pp. 517 ff.
27. Soon after the amendment to Article 2013 c.c. the Tribunal of Rome has confirmed that the judgment of equivalence must be conducted by adopting as measure the abstract scheme of the collective agreement and not the previous tasks of the worker. Trib. Roma, n. 8195/2015, in *Lav. giur.*, 2015, 11, p. 1031, with note to F. Aiello, *Il nuovo art. 2103 c.c.: equivalenza senza*

In this respect, the role of collective autonomy in terms of horizontal mobility is strongly reinforced, although the known critical aspects of our contractual system, caused by the failure to implement Article 39 of the Constitution, remain unresolved.

17.2.1 Briefly on Practical Experience

The social partners seem to have taken note of the new needs. In the unitary agreement signed on 9 March 2019 (between Confindustria and Cgil, Cisl, Uil), for instance, they indicated that the goal of the collective bargaining is – *inter alia* – to find suitable spaces to 'enhance the professional contents and the technical and organisational skills that people's work can express'.[28] But its practice certainly proves to be more complex than its formulation: sufficient adjustment levels do not seem to have yet been achieved. The reformist attempts appear to have lessened and their capacity for adaptation is still sensibly reduced. At the time of writing we are still far from 'refined clauses of evaluation of workers position';[29] apart from some modifications, it has not just been an incisive remodulation of classifications.

This holds true with regard to national collective agreements but also to the second level of bargaining, whose relevance cannot be ignored given the growing decentralisation, also receipted by interconfederal agreement, and the openness to this level of bargaining by lawmaker.

Considering some company collective contracts, not satisfactory in terms of principles of representativeness due to ontological reasons linked to the very nature of such agreements, it could be claimed that the corporate supplementary collective bargaining generally opts almost exclusively for the 'entrustment' to the national one. The hypotheses in which the former intervenes directly on the classification systems defined by the bargaining category appear to be rare.

The negotiation of mandatory clauses regarding information procedures and scheduling of meetings to monitor the adequacy of workers' classification is expected.[30]

This suggests on the one hand the need for the negotiating parties to innovate, also due to the emergence of new professional figures. On the other hand, it reveals all the sensitivity of the matter and the fear of losing control, which eventually leads the social partners to implement simple adaptations with respect to an already existing and

professionalità pregressa?. Since then, this position was confirmed by other judgments, as Cass. 18 February 2016, n. 3216, in *Giust. civ. mass.*, 2016; Trib. Roma, n. 8253/2018, unpublished.

28. F. Liso, *Quale erratica considerazione sul recente accordo interconfederale Confindustria, Cgil, Cisl, Uil del 9 marzo 2018*, in *BollettinoADAPT*, 23 April 2018, n. 16.
29. M. Brollo, *La disciplina delle mansioni dopo il Jobs Act*, *supra*, p. 1162.
30. This is generally done with repeated formulas, such as 'The company remains ready to annually review with the RSU the application of the rules on classification and professionality', Supplementary Company Agreement of Philip Morris Manufacturing & Technology Bologna Spa, 21 September 2016. *See also* Supplementary Company Agreement of L'Orèal Italia Spa, 7 July 2016 (with Femca-CISL, Filctem-CGIL).

consolidated structure, without undertaking reforming initiatives which are effective and radical.[31] Despite of the opening of the law we are far from a suitable system.[32]

But instead, the broad appeal of collective bargaining to the subject of training and updating can conversely be evaluated positively as it is closely linked precisely to the needs of constant adaptation of professional skills. It seems to be transversally a subject of constant negotiation between the social partners, given the strategic importance of the subject in terms of competitiveness and innovative development of the company.[33] Training and development of human resources are considered fields in which companies tend to invest, in accordance with the need for growth and business evolution, as well as to better respond to economic, organisational and productive needs. This confirms the need to understand professionalism in a dynamic and evolutionary sense and in terms of the personal background of the worker, which is not tied to the individual workplace, but rather expendable in the labour market and is able to ensure the worker's operability in the new organisational systems, also through a continuing training activity complying with the principle of lifelong learning.

17.3 A STRATEGIC ROLE OF SOCIAL PARTNERS FACED WITH THE GUARANTEES OF LABOUR LAW?

At least two observations emerge from these few inputs. First, within this complex context, the idea that the protection of work passes through a guarantee of stability seems now outdated, at least from the point of view of the professionalism acquired. Protection today would not correspond to safeguarding stability at all costs; it rather refers to the protection of those fundamental of the worker with the needs of the company, considering changes and emerging challenges, in a win-win perspective that is the result of a mediation of interests and that follows a logic that does not undermine either of the parties involved or their expectations.

It involves the necessity to challenge the traditional categories of the 'old' labour law, but without undermining its axiological dimension, since it is concerned with a 'material' which has in itself a value different from the commodity.[34] This is why one of the tools that makes effective the protection of the man who works effectively must be preserved: the binding nature of the laws and of the collective contract clauses, which aims to protect the weak part of the relationship.

31. An example, but an isolated case, of integration of collective national agreements is that one of the Supplementary Company Agreement of Club Mediterranèe S.A., 4 March 2015 (with Fisascat, UILTuCs, Filcams).
32. It should be pointed the case of the Agreement Automobili Lamborghini Spa, 7 March 2017 (with Fiom-CGIL, Fim-CISL), defined 'Anti-Jobs Act', continuing to ensure protection of professionalism acquired (in the old sense) in exception to the law.
33. For example, Agreement on continuing education of Esselunga Spa, 25 February 2013 (with Fisascat, UILTuCs, Filcams); Supplementary Company Agreement Automobili Lamborghini Spa, 22 May 2015, Article 6 (*Training and Professionalism*) and that one of 17 March 2017.
34. The values prospective (emphasised, i.e., by the studies of Mengoni, L. Mengoni, *Diritto e valori*, Il Mulino, 1985) depends on human dimension of work, as it is summarised in the famous formula 'labor is not a commodity' of the Declaration of Philadelphia (1944). *See* M. Grandi, *Il lavoro non è una merce: una formula da rimeditare*, in *Lav. dir.*, 1997, 4, pp. 557 ff.

Even though this approach is not unanimously shared and the instability of the structure of the sources, resulting from the most recent reforms, undermines the substantial binding nature,[35] the idea of the necessary conservation of the technique appears essential. In accordance with the historical function of labour law, the subject must guarantee the right balance between the reasons for development and the needs for the protection of the human person. In doing so – faced with the risk of consequences related to the problems of digital work in platform, its representation and its classification – collective bargaining in this way has increasingly played a key role.[36] It has always been – better than law – not only an extremely valuable tool to deal with changes, to ensure the adaptability, but also to provide for the safety of workers.

Hence, a second observation emerges. If the cycles of technological innovation linked to the digitalisation of work make it increasingly hard for the legislator to 'keep pace with changes',[37] the role of the social partners should be deemed to be crucial, to the extent that they are able to take into account the variability of the possible models and find suitable solutions to effectively balance the needs of the company and of the job with those of the workers.

Although it is certainly not possible to think of stopping progress, it is rather possible to face changes by adapting tasks, places and timetables to the needs of production contexts also through the bargaining tool. This could be achieved by reconciling the different interests of capital and labour, and it entails a cooperation between the employer and the employee representatives, the latter being involved not only through forms of greater participation.[38]

This awareness has equally been achieved by the trade union actors. The idea of a participatory dimension of industrial relations, characterised by the identification of the good performance of the company and a better working conditions as a common goal for both parties, is not new, but it seems to be enriched today by driving forces, as an additional effect. Once again in the mentioned interconfederal agreement of 9 March 2018, having taken into account the gradual devaluation of the concertation, the same social partners have expressed their intention to modernise the industrial relations in a participative prospective and collective bargaining in order to actively contribute to promoting the competitiveness of companies and the valorisation of work. Furthermore, with regard to second-level contractual practice, recently the reference to the needs of innovation has often been accompanied by the reference to improve the profiles of participation and involvement of workers in the growth dynamics of the company.[39] It would seem that indirectly the industrial revolution causes an additional

35. A. Pizzoferrato, *L'autonomia collettiva nel nuovo diritto del lavoro*, *supra*, pp. 447 ff.
36. Labour law has not only been based on the legislation of the work relationship and the market, but also has always breathed with two lungs: in addition to binding legislative previsions, the other lung is the collective bargaining, M. Napoli, *La tutela del lavoro tra legge e contrattazione collettiva*, in M. Napoli, V. Ferrante, M. Corti, A. Occhino, *Nuove tendenze nelle fonti del Diritto del lavoro. Dagli accordi del 2009 e 2011 al decreto legge 138*, Vita e Pensiero, 2014, p. 4.
37. M. Weiss, *Digitalizzazione: sfide e prospettive per il diritto del lavoro*, *supra*, p. 660.
38. *See* A. Gabriele, *I diritti sindacali in azienda*, Giappichelli, 2017.
39. For instance, Integrating Agreement of chemical-pharmaceutical group Bayer, 30 July 2014 (with Fisascat, UILTuCs, Filcams); Supplementary Company Agreement Eataly Distribuzione Srl, 28 October 2015 (with Fisascat, UILTuCs, Filcams); Agreement on Industrial Relations of

effect: a constant – and perhaps never resolved – need to rethink collective bargaining and industrial relations, as well as the labour law discipline, for their undeniable strategic importance.[40]

Euronics Italia Spa, 5 October 2016 (with Fisascat, UILTuCs, Filcams); Supplementary Company Agreement Luxury Goods Italia Spa – Divisione Retail Gucci, 30 January 2017 (with Fisascat, UILTuCs, Filcams).

40. *See* the observations in A. Bellavista, *Gli orizzonti del diritto del lavoro post-statutario*, in AIDLASS, *Legge e contrattazione collettiva nel diritto del lavoro post-statutario*, Acts of Study-days of Labour Law, Naples 16-17 June 2016, Giuffrè, 2017, pp. 342 ff.

PART V Platform Work and Business 4.0: Analysis of Some National Cases

CHAPTER 18

Gig Work: Employees or Independent Contractors? Data and Regulatory Challenges in the Swedish Experience

Federico Fusco

18.1 INTRODUCTION: LABOUR IS NOT A COMMODITY ... BUT A SERVICE IS

One of the basic principles of labour law is the well-known principle: 'labour is not a commodity'.[1] As it always happens when designing a law also this statement has been shaped moving from the existent reality. In the Taylorism and Fordism models, almost the entire production process took place within a big firm. Thus, there was the need to state that the labour was different from the other input of the production and had to be treated differently.

The technological development of the production processes made this model obsolete. Nowadays, the in-house production has been largely replaced by the outsourcing, with companies focusing on their core business and buying on the market all the other necessary goods or services.

In the beginning, this shift form the 'make' towards the 'buy' affected the labour relationship only in an indirect way. Even if the outsourcing processes had a big impact on the workers, to the extent that they have been protected by specific norms on the transfer of undertakings (or part of them),[2] the survival of the notion of 'employee' was not challenged.[3] Therefore, regulative issues have concerned only subjects that, being on the border between employees and self-employed (or, better, being self-employed

1. Article 427 of the Treaty of Versailles (1919) and Art. 1 of the Declaration of Philadelphia (1944).
2. *See* EC Directive 2001/23.
3. In fact, the legal provisions focus on the safeguarding of the employees' rights and on how to identify who is the (new) employer.

who shared with the employees some of their weaknesses), have been typically protected thanks to the extension of some right typical of the employment relationship.

However, in the last years the technological progress is reshaping the features of the processes of externalization. In this regard, a number of new web platforms connect in real time and with low costs economic actors from all over the world. Thus, for a growing set of tasks it is no longer necessary the physical presence of a human being within the perimeter of the firm (and under the scheme of the employment relationship).

To obtain this result a complex activity is split into a series of elementary tasks, which are than allocated, via the platforms, to a multitude of people. The key element of this scheme is that those economic actors are not providing a 'working activity', but are committed to achieve a specific result.

This difference between 'working activity' and 'specific result' is very important. In fact, an actor providing the latter is not offering to the capitalist his time and working energies such as the classic blue-collar. Instead, he is fulfilling a contract of service delivering, whose elements have been freely negotiated by the parties on the (digital) market. This feature is exploited in order to claim that such economic actor is not an employee, but an independent contractor.

Now if it is true that labour is not a commodity, it is also true that a service can be. However, as clearly pointed out by Prassl the new technologies are making the link between service and provider so thin that it is possible to speak of 'humans as a service'.[4] In fact, the web platforms exploit the lack of physical contact, the depersonalization of the activity and the automation of certain operations such as billing and payment in order to create a curtain between the contracting parties. Thus, it is presented as a service something that in its core features is not very different from the process of making available for the employer his own working energies.

In this regard it is possible to claim that web platforms creates distance, eliminating distance: while the physical distance is no longer a matter thanks to the information and communication technologies, the aseptic environment of the net glosses with a polished surface something that otherwise would pretty much look like a labour relation.

In this light, if we want to respect the essence of the recalled fundamental principle 'labour is not a commodity', there is the need for further investigation of the phenomenon of the gig economy and of its regulatory challenges.

18.2 THE SWEDISH EXPERIENCE

A common initial obstacle in the analysis of the gig economy is the lack of data concerning its dimension and features. In fact, the public records, such as the ones of tax and social protection authorities, do not register if an activity is related to the gig

4. Prassl, J. 2018. *Humans as a Service: The Promise and Perils of Work in the Gig Economy*, Oxford University Press.

economy.[5] On the other hand, the empirical researches are hindered by the lack of geographical fences for the activities carried using the net. Thus, it is difficult to identify the sample to analyse. The issue has been addressed Prof. Vili Lehdonvirta and Dr Otto Kässi of the Oxford Internet Institute with the creation of the Online Labour Index. It consists in a software that automatically crawls the five largest English-language online labour platforms, tracking the number and type of available tasks. The comparison of the results of two succeeding crawls provides a measure of the jobs that have been accepted. Those data are used in order to create an index that measures the variation of the supply and demand of online tasks, using as conventional benchmark the daily average of May 2016.[6] This method gives a picture of the gig economy from an employer perspective (the tasks are sorted in relation with the employer's country), but a similar system is used also in order to investigate the geographical origin of the workers.

Thanks to their constant update, those instruments are undoubtedly useful in order to observe that part of the gig work that does not require a physical contact between the parties involved. However, among the platforms that are studied are not listed the major ones providing the so-called work on demand via internet. This is a sector of the gig economy in which the service must be locally delivered. Thus, it involves a physical contact between the two parties (such as transports service via Uber or food delivery via Foodora). Even if this share of the gig economy is comparatively smaller, under a labour law perspective it generates relevant problems, due to the social dumping that creates within the same nation.

For this reason for the extent of this study, we have preferred to rely on data collected with the classic instrument of the survey and that offer the benefit to give a full-scale picture of the gig economy.

As a general introduction it should be pointed out that a major share of the Swedish work-age population is somehow involved in the online economy: without counting online grocery shopping and online home rental schemes (such as Airbnb), the 68% of Swedes are either obtaining an income from online activities or buying labour via online platforms.

However, in spite of those data the web workers are not widely spread in Sweden, even if they have a good potential of growth.[7]

In fact, there are a good number of platforms, which allow web working. The most important one are, for crowd working, Upwork and Clickworker (Amazon Mechanical Turk is not very used by Swedish workers) and, for work on demand via internet, Uber, Foodora, Hungrig and Care.com.

5. Often there is no official definition for gig economy, web work, etc. Moreover, the literature points out the risk that economic operations related to the gig economy could not been reported to the tax authorities, which struggle to surveil it. *See* OECD 2018. *The Future of Social Protection: What Works for Non-standard Workers?*, Paris, OECD Publishing, https://doi.org/10.1787/9789264306943-en.
6. *See* Online Labour Index at https://ilabour.oii.ox.ac.uk/online-labour-index/.
7. For this result, *see* both Eurofound 2015. New forms of employment. Publications Office of the European Union Luxembourg, 108 and Pesole, A. et al., 2018. Platform Workers in Europe: Evidence from the COLLEEM Survey. Joint Research Centre (Seville site), 5 ss.

A survey from 2016[8] shows that there are around 737,000 workers active in the gig economy in this Nordic country, representing the 12% of the working force (adults aged 16-65). For most of them, it is and occasional activity and only 3% of Swedes do it at least one a week (4% at least one a month). However, the rate of people willing to find a job thanks to the crowd economy appears to be relevant (24% of the workforce).

In addition, the web work seems to be a supplementary source of income, rather than the main one. In fact, for the 33% of the gig-workers the revenues from this activity accounts to less than 10% of the global income. Only about 23% of them (that correspond to the 2.8% of the active population) get from this activity more than the 50% of their total revenues.

The income from web working is generally low, with the 53% of web workers earning less than SEK 300,000 per year and 87% less of SEK 500,000 per year. High earners (more than SEK 700,000 per year) comprise only 4% of web workers. Slightly higher is the average income of people purchasing web work (around 31% of the population): the 7% earns more than SEK 700,000 per year and the 76% less than SEK 500,000 per year.

Swedish web workers are mostly concentrated in the main centres of population, with Stockholm and Gothenburg areas (the two biggest metropolitan areas of the country) accounting the 44% of them. They are largely young: the 28% of them is between 16-24 years old and 29% between 25-34. However, only minor parts of them (around 12%) are students, thus suggesting the idea that the majority people are fully available on the labour market.

Coming to the major distinction between crowd workers and workers on demand via internet in Sweden the most of the web workers is willing to perform both types of jobs. The typical web worker performs a variety of different activities, suggesting the idea of a very flexible work force not only considering the working time and load, but also with regard with the type of job.

However, the crowd working is the most common option (87% of web workers perform it). This choice puts them in a weaker position on the labour market because most of the tasks can be performed from everywhere, so that they compete on a global labour market with workers from India, Eastern Europe and other low-wage countries. Also because of this reason, the average pay of this type of task is low, especially if compared to the Swedish standard.[9] A more in deep analysis shows that they are mostly performing office work, short tasks or 'click work' (70%) or creative or IT work from home (63%).

The ratio of Swedish web workers willing to be workers on demand via internet is, instead, of 62% and the most commonly tasks are cleaning, carpentry and gardening activities performed in other people's homes (55%). Finally, the 35% seeks for a work as driver, but this figure could be influenced by the fact that in 2016 an important web based driving service such as Uber Pop was deemed illegal and shut down.

8. Huws, U., Joyce, S. *Size of Sweden's 'Gig-Economy' Revealed for the First Time*, Foundation for European Progressive Studies UNI Europa 2016.
9. Eurofound 2015. New forms of employment. Publications Office of the European Union Luxembourg, 115.

In fact, in Sweden as in other European countries, some of the sectors interested by the web work are heavily regulated, thus creating several normative obstacles. This happens especially in the transport sector, where are often required some types of administrative authorizations. In this light in 2016, the Uber Pop service was deemed to be against the law on taxi licenses and shut down. In addition, other controversial aspects concern the status of the drivers as employee or independent contractors. Claiming a misclassification from the company, the Swedish Tax Authority (*Skatteverket*) has recently requested to Uber to pay SEK 16.8 million for unpaid employer's contributions and taxes only with regard to 2015.

Moving back to the wage issue, the crowd work, also because of the social dumping created by the international competition between workers, is generally lower paid compared to the work on demand via internet. However, even the latter presents some problems, being the average income lower than the one provided by the Swedish collective agreements for similar activities. This gap stems from the fact that most of the web workers are freelancers and not employee. Thus, they are devoid of collective agreement that in the Swedish labour market is an essential source of rights. An example of this situation is offered by the Foodora case (which is one of the few platforms resorting also to employee), where, accordingly to the Swedish Union for transport workers (*Transportarbetarförbundet*) only, in few cases the workers reached the minimum wage of the sector.

Nevertheless, the lack of unionization of the Foodara's deliverers hinders the trade union's efforts to persuade the firm to sign a collective agreement. This aspect drives the attention upon another essential flaw of the gig economy. In fact, the regulation of the Swedish labour market is grounded on the existence of a high rate of both trade union density and collective agreements coverage. Thus, most of the standards stems from the collective agreements, rather than being granted by the law. For those reasons, the lack of members among a firm's workforce is a great obstacle for the implement of working conditions, but this situation is the most common when it comes of web work.[10]

18.2.1 The Challenge Posed by the Gig Economy to the Grounds of the Employment Relationship Itself

One of the most important aspects of the web work is that it is mostly regulated as self-employment.

This is a common thread of the gig economy, whose profitability stems not only from the reduction of the transaction costs thanks to the technological platforms. In fact, an important feature of this economic sector consists also in the avoidance of the labour legislation,[11] which in some analysis has been pinpointed as its driving force.[12]

Under an economic perspective, this trend is perfectly rational. In fact, as Coase pointed out, the firm exists in order to reduce transaction costs. Thus, a firm prefers to

10. *See* Unionen, *Plattformsekonomin och den svenska partsmodellen*, Stockholm, 2016.
11. *See* Prassl, J. 2018. *Humans as a Service: The Promise and Perils of Work in the Gig Economy*, Oxford University Press. Ch. 6. A quick idea of the dimension of this matter in a country with

organize something by itself if its cost is inferior compared to the one of carrying out the transactions thought the market. This implies that 'the limit to the size of the firm is set where its costs of organizing a transaction become equal to the cost of carrying it out through the market'.[13] In other words, the essence of the firm is to organize and direct with a certain degree of authority a set of resources as long as this leads to costs savings.[14] Towards the human resources, this authority relationship is crystalized in the employment contract and in the subsequent subordination of the employee.

It is now clear that if the cost of carrying out an operation through the market diminishes during the time, the entrepreneur will downsize the firm. In fact, it would be more convenient to revert to the open market. This is a well-known trend and, during the twentieth century, it led to the overcoming of the Fordism. However, until the rise of the gig economy, most of the activities were outsourced to other firms that were fulfilling them using their own employees. Thus, the problem that arose concerned the labour standards granted by those firms, but not the existence of the labour relation itself.[15]

Nowadays, instead, the online platforms allow to outsource an increasing number of activities to individuals that fulfil them acting as service providers. This implies that among the whole value chain the task is completed without involving any employment contract.

In other words, the employment relationship stems from the need to organize a firm, which, in turn, aims to save the greater costs of using the price mechanism on the market. For this reason, if those costs drop under a certain level, there is no point in using the employment contract anymore.

Moving from those remarks, we can argue that the gig economy is undermining the economic ratio that grounds the employment contract.

On the other hand, if we agree that the labour law is something more than a simple tool of rationalization of the economic activity, the reasoning explained above is not sufficient to justify its overcoming. In particular, if we focus on the need to rebalance the power between the economic actors, we can argue that the gig economy imposes new regulations, rather than a deregulation. In fact, the online platforms act as a filter between supply and demand and have an exclusive and complete information about the size and features of both of them. Thus, they can exploit this asymmetric information in order to shape the market to their advantage.

high labour costs such as Sweden is provided by the already mentioned ongoing claim of SEK 16.8 million raised by the Swedish Tax Authority against Uber for a solely year of operation of the Uber Pop service.

12. With specific regard to the Uber case the 'regulatory arbitrage' – i.e., the circumvention of the employment law – is identified as the major source of the gig economy profits by Tomassetti, J. *Does Uber Redefine the Firm? The Postindustrial Corporation and Advanced Information Technology, Hofstra Labor & Employment Law Journal*, Vol. 34: Iss. 1, Art. 3, 34, 2016.
13. Coase, R.H. 1998. *The Firm, the Market and the Law*, University of Chicago Press, 7.
14. Coase, R.H. 1937. *The Nature of the Firm, Economica*, Vol. 4, 392.
15. Davidov, G. *Indirect Employment: Should Lead Companies Be Liable?, Comparative Labor Law and Policy Journal*, 2015, 37, 6-7.

For those reasons, as we will see below, the labour law has not completed its function. Nevertheless, considering that the classic scheme of the employment relationship is losing its economic ground, there is the need of new criteria of allocation of the labour protections.[16]

18.2.2 The Legal Challenges under the Present Legal Frame

As we have mentioned at the beginning of the previous section, the gig economy platforms in their contractual relationship with the gig-workers tend to exclude any employment relationship.

This regulatory arbitrage can be of course challenged I front of the national courts, which can reclassify the gig-worker as an employee. However, the length and costs of the processes, together with the uncertain concerning their outcome caused by the peculiar features of the gig work, hinder this solution. Thus, it result a sector still characterized by the self-employment.[17]

Those features are present also in Sweden,[18] even if this regulatory arbitrage has recently been partially challenged. In fact, as mentioned, the Swedish Tax Agency is currently running an investigation, which could end in the reclassification of the Uber Pop drivers as employees.

The picture of the Swedish gig economy is completed by the existence of the so-called umbrella companies (*egenanställningsföretag*). Those companies hire the freelancers (also, but not only, working in the gig economy), which then become, from a formal point of view, their employees. However, this scheme does not ensure the typical employee's rights. In fact, the workers have no right to a fixed wage, but must find the clients by themselves. Once the worker-freelancer has found one, the contractual relationship is established between this client and the umbrella company. This means that that is the company, which invoices the client and, after the payment, transfers the amount to the freelancer. The advantage lies in the fact that this scheme

16. Hendrickx, F. *Regulating New Ways of Working: From the New 'Wow' to the New 'How'*, *European Labour Law Journal*, Vol. 9, Iss. 2, 2018, 202, where the A. points out that: 'the real contrast is perhaps not employee versus employer, but labour versus capital'.
17. For example, Uber drivers have been considered limb (b) workers in UK (dependent contractors that enjoy only some employee rights. *See* Employment Tribunal of London, case n. 2202551/2015 *Mr. Y Aslam, Mr. J Farrar & others v. Uber*, reasons of 28 October 2016). In France, it was stated that they are self-employed (Conseil de Prud'hommes de Paris, Case F 16/11460 of 29 January 2018, *F. Menard v. Uber France*). Finally, in California - USA - an ongoing class action has almost been settled with an USD 100 million lump sum agreement that was, however, refused by the judge on the basis that the claims must be solved under the arbitration procedures and not with a class action (*see Douglas O'Connor et al. v. Uber Technologies Inc.*, Case No. 13-cv-03826-EMC - ND Cal. For the appeal, *see* US Court of Appeal for the Ninth Circuit, 25 September 2018). In Italy the riders from Foodora have been considered to be self-employed by the decision of Tribunale di Torino of 7 May 2018, n. 778. In France, the ones of Take Eat Easy have been classified as employee (*see* Cour de cassation - Chambre sociale - arrêt n°1737 of 28 November 2018).
18. *See* Huws U., Joyce, S. *Size of Sweden's 'Gig-Economy'*, *supra* and OECD 2018. *The Future of Social Protection: What Works for Non-standard Workers?*, Paris, OECD Publishing, 205.

relieves the freelancer from a diverse number of administrative burdens and paperwork. In fact, the company, because of its formal status of employer, carries out those tasks, charging on the freelancer a cost, usually as a share of his revenues.

It is important to specify that the adoption of this scheme is fully voluntary, so that a gig-worker, as well as any other self-employed, can freely decide if join an umbrella company or not. For this reason, the data collected by organization of those companies (*Egenanställningsföretagens branschorganisation*) are not sufficient to track the dimension of the gig work. In addition, it should be pointed out that the recent OECD report is deceiving because it mentions the registration with an umbrella company as a legal requirement.[19]

Concerning the qualification of the contract is should also be mentioned that the Swedish employment law is based on the principle of the 'primacy of facts'. According to this rule, the work relationship must be qualified because of its actual features. Thus, the qualification contained in the contract can be challenged in court in order to obtain a requalification of the agreement. However, as it has been pointed out, this is a theoretical possibility, rather than an actual one. In fact, 'many self-employed persons holding a registered Business Tax Certificate would ... never challenge their contractual status as self-employed persons, since they, and their contractor, might prefer this contractual arrangement'.[20]

Nevertheless, the diverse classification of workers may create imbalances on the market under the aspect of an unfair competition based on social dumping. This happens even admitting that a self-employed gig-worker would get the same remuneration that he would obtain performing the activity as an employee.[21] In fact, the diverse legislation on social protection generates a different final cost, making a gig-worker cheaper (under the same average hourly wage) than an employee. This divide depends from the combination of several factors. First of all, even if self-employed are covered by (and must pay contributions to) a series of social schemes (as unemployment and disability insurance), they are exempted from the one aimed to finance the wage guarantee (*lönegaranti*). In fact, not having any employee they are not exposed to the risk of not being able to pay wages. Thus, their global social insurance contribution is equal to 28.97%, while for an employee is 32.14%.

Another important difference is the lack of collective agreement, which in Sweden usually introduces additional contributions for the pension scheme. In average, this generates a raise of the labour cost of 5% for lower wages and significantly greater for the higher ones.[22]

---

19. *Ibid.*
20. Inghammar, A. 2017. The Concept of 'Employee': The Position in Sweden. *In:* Waas, B. & Voss, G.H.V. (eds) *Restatement of Labour Law in Europe: Vol I: The Concept of Employee.* Hart Publishing Limited, 687.
21. *See* the *Transportarbetarförbundet* (Transportation Workers Union) campaign: 'How tasty is 39 kr per hour?' (*Hur gott smakar 39 kr i timmen?*). This pay rate refers mainly to Uber eat. In Foodora, part of the riders has an employment contract with fixed shifts and a minimum pay of SEK 70 per hour.
22. *See* OECD 2018. *The Future of Social Protection: What Works for Non-standard Workers?*, Paris, OECD Publishing, 205-206.

For all of those reasons only taking into account social contributions the cost of a self-employed is around 8% lower than the one of an employee. This difference is narrowed if the gig-worker operates under an umbrella company because in this case he formally is an employee. Thus, it should be paid also the share of social contribution for the wage guarantee. However, depending from the platform's structure, the worker could not be able to transfer this extra cost on the client, with the result of a decrease of his net income.[23]

Moving from this theoretical legal framework to its practical implementation, there are two other issues that must be investigated.

The first consist in the difficulties of enforce the social security and fiscal provisions towards a huge number of self-employed, each of whom is liable for only relatively small amount of money. In contrast to what happens with the employment contract, where all the payments to the tax and social security agencies are made by the employer, the platforms are not usually subject to this burden, which, instead, lies on the gig-workers. In case of non-compliance it is, then, necessary to recover the due amounts from each individual worker. This raises both costs and time of the enforcement procedure and, so, hinders them.[24] Moreover, the available data suggest that, when the working performance can be delivered over the net, the worker often performs the activity from a different country from the client's one.[25] In this case, it can be even more difficult to identify and implement the proper fiscal provisions, especially if the activity involves a subject living outside of European Union. Moreover, if those provisions create an obligation to pay some taxes in Sweden, it is can be very difficult for the Swedish Tax Authority to discover the lack of reporting and, therefore, to enforce the payment.[26]

The second problem consists in the difficulties for the Swedish gig-workers to obtain the unemployment benefits for whom they have paid the social contributions. The main problem is that they struggle in demonstrating the condition of involuntary unemployed, which is needed in order to obtain those benefits.[27] This happens because self-employed do not have a former employer that can certify the dismissal. Thus, they are asked for a self-declaration, but this method raises the risk of abuses. For this reason, the legislation requires to shut down the firm, but this operation and the

23. This is the typical case of the transport and delivery platforms where the remuneration is calculated by an algorithm taking into account a set of elements such as time, distance, level of global request, etc.
24. For example, the Swedish Tax Authority highlights the trend of the Uber Pop drivers of misreport their incomes. *See* Skatteverket 2017. Slutrapport för kontroller av UberPop-förare inkomstår 2015, 2 ss.
25. *See* Online Labour Index, *supra*.
26. It can be argued that all the payments of the web platform are performed by electronic means and, thus, are trackable. However, even admitting that the Tax Agency has direct access to all the electronic transfers related to a Swedish account (and it has not), in most of the cases the platform acts as an intermediary (or filter) between the parties. This makes more difficult to link the payments made by the clients to the single gig-worker. Moreover, additional obstacles are represented by the fact that most platforms are registered in foreign countries and hosted on foreign servers.
27. OECD 2018. *The Future of Social Protection: What Works for Non-standard Workers?*, Paris, OECD Publishing, 211.

following necessary investigations from the unemployment funds usually take a longer time. Moreover, there is the risk that self-employed abuse of the unemployment benefits in order to maximize their incomes during periods in whom a lowering of the income would be normal. Therefore, when the business is resumed after obtaining those benefits, it is imposed a cool down of five years before being able to obtain the benefit again.

The situation remains critical even if the gig-worker is hired via an umbrella company. In fact, being formally an employee, he should obtain from the former employer a declaration assessing the condition of involuntary unemployed. However, the umbrella company is only a façade and, thus, cannot provide it.

18.3 CONCLUSION

The analysis conducted in this chapter shows that the gig work in Sweden is actually wrapped in a coat of uncertainty: the shortage of data concerning its dimension hinders a complete understanding of the phenomenon and of the related need of a specific regulation.

In such a situation platform companies argue that their services foster a more inclusive labour market. In fact, they would allow people that otherwise would be (at least partially) inactive to perform some working activities during a 'transition period' towards a more stable job. Some examples would be people with caring responsibilities or the ones performing for most of their times another activities, such as students or people that already have another job. For those reasons the gig work would be a marginal phenomenon, unsuitable for a specific legal intervention.

However, on the other hand there is the risk for a part of population to be trapped in those low productivity jobs. This would create a social cost that, in the absence of specific rules aimed to internalize it, would be borne by the society.

The analysis conducted above shows that the classic employment rules struggle to fit to the gig economy. In fact, they are based on the major divide between employees and self-employed. However, the changes in the way of working caused by the web platforms make this classification unfit to describe the contemporary reality.

This finding highlights that our labour law is missing one of its aims: it is leaving outside of its protective shelter people who, accordingly with the scope of labour law itself, should enjoy its protection. The same happens with the social security system, whose benefits cannot be fully enjoined by the gig-workers, which is a cause of the high degree of fragmentation of their working life.

For those reasons, there is the need to recalibrate both the area of intervention of labour law and the functioning of the welfare system in order to protect also the above-mentioned subjects.

In fact, the gig-workers, unlike the normal self-employed, are not able to achieve by themselves a level of working condition and social security rights in line with the Swedish standards. Therefore, without a proper intervention they will be segregated in the lower part of the society.

Besides the ethical issues, the outcome of such situation would be that those people:

(1) get an income level far below the average Swedish standard, thus motivating the companies to substitute their (more expensive) employees with this cheaper form of job;
(2) get very low level of social benefits (included pensions) because of the low contributions to the related insurances;[28]
(3) will be keener to need financial aid, thus becoming a cost for the society.

For those reasons, we think that the labour rights should be allocated using criteria other than the classic dichotomy 'employee – self-employed'. A possible solution could be to resort to a risk-based approach.

The fundamental reason for whom the labour law protects certain subjects does not rely on the status of employees. In fact, this merely constitutes a legal category used to group together people whom, because of their situation, need some protection. In other words, it represents a superstructure used to describe individuals that share a weak position on the labour market and, thus, deserve special attention.

However, as explained above, the gig economy is eroding the economic need of the employment contract. At the same time, it is creating economic actors that, despite being devoid of many of the classic features of the employee, share with him the economic weakness.

This shift of the way of production suggests the need of an adaptation of the allocation criteria of the labour protections. In fact, if in the past the category of 'employee' encompassed all the economic actors needing protection, nowadays it leaves out an increasing number of subjects.

In our opinion, this problem can be solved allocating the labour law protections with regard to the possible economic outcome of the activity done by each subject. Generally, people perform an economic activity because they expect a profit from it. Depending on the features of such activity the possible profit can be higher or lower. In the former case, the economic actor does not need a specific protection from the law; in the latter, he does.

Thus, the labour law protections should be allocated according to the economic power. People performing activities from whom they can get lower profits should enjoy higher protections. The contrary should happen for those who can make higher profits.

Such scheme would grant protections not only to the classic employees but also to the gig-workers. In fact, most of them do not have the power to shape their activity in order to make it more profitable.[29]

28. *See* Kommittédirektiv Dir. 2018:8, *En ny arbetslöshetsförsäkring för fler, grundad på inkomster*; Kommittédirektiv Dir. 2017:56, *Trygghet och utveckling i anställningen vad gäller arbetstid och ledighet*.
29. *See* Employment Tribunal of London, case n. 2202551/2015, *supra*, where concerning the Uber drivers is stated: 'no driver is in a position to (grow his business), unless growing his business simply means spending more hours at the wheel'.

In addition, it would allow to adjust the type and strength of protection according to the effective economic power of the individual. This would prevent one of the main issues of the dichotomy 'employee/self-employed' in which, in theory, either is granted a whole set of protection, either none. It can be objected that this is not true, because when there is an individual who has features of both the categories, usually special rules are applied. For example, managers are devoid of some of the protections, while some additional rights are usually extended to economically weak self-employed. This objection would be naturally true. Nevertheless, it omits to consider that such scheme works thanks to derogations and special exemptions to the general rule 'employees are protected, self-employed are not'.

However, as demonstrated by the gig economy, the adaptability of this scheme faces some limits. The outcome is that nowadays the gig economy is dumping on the society part of the (social) costs that it generates.[30]

Thus, it seems more appropriate to adopt a new mechanism of allocation of the labour law protections that would force the economic actors to bear the costs created by their activity.

However, a similar solution requires an extensive intervention of the legislator and, thus, it is not feasible in the short term.

30. Tomassetti, J. *Does Uber Redefine the Firm?, supra.*

CHAPTER 19

Protection from Discriminatory Dismissal According to ILO Norms in the Context of German and Turkish National Law

*Ceren Kasım**

19.1 INTRODUCTION

Can the existing international labour law protections also potentially protect workers, employees or independent contractors working in new forms of work? The aim of this chapter is to discuss this question in terms of the meaning of International Labour Organization (ILO) law in the context of discriminatory dismissal from a comparative perspective, namely by comparing German and Turkish law.

Indeed, there are already existing protections according to ILO norms which are applicable to all people under employment relationship or occupation regardless of their legal status as employees or independent contractors. Protection against discrimination is one of them; this protection is also the main topic of this chapter. Protection against discriminatory dismissal on the other hand is the intersection point of the anti-discrimination law and the dismissal protection law as shown in the figure below:

* This chapter is based on a part of the author's ongoing doctoral research.

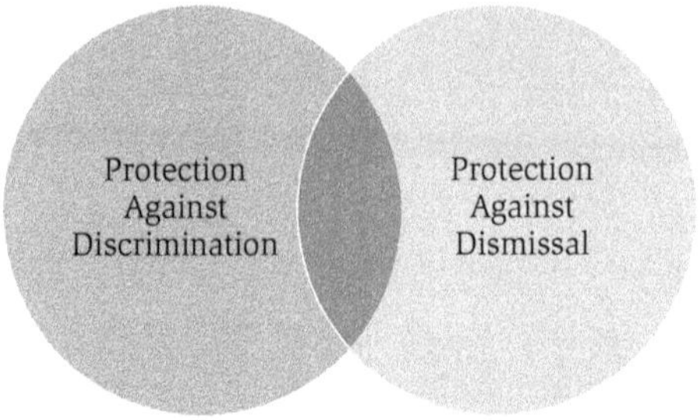

Source: Author's own work.

Anti-discrimination laws' legal roots in international law can be traced back to the UN Charter. Currently, the obligation of states not to discriminate against citizens is found in core human rights norms. As an independent field of law governing pre-contractual and contractual relationships between individuals, anti-discrimination law emerged in the US after the Second World War. Other countries developed anti-discrimination norms beginning in the 1960s. At present, the vast majority of states ban discrimination. Anti-discrimination law has a broad scope. Among other things, it deals with employment relations. In the ILO system the elimination of discrimination with respect to employment and occupation is considered to be one of the fundamental principles and rights at work. ILO Convention No. 100 (Equal Remuneration Convention) (C100) and ILO Convention No. 111 (Discrimination (Employment and Occupation) Convention) (C111), both dealing with discrimination, are accepted as fundamental ILO Conventions.

On the other hand, dismissal protection has a very different status. The termination of an employment contract can take various forms. The most common way is the dismissal. Dismissal protection makes the termination of a contract difficult or bans it and requires the employer to comply with prescribed conditions at the termination. Protection against dismissal emerged from the European workers' movement and European legal history. Today, despite the efforts of the ILO, there is no global consensus on a protection against dismissal. Only a few ILO Member States (36 out of 187 states) have ratified the ILO Convention on the Termination of Employment by the Employer (ILO Convention No. 158) (C158). Even in the countries with statutory dismissal protection regulations, a reduction of the degree of dismissal protection can be observed, especially in times of economic crisis.

The ILO, as the oldest United Nations specialized agency with 187 Member States, has a unique structure within the UN system with its tripartite system and since its inception has been at the forefront of developing and internationalizing labour and social standards.[1] Since its founding in 1919, the ILO has passed 189 conventions.[2]

1. The ILO was established as an agency of the League of Nations with the Treaty of Versailles in 1919 following World War I. *International Labour Office*, The Labour Provisions of the Peace Treaties, Geneva 1920.
2. https://www.ilo.org/dyn/normlex/en/f?p=1000:12000:::NO::: (20.1.2019).

Nonetheless, today fewer than half of these, i.e., 76 ILO conventions, contain up-to-date regulations, and deal with a variety of subjects, from working conditions and social security, to the special needs of certain professions.[3] A characteristic of ILO norms is that they are generally not self-executive. ILO conventions do not have any direct effect after their adoption, as is the case with other international treaties.[4] Regardless of the vote of the country's delegates on the adoption of the ILO standard, a Member State's affiliation with an ILO convention is only possible after its ratification.[5] With regard to this, in this chapter the application, effectiveness and promotion of ILO norms which govern the protection against discriminatory dismissal (which on the one hand has a fundamental character, thanks to the protection against discrimination, but on the other does not, because of the protection against dismissal) will be discussed in the context of German and Turkish law (*see* Table 19.1).

Table 19.1 Germany Versus Turkey

	Federal Republic of Germany	*Republic of Turkey*
Area	357,386 km^2 (62nd)	783,356 km^2 (36th)
Population	83,000,000 (17th)	82,003,882 (19th)
Government	Federal	Unitary
	Parliamentary Republic	Presidential Constitutional Republic (Since 2018)
Secularity	Not Secular	Secular
Formation	German Empire 1871	Ottoman Empire 1299
	Weimar Republic 1918	War of Independence 1919
	NS-State 1933	Declaration of Republic 1923
	West and East Germany 1945-1990	Parliamentary Representative Dem. 1923-2018
	Reunification 1990	Presidential System 2018 (1961, 1971 and 1981 Military Coups)
GDP (PPP)	total USD 4.555 trillion (5th)	total USD 2.274 trillion (13th)
	per capita USD 54,983 (18th)	per capita USD 27,390 (45th)
HDI	0.936 – very high (5th)	0.791 – high (64th)
Official Language	German	Turkish

3. https://www.ilo.org/dyn/normlex/en/f?p=1000:12020:::NO::: (20.1.2019).
4. Zimmer, R., Wirkungsweise, Auslegung und Implementierung der Standards der Internationalen Arbeitsorganisation in Deutschland, in W. Däubler/R. Zimmer (Hrsg.), Arbeitsvölkerrecht, Festschrift für Klaus Lörcher, Baden-Baden 2013, P. 29 (30).
5. Zimmer, FS-Lörcher, P. 29 (30).

	Federal Republic of Germany	*Republic of Turkey*
State and Ethnicity	Immigration Country	Multinational State/Multi-ethnic Society
Ethnic Groups	80.8% Germans	Turks
	11.7% Europeans	Kurds
	3.4% Turks	Arabs
	1.3% Arabs	Laz
	0.6% Africans	Circassians
	0.5% Americans	Bosnians
	0.1% Other	Other
State and Religion	Religious Communities	Secular State
	Statutory Corporations	
Religions	57% Christians	98% Muslims
	Catholics	(Automatic Registration of the Population by the State as Muslim)
	Protestants	
	36% No Religion	
	5% Muslims	Hanafis
	2% Others/Undeclared	Shafiìs
	Alevis	Christians
		Jews
		Others
Immigration	Second-highest Number of International Migrants Worldwide	19
Foreign Born Population	Foreign Born Population	
	12,005,690 (4.9%)	2,964,916 (1.3%)
	12% of residents do not have German Citizenship	
	22.5% of residents have an immigrant background	

Source: 'Bevölkerung nach Geschlecht und Staatsangehörigkeit', Destatis, 15 July 2018; 'Germany' and 'Turkey' CIA World Factbook, 11 February 2016; 'World Economic Outlook Database, October 2018', International Monetary Fund; 'Bevölkerung in Privathaushalten nach Migrationshintergrund im weiteren Sinn nach ausgewählten Geburtsstaaten', Statistisches Bundesamt (Destatis); 'Population by migrant status and sex', Statistisches Bundesamt (Destatis) 2017; 'Numbers and Facts about Church Life in the EKD 2018 Report', Evangelical Church of Germany, 2018; 'Human Development Report 2019', United Nations Development Programme, 2017; Ethnologue: Ethnologue Languages of the World – Turkey, 2017; 'Adrese Dayalı Nüfus Kayıt Sistemi Sonuçları' Türkiye İstatistik Kurumu; 'World Migration Report 2018' International Organization for migration (IOM), The UN Migration Agency.

The legal systems of Germany and Turkey differ in terms of the date when the countries became an ILO member, their ratified conventions (Turkey has ratified all three mentioned conventions – ILO Convention No. 100, ILO Convention No. 111 and ILO Convention No. 158, whereas Germany did not sign ILO Convention No. 158 but ratified Convention No. 100 and Convention No. 158), and the number of cases they were subjected to through the ILO regular or special supervision system (*see* Table 19.2).

Table 19.2 ILO: National German and Turkish Law

	Federal Republic of Germany	*Republic of Turkey*
Member of the ILO	from 1919 to 1935 since 12.6.1951	since 18.7.1932
Ratified Conventions	85	59
Conventions in Force	59	55
Denounced Con.	25	3
Fundamental Con.	8 of 8	8 of 8
C100	in force since 1956	in force since 1967
C111	in force since 1961	in force since 1967
C158	–	in force since 1995

Source: Author's own work.

Both Germany and Turkey are Member States of the ILO. The Federal Republic of Germany was a member between 1919 and 1935, and since 12.6.1951 it has been again having ILO member status. Eighty-five ILO conventions and one ILO Protocol, including all eight Conventions on ILO Core Labour Standards, have been ratified by Germany.[6] Currently there are 59 conventions, including all eight fundamental Conventions, in force in German territory, and the others have either been automatically terminated, terminated on the basis of more recent ILO conventions on the same subject, or for other reasons.[7] The Republic of Turkey has been an ILO Member State since 18.7.1932.[8] Fifty-nine ILO conventions, including all eight Conventions on ILO fundamental labour standards, have been ratified by Turkey; 55 of them, including all eight fundamental conventions, are in force in Turkey.

6. http://www.ilo.ch/dyn/normlex/en/f?p=1000:11200:0::NO:11200:P11200_COUNTRY_ID:102643 (30.11.2018).
7. http://www.ilo.ch/dyn/normlex/en/f?p=1000:11200:0::NO:11200:P11200_COUNTRY_ID:102643 (30.11.2018).
8. http://www.ilo.ch/dyn/normlex/en/f?p=1000:11110:0::NO:11110:P11110_COUNTRY_ID:102893 (30.11.2018).

19.2 PROTECTION AGAINST DISCRIMINATION

The Constitution of the International Labour Organization admits the fact that a universal and lasting peace can only be created if it is based on social justice (Preamble ILO Const.). This understanding of social justice in connection with protection from discrimination is first reflected in the unanimously adopted Declaration Concerning the Aims and Purposes of the International Labour Organization, from 10 May 1944, namely the Declaration of Philadelphia, which was later inserted into the Preamble to the ILO Constitution (ILO Const.) and is now an integral part of the ILO Constitution.[9] The Declaration of Philadelphia emphasizes and affirms that all human beings, regardless of race, creed or sex, have the right to seek material well-being and spiritual development in conditions of freedom and dignity, of economic security and equal opportunity. It constitutes the first international declaration of rights with international vocation, *applicable to all people everywhere*, guaranteeing the reproduction of democratic freedom and at the same time social rights. [10] In this way it presents itself as the first document of international law focused on human rights, later inaugurated in the Universal Declaration of Human Rights of 1948 and the Charter of the United Nations of 1951.[11] The Declaration is a binding document for all 187 Member States of the ILO, as it is a fundamental and essential part of the Organization's Constitution.[12] This means that countries cannot avoid taking account of the content of the declaration when formulating their social, economic and financial policies.[13]

The second major declaration of ILO about its principles and values, the ILO Declaration on Fundamental Principles and Rights at Work and its follow-up of 1998, put the elimination of discrimination in employment and occupation as one of the responsibilities of ILO Member States.[14] This was reaffirmed in the third major ILO Declaration, the Declaration on Social Justice for a Fair Globalization of 2008.[15]

In the next sections, several ILO conventions on protection against discrimination that are relevant in the context of this chapter will be examined. While the core labour

---

9. ILO, Declaration Concerning the Aims and Purposes of the International Labour Organization (Declaration of Philadelphia) General Conference of the International Labour Organization from 10.5.1944. In 1946 it was incorporated into the ILO Constitution, which sets broader objectives compared to the objectives contained in the previous Preamble. Perulli, A., The Declaration of Philadelphia (DoP), in E. Ales/M. Bell/O. Deinert/S. Robin-Olivier (eds), International and European Labour Law, Baden-Baden 2018, paras 1, 2; Evju, S., The European Social Charter and the International Labour Organisation – Interlinks Past and Present, in W. Däubler/R. Zimmer (Hrsg.), Arbeitsvölkerrecht, Festschrift für Klaus Lörcher, Baden-Baden 2013, P. 146 (146). https://www.ilo.org/dyn/normlex/en/f?p=1000:62:0::NO:62:P62_LIST_ENTRIE_ID:2453907:NO (30.11.2018).
10. IELL/Perulli DoP para. 1, 4.
11. IELL/Perulli DoP para. 1, 4.
12. IELL/Perulli DoP para. 34.
13. IELL/Perulli DoP para. 34.
14. ILO, Declaration on Fundamental Principles and Rights at Work, from 18.6.1998, adopted by the International Labour Conference at its 86th Session.
15. ILO, Declaration on Social Justice for a Fair Globalization, from 10.6.2008, adopted by the International Labour Conference at its 97th Session.

standards of Convention No. 100 and, in particular, Convention No. 111, are investigated, other conventions, such as Conventions Nos 118 and 159, which in fact also address discrimination protection, are not dealt with.

19.2.1 Convention No. 100

Convention No. 100 concerning Equal Remuneration for Men and Women Workers for Work of Equal Value from 29.6.1951 has been in force internationally since 23.5.1953. Since 1988, it has been one of the fundamental labour standards of the ILO. This means that all members of the ILO, even if they have not ratified the relevant fundamental conventions, have an obligation arising from their membership of the Organization alone, to uphold, promote and implement the principles of the fundamental rights covered by these Conventions in good faith and in accordance with the ILO Constitution.[16] Therefore, the obligation of states to respect, promote and implement these core labour standards arises from their membership of the ILO alone.[17] So far, 173 ILO Member States have ratified Convention No. 100. The Convention on Equal Remuneration for Men and Women Workers for Work of Equal Value has been in force since 8.6.1956 in Germany and since 19.7.1967 in Turkey.[18]

ILO Convention No. 100 deals with equal pay in terms of gender differences, which is a global phenomenon to which no country is immune.[19] States parties undertake to promote and ensure the application of the principle of equal remuneration for work of equal value to all men and women workers by national legislation, by statutory or recognized wage-setting bodies, by collective agreements or by a combination of these various means (Article 2 C100). Because of a multitude of factors causing gender pay-gaps, Convention No. 100 should be read in conjunction with other ILO conventions.[20] In particular, Recommendation No. 90 offers a wide range of policy instruments.[21] However, the details of Convention No. 100 cannot be addressed in this work.

16. ILO, Declaration on Fundamental Principles and Rights at Work, from 18.6.1998, adopted by the International Labour Conference at its 86th Session, P. 2; Seifert, A., Die Internationale Arbeitsorganisation und der deutsche Radikalenerlass, in W. Däubler/R. Zimmer (Hrsg.), Arbeitsvölkerrecht, Festschrift für Klaus Lörcher, Baden-Baden 2013, P. 42 (45).
17. Carinci, M.T., ILO Convention 158, Termination of Employment Convention, 1982 (No. 158), in E. Ales/M. Bell/O. Deinert/S. Robin-Olivier (eds), International and European Labour Law, Baden-Baden 2018, para. 3.
18. Republic of Turkey: signed 13.12.1966, Decision of the Council of Ministers 2.9.1967, entered into force 19.7.1967 (RG 22.12.1966, 12484; RG 21.9.1967, 12705).
19. Teklè, T., ILO Convention 100, Equal Remuneration Convention, 1951 (No. 100), in E. Ales/M. Bell/O. Deinert/S. Robin-Olivier (eds), International and European Labour Law, Baden-Baden 2018, para. 2.
20. IELL/Teklè C 100 para. 2.
21. IELL/Teklè C 100 para. 2.

19.2.2 Convention No. 111

Convention No. 111 on discrimination in employment and occupation of 4.6.1958 has been in force since 15.6.1960 under international law. It is supplemented by Recommendation No. 111, which was adopted at the same time, concerning discrimination in employment and occupation. Like Convention No. 100, Convention No. 111 is one of the core conventions of the ILO. About 175 out of 187 ILO Member States have ratified Convention No. 111.[22] Thus the Convention is one of the most ratified ILO conventions.[23] Since 15.6.1961 in Germany and since 19.7.1967 in Turkey, the Convention on Discrimination in Employment and Occupation has been in force.[24]

Convention No. 111 limits itself to employment and occupation. It is the first global convention of the United Nations, and its institutions are explicitly dedicated to providing protection from discrimination in employment.[25] Above all, it has proved to be a living document that can respond to evolving understandings of work, discrimination and equality.[26]

A definition of discrimination can be found in the first article of the Convention, which serves as a reference for subsequent international human rights treaties and national legislations in the field of discrimination.[27] For the purposes of the Convention, discrimination is any distinction, exclusion or preference made on the basis of the enumerated characteristics of discrimination which results in nullifying or impairing the equality of opportunity or treatment in employment or occupation (Article 1, I, a C111). Therefore crucial for the existence of discrimination under Convention No. 111 is the effect of a distinction, exclusion or preference in employment or occupation.[28] In this sense, Convention No. 111 covers *all discriminations* that may affect equal opportunity and equal treatment.[29] Any discrimination, formal or substantive, direct or indirect, falls within the scope of the Convention.[30] *Motive* is not a constitutive element of discrimination.[31] *Employment and occupation* within the meaning of Convention No. 111 include access to vocational training, access to employment and particular occupations (Article 1, III C111). *Employment* includes employment in the public

22. https://www.ilo.org/dyn/normlex/en/f?p=1000:11300:0::NO:11300:P11300_INSTRUMENT_ID:312256 (16.1.2019).
23. The most ratified convention is the C182 with 182 ratifications. C29 was ratified by 178 and C105, like C111, was ratified by 175 ILO Member States. https://www.ilo.org/dyn/normlex/en/f?p=NORMLEXPUB:12001:0::NO::: (16.1.2019).
24. Federal Republic of Germany: ratification 8.4.1961, entered into force 15.6.1961 (BGBl 1961 II, 97). Republic of Turkey: signed on 13.12.1966, Decision of the Council of Ministers on 2.9.1967, entered into force on 19.7.1967 (RG 22.12.1966, 12484; RG 21.9.1967, 12705).
25. Teklè, T., ILO Convention 111, Discrimination (Employment and Occupation) Convention, 1958 (No. 111), in E. Ales/M. Bell/O. Deinert/S. Robin-Olivier (eds), International and European Labour Law, Baden-Baden 2018, para. 1.
26. IELL/Teklè C 111 para. 1.
27. IELL/Teklè C 111 para. 1.
28. Schiek, D. (Hrsg.), Allgemeines Gleichbehandlungsgesetz (AGG), Ein Kommentar aus europäischer Perspektive, 1. Aufl., München 2007 AGG, Einl. para. 16.
29. ILO, Giving Globalization a Human Face, International Labour Conference 101st Session, 2012, para. 743.
30. ILO, Giving Globalization a Human Face, paras 743 ff.
31. IELL/Teklè C 111 para. 6.

sector, including civil servants, and in the private sector, as well as both wage and non-wage labour.[32] These include self-employment and unpaid family work.[33] *So the Convention applies to all types of work, including those not covered by labour law.*[34] Above all, it includes the employment conditions and the security for the term of employment (security of tenure of employment) (Article 1, III C111; Article 2, b, iv R111).[35]

Race, colour, sex, religion, political opinion, national extraction and social origin are *grounds of discrimination protected under Convention No. 111*. Notably, unlike in the Universal Declaration of Human Rights (UDHR), the International Covenant on Civil and Political Rights (ICCPR) and the International Covenant on Economic, Social and Cultural Rights (ICESCR), the characteristics of language, property or birth are not enumerated within the scope of protection afforded by the Convention's anti-discrimination protection. According to Convention No. 111, grounds of discrimination are understood as a developing area.[36] In agreement with this, Article 1, I, b C111 sees a possibility of the Member States recognising *additional grounds* as grounds of discrimination with the agreement of the social partners. Although not directly regulated by the Convention, the *intersectional nature of the concept of discrimination* is addressed frequently, in particular by the Committee of Experts on the Application of Conventions and Recommendations (CEACR).[37]

The *occupational requirements*, 'Any distinction, exclusion or preference in respect of a particular job based on the inherent requirements ...', and the *special measures* of protection and assistance are not to be considered as discrimination under ILO Convention No. 111 (Articles 1, II and 5 C111). However, the *occupational requirements* should not be broadly interpreted, and any exclusion must be proportionate to the task to be performed (e.g., the termination of a worker's employment by a Lutheran school after his conversion can be considered a discriminatory termination, because the Lutheran faith cannot be considered as an inherent requirement for the performance of his work as a statistician).[38] In terms of *special measures* it should, in particular, be noted that measures intended to protect disadvantaged groups can have a discriminatory effect (e.g., night work ban for women).[39] In addition, the measures taken against a person suspected of engaging in activities prejudicial to the security of the state or indeed confirmed as such shall not be considered as discrimination (Article 4 C111). Anyhow, that provision should be interpreted narrowly too, with due respect for the principle of proportionality and limited to the necessary characteristics of a particular post.[40]

---

32. IELL/Teklè C 111 para. 27; Seifert, FS-Lörcher, P. 42 (48).
33. IELL/Teklè C 111 para. 27.
34. IELL/Teklè C 111 para. 27.
35. ILO, Discrimination (Employment and Occupation) Recommendation No. 111, 1958.
36. ILO, Giving Globalization a Human Face, para. 761.
37. ILO, Giving Globalization a Human Face, para. 764; IELL/Teklè C 111 para. 22. ILO Committee of Experts on the Application of Conventions and Recommendations (CEACR).
38. IELL/Teklè C 111 para. 24.
39. IELL/Teklè C 111 para. 36.
40. IELL/Teklè C 111 para. 34; Seifert, FS-Lörcher P. 42 (49); ILO, Complaint (Art. 26) - 1985 - Federal Republic of Germany - C 111, Report of the Commission of Inquiry, para. 585.

In view of the human rights nature of the right to not be discriminated against, Convention No. 111 is established for everyone. Under Convention No. 111, states parties undertake to establish and implement a national policy that promotes equal opportunities and equal treatment in employment and occupation, with the aim of eliminating any discrimination in this field (Article 2 C111). The methods used to carry out this policy may be adapted to national circumstances and practices (Article 2 C111). Further, the prohibition of discrimination should not only have a preventive function but should also eliminate the effects of discrimination.[41] In the context of employment, it means, on the one hand, the elimination of discriminatory practices in employment.[42] But, on the other hand, it also requires the indemnification of the person who, as a result of unlawful discrimination, has suffered an injustice that creates the situation that would not have existed, if the discriminatory behaviour had not occurred.[43] In this context, for example, *in the case of a discriminatory dismissal, it is not enough just to make a severance payment; reinstatement would be advisable.* The comprehensive mandate to act that is placed on the individual states, including immediate obligations such as the removal of discriminatory legal provisions or modifying administrative practices, and medium-term commitments such as legislation, education or cooperation with appropriate bodies, also includes combating indirect discrimination and de facto obstacles to effective equal treatment (Article 3 C111).[44]

However, the obligation of non-discrimination under ILO Convention No. 111 applies not only to the state, but according to Recommendation No. 111 also applies to *private employers* and *social partners*, both in collective bargaining and industrial relations, as well as in the admission, membership or participation in their affairs (Article 2 R111).[45] In this way, the vertical applicability of the Convention and its authorization, including in cases of discrimination by private entities, are explicitly set out in ILO Recommendation No. 111.[46] However, there is still uncertainty about the extent to which Convention No. 111 confers individuals' subjective rights or at least leads to a corresponding interpretation of national labour law norms in conformity with international law.[47] It is particularly controversial with regard to characteristic political opinion according to German law.[48]

A more positive example of the consideration of the Convention by German courts is the decision of the German Federal Constitutional Court on maternity pay

41. IELL/Teklè C 111 para. 32; Constitutional Court of South Africa, *Jacques Charl Hoffman v. South Africa Airways*, 28.9.2000, Case No. CCT 17/00, para. 50.
42. IELL/Teklè C 111 para. 32; Constitutional Court of South Africa, *Jacques Charl Hoffman v. South Africa Airways*, 28.9.2000, Case No. CCT 17/00, para. 50.
43. IELL/Teklè C 111 para. 32; Constitutional Court of South Africa, *Jacques Charl Hoffman v. South Africa Airways*, 28.9.2000, Case No. CCT 17/00, para. 50.
44. Däubler, W./Bertzbach M. (Hrsg.), Allgemeines Gleichbehandlungsgesetz, Handkommentar, 2. Aufl., Baden-Baden 2008, Einl. para. 179; IELL/Teklè C111 para. 33.
45. IELL/Teklè C 111 para. 33.
46. IELL/Teklè C 111 para. 33.
47. Däubler/Bertzbach/Däubler Einl. para. 180.
48. Däubler/Bertzbach/Däubler Einl. para. 180; Seifert, FS-Lörcher, P. 42 (42 ff.); ILO, Complaint (Art. 26) - 1985 - Federal Republic of Germany - C111.

from 2003. Here, the Court explicitly referred to ILO Convention No. 111 in order to further define the content of the constitutional principle of equality. Based on this ILO Convention, the UN Convention of 18 December 1979 on the Elimination of All Forms of Discrimination Against Women and the European Anti-discrimination Law, the Court concluded that the equality requirement does not just mean formal equality between men and women, but also the elimination of 'indirect and factual discrimination'. This example shows that ILO conventions can make a meaningful contribution to the interpretation of German constitutional norms.

19.3 PROTECTION AGAINST UNFAIR DISMISSAL: CONVENTION NO. 158

Although some other ILO conventions also provide special provisions regarding the termination of employment contract and unfair dismissal, such as Convention No. 98, concerning the application of the principles of the right to organise and to bargain collectively from 1949, ILO Convention No. 158, concerning the Termination of Employment at the Initiative of the Employer adopted on 2.6.1982 with ILO Recommendation No. 166 concerning the Termination of the Employment Recommendation (22.6.1982) is the central part of the dismissal protection regulations of the ILO system. Convention No. 158 has been in force since 23.11.1985 under international law and is the successor to Recommendation No. 119 of 1963, which was the first ILO instrument dedicated specifically to the termination of the employment relationship.[49] Since Convention No. 158 is not one of the core labour standards of the ILO, it is only binding for states which have ratified the Convention.[50] These states are obliged to take all necessary measures to implement its content and make its provisions enforceable.[51] States can employ different implementation methods according to their legal system and national practice, taking into account national differences (Article 1 C158).[52] Ratifications with reservations are, on the other hand, frequently not permitted, except those expressly provided for in the Convention.[53] It should be stressed, however, that the prohibition on dismissals for discriminatory reasons enjoys the same level of forced protection provided for in the ILO Declaration on Fundamental Principles and Rights at Work and Its Follow-Up Measures of 1998, for core labour standards.[54] However, compared to C100 and C111, the number of ratifications is quite low. So far, only thirty-six states have ratified Convention No. 158, and one state has already terminated it.[55] The claim that some countries already meet or over-fulfil the standards of the Convention, and that the principles of the Convention are already part of their common

49. IELL/Carinci C 158 para. 1.
50. IELL/Carinci C 158 paras 2, 3.
51. IELL/Carinci C 158 para. 2.
52. ILO, Protection against Unjustified Dismissal, para. 24.
53. IELL/Carinci C 158 para. 2.
54. IELL/Carinci C 158 para. 2.
55. https://www.ilo.org/dyn/normlex/en/f?p=1000:11300:0::NO:11300:P11300_INSTRUMENT_ID:312303 (21.1.2019). Brazil has terminated Convention No. 158 on 20 November 1996.

legal traditions, plays a role in the limited number of ratifications.[56] On the other hand, the strict structure of the Convention requires Member States to adapt their national clauses to the detailed regulations of the Convention as soon as it is ratified.[57] However, the crucial point is the conflict between fundamental principles of the liberal market economy such as freedom of enterprise, flexibility or the primacy of economic requirements and the protection of workers from dismissal.[58] The influence of the Convention is not limited to the ratification states. The fundamental principles of the Convention are applied by more countries than the ratification states alone.[59] It also affects the European Social Charter (revised).[60]

The Republic of Turkey is one of the ILO Member States which have ratified Convention No. 158. By contrast, the Federal Republic of Germany has not yet signed Convention No. 158. The ratification of Convention No. 158 by Turkey took place on 12.10.1994 and has been in force since 4.1.1995.[61] Existing provisions of the Turkish Labour Law regarding the right of dismissal protection are the implementation of the Convention into national Turkish law.

The definition of termination and the termination of the employment relationship is given in Article 3 C158. In the sense of C158, termination only includes termination of employment as a result of the employer's initiative (Article 3 C158).[62] *Regardless of the branch of economic activity* (e.g., public officers are also included) and to all employed persons (e.g., regardless of *the nationality of the employee*) the protection regulated by Convention No. 158 should apply (Article 2 I C158).[63] In principle, fixed-term employment is also included.[64] Yet, the Member States are entitled to exclude the application of all or some of the provisions of the Convention to certain categories of workers based on the employment contract; such as engagements for a certain period of time or for a specific task, probationary assignments, or based on the groups of the employee concerned (Article 2 II, IV, V C158). However, the exclusion of certain groups of workers from the rules on dismissals can only be enforced if the signing state consults with the employers' and workers' organizations concerned and, second, the signing state indicates in its first report under Article 22 ILO Constitution the excluded groups (Article 2 IV, V, VI C158; Article 22 ILO Const.). This procedure is very strict, and the provision is very narrowly interpreted so that Member States are not allowed to introduce any other exceptions not listed in the first report.[65] Recently, the ILO CEACR, in its 2015 Observation on Turkey, addressed the categories of workers

56. IELL/Carinci C 158 para. 5; Schubert, J.M./Buschmann, R. (unter Mitarbeit von), Arbeitsvölkerrecht, Berlin 2017, P. 31.
57. IELL/Carinci C 158 para. 5.
58. IELL/Carinci C 158 para. 5.
59. Buschmann, R., Soziale Menschenrechte im Blick, in W. Däubler/R. Zimmer (Hrsg.), Arbeitsvölkerrecht, Festschrift für Klaus Lörcher, Baden-Baden 2013, P. 257 (269).
60. Buschmann, FS-Lörcher, P. 257 (270).
61. Law No. 3999 from 9.6.1994 (RG 18.6.1994, 21964); Parliament Decision on 10.8.1994, No. 94-5971 (RG 12.10.1994), in force from 4.1.1995.
62. ILO, Protection against Unjustified Dismissal, para. 20.
63. IELL/Carinci C 158 para. 9, Fn. 22; CEACR – adopted 2015, published 105th ILC session 2016 – Slovakia.
64. Buschmann, FS-Lörcher, P. 257 (266).
65. IELL/CARINCI C 158 para. 15.

excluded from dismissal protection.[66] The Committee of Experts drew attention to the fact that Turkey has exempted small and medium-sized enterprises from the obligations of dismissal protection by excluding establishments with less than thirty employees from the scope of application for protection against unfair dismissal (Article 18, I Labour Law No. 4857). These workers have the option of claiming a compensation, but there is no possibility of reinstatement. However, it has emerged that the vast majority of companies in Turkey are small and medium-sized enterprises. In addition, the number of enterprises with fewer than thirty employees is increasing in order to benefit from the derogation. Therefore, a large number of workers do not enjoy job security. For these reasons, the Committee of Experts called on the government to provide updated information on any developments concerning the application of the Convention in small and medium-sized enterprises, which may be excluded from the employment protection provisions; including the data on the growth of establishments with fewer than thirty employees compared to other facilities. Worker categories excluded from dismissal protection in Turkey continued to find a place in the observation of the Expert Committee of 2016 with a renewed call for the provision of detailed statistical data on the subject.[67]

The termination of the employment relationship must be based on a valid reason: this is the cornerstone of the provisions of Convention No. 158.[68] In accordance with the principle of justification for termination, the termination of an employee's employment relationship may only occur as the result of a valid reason for doing so (Article 4 C158).[69] The obligation to justify terminating the employment relationship for a valid reason applies only to the employer.[70] In addition, the issue of termination of employment for a valid reason is different from the worker's right to a notice period and/or a severance payment.[71] Irrespective of whether or not the employer dismisses after giving notice, the existence of a valid reason for terminating the employment relationship is required.[72] A valid reason must be either related to the capacity or conduct of the worker, namely subjective reasons, or based on the operational requirements of the undertaking, establishment or service, namely objective reasons (Article 4 C158).[73] An additional set of reasons, which are not related to the subjective or objective justifiable reasons, but nevertheless cannot justify the termination, are included in Articles 5 and 6 C158.[74] It covers, *inter alia*, the reasons relating to the personal characteristics of the employee and the reasons relating to the legitimate exercise of a fundamental right by the employee, such as membership of a trade union, employee representation or legal action against the employer (Article 5 and Article 5 a,

66. CEACR – adopted 2015, published at 105th ILC session 2016 – C 158 Turkey.
67. CEACR – adopted 2016, published at 106th ILC session 2017 – C 158 Turkey.
68. ILO, Protection against Unjustified Dismissal, para. 76; IELL/CARINCI C 158 para. 16; Buschmann, FS-Lörcher, P. 257 (268).
69. Buschmann, FS-Lörcher, P. 257 (268).
70. ILO, Protection against Unjustified Dismissal, para. 77.
71. ILO, Protection against Unjustified Dismissal, para. 76.
72. ILO, Protection against Unjustified Dismissal, para. 76.
73. IELL/Carinci C 158 para. 16.
74. IELL/Carinci C 158 para. 20.

d C158).[75] Personal discrimination grounds listed in Article 5 C158 which do not constitute a valid reason for dismissal are race, colour, sex, marital status, family responsibilities, pregnancy, religion, political opinion, national extraction or social origin. ILO Recommendation No. 166 adds to these distinguishing features the characteristic of age. A similar clause in the Turkish Labour Code additionally includes the ground of birth, but does not take into account the characteristics of national descent or social origin. However, an opening clause is included (Article 18, III, d Labour Law No. 4857). In many cases, the unlawful causes of termination listed in Article 5 C158 are also discriminatory under other ILO conventions.[76]

The practical application of Articles 4 and 5 C158, with regard to valid reasons for dismissal, occupied the Committee of Experts in its 2016 observation of Turkey.[77] 'A massive wave of dismissals ...' by the Turkish Government after July 2016, especially in the public sector, aroused concern.[78] The Committee pointed out that the employment of an employee should not be terminated unless there is a valid reason. In this regard, it requested the Turkish Government to provide detailed information on the practical application of Articles 4 and 5 of the C158 in relation to the massive wave of dismissals.[79]

ILO Convention No. 158 provides very detailed procedural requirements, which include the period before or at the time of termination, but also the time after unfair dismissal. Among other things it concerns the employee's hearing before a behavioural or performance-related dismissal (Article 7 C158), notice periods (Article 11 C158), the burden of proof, which in principle is borne by the employer (Article 9, II C158), and the hearing of worker's representatives against dismissals for economic, technological, structural or similar reasons (Article 13 C158). The right of the employee to dispute the termination of his/her employment contract with an impartial body is guaranteed (Article 8 C158). The body must also have the power to examine the reasons for the termination of the employment relationship and the other circumstances of the case and to decide whether the termination is justified (Article 8 C158). However, in the event of termination based on the operational requirements of the undertaking, establishment or service, the impartial body may decide on the justification of the termination only if the internal rules of the Member State allow such a justification to be verified (Article 9, III C158).[80] Legal consequences in the case of unjustified dismissal are invalidity, reinstatement, adequate compensation or other relief as may be deemed appropriate (Article 10 C158).

75. IELL/Carinci C 158 para. 21.
76. IELL/Carinci C 158 para. 21. ILO C98; ILO C135; ILO C111.
77. CEACR - adopted 2016, published at 106th ILC session 2017 - C 158 Turkey.
78. CEACR - adopted 2016, published at 106th ILC session 2017 - C 158 Turkey.
79. CEACR - adopted 2016, published at 106th ILC session 2017 - C 158 Turkey.
80. IELL/Carinci C 158 para. 27.

19.4 ENFORCEMENT MECHANISMS

Regular Supervisory Mechanisms *Periodic Reports *Committee of Experts on the Application of Conventions and Recommendations - Observations - Direct Requests - Annual Report *Conference Committee on the Application of Standards - Review - Selection of some observations for discussion (Request to Respond)	
Germany: Total 4	**Turkey:** Total 26
C111 - 2 times (1988, 1989) C87 - 1 time (1994) C29 - 1 time (2002)	C111 - 4 times (1987, 1989, 1990, 1991) C 98 - 11 times C 87 - 6 times C 135 - 1 time
- Highlighting situations of special concern **Special Supervisory Mechanisms** *Representations (National and international employers' or workers' organisations, ILO Governing Body)	
Germany: Total 14	**Turkey:** Total 46
10 about FOA	38 about FOA
*Complaints (Member States, International Labour Conference delegate, ILO Governing Body)	
Till now total 32 cases	
Germany: 1 (Decree on Radicals)	**Turkey:** None

When an ILO Member State ratifies a convention, it undertakes to submit periodic reports on its application of the convention within the differentiated regular supervisory mechanisms.[81] The Committee of Experts set up in 1926 examines the government reports on ratified conventions.[82] In examining the application of international labour standards, the Committee of Experts makes two types of comments: observations and direct requests. It also prepares an annual financial report to be submitted to the International Labour Conference each year, during which the Conference Committee examines the report for the application of labour standards.[83] The Conference Committee on the Application of Standards reviews the report in a tripartite environment

81. ILO, Rules of the Game, P. 102 ff; Zimmer, FS-Lörcher, P. 29 (29); Wendeling-Schröder, U./Stein A., Allgemeines Gleichbehandlungsgesetz, Beck'sche Kommentare zum Arbeitsrecht, 1. Aufl., München 2008, Einl. para. 25; Süzek, S., Iş Hukuku, Yenilenmiş 9. Baskı, Istanbul 2013, P. 86.
82. ILO, Rules of the Game, P. 102; Süzek, P. 106.
83. ILO, Rules of the Game, P. 102, 103; Süzek P. 106.

and selects a number of observations for discussion.[84] The observed governments are invited to respond to the Conference Committee and to provide information about the situation.[85] Between 1986 and 2018, Germany received four requests to respond to the Conference Committee's comments.[86] In 1988 and 1989 the requests were concerned with the Decree on Radicals in connection with ILO Convention No. 111.[87] In 1994, the topic was the prohibition of strikes for officials in connection with ILO Convention No. 87.[88] In 2002, the topic was work done by prisoners in connection with ILO Convention No. 29.[89]

In contrast with the small number of German cases, the Republic of Turkey had to testify before the Conference Committee twenty-six times between the years 1986 and 2018 (twenty-six times within thirty-two years) to answer questions concerning the observations.[90] Eleven of these cases dealt with ILO Convention No. 98 on the Right to Organise and Collective Bargaining – a fundamental convention. Six cases dealt with ILO Convention No. 87 on the Freedom of Association and Protection of the Right to Organise Convention – another fundamental convention. One case in 2017 concerned Convention No. 135 on Workers' Representatives in connection with the massive wave of dismissals after the 2016 coup attempt in the country. More than two-thirds of the cases have therefore referred to the rights of association and trade union rights.

Another wave of dismissals after the 1980 coup, triggered by an amended article in a law called State of Emergency Law No. 1402, was the subject of observations for a number of years at the end of the 1980s.[91] This happened in conjunction with Convention No. 111. Following the 1980 coup and the declared state of emergency, 4,530 officials were dismissed.[92] The dismissals affected around 8,500 people, including university teachers, teachers, civil servants, public sector workers and civil

84. ILO, Rules of the Game, P. 103; Süzek P. 86.
85. ILO, Rules of the Game, P. 103.
86. https://www.ilo.org/dyn/normlex/en/f?p=1000:11110:0::NO:11110:P11110_COUNTRY_ID:102643 (29.1.2019).
87. Individual Case (CAS) – Discussion: 1988, Publication: 75th ILC session (1988) Discrimination (Employment and Occupation) Convention, 1958 (No. 111) – Germany (Ratification: 1961) and Individual Case (CAS) – Discussion: 1989, Publication: 76th ILC session (1989) Discrimination (Employment and Occupation) Convention, 1958 (No. 111) – Germany (Ratification: 1961).
88. Individual Case (CAS) – Discussion: 1994, Publication: 81st ILC session (1994) Freedom of Association and Protection of the Right to Organise Convention, 1948 (No. 87) – Germany (Ratification: 1957).
89. Individual Case (CAS) – Discussion: 2002, Publication: 90th ILC session (2002) Forced Labour Convention, 1930 (No. 29) – Germany (Ratification: 1956).
90. https://www.ilo.org/dyn/normlex/en/f?p=1000:11110:0::NO:11110:P11110_COUNTRY_ID:102893 (29.1.2019).
91. Sıkıyönetim Kanunu No: 1402 Kabul Tarihi: 13.5.1971. Individual Case (CAS) – Discussion: 1987, Publication: 73rd ILC session (1987) Discrimination (Employment and Occupation) Convention, 1958 (No. 111) – Turkey; Individual Case (CAS) – Discussion: 1989, Publication: 76th ILC session (1989) Discrimination (Employment and Occupation) Convention, 1958 (No. 111) – Turkey; Individual Case (CAS) – Discussion: 1990, Publication: 77th ILC session (1990) Discrimination (Employment and Occupation) Convention, 1958 (No. 111) – Turkey; Individual Case (CAS) – Discussion: 1991, Publication: 78th ILC session (1991) Discrimination (Employment and Occupation) Convention, 1958 (No. 111) – Turkey.
92. Individual Case (CAS) – Discussion: 1987, Publication: 73rd ILC session (1987) Discrimination (Employment and Occupation) Convention, 1958 (No. 111) – Turkey.

servants.[93] The highly likely discriminatory nature of the terminations resulting from political opinions raised the ILO's concerns.[94] From 1987 to 1991, the Government of the Republic of Turkey had to answer to the Conference Committee each year to answer questions on this subject. After the reinstatement of the dismissed according to the decision of the State Council and the repeal of the Law No. 1402 the situation de-escalated. The year 2001, in which the government had to answer questions concerning the implementation of Convention No. 158, which played an important role in shaping today's Turkish legislation on protection against dismissal, is of particular importance.[95]

The regular supervisory mechanisms based on state reporting procedures are complemented by special supervisory mechanisms.[96] Special supervisory mechanisms provide on the one hand a special representation procedure for employee and employer organizations and for the ILO Governing Body, when a Member State has failed to secure the effective observance within its jurisdiction of any Convention to which it is a party (Articles 24, 25 ILO Const.). Germany has received ten representations about freedom of association and four representations about other issues.[97] The Republic of Turkey has so far received thirty-eight complaints about freedom of association and eight complaints on other issues.[98] On the other hand, the special supervisory mechanisms give Member States, International Labour Conference delegates and the ILO Governing Body the possibility of bringing a complaint against a Member State (Article 26 ILO Const.). Taking into account the relatively low number of complaints made against all Member States, a total of thirty-two cases from 1919 to 2019, it can be concluded that this supervisory mechanism has relatively limited practical significance.[99]

However, one of these thirty-two cases was against Germany: Decree on Radicals.[100] The case concerned a decision of the German federal states of 28.1.1972, which presupposed for the placement into the public service, the examination of the fidelity to 'the liberal democratic basic order in the sense of the constitution ...' (*der freiheitlich demokratischen Grundordnung im Sinne des Grundgesetzes* ...) of the applicants or civil servants.[101] As a result of abstract doubts about the constitutionality of applicants or civil servants, even membership of an organization with anti-constitutional goals, *verfassungsfeindlichen Zielen* was enough to be evaluated as enemy of the liberal

93. Individual Case (CAS) - Discussion: 1989, Publication: 76th ILC session (1989) Discrimination (Employment and Occupation) Convention, 1958 (No. 111) - Turkey.
94. Individual Case (CAS) - Discussion: 1987, Publication: 73rd ILC session (1987) Discrimination (Employment and Occupation) Convention, 1958 (No. 111) - Turkey.
95. Individual Case (CAS) - Discussion: 2001, Publication: 89th ILC session (2001) Termination of Employment Convention, 1982 (No. 158) - Turkey.
96. ILO, Rules of the Game, P. 106 ff.
97. https://www.ilo.org/dyn/normlex/en/f?p=1000:11110:0::NO:11110:P11110_COUNTRY_ID:102643.
98. https://www.ilo.org/dyn/normlex/en/f?p=1000:11110:0::NO:11110:P11110_COUNTRY_ID:102893 (28.1.2019).
99. Seifert, FS-Lörcher, P. 42 (47).
100. ILO, Complaint (Art. 26) - 1985 - Federal Republic of Germany - C111.
101. Seifert, FS-Lörcher, P. 42 (43); § 35 I Satz 3 BRRG; ILO, Complaint (Art. 26) - 1985 - Federal Republic of Germany - C111, para. 2.

democratic constitution.[102] All who were regarded as enemies of the liberal democratic constitution experienced exclusion from public service or removal from public service.[103] In this context, every candidate for the civil service received a regular inquiry on security. A decision of the Federal Constitutional Court of 22.5.1975 declared the Decree on Radicals to be lawful. In 1985, following numerous complaints against Germany and the increased attention of the ILO Committee of Experts to the subject in many of its reports, the ILO Governing Body decided for the first and so far for the only time in the history of the ILO to bring a complaint against the Federal Republic of Germany and set up an ILO inquiry committee.[104] After a lengthy 'quasi-court-shaped' procedure, the Committee of Inquiry drafted a comprehensive report stating that the decree indeed violated the Convention and ended with recommendations to amend the Convention practice in dealing with political radicals in public service.[105]

This raises the question of the legal nature of the ILO's recommendations after implementation into national law. Following the forwarding of the report of the Committee of Inquiry to the governments concerned, the report will be published. After that, the government concerned shall inform the Director-General of the International Labour Office within three months whether or not it agrees with the recommendations contained in the report of the Committee of Inquiry. If it does not agree, it must state whether it proposes to appeal to the International Court of Justice by means of a complaint (Articles 28, 29 ILO Const.). In the case of the Decree on Radicals, the German Government informed the Director-General that it did not agree with the recommendations of the Committee majority, but refrained from appealing to the International Court of Justice.[106] Now the question is whether the recommendations of the ILO have a legally binding character. The recommendations of the ILO are not non-binding proposals, but rather binding instructions that the parties to the conflict have to implement into national law.[107] Article 33 of the ILO Constitution states that should a member fail to implement the recommendations contained in the report of the Commission of Inquiry or, as the case may be, in the decision of the International Court of Justice within the specified period, the Board of Directors may recommend to the Conference a measure that it considers reasonable, convenient and appropriate to ensure compliance. However, the country concerned may decide how to implement that recommendation, which is binding under international law, into national law.[108]

In addition, an individual complaint option is not provided. Since both Germany and Turkey have ratified all eight core Conventions, this chapter will not elaborate on

102. Seifert, FS-Lörcher, P. 42 (43).
103. Seifert, FS-Lörcher, P. 42 (43).
104. ILO, Complaint (Art. 26) – 1985 – Federal Republic of Germany – C111; https://www.ilo.org/dyn/normlex/en/f?p=1000:11110:0::NO:11110:P11110_COUNTRY_ID:102643 (29.1.2019).
105. Seifert, FS-Lörcher, P. 42 (48).
106. Seifert, FS-Lörcher, P. 42 (49).
107. Seifert, FS-Lörcher, P. 42 (50).
108. Seifert, FS-Lörcher, P. 42 (50).

the follow-up measures provided specifically in the 1998 Declaration on unratified core labour standards.[109]

19.5 CONCLUSION

The ILO system is based on the responsibility of individual states.[110] So, its reach is limited, not only in terms of standard-setting activity or the low rate of ratification, but also in view of the weakness of its supervisory mechanisms and the lack of effective sanctions.[111] However, with respect to Turkish industrial relations and the Turkish legal system, these limited monitoring mechanisms are more frequently used compared to Germany. The ILO's tripartite system allows social parties to seek support from the ILO mechanisms, even if they are poorly enforceable. They serve as a place to make the voice of the others heard, whose voices cannot be heard in the national systems for various reasons. It is a place where they can express themselves, seek support and demand their rights are met.

109. Weiss, M., Die Metamorphose der internationalen Arbeitsorganisation, in W. Däubler/R. Zimmer (Hrsg.), Arbeitsvölkerrecht, Festschrift für Klaus Lörcher, Baden-Baden 2013, P. 21 (24 ff.).
110. IELL/Perulli DoP para. 36.
111. Weiss, FS-Lörcher, P. 21 (22).

Chapter 20

Digital Nomads on Polish Labour Market: Legal Situation, Risks and Expectations

Kamila Naumowicz

20.1 INTRODUCTION

Human mobility – and thus the possibility of changing places – is an important factor in creating and determining not only legal forms or social forms, but also culture.[1] Nomadism is not a new phenomenon. Since antiquity, people have travelled around the world in search of work, being in a constant motion and moving from place to place depending on the demand for a given type of goods or services they provided. As defined by Encyclopaedia Britannica the term 'nomadism' is to be understood as a 'way of life of people who do not live continually in the same place but move cyclically or periodically. ... Nomadism does not imply unrestricted and undirected wandering; rather, it is based on temporary centres whose stability depends on the availability of food supply and the technology for exploiting it'.[2]

This phenomenon has been almost entirely eliminated by the spread of agriculture and industry – nowadays there are only few examples of nomadic societies still existing in the twenty-first century. In the anthropological studies of primitive cultures the common characteristics of nomads have been identified as a restricted amount of baggage or material culture, small and impermanent camps and shelters, family-based

1. F. Gross, *Koczownictwo: Studia nad nomadyzmem I nad wpływem tegoz na społeczeństwo, ustró j i prawo*, Wydawnictwo Kasy im. Mianowskiego – Instytut Popierania Nauki, 1936, p. 1. After, E. Nowicka, *Wartość przestrzennej ruchliwości. Pochwała nomadyzmu i jej ograniczenia*, in *Studia Migracyjne – Przegld Polonijny*, 2016, vol. 4, n. 162, pp. 35-55 (translated by the author).
2. Encyclopaedia Britannica, term *Nomadism*, available at: https://www.britannica.com/topic/nomadism, 2016 (accessed 10 November 2019).

social organization.[3] But who are the contemporary 'nomads' and do these elements apply to 'digital nomadism'?

Nowadays, the term 'nomadism' in relation to labour market is often being confused with labour migration or travelling and is often used as their synonym. There is no legal definition of this term, and the concept itself includes many different types of working performances. Nevertheless, one thing is certain – the use of modern technologies has influenced not only the conditions of work but also the worker himself – his physical and mental functioning, his way of communication, use of language, expectations on the place of work and living.

Thus, nomadism has become a field of interest and study for jurists, anthropologists, psychologists, linguistics and even architects, property developers or urban planners that need to adapt the cities and accommodations for the needs of this type of workers. In order to better understand the needs, risks and challenges connected to the digital revolution, it is therefore necessary to study carefully what contemporary nomadism is and what makes it have so far-reaching influence on the functioning of not only the labour market, but also entire societies.[4]

20.2 DIGITALIZATION AND NOMADISM

It is believed that the term 'digital nomad' has been used for the first time in the 1990s by Tsugio Makimoto and David Manners who jointly wrote a book with the phrase 'digital nomad' in the title.[5] Since then, the term has become a catchphrase that describes a new way of life and work. It is understood as a freedom from the traditional constraints of time and location in the working performance, owed to the technological progress, as far as the use of internet and mobile intelligent devices in the work process.[6]

Digital nomadism has been a growing trend in the international labour market. The exact number of digital nomads is difficult to be estimated because of different forms of working performance they are engaged in (mainly civil contracts or self-employment but also so-called grey zone).[7]

3. Encyclopaedia Britannica, term: *Primitive culture*, available at: https://www.britannica.com/topic/primitive-culture, 2016 (accessed 10 November 2019).
4. An example of the influence of digital nomadism on the international regulations might be the concept of Special International Residency and Work Zones created by some host countries that are trying to attract digital nomads offering special working permits, immigration procedures and other legal benefits, *see* more T.W. Bell, *Special International Zones in Practice and Theory*, Chapman Law Review, vol. 21, 2018, pp. 299-301, available at: https://ssrn.com/abstract=3271942 (accessed 10 November 2019).
5. T. Makimoto, D. Manners. *Digital Nomad*, vol. 354. Chichester: Wiley, 1997.
6. T. Makimoto, *The Age of the Digital Nomad: Impact of CMOS Innovation*, IEEE Solid-State Circuits Magazine, vol. 5 (1), 2013, p. 40-47, available at: https://ieeexplore.ieee.org/abstract/document/6449377 (accessed 10 November 2019). *See also*: *Nomads at last. Special report*, The Economist, 12 April 2008, available at: https://www.economist.com/special-report/2008/04/10/nomads-at-last (accessed 10 November 2019).
7. The way the digital nomads define themselves also differs and evolves – according to the 'State of the Freelance Nation 2018' survey 50% of respondents identify themselves as self-employed, 19% as small business owners, 19% call themselves entrepreneurs and only 12% identify as

As the authors of the Eurofound report on platform work indicate 'In Poland, where the concept of platform work is less well known, it is often associated with working remotely and is linked to outsourcing, freelancing or independent work'.[8] Thus, in various reports referring to digital nomads they are identified as independent contractors, platform workers, individual entrepreneurs, independent professionals (iPros), etc.

The predictions for the nearest future show that this global phenomenon will become increasingly popular.[9] Data taken from online surveys indicate that in the US 35% of workforce (nearly 55 million Americans) are working in microbusinesses or freelancing.[10] These numbers differ for European Union (EU), where the participation of the digital nomads in the market is estimated to be around 5% of the European workforce with about 11,000,000 of freelancers in Europe. The iPros, known as 'freelancers', are defined for the purpose of these surveys as 'people working in the service sector who are self-employed and do not have any employees'.[11] They are believed, though, to be the fastest growing segment of European labour market.

20.3 POLISH LEGAL FRAMEWORK FOR DIGITAL NOMADISM

In order to better understand the complexity of the legal status of digital nomads in Poland, it is necessary to indicate the most common forms of performing work in Polish labour market, that are as follows:

- an employment relationship (regulated by labour law);
- different civil law contracts (regulated by civil law); and
- self-employment (regulated by a set of acts referred to as 'Constitution for Business').[12]

The key legal act regulating relations between employers and employees in Poland is the Labour Code.[13] According to the Article 22 of the Polish Labour Code: '§ 1. By establishing an employment relationship, an employee undertakes to perform work of a specified type for the benefit of an employer and under his supervision, in a place and at the times specified by the employer; the employer undertakes to employ

'freelancers'. *See* 'State of the Freelance Nation 2018' survey, available at: https://wisebrand.co/state-of-the-freelance-nation-survey/press-release/ (accessed 10 November 2019).

8. I. Mandl, Z. Kilhoffer et al., *Employment and working conditions of selected types of platform work*, Eurofound, 2018, p. 10, available at: https://op.europa.eu/en/publication-detail/-/publication/8a892648-c782-11e8-9424-01aa75ed71a1/language-en/format-PDF/source-77270770 (accessed 10 November 2019).
9. For example a platform dedicated to nomads based on the number of its users called NomadList predicts that in the next twenty years more than 1 billion people will become digital nomads. *See* https://nomadlist.com/ (accessed 10 November 2019).
10. V.G. SNYDER, *The Surprising Reality Is Freelancers Are Happy and Prospering*, available at: https://www.entrepreneur.com/article/308524 (accessed 10 November 2019).
11. According to European Forum of Independent Professionals, available at: https://freelancersweek.org/about/ (accessed 10 November 2019).
12. *See* https://www.gov.pl/web/przedsiebiorczosc-technologia/konstytucja-biznesu (accessed 20 October 2019).
13. Act of 26 June 1974 Labour Code (Journal of Laws of 2019 item 1040 with amendments).

the employee in return for remuneration'. This relationship is characterized by subordination and power of control over the employee on the one hand, and the obligation to perform work personally on the other.[14]

What needs to be underlined, is that according the provisions of the Article 22 of the Labour Code § 1^1 and 1^2, in each case where the working performance meets the conditions specified in § 1 of the Article 22, it is considered employment on the basis of an employment relationship, regardless of the name of the contract concluded between the parties. Furthermore, it specifies that, in such case, employment contracts cannot be replaced with a civil law contracts – concluding a civil law contract where an employment contract should be concluded is considered an offence against the rights of an employee (Article 281 point 1) of the Labour Code).

Regarding the use of communication technologies in the working performance, a particular type of work in the form of telework is also regulated by the Labour Code, which defines it as '§ 1. Work may be performed away from the premises of an employer, on a regular basis, by means of information and communications technologies (ICTs) in the meaning of the provisions on rendering services by electronic means (telework)' (Article 67^5 of the Labour Code). Telework as defined above is regulated by Polish Labour Law as a type of employment relationship, characterized by the use of different technologies in the working performance, but still considered a subordinate type of work.

The common form of working performance used by digital nomads is self-employment. Thus, they are often being referred to as freelancers. In this case, their professional activity is not regulated by Labour Code, and they are not granted the rights and social protection regarding employees under the labour law regulations. In the Polish legal framework freelancers are considered individual entrepreneurs and – contrarily to employment relationship – their working performance is supposed to be autonomous.

One of the problems, occurring in Polish labour market in recent years, is the fact that non-standard forms of employment (including civil law contracts or 'business to business' B2B model of cooperation), have been over-used to substitute traditional employment relationship in order to reduce risks, employment costs and responsibilities of the employers in the gig economy, often in violation of the Article 22 as mentioned above.[15]

This tendency has been increased by the technological revolution that made remote work and different organization of working conditions even easier for the companies. The growing popularity of platform work puts new challenges in the application and interpretation of the traditional concept of subordination as defined by the Article 22 § 1 of the Labour Code – regarding the elements of time and place of work in the digital era, or the necessity to balance work and life with the right to privacy put

14. *See* K. Jaśkowski, E. Maniewska, Komentarz aktualizowany do Kodeksu pracy, 2019, LEX/el., commentary to Art. 22.
15. M. Wojciuk, *Labor taxation versus employment models in Poland*, 'Optimum. Economic Studies' No 2 (92) 2018, p. 139.

at risk by the use of new forms of supervision and control offered by technological revolution.

As indicated in the Preamble of the General Data Protection Regulation (motive 6) 'Rapid technological developments and globalization have brought new challenges for the protection of personal data. ... Technology allows both private companies and public authorities to make use of personal data on an unprecedented scale in order to pursue their activities'.[16] Same risk has been highlighted by the Article 29 Data Protection Working Party in the Opinion 2/2017[17] on data processing at work, which empathized that in the working environment 'The rapid adoption of new information technologies in the workplace, in terms of infrastructure, applications and smart devices, allows for new types of systematic and potentially invasive data processing at work'.

20.4 FREELANCERS' REPORTS: WORKING CONDITIONS VERSUS EXPECTATIONS

The analysis of surveys on digital nomads shows a strong difference between their social image and expectations on the one hand, and the real working conditions offered by the labour market, on the other. Comparing the status of freelancers in the United States (US) and Poland might be an answer to the question, how the expectations and media portrait of freelancers have been created to better understand their needs and legal status.

The FlexJobs[18] portal in US conducted a survey of over 500 people declaring themselves to be digital nomads in September and October 2018. The data shows that the 'statistic' digital nomad is not a young freelancer traveling with a backpack around the world or an owner of a technological start-up. Contrary to what we expect from the image that the media promote, a 'statistic' digital nomad is a woman (70% of women in relation to 30% of men), married (61%), representing generation X (41% of respondents), experienced employee of the company (32%), employed at least forty hours per week and performing work in the following industries: writing, education and training, administration (the broadly understood IT sector was only mentioned on the 6th position). She has health insurance (72% of respondents), pays retirement contributions and has at least bachelors' degree (72%) or higher (33%). As far as the form of work is considered more digital nomads are employed by a company (35%)

16. Regulation (EU) 2016/679 of the European Parliament and of the Council of 27 April 2016 on the protection of natural persons with regard to the processing of personal data and on the free movement of such data, and repealing Directive 95/46/EC (General Data Protection Regulation, GDPR), OJ L 119, 4 May 2016, pp. 1-88.
17. Article 29 Data Protection Working Party, Opinion 2 /2017 on data processing at work, available at: https://ec.europa.eu/newsroom/article29/item-detail.cfm?item_id=610169 (accessed 20 October 2019).
18. B.W. Reynolds, *FlexJobs Digital Nomad Survey: Insights into the Remote Lifestyle*, available at: https://www.flexjobs.com/blog/post/flexjobs-digital-nomad-survey-insights-remote-lifestyle/ (accessed 10 November 2019).

than freelancers (28%) or business owners (18%). Other important statistics influencing social portrait of the digital nomad consider the time and place of work and their social status and are shown by the answers to the following questions:

- how many countries they visit in a year: one to two countries (73%);
- working hours: 70% work forty hours per week or fewer, one-third of digital nomads work more than forty hours per week;
- health insurance: 74% of digital nomads have health insurance;
- income: 18% earn more than USD 9,999 per year and 22% earn between USD 50,000 and USD 99,999, while according to the Social Security Administration, the average US worker earns USD 46,641 a year; comparing to traditional work, 31% of nomads declare to earn similar amounts of money, 18% earn more money as a digital nomad than when they worked traditionally, while 46% earn less money as a digital nomad;
- additional financial support: 32% have occasionally received financial support beyond income from an outside source like a friend or family member;
- financial stress: 38% respond they feel less stressed financially as a digital nomad, and 34% declare there is no difference in financial stress than when they worked in a traditional job.

Similar results have been received by WiseBand, a marketing platform for independent workers, in a survey 'State of the Freelance Nation 2018' conducted in December 2017 among 2,000 Americans.[19] The report dispels some major myths about freelancers and their working conditions – regarding their age, incomes and working habits. According to the data collected in the survey freelancing is no longer seen as a temporary phase between full-time employment relationships but a separate and stable career path, guaranteeing financial security within one to two years. Fifty-four per cent of freelancers declare not being interested in turning back to a full-time employment. Among the rest, surprisingly, Millennials are more likely to return to full-time employment than the freelancers of age 35 + , who declare to be rather satisfied with their work life balance as freelancers.

Putting these results aside, the analysis of Polish surveys demonstrates a quite different image of a digital nomad and his working conditions. An analogical report has been published by useme.eu, which is the largest remote work platform in Poland for specialists in the IT, media, graphics and design industries with over 40,000 registered users, including over 30,000 freelancers and 12,000 companies. The 'Freelancers in Poland' survey was conducted by the platform on a group of 1,002 respondents using the questionnaire method available on the website.[20] For the aims of the report, a

19. This online survey was conducted between 10 December 2017 and 21 December 2017 and studied the working habits of 2,000 North American adults (age 18 +) registered at the platform. Full results are available in the report on the website: https://wisebrand.co/state-of-the-freelance-nation-survey/ (accessed 20 October 2019).
20. Previous research carried out between April and August 2016 using the survey method on a group of 723 mobile specialists. Full data available at: https://useme.eu/pl/help/image/Raport%3A_Polski_Freelancer_2016 (accessed 20 October 2019).

freelancer was defined as every person earning on their own account on the basis of performed orders regardless of the legal form of cooperation.

The major differences between the status of American and Polish freelancers are the following – according to the 'Freelancer Report 2018'[21] over 25% of freelancers in Poland work in the 'grey zone' with unclear legal status or no legal contract whatsoever. Their working time is often longer than forty hours per week, and they gain lower income than the minimum wage guaranteed by legislation for employees and some civil law contractors.[22]

A statistic freelancer in Poland is primarily a young or middle-aged person. More than a half (51.1%) are people aged 25-34, 21% are 18-24, and every fifth (19.5%) has between 35-44 years. Nearly 8% of people are people over the age of 45. In relation to the survey from the previous edition, the number of people under 18 years of age and in the range of 18-24 years decreased, but increased in the above-mentioned middle group and among people over 45. In the group of respondents, men predominate slightly (56.7% of respondents).

Nearly two-thirds of freelancers live in large cities, with 40.4% of respondents living in cities with over 400,000 habitants. In relation to the previous year, the number of people living in rural areas and smaller cities has increased, which may indicate a growing popularity of the freelance profession in these regions.

The most popular fields represented by these professionals are graphics (37%), copywriting (31%) and programming (26%). While asked about the place of work Polish freelancers replied as usually work at home. Few use the opportunity to work in the client's office (16%) or in the co-working spaces (only 7%). 28% of respondents declared to affront the problem of separation between 'home' and 'office' area.

As far as the working time is considered, only people having regular jobs work up to four hours a day as freelancers. The vast majority spends four to ten working hours or more during the day. Working time is described as quite flexible, among all respondents only 5.1% answered that they always work at regular times. As far as leisure time is concerned, 42% declared that they were able to have two weeks of vacation during the year, 23.7%, however, admitted that they were able to organize at most weekend holidays or not to go anywhere. The others referred to be departing for a week or less during the year.

Earnings depend primarily on the industry and the number of orders accepted by freelancers. More than half of the respondents answered that they earn from PLN 1,000[23] (42%) to PLN 2,000 (24%) as freelancers, and that is considered by 63% of them as low remuneration. Respondents who complained about their earnings are mainly copywriters and graphic artists with low experience in the field. Higher amounts in the ranking were indicated by graphic designers with more seniority as well as programmers and specialists from the IT industry. In comparison to last year's

21. The 'Freelancers in Poland 2018' survey conducted by the platform useme.eu: https://useme.eu/pl/blog/raport-freelancing-w-polsce-edycja-2018,98/ (accessed 21 October 2019).
22. Act of 10 October 2002 on minimal wage for work (Journal of Laws of 2018 item 2177 with amendments).
23. EUR 1 corresponds approximately to PLN 4.4.

report, the number of people who earn over 1,000 and over PLN 2,000 increased – up to 23% and 14.5% respectively. The number of people earning PLN 3,000-PLN 5,000 has also slightly improved – in the last year such income was declared by 9.5% of respondents, this year by 13.1%.

The analysis of the form of cooperation from the questionnaires shows that 48.6% of respondents declare the combination of full-time and commissioned work, treating remuneration received as freelancers only as an addition to the payment received from a labour law based contract. Almost the same group (48.4% of respondents) declared that they do not combine work as a freelancer with a full-time job or contract.

An interesting result comes in terms on the willingness of becoming independent from a subordinate work. Only 10.3% of respondents declared willingness to give up their full-time job, 42.6% prefer to combine regular job with freelancing, seeing it as an addition to more stable and regular income from a full-time work. As a consequence, only 23% of respondents declared to register their own business, the same number declares to earn occasionally without any legal contracts, 12.4% of respondents offer their services always 'without bill'. That means that over 25% of remote work and freelance settlements take place in the 'grey zone', without paying any taxes or social contributions.

When the seniority of cooperation is considered, half of the respondents declare to work as freelancers for less than two years – it can be assumed that they use platforms to build their base of regular customers. In the group of those freelancers who work remotely for more than two years, people with three to five years of experience are predominant (22%). Polish freelancers find orders from recommendations and cooperation with regular clients. A significant source of 'gigs' for Polish freelancers is the use of Polish platforms for freelancers, while foreign portals and advertising websites are used randomly. Statistically, the Polish freelancer works for around two to three regular customers a month and tries to acquire five to seven new ones. For the most part of respondents (68%) the clients are mainly small and medium Polish companies, natural persons and micro-enterprises.

The analysis of the data demonstrated above allows to identify the most important problems indicated by respondents, which are connected with financial security (irregular payments from customers affect 25% of respondents, while another 34% declared to affront these problems sporadically). It might be due to the fact that Polish freelancers rarely decide to collect a down payment (half of the respondents declare that they do it rarely or never, while another 26% do it sometimes). The other negative aspects frequently mentioned by freelancers include lack of good orders, low wages as well as high competition on the market. Freelancers also declare to face problems with the lack of social and health protection.

20.5 WORKING CONDITIONS BASED ON PLATFORM REGULATIONS

Freelancers to register as users of a certain advertising platform in search for 'gigs' are obliged to accept the working conditions stipulated by platform regulations that may be highly limiting to their autonomy as 'independent entrepreneurs'. These regulations regard the power of control of the client or the platform itself over freelancer's work, stipulation of wage or limitations to freelancers' privacy.

For example the platform Upwork enables the client to have a far-reaching control of the freelancer's work – it creates an automatic Job Log, takes pictures of the contractor's computer six times within an hour, so that the client has a continuous preview of what the freelancer is currently doing. In addition, the platform provides chat for a direct communication with a freelancer.[24]

This excessive power of control brings questions in the field of privacy and data protection, especially when we consider the fact that freelancers are mainly working on their own private devices, that might be used also by others (e.g., members of the family) and for private purposes (e.g., in fact a print screen automatically taken by the platform may show a private picture of the family member put on the desktop which would be already considered a violation of privacy under GDPR regulations).

Another example of difficulties faced by Polish freelancers came from a Polish platform zlecenia.przez.net[25] regarding the policy of the stipulation of wages. The platform is organized in a form of an auction of offers, where the customer presents a project without indicating a remuneration, and freelancers participate in the auction presenting their proposals along with the price of the service. Usually the first contractor is put in the most difficult situation, because the others will lower the price in order to win the auction and the competition between freelancers is not regulated or controlled anyhow by the platform. A similar strategy is applied by a platform freelancer.pl, which describes the right of a buyer to choose his collaborator for the order with a phrase 'Choose the Winner'. The same portal charges the parties of the contract unequally – the fee is paid by both parties of the contract but in such a proportion:

- 3% of the project value from the buyer;
- 10% of the project value from contractors (freelancers).

24. According to Upwork Privacy Policy: 'As part of the Service, we collect information about a Freelancer's work on a project for a Client. This feature is known as Work Diary. Work Diaries include information provided by the Freelancer, such as a memo, as well as automatically gathered information about work on a project, such as number of mouseclicks and keyboard strokes and regularly taken screenshots (which may include a webcam picture of you if you have not disabled this feature in your settings). ... We will share information contained in Work Diaries with the relevant Client and with any manager or administrator of any applicable Freelancer Agency. We inform Freelancers each time we capture information for Work Diary ... a Freelancer may choose to block or delete the screen shot and associated data for a recorded work interval, but then the *Freelancer may not be paid for that work interval.* Upwork may use general information from Work Diaries for statistical analysis, product development, marketing and research'. *See* at: https://www.upwork.com/legal#privacy (accessed 20 October 2019).
25. The platform zlecenia.przez.net has been taken over by the freelancer.pl platform, which continues the same policy in the stipulation of wages, adding also a possibility for the buyer – instead of a publication of a task/project for the order – an organization of a 'contest' for freelancers who are supposed to submit one or more solutions via the website. According to the User's Agreement the payment will be guaranteed only to 'a Project awarded by a Buyer (for example through HireMe), a service bought by a Buyer from a Seller, and service awarded by a Buyer to a Seller as a result of a Contest or competition hosted via the Website'. *See* at: https://www.freelancer.pl/about/terms (accessed 20 October 2019).

20.6 CONCLUSIONS

As it has already been mentioned above, in 2016 the European Forum of Independent Professionals (EFIP) has established a report on 'Future Working: The Rise of Europe's Independent Professionals (iPros)'[26] defining iPros as 'highly skilled self-employed individuals who work for themselves but do not employ others'. According to the authors of the report, the current legal frameworks, within which iPros provide work, differ from country to country and require further adjustments.

But digital nomads are not simply iPros with their own registered businesses. They are not a homogeneous group but rather a social phenomenon that from a legal perspective includes various types of working performance, difference in terms of form, time, place, methods, wages and organization. They do not enter in the strict category of typical self-employment and the traditional division between autonomous and subordinate work. Furthermore, as it has been proved by the social researchers in Poland, the expectations of the nomads themselves in relation to the labour market do not correspond with the reality that the labour market offers.

The legal response to their needs and problems as identified by the surveys on a national level is insufficient. On the European level the Directive of the European Parliament and Council on transparent and predictable working conditions in the EU was believed to bring a significant improvement of the working conditions of platform workers, including digital nomads. It was supposed to broaden the definition of a worker in European law, but this proposal was abandoned from the final version of the approved regulation.

The Directive is certainly an important step towards improving the situation of people providing work in the so-called atypical forms, including those working via online platforms, however, a cautious and insufficient step to talk about their full protection. Above all, the relation between the definition of worker as defined by the EU and Polish regulations of employee within the meaning of Article 2 of the Labour Code remains unclear, which, according to court judgments, raises interpretational doubts not only in Poland but also in various EU Member States. Dynamic technological development and significant growth of employment within the framework of the gig economy make it urgent and necessary to redefine the classic terms of the employee and employer and their legal relationship in Polish Labour Law, and – as the EU legislator shows – such elements of this relationship as time and place of work (not forgetting the mutual obligations of the parties, the limits of control or the need to respect private life of the worker) have to be redefined.

26. EFIP, *Future Working: The Rise of Europe's Independent Professionals (iPros)*, previously available at: http://www.efip.org/sites/default/files/Future_Working_Full_Report.pdf (accessed 20 April 2019).

Therefore, given the pace of change and the growth of people engaged in non-standard forms of work, such comprehensive regulation should appear in Polish law as soon as possible, because the existing gaps are not conducive to building fair and predictable working conditions for all types of workers.

CHAPTER 21

Platform Work and 'Double Alienness'

Simone D'Ascola

21.1 INTRODUCTION

This chapter is aimed to suggest that one of the most devaluated paradigms of subordination in Italian Labour Law can still produce interesting heuristic results with regard to one of the most peculiar phenomenon of contemporary capitalism: the work through digital and web platforms.

Honestly, this paradigm can surely be considered as an old one in Italian Labour Law, while it receives definitely more consensus within other geographical contexts, such as the Spanish one (*see* below).

I am referring to the idea of double alienness.[1] The brief reflection I propose tries to answer the following simple question: is it possible to use the Italian theory of the subordination as 'double alienness' of the worker[2] as a relevant contribution to the debate about the uncertain and questioned *salaried* nature of the work given in the gig economy, especially (but not only) in the food delivery through platforms?

In Italian Labour Law it is possible to state that the qualification process is the 'access gate' to the whole set of protections: in fact, the kind of protections and guarantees assured to the dependent workers – whose relation is 'salaried' – is still largely superior to the features and guarantees recognized to autonomous workers or independent contractors.

1. I prefer to use 'alienness' to make this expression clear in English: in fact, the alternatives of 'alienation' (cf. Marx) or 'estrangement' seem to have a too dynamic meaning, while the Italian *alienità*, which I intend to translate, refers to a more static condition.
2. Which is 'the alienness (meaning exclusive destination to others) of the result whose achievement the provision of labour is used for, and the alienness of productive organization the service is part of': Italian Constitutional Court, 12 February 1996, No. 30 (*see* below).

As a consequence, the question about how to apply qualification categories to platform work is crucial. It is not only currently discussed by many of the scholars,[3] but also the case law, all around the world as in Italy, is now facing this topic. It is absolutely necessary to adopt an open-minded approach, otherwise the new phenomena's destiny is to escape from juridical control.

21.2 THE IDEA OF 'DOUBLE ALIENNESS' IN ITALIAN LABOUR LAW

The salaried relation of work (*subordination*) can be divided into two main approaches historically spread within the main twentieth century's Italian Labour Law doctrine.

One is the technical approach and the other is the socio-economic. The first takes mainly into account the directives that the employer gives to his employees and focuses on the exercise of powers of the first towards the seconds.

The other approach enhances the condition of dependence experienced by the worker with regard to the employer. Both approaches are possible because the legal definition is very essential and requires analytic development and interpretations to be applied.

The idea of double alienness is a face of the second approach because the condition of 'dependence' (mentioned in the fundamental Article 2094 of Italian Civil Code) of the workers requires economic holds to be recognized.

That is why some authors proposed this particular kind of reconstruction about the subordination.[4] In different moments of their juridical productions they recognized that the salaried worker is extraneous both from the means of production (which belong to the capitalist) and from the result of his work (which similarly belongs to the capitalist) and, as a consequence, he is just owner of its energies which are sold to the employer.

This is the condition of double alienness (from the means of production, or the organization of them, *and* from the result of the job), which implies that for the qualification of the work relationship it is possible to investigate also these elements.

Also Gaetano Vardaro[5] considered the condition of alienness and stated that the proper consideration of a subjective labour law requires to consider both the so-called technical subordination and the existential one, where the second, even sliding from the formal elements of dependent work, allows to appreciate the personal relation of subjection in which the worker is overall included.

3. *See*, also for details and references, A. Donini, *Il lavoro attraverso le piattaforme digitali*, Bononia University Press, 2018.
4. For instance, U. Romagnoli, *La prestazione di lavoro nel contratto di società*, Giuffrè, 1967; L. Mengoni, *Lezioni sul contratto di lavoro*, Celuc, 1971; F. Mazziotti, *Contenuto ed effetti del contratto di lavoro*, Jovene, 1974; M. Roccella, *Manuale di diritto del lavoro*, Giappichelli, 2015.
5. G. Vardaro, *Tecnica, tecnologia e ideologia della tecnica nel diritto del lavoro*, in *Politica del diritto*, 1986.

21.3 RELEVANT CASE LAW

In 1996 a very famous leading case of the Italian Constitutional Court (Judgment of 12 February 1996, number 30, drafted by Luigi Mengoni) gave very important suggestions about double alienness.

It was actually dedicated to cooperative work, and Mengoni used in the decision the theory of double alienness in order to state what was 'technically' salaried work, detailing that the condition of alienness from the employer's organization and from the product (or result) was indefectible.

Although the decision was given with regard to a specific case (and it excluded subordination in cooperative work, where the worker is partially owner of the economic activity) it remained as a fundamental moment for the recent domestic evolution of Italian Labour Law.[6]

This judgment was followed by some decisions of the Supreme Court (*Corte di Cassazione*)[7] which somehow recalls this theory, because they consider the socio-economic approach in solving the dispute and mentions the double alienness.

In fact, rather than being based on the occurrence of the single elements of the so-called eterodirezione,[8] it takes into consideration some more material and socio-economic factors:[9] the absence for the worker of any kind of property or control on the product/result of his labour provision and on the means used for the production.

Double alienness criterion appears also in the recent Court of Cassation's Judgment No. 29761/2018. This decision, even if does not entirely support the idea of double alienness, gives a clear definition of it: 'alienness in the sense of exclusive destination to others of the result for which the worker's performance is used and alienness from the productive organization in which the performance takes place'.[10]

The Judgment No. 29761 takes into consideration both Constitutional Court Judgment Nos 30/1996 and 76/2015 in order to assert that the second one proposed a different concept of subordination upholding a very narrow concept of subordination.

In fact, about five years ago the Constitutional Court had the chance to focus again on this topic (the notion of salaried employment), but, according to some scholars, not denying the Judgment No. 30/1996.[11]

Among the case law of the Court of Cassation there are also judgments not directly referred to double alienness which though dedicate some consideration to it. For example, the worker's *organizational insertion* in the enterprise structure is

---

6. A positive evaluation of that decision is recently given by M. Barbieri, *Della subordinazione dei ciclofattorini*, in *Labour and Law Issues*, 2019.
7. For instance, Court of Cassation, Judgments No. 21646/2006; No. 820/2007 and No. 18692/2007. More recently No. 14660/2017.
8. The condition of being subjected to the employer's powers and directives.
9. In order to distinguish from self-employment. *See also* L. Mariucci, *Il lavoro ddecentrato*, Franco Angeli, 1979, p. 90: 'it is precisely this separation from the product of work and from the organization in which it is inserted that marks the discriminant with self-employment'.
10. Literally 'alienità nel senso di destinazione esclusiva ad altri del risultato per il cui conseguimento la prestazione di lavoro è utilizzata e alienità dell'organizzazione produttiva in cui la prestazione si inserisce' (author's translation).
11. M. Barbieri, *supra*, p. 13.

enhanced also with reference to his alienness from work instruments by Court of Cassation, 4 March 2015, No. 4346.

21.4 THE 'DOUBLE ALIENNESS' OF THE PLATFORM WORKER

As long as it appeared in the reality that labour law is called to regulate, the phenomenon of platform work has been largely discussed with reference to the qualification topic.[12]

In this paragraph the intention is neither to solve the problem of the qualification of the work relation in the different contexts of platform work, nor establishing which is the best qualifying *technique* to explain such an innovative and complex phenomenon.

I will just try to develop this 'old' idea about subordination with regard to some kinds of platform work relations. In particular, we will figure out in which terms it is possible to recognize a condition of double alienness in the working position of all the workers involved in the sector of food delivery through digital Apps. It is in fact one of the most relevant sectors in *gig economy* (but also transport services such as Uber can be involved by the same ideas).

In a context where evolutions and transformations are so rapid and relevant, it is not easy to keep on using the consolidated criteria to find out a subordinate relation, because the relation itself presents new features.

Surely not all the jobs on digital platforms present the condition of double alienness. Nevertheless, it seems to be interesting to look at the phenomena from this point of view. In fact:

- the job relation between the worker and the digital platform (e.g., Foodora, Deliveroo) requires the interpreter to 'identify the legal status of subordination' (Tullini);
- the dimension of the social and economic condition of the platform worker is crucial in the current scenario and should not be completely overlooked, though intersecting it with many more strictly technical nodes (Perulli);
- the debate on the qualification of these work relations in Italy has been so far based mainly on the use of the classic categories of 'heterodirection' or on elements such as the subjection (or not) to the employers' powers (e.g., disciplinary power, even if exercised through exclusion from the platform as a consequence of negative feedbacks);

12. P. Tullini, *Economia digitale e lavoro non-standard*, in LLI, 2016, 2; A. Perulli (dir. by), *Lavoro autonomo e capitalism delle piattaforme*, Cedam, 2018; M. Biasi, *Dai pony express ai riders di Foodora. L'attualità del binomio subordinazione-autonomia (e del relativo metodo di indagine) quale alternativa all'affannosa ricerca di inedite categorie*, in G. Zilio Grandi, M. Biasi (dir. by), *Commentario breve allo statuto del lavoro autonomo e del lavoro agile*, Cedam, 2018, pp. 67 ff. (also for a detailed summary of the scholars' positions); E. Signorini, *Il diritto del lavoro nell'economia digitale*, Giappichelli, 2018.

- in some cases it could appear clear that taking into account the double alienness (in the specified sense) the qualification process in the Italian system could be (not solved but) helped.

In order to use double alienness as required is to go through the notion of 'means of production'. This is one of the most interesting and original aspects of the effort to apply the double alienness to this field.

Moreover, it helps to be more specific in the individuation of which kind of platform jobs can be considered: it will be necessary to answer to the following (and perhaps provocative) questions: in the Uber business what is the most important means of production? The driver's vehicle or the digital App? And what about services such as Foodora or Deliveroo? Can we consider the bicycle and the smartphone as a relevant means of production or are we supposed to value the App in this perspective?

Even though the App is totally dematerialized, it can probably be affirmed that its features, technology (the algorithm) and strategic importance (giving the concrete possibility to exist to a service like those mentioned) make *the App being the key element of the means of production*. An in-depth study of the App mechanisms would demonstrate this, even if it is almost impossible because the algorithms are secret.

From a methodological point of view it is necessary to adopt a substantially 'typological' qualifying method. In fact, even considering the absence of formal modification to the prototype given by the Article 2094 of the Italian Civil Code (but the new Article 2 of the Legislative Decree No. 81/2015 is challenging in this regard),[13] the sociological scenario of work performances is evolving considerably and the difficulty of grabbing certain forms of work are very remarkable (especially the most advanced and digitalized tertiary sector which includes the examples just made).

The point of view of the 'Mengonian' theory of double alienation could lead to interesting results, although it must be borne in mind that the main obstacle to achieving definitive and satisfying answers is the non-unity of the phenomenon taken into consideration. Not all the Apps work in the same way: as a consequence not all the platform workers could be considered subordinate with respect to the multinational companies which own these Apps. This does not mean that it is not worth attempting a new reconstruction, both for trying to enrich a theoretical reflection and to contribute in a possible future to solve practical and judicial cases.

21.5 PLATFORMS CASE LAW AND DOUBLE ALIENNESS

It is now necessary to briefly verify if the case law so far appeared in Italy about platforms considered the double alienness approach.

The answer is substantively negative: the recent important judgments given by the Tribunal of Torino, the Tribunal of Milano and the Court of Appeal of Torino about some Foodora workers, which pretended to be qualified as subordinate workers, basically did not take into consideration this argument.

13. After the changes introduced by Act No. 128/2019.

Since these judgments have been severely criticized by the doctrine because of their aporias and contradictions (especially the first two), a larger, even if doubtful, approach to the topic is essential: what would have happened if the judges had wanted to enhance this element? Would the outcome have been different? If one thinks about the structure of the employment relationships examined, it is legitimate to think that yes, it would have changed. In fact, the workers were completely unrelated and extraneous both to the digital means of production (the Apps) and to the result of their performance (the delivery service).

While Italian case law so far in this field basically ignored the approach of double alienness or, more precisely, avoided to consider its presence as relevant for the qualification decision, a comparative overlook gives some cues: for instance, in Spain it is common to give value to the element of alienness (*ajenidad*). Actually the reason is also that it is included in the fundamental Spanish Labour Law Act (*Estatuto del los trabajadores*).[14]

So, in Spain, a recent case qualified some workers of Deliveroo as subordinate workers recognizing a decisive role to the double alienness theory.[15]

Another important, more recent Spanish judgment states, in detail, that:

> The unfeasibility for the distributor that, with its means and unlinked from the platform, can carry out its own economic activity, is connected with the other element that qualifies as *working* the contractual relationship: the alienness.
>
> The work of the dealer is meaningless if it is not integrated into the business activity of G. SL, integration that takes place from the moment each micro-task is entrusted and accepted. Since then, G. SL assumes it as its own and responds of it in front of suppliers and customers. It is not known that the dealer assumes some type of responsibility towards these and even when, as indicated above, this is stated in the contract. It is also G. SL who invoices for its activity of transporting goods to suppliers and customers, integrating in the cost of the service the price that for the task will then be paid to the dealer.
>
> The alienness in the results is evident because the defendant endorses the result of the activity of the distributor, also moving to G. SL the risks of the work provided. And there is also the *alienness* in the market because the demand is constituted as an essential intermediary between the task of the dealer and its final recipient.[16]

It is easy to recognize what kind of reasoning was carried on by the Spanish judge: precisely the kind of analysis which is being suggested in this page.

14. *See* A. Ojeda Aviles, *Ajenidad, dependencia o control: la causa del contrato*, in *Derecho Puc, Revista de la facultad de derecho*, 2007, pp. 375 ff.
15. Juzgado de lo Social, VI sección, 1 June 2018, No. 244 – Ana Belen Diez Farto Est. – Jose Enrique (avv. Rafael Martínez Simón) c. Roofoods Spain S.L. – Marco Civolani (avv. Román Gil Alburquerque). About Spanish judgments, *see* G. Pacella, *Alienità del risultato, alienità dell'organizzazione: ancora una sentenza spagnola qualifica come subordinati i fattorini di Deliveroo*, in *Labour and Law Issues*, No. 4, 2018, 61; J. Pérez Rey, *Son los riders trabajadores?, Comentario a los primeros escarceos judiciales en torno a las identidades debiles de la economia uberizada*, in www.actumsocial.es, 2018, p. 2.
16. Juzgado de lo Social de Madrid, 11 February 2019.

21.6 FINAL REMARKS

The topic offers many handholds for deepening that are not possible here. More and more Italian scholars seem to be sensible to these aspects.[17]

The digital economy requires to adopt these kinds of flexible views at a double level: in terms of handling legal categories and in terms of establishing the fair protections for the people who work.

That is why it is possible to suggest that the double alienness approach should at least be taken into consideration (from judges and scholars) for the contribution it can give.

In fact, as long as Italian Labour Law continues to be structured on the self-employment/subordination dichotomy, it is inevitable that all the reconstructive paths are followed to find the appropriate way to offer adequate guarantees to platform workers.

17. About alienness in platform work, *see also* G. De Simone, *Lavoro digitale e subordinazion. Prime riflessioni*, in *Rivista giuridica del lavoro e della previdenza sociale*, 2019, p. 15. Also V. Pietrogiovanni, *Redefining the Boundaries of Labour Law: Is 'Double Alienness' a Useful Concept for Classifying Employees in Times of Fractal Work?*, in A. Blackham, M. Kullmann, A. Zbyszewska, Hart (dir. by) *Theorising Labour Law in a Changing World: Towards Inclusive Labour Law*, 2019, pp. 55 ff. discusses double alienness as he had already done in V. Pietrogiovanni, *Reality Still Bites: A First Look on Labour Law and Jobless Youth in Nordic and Southern European Countries*, in *European Journal of Social Law*, 2014, pp. 141 ff.

CHAPTER 22

Some Thoughts on Industry 4.0 and Trade Unions

Pasquale Monda

22.1 THE CONSIDERABLE DECLINE OF THE FOURTH INDUSTRIAL REVOLUTION

The role of the union in the era of the fourth industrial revolution is extensively discussed. This is partially due to the tendency of disintermediation that overcomes the intermediate bodies of the production process, which does not consider the collective representations of the workers. Besides, it neglects to consider among the main problems of the digitisation of productive activities the difficulty of the union in carving out its role within the change, above all organisational changes in progress.[1]

The reflection on these aspects is not at all simple even if, as in the following pages, the analysis is limited to the national dimension only. This is because the phenomenon in question is variously influenced by the multiple expressions of the digital economy, whose correct identification is crucial to develop any consideration on the point.

Well, although lacking 'a paradigm or a theoretical formulation' inclined to specify its contours, it is possible,[2] following an approach that begins to make its way in literature,[3] to 'simplify the digital economy', enucleating the 'most qualifying components'. At least two macro-areas derive from this: the first includes all the hypotheses in which digital technology acts as an intermediary for the delivery of goods and services; the second, according to the first reconstructions of the phenomenon,

1. Caruso, *La rappresentanza delle organizzazioni di interessi tra disintermediazione e re-intermediazione*, WP CSDLE 'Massimo D'Antona'.IT – 326/2017.
2. Tullini, *La digitalizzazione del lavoro, la produzione intelligente e il controllo tecnologico nell'impresa*, Tullini (edited by), *Web e lavoro*, Giappichelli, 2017, p. 4.
3. Spinelli, *Tecnologie digitali e lavoro agile*, Cacucci, 2018, p. 17.

includes all the variegated forms of 'aggregation between digital technologies aimed at taking decisions oriented to the efficient management of resources, flexibility, productivity and product competitiveness'.[4]

The first component of the digital economy is, in some respects, the most controversial and, at the same time, the one that is developing most rapidly.[5] The use of sophisticated digital platforms to carry out the work of distributing goods and services is a complex phenomenon, where the platform relates not only to those who request a service and those who provide it but also organises the execution of a large portion of the work itself.[6] There are numerous problems linked to these events: 'economy of chores' (or, to use a well-known expression, 'gig economy') – it is claimed – favours the avoidance of rules and rights, spreading serious distortions in the labour market. What is most interesting to highlight, in the wake of the recent litigation, is the difficulty of qualifying the work through the platform: if the need for qualification is not in question,[7] to make it difficult is the presumed freedom of the worker in deciding whether and when to perform the service, a freedom in itself incompatible with the obligation of obedience related to the managerial power.

The second component of the digital economy, called 'Industry 4.0', has very broad and complex contents, which make its implementation paths extremely varied. Despite their extreme variety, however, such paths, using digital technologies, intend to connect people and things to a single network to allow both their identification and the transfer of information concerning them (Internet of Things and Internet of Services, wearable devices), in order to manage the organisation in a dynamic and automated way. The production process, thus, becomes extremely fluid, capable of rapidly changing according to the changing expectations of the market: revealed expectations often anticipated or even conditioned by the same forms of automation underlying the production.[8] Coming to the stricter aspect of work, with 'Industry 4.0' the subordinated nature of the employment relationship is not questioned; this is not the striking factor we are concerned with, but the effects of a 'substitute' and/or 'complementary' type that the integration of the work in the so-called smart factory – i.e., the company that uses digital technologies in the sense indicated – generates.

The 'substitute effect' is expressed in the transition from a worker with standardised tasks and very limited skills to one with high professionalism and whose tasks are managed dynamically: those who carry out their work, far from executing the

4. *See* the document entitled *Sviluppo economico e politiche energetiche. Industria 4.0* elaborated by the X Commissione della Camera dei deputati.
5. This explains the need for a specific regulation: the reference is to the Law Decree n. 101/2019 and the Law n. 128/2019.
6. *See* Corte d'Appello di Torino 4 February 2019 n. 26 and Tribunale di Torino n. 778/2018.
7. Delfino, *Il lavoro mediante piattaforme digitali tra tradizione e innovazione: il caso* Uber, *DLM*, 2018, p. 2.
8. In this regard, it is observed that Industry 4.0 aims to define an organisation of production processes based on technology and devices that communicate with each other: a factory model where computer-guided systems monitor physical processes and make decentralised decisions based on auto mechanisms' organisation. In this sense v. Camera dei deputati Digitalizzazione dell'industria europea – Cogliere appieno i vantaggi di un mercato unico digitale *(Comunicazione COM(2016)180)*.

directives of the employers, are increasingly committed to improving both the development and the design of the production cycle. In short, the 4.0 worker is, at the same time, the 'protagonist' as well as someone who is 'responsible' for the production efficiency and no longer a mere 'producer' limited to a single role.[9]

The substitute effect - mentioned above - involves the relationship between work and technology which simultaneously complement one another: the organisation of the service takes place via the technologies through which the work itself is carried out. The benefits of this relationship are important and a few examples are as follows: the control on the performance of the service, companies destined to become much more pervasive and a place of high potential performance to be found nowhere else but exclusively within the material boundaries of the company.[10]

22.2 LOOKING AT SOME IMPLEMENTATION EXPERIENCES OF INDUSTRY 4.0

Much more should be said about the relationship between the digital economy and work, but, to stay within the boundaries of reflection, it is advisable not to go further and to start thinking closely about the role of the union.

In order to proceed in this direction, however, it requires further clarification.

The considerations expressed show that the 'digital revolution' in progress is heterogeneous and suggests keeping the two macro-areas identified very distinct. This is because, in addition to enhancing the intrinsic peculiarities, such diversification makes it possible to give the right weight to a leading element in the development of the analysis: the reference is to the qualification of the case. More precisely, given that Italian trade union law is still very much tied to the subordinate nature of the employment contract and the trade union disintermediation binomial - digital economy can only be declined differently depending on whether we are talking about a 'gig economy' or an 'Industry 4.0' economy: only in the case of the 'gig economy' is the legal nature of the work performed uncertainly. However, it is not possible here to bite into the wide debate on the qualification of the so-called gig workers, the following pages will look more closely at 'Industry 4.0' only.

What has been said allows resuming the threads of the discourse and confronting ourselves with those authors who, moving from the careful analysis of some empirical experiences, place the accent on the 'substitute' effects of 'Industry 4.0'. This is to highlight that, in order to promote a worker with an increasingly active role in business processes, organisational models based on the widespread use of job rotation, job enrichment and job enlargement practices are spreading. The aim is to increase the knowledge that the worker has of the production system, amplifying the opportunities

9. Del Punta, *Un diritto per il lavoro 4.0*, Cipriani, Gramolati, Mari (edited by), *Il lavoro 4.0. La Quarta Rivoluzione industriale e le trasformazioni delle attività lavorative*, Firenze University Press, 2018, pp. 225 ss.
10. *See* the new Art. 4 Law 300/70, on the power of control, and the recent regulation on smart working.

to consciously participate in organisational innovation projects.[11] It is not by chance that the experiences in question associate a marked recourse to rewarding work on the tasks, to make the staff more 'responsible' for production trends.

It is too easy to observe how such practices are anything but innovative and, in themselves, hardly inclined to foster forms of trade union disintermediation: an outcome, rather, attributable to the choice of entrusting their development to the individual contract. To be precise, the organisational models considered here resort to individual agreements both to implement fruitful job rotation, job enrichment and job enlargement programmes and to distribute collective bonuses. And, again with individual agreements, 'participatory' relationships are established between the lender and the employer, on company improvement programmes, through which the former expresses its increased skills.

Of course, enhancing individual negotiation does not necessarily mean sacrificing trade union input: this is demonstrated by the wide debate on the possibility of increasing its space without renouncing its virtuous relationship with the main expression of trade union action, i.e., the collective agreement. The experiences considered, however, highlight the attempt to propose a marked centrality of the individual contract in dealing with decisively crucial issues. Giving some examples, through the individual contract the most suitable training paths are identified for a profitable job rotation and for the exercise of new tasks in the context of a vertical expansion (job enrichment) or horizontal projects (job enlargement) of the job and, passing to the awarding side, to determine the objectives, the verification techniques, the criteria and the timing of delivery of the prize. Thus, the main protagonists of the managerial affair are the employer and the employee, while the union – it is stated – 'plays, at most, of remittance':[12] it is in this way, therefore, that the first experiences of implementation of Industry 4.0 take the road to disintermediation.

22.3 THE EMPHASIS OF THE INDIVIDUAL CONTRACT: SOME DOUBTS

In this way, the attempt to intertwine the development of Industry 4.0 with the 'captivating idea' of focusing on the individual contract to make organisational work more flexible and dynamic emerges: this is not an obligatory path, and such a characteristic leads us to pay great attention to its risks.

To immediately come to the essence of the problems, it should be noted that the main doubts related to the drive towards 'contractualism' derive from the nature of the service, whose inclusion in the context of subordination of course is not our concern in this text. Many considerations could be made in this regard, as the debate is very rich, but it is useful to focus the attention on just two essential points.

11. *See* Caruso, Il sindacato tra funzioni e valori nella 'grande trasformazione'. L'innovazione sociale in sei tappe, WP CSDLE 'Massimo D'Antona'.IT – 394/2019, p. 26.
12. Pero, Ponzellini, Il nuovo lavoro industriale tra innovazione organizzativa e partecipazione diretta, Carrieri, Nerozzi, Treu (edited by), La partecipazione incisiva. Idee e proposte per rilanciare la democrazia nelle imprese, Il Mulino, 2015.

In the first place, it does not seem that the greater margins of autonomy and involvement of the 4.0 worker detract from the typical characteristics of subordination: the 4.0 worker, therefore, remains without complete management power to have autonomy over the final result without any further intermediation. The point posed prior is not insignificant, which relates – and leads us to the second aspect – the '4.0 worker', despite being at the centre of profound organisational renewal, still manifests the typical, though not exclusive, trait of every employed worker: the socio-economic weakness, a weakness already present in the market and perpetuated by the so-called smart organisation on par with what happens in all organisational models focused on employment. The presence of a 'cyber conscience',[13] around which the organisation of work revolves, does not change in any way, and since the 4.0 worker does not directly exercise organisational-managerial power, his performance remains functionally absorbed in the structure of the employer, not gaining any visibility in the labour market.

Therefore, in pursuing the path of Industry 4.0, one cannot ignore considering a crucial profile in the reflection: the weakness of the employed as a paradigmatic trait of labour law. This profile is so important that the Italian constitutional text already insists on it: while giving importance to work in all its forms, a particular accent is placed on work carried out under conditions of socio-economic dependence, imposing, through the principle of substantial equality, the removal of all obstacles to the possibility of making this form of work a real expression of the person as well as an instrument of participation in the life and development of the country.

Against the background of the clarifications made, there is no doubt that even for the '4.0 worker' the perspective of 'hetero-protection' deserves the utmost attention and, above all, keeps its timeliness unchanged: if the '4.0 worker' lacks an 'economic individuality' autonomous from that of employers, the heteronomous production of the rules for the employment relationship contributes significantly to restoring the identity of the person. And, given that the collective agreement also contributes to 'rebalancing and moderating social disparities', it is frankly difficult to avoid its contribution.

Of course, we do not intend to argue that individual autonomy is deprived of any space, which, in implementing Industry 4.0, takes on a very precious role:[14] after all, even for 4.0 worker the civil law principle applies, according to which each individual, including those who work at other people's dependencies, can self-determine their interests. To be avoided – to use authoritative doctrine – is the danger of making recourse to individual autonomy no longer the opportunity to 'choose one's life plan',[15] fatally sacrificing the opportunity to develop virtuous organisational innovations. In other words, by focusing on the individual contract alone, there is the risk of accentuating the asymmetry of intrinsic power in the employment relationship, compromising at the root the development of a healthy balance between the reasons of a 'digitalised' organisation, destined to take over, and the lender's interests.

---

13. Faioli, Mansioni e macchina intelligente, Giappichelli, 2018.
14. Many scholars show that for new 4.0 workers collective bargaining is required differently from workers tout court; a negotiation that traces a sure path to satisfy the demands of autonomy and individual freedom coming from 4.0 workers.
15. Zoppoli L., *Contratto, contrattualizzazione, contrattualismo: la marcia indietro del diritto del lavoro*, RIDL, 2011, p. 193.

22.4 THE COLLECTIVE AGREEMENT, THE RECENT ARRANGEMENTS OF THE UNION SYSTEM AND THE RENEWED ATTENTION TO UNION DEMOCRACY

The choice to implement Industry 4.0 in the manner envisaged by the experiences examined is anything but consistent with the attempt by the social partners to relaunch a decisive 'trade union re-intermediation',[16] making it an essential piece of the 'transformation and digitalisation processes'. This is the belief that 'authoritative, dynamic and qualified industrial relations constitute a factor of development, capable of positively affecting an economic-productive system that must be able to overcome the challenges posed by increasingly globalized markets, technology and the consequent changes of the work'.[17]

Much could be said about the strategies adopted to 'rediscover the vital circuits of trade union dialectics, in relations between collective bodies such as, if not above all, with and among workers'. However, the collective agreement is undoubtedly at the centre of these strategies, as a tool that best manages to mediate the need to relaunch the 'competitiveness of companies' in the current historical situation and, at the same time, 'enhance the work'. Not surprisingly, most recently with the intersectoral agreement of 9 March 2018, the collective agreement reiterates its competence to deal with crucial issues in the implementation of Industry 4.0, such as the incentive for remuneration and, to the point of providing a specific agreement, training. To better clarify the centrality mentioned above, it is important to point out that this collective agreement is no longer the expression of a trade union system centred on the so-called unity of action, but, to compensate for its failure, of a system that values a real and effective representative capacity, making it the basis of legitimacy to carry out the same trade union activity. Moreover, to avoid the danger of separate agreements, the measure of representativeness is the objective fact to anchor the introduction of the majority rule, which replaces that of unanimity. The collective contract, therefore, is considered validly concluded no longer when the assent of all the unions occurs but when the majority requirement is satisfied: a system, therefore, profoundly renewed with respect to the past, although – it is important to observe it – still weak due to the lack of a law regulating trade unions.[18]

16. Caruso, *La rappresentanza delle organizzazioni di interessi tra disintermediazione e re-intermediazione*, WP CSDLE 'Massimo D'Antona'.IT – 326/2017.
17. *See* intersectoral agreement of 9 March 2018.
18. The system discussed in the text finds its source in the 2011 Agreement, in the 2013 Protocol and the TU on the representation of 2014, containing the first two, who intervene for the first time on union representation, selecting the negotiating actors and specifying when the collective contract is validly stipulated. Well, to understand the weakness mentioned above, it is important to note that the collective agreement stipulated according to the procedural rules of the aforementioned agreements, although the same discuss generalised effectiveness, in reality, can only have relative efficacy. This is because such agreements, being of a negotiating nature, must be interpreted according to the private scheme, with the effect that what is declared in the TU becomes irrelevant, as it cannot be 'the parties who can give themselves what they do not have'. In this regard, the literature is very broad, *see*, among the many and for the necessary in-depth analysis.

The observations made confronted the opinion of those who believe that the reform pressure of Industry 4.0 accentuates the need for a profound and indispensable union change to carve out space in the ongoing organisational review processes. It is pointed out – and it is significant that representatives of the trade unions are also doing this – that Industry 4.0 requires an awareness of how the organisational innovations in place led the union to have to represent a 'high variety of people and new and extremely disintegrated interests'.[19] So – it is adds – the union's leading role, in this delicate phase of change, depends on its ability to act as a stable and reliable mediator of the variegated new generations interests: stability and reliability – it is specified – follow a renewed democracy of the union, without which 'there is a risk that all new factories will be factories without a union, and unfortunately there are already many new factories in which workers do not consider the union a representative'.[20]

To clarify the statement, it is worth noting that, despite the new union season, the persistence of a still firm legal framework to privatise paradigms does not exclude 'actions' inclined to compromise the application of the only collective agreement applicable according to the intersectoral agreement of 2014. It is sufficient to consider that nothing prevents the individual from taking part or not taking part anymore in the intersectoral agreement of 2014 member union, to participate in a different union, to constitute a new union or to join other workers in a new union or to simply follow the path of the individual contract. This is why the centrality of trade union democracy is emphasised in a labour market where the fragmentation of interests makes their aggregation difficult.

It is necessary to ask what democracy means.

The question is not insignificant; of course, looking for an answer is not easy: a lot should be covered, but here we can only confine ourselves to a fraction of essential observations.

Well, as an 'inelastic principle' connected 'to the organization of union pluralism',[21] democracy beats both the relations among unions and the relations between trade unions and workers: and in the latter, it takes on this importance. It has been at the centre of a careful historical and evolutionary reconstruction process, which has identified its essential nucleus in the 'adequate opening of the union representation system' to the interests of all workers: an opening to be realised – it was authoritatively specified – also ignoring the 'endo-associative dynamics, to which, on the contrary, we have too often limited ourselves to looking'. Therefore – more recent analyses point out – it is democracy in the relations between trade union and worker that allows the trade union system to realise one of its 'minimal functions of constitutional importance':[22] to

19. Bentivogli, *Sindacato futuro nell'era dei big data e Industry 4.0. Industry 4.0: la* smart factory necessita *della* smart union, Bentivogli, Di Vico, Pero, Viscardi, Nvaretti, Mosconi, *#SindacatoFuturo in Industry 4.0*, p. 3.
20. *See* again Bentivogli, *Sindacato futuro nell'era dei big data e Industry 4.0. Industry 4.0: la* smart factory necessita *della* smart union, Bentivogli, Di Vico, Pero, Viscardi, Nvaretti, Mosconi, *#SindacatoFuturo in Industry 4.0*, p. 19.
21. D'Antona, *Il quarto comma dell'art. 39 della Costituzione, oggi*, DLRI, 1998.
22. Zoppoli L., Una nuova costituzione per il sistema sindacale italiano? Riflessioni introduttivie, Zoppoli L., Zoppoli A., Delfino, Una nuova costituzione per il sistema di relazioni sindacali?, Editriale Scientifica, 2014, p. 23.

base the choices concerning labour relations 'on a sufficient if not ample consent'[23] among the workers themselves.

At this point, the initial observation appears sharper.

If the large unions increasingly value their real and effective representative capacity, to make it the basis of legitimacy to carry out their activity, it is not surprising that, in a historical moment marked by the push towards Industry 4.0, the way to allow the union to carve out a leading role is assumed to start from the 'care' of its relationships with individuals and from the construction of that 'dialogue' indispensable to aggregate the multiple and fragmented interests that appear on the labour market. Only in this way the collective action can be made more accurate in assessing the congruence of its interventions to the quota, avoiding the escape of the worker from the union: an eventuality inclined to feed the double risk of jeopardising the possibility of facing the challenges of the so-called fourth industrial revolution within the coordinates of the intersectoral agreement of 2014 and to stimulate or boost – it is the case examined above – towards the individual contract or adherence to forms of 'struggle' promoted by 'more impetuous' subjects (committees or base unions, spontaneous groups, etc.), considered much more incisive and therefore 'shareable'.[24] Ultimately, only in this way the union can express a power from the legitimacy prone to prolong itself in time and satisfy the guarantees of reliability as well as stability considered, today more than ever, essential.

22.5 TOWARDS AN UNCERTAIN FUTURE, BUT WITHOUT LOSING THE AWARENESS OF THE PRESENT

Given the aforementioned terms, it is clear that the question of democracy undoubtedly arises before Industry 4.0 and, above all, goes far beyond its borders.[25] However, Industry 4.0 makes it a matter of urgent need to study it further, since it 'Accelerates and sharpens the known weaknesses of the trade union system'. This is why the opinion that identifies democracy as an issue on which to insist on is becoming increasingly common by examining the solutions adopted by the often-mentioned intersectoral agreements, by the trade unions themselves and, not least, practised beyond the strictly national boundaries to declare its contents.

As it is not possible to examine these aspects, it is difficult and, in some ways, inappropriate to hypothesise a 'conclusion'. The fact is that digital economy feeds a profound renewal of work; a process by which the legal labour system has recently established a proper comparison – it has recently been written – 'even at the cost of deeply reviewing' its regulation techniques: on the other hand – it has been added –

23. *See* again Zoppoli L., Una nuova costituzione per il sistema sindacale italiano? Riflessioni introduttivie, Zoppoli L., Zoppoli A., Delfino, Una nuova costituzione per il sistema di relazioni sindacali?, Editriale Scientifica, 2014, p. 23.
24. Rusciano, Sul metodo delle riforme del Diritto del lavoro, DLM, 2018, p. 199.
25. Dufour, Hege, *The legitimacy of collective actors and trade union renewal*, www.bollettinoadapt.it.

'change is in the nature of law and, in particular, labour law'.[26] Imagining the results of this comparison is certainly difficult since in an extremely 'liquid' modernity 'the only constant of it is change and the only certainty is uncertainty'.[27] But – in the words of Bauman – in dealing with the uncertainty of the future one cannot lose one's cultural identity and, as far as it is more interested, juridical identity. The roads to modernity, therefore, must be travelled without ever forgetting the teaching of those who invite us to develop the legal system in relation to the changes of reality but always filtering the necessary gnoseological opening through the founding principles of the legal system. And there is no doubt that these principles require the utmost consideration to be given to the role of the union, the absence of which, in the current 'organisational reorganisation', risks determining the absence of an important 'vehicle of non-economic solidarity values or counterpower in the company'.[28]

Therefore some attempts, although not numerous, to develop Industry 4.0 without the role of the collective bodies will be more than welcome. On the other hand, despite the blunt weapons in its possession, the European Union tries to follow this path, giving a role to the union in the context of the European social dialogue: these considerations are demonstrated by a Communication from the European Commission[29] and an Opinion from the Economic Committee European social policy.

The Communication, in particular, promotes a 'widespread social dialogue on the social aspects of digitalisation':[30] social partners – it is stated – are invited to 'include the digital single market in the social dialogue at European level'. This is because – continues the Commission – 'digitalization, far from being solely a technological issue, has broad implications in the social, labour and economic spheres'.

In concurrence, the European Economic and Social Committee released the *Industry 4.0 and Digital Transformation: The Direction to Follow*', which states that companies and trade unions must cooperate to promote functional and sustainable digitalisation. To this end, the opportunity of social dialogue is further enhanced, specifying its development at European, national, regional as well as corporate level. And, having specified the subjects covered by the 'European social dialogue in the context of Industry 4.0',[31] a 'sectoral' social dialogue is supported at national level.

26. Zoppoli L., *Valori, diritti e lavori flessibili: storicità, bilanciamento, declinabilità, negoziabilità*, WP CSDLE 'Massimo D'Antona'.IT – 400/2019.
27. Bauman, Modernità liquida, Laterza, 2011.
28. *See* again Zoppoli L., *Valori, diritti e lavori flessibili: storicità, bilanciamento, declinabilità, negoziabilità*, WP CSDLE 'Massimo D'Antona'.IT – 400/2019.
29. 'Digitalizzazione dell'industria europea. Cogliere appieno i vantaggi di un mercato unico digitale'.
30. According to the Commission, the challenges discussed in the text must be found in the structural modification of the labour market and the nature of work and in the effects that such changes may have about working conditions, employment levels and income distribution.
31. The analyses of economic and social complexities and the anticipation of change at the sectoral level, promoting a shared understanding; mapping the consequences for different segments of the labour market – low, medium and high – as well as for vulnerable groups; changes in the relationship between employer and employee; responsibility for health and safety in the workplace with regard to the use of automatic and connected machines and vehicles; job descriptions; 'flexicurity' and mobility due to further fragmentation of value chains; the skills and qualifications focused on the needs of digital technology users, as well as the requalification, which thus become key aspects; education, from elementary schools to universities; continuous

Whereas, at the regional and company level, it is encouraged a social dialogue centred on 'changes in business models and on specific situations concerning individuals, mutual enrichment between companies, schools and higher education institutions and corporate campuses'.

requalification and constant improvement of skills; attention to gender balance; good practices, attention to promoting convergence between Member States; mobility (Schengen); communication and information.

STUDIES IN EMPLOYMENT AND SOCIAL POLICY

1. W. Beck, L. van der Maesen & A. Walker (eds), *The Social Quality of Europe*, 1997 (ISBN 90-411-0456-9).
2. R. Blanpain, M. Colucci, C. Engels, F. Hendrickx, L. Salas & E. De Smyter, *Institutional Changes and European Social Policies after the Treaty of Amsterdam*, 1998 (ISBN 90-411-1018-6).
3. V. Lo: *Law and Industrial Relations: China and Japan after World War II*, 1998 (ISBN 90-411-1075-5).
4. A. Den Exter & H. Hermans (eds), *The Right to Health Care in Several European Countries*, 1998 (ISBN 90-411-1087-9).
5. M. Biagi (ed.), *Job Creation and Labour Law from Protection towards Pro- Action*, 2000 (ISBN 90-411-1432-7).
6. W. Beck, L. van der Maesen, F. Thomése & A. Walker (eds), *Social Quality: A Vision for Europe*, 2000 (ISBN 90-411-1523-4).
7. F. Pennings, *Introduction to European Social Law*, 3rd ed., 2001 (ISBN 90-411-1628-1).
8. J. Murray, *Transnational Labour Regulation: The ILO and EC Compared*, 2001 (ISBN 90-411-1583-8).
9. R. Blanpain & C. Engels (eds), *The ILO and Social Challenges of the 21st Century*, 2001 (ISBN 90-411-1572-2).
10. M. Biagi (ed.), *Towards a European Model of Industrial Relations? Building on the First Report of the European Commission*, 2001 (ISBN 90-411-1653-2).
11. J. Clasen (ed.), *What Future for Social Security? Debates and Reforms in National and Cross-National Perspective*, 2001 (ISBN 90-411-1671-0).
12. A. Numhauser-Henning (ed.), *Legal Perspectives on Equal Treatment and Non-Discrimination*, 2001 (ISBN 90-411-1665-6).
13. R. Blanpain (ed.), *Labour Law, Human Rights and Social Justice* 2001 (ISBN 90-411-1697-4).
14. M.-C. Kuo, H.F. Zacher & H.-S. Chan (eds), *Reform and Perspectives on Social Insurance: Lessons from the East and West*, 2002 (ISBN 90-411-1819-5).
15. P. Foubert, *The Legal Protection of the Pregnant Worker in the European Community*, 2002 (ISBN 90-411-1842-X).
16. M. Biagi (ed.), *Quality of Work and Employee Involvement in Europe*, 2002 (ISBN 90-411-1885-3).
17. F. Pennings, *Dutch Social Security Law in an International Context*, 2002 (ISBN 90-411-1887-X).

18. T. Carney & G. Ramia, *From Rights to Management: Contract, New Public Management and Employment Services*, 2002 (ISBN 90-411-1889-6).
19. R. Blanpain & M. Colucci, *European Labour and Social Security Law, Glossary*, 2002 (ISBN 90-411-1905-1).
20. I.U. Zeytinoglu (ed.), *Flexible Work Arrangements: Conceptualizations and International Experiences*, 2002 (ISBN 90-411-1947-7).
21. J. Berghman, A. Nagelkerke, M. Boos, R. Doeschot & G. Vonk (eds), *Social Security in Transition*, 2002 (ISBN 90-411-1969-8).
22. R. Blanpain, *The Legal Status of Sportsmen and Sportswomen under International, European and Belgian National and Regional Law*, 2003 (ISBN 90-411-1980-9).
23. R. Blanpain & M. Weiss (eds), *Changing Industrial Relations & Modernisation of Labour Law, Liber Amicorum in Honour of Professor Marco Biagi*, 2003 (ISBN 90-411-2008-4).
24. J. Malmberg (ed.), *Effective Enforcement of EC Labour Law*, 2003 (ISBN 90-411-2160-9).
25. M. De Vos (ed.), *A Decade Beyond Maastricht: The European Social Dialogue Revisited*, 2003 (ISBN 90-411-2163-3).
26. M. Sewerynski (ed.), *Collective Agreements and Individual Contracts of Employment*, 2003 (ISBN 90-411-2190-0).
27. R. Blanpain & M. Van Gestel, *Use and Monitoring of E-Mail, Intranet and Internet Facilities at Work: Law and Practice*, 2004 (ISBN 90-411-22-66-4).
28. A. C. Neal (ed.), *The Changing Face of European Labour Law and Social Policy*, 2004 (ISBN 90-411-2312-1).
29. E. Sol & M. Westerveld (eds), *Contractualism in Employment Services: A New Form of Welfare State Governance*, 2005 (ISBN 90-411-2405-5).
30. F. Pennings (ed.), *Between Soft and Hard Law – The Impact of International Social Security Standards on National Social Security Law*, 2006 (ISBN 978-90-411-2491-3).
31. L. Dickens & A. C. Neal (eds), *The Changing Institutional Face of British Employment Relations*, 2006 (ISBN 978-90-411-2541-5).
32. G. Sebardt, *Redundancy and the Swedish Model in an International Context*, 2006 (ISBN 978-90-411-2503-3).
33. A.M. Swiatkowski, *Charter of Social Rights of the Council of Europe*, 2007 (ISBN 978-90-411-2608-5).
34. M. Sargeant (ed.), *The Law on Age Discrimination in the EU*, 2008 (ISBN 978-90-411-2522-4).
35. G. Di Domenico & S. Spattini (eds), *New European Approaches to Long- Term Unemployment: What Role for Public Employment Services and What Market for Private Stakeholders?*, 2008 (ISBN 978-90-411-2614-6.)
36. C. Welz, *The European Social Dialogue under Articles 138 and 139 of the EC Treaty: Actors, Processes, Outcomes*, 2008 (ISBN 978-90-411-2744-0).
37. M. Rönnmar (ed.), *EU Industrial Relations v. National Industrial Relations: Comparative and Interdisciplinary Perspectives*, 2008 (ISBN 978-90-411- 2770-9).

38. F. Pennings, Y. Konijn & A. Veldman (eds), *Social Responsibility in Labour Relations: European and Comparative Perspectives*, 2008 (ISBN 978-90- 411-2783-9).
39. F. Pennings & C. Bosse (eds), *The Protection of Working Relationships: A Comparative Study*, 2011 (ISBN 978-90-411-3289-5).
40. S. Devetzi & S. Stendahl (eds), *Too Sick to Work?: Social Security Reference in Europe for Persons with Reduced Earnings Capacity*, 2011 (ISBN 978-90- 411-3426-4).
41. Ulrich Becker, Frans Pennings & Tineke Dijkhoff (eds), *International Standard Setting and Innovations in Social Security*, 2013 (ISBN 978-90-411-3233-8).
42. E. Ales (ed.), *Health and Safety at Work: European and Comparative Perspective*, 2013 (ISBN 978-90-411-4661-8).
43. F. Pennings, T. Erhag & S. Stendahl (eds), *Non-public Actors in Social Security Administration: A Comparative Study*, 2013 (ISBN 978-90-411-4917-6).
44. A. Neal (ed.), *Cross-Currents in Modern Chinese Labour Law*, 2014 (ISBN 978-90-411-4763-9).
45. B. Waas (ed.), *The Right to Strike: A Comparative View*, 2014 (ISBN 978-90-411-5007-3).
46. A. Ojeda-Avilés, *Transnational Labour Law*, 2015 (ISBN 978-90-411-5858-1).
47. A. Numhauser-Henning & M. Rönnmar, *Age Discrimination and Labour-Law: Comparative and Conceptual Perspectives in the EU and Beyond*, 2015 (ISBN 978-90-411-4979-4).
48. A. Perulli & T. Treu (eds), *Enterprise and Social Rights*, 2017 (ISBN 978-90-411-8234-0).
49. Dr F.C.A. van Haasteren, *Decent Flexibility: The Impact of ILO Convention 181 and the Regulation on Temporary Agency Work*, 2017 (ISBN 978-90-411-9236-3).
50. T. Dijkhoff & L.G. Mpedi (eds), *Recommendation on Social Protection Floors: Basic Principles for Innovative Solutions*, 2018 (ISBN 978-90-411-8623-2).
51. A. Perulli & T. Treu (eds), *Sustainable Development, Global Trade and Social Rights*, 2018 (ISBN 978-90-411-9235-6).
52. M. Mironi & M. Schlachter (eds), *Regulating Strikes in Essential Services: A Comparative 'Law in Action' Perspective*, 2019 (ISBN 978-90-411-8997-4).
53. A. Perulli & T. Treu (eds), *The Role of the State and Industrial Relations*, 2019 (ISBN 978-94-035-0661-6).
54. T. Gyulavári & E. Menegatti (eds), *The Sources of Labour Law*, 2020 (ISBN 978-94-035-0284-7).
55. V. Cagnin, *Labour Law and Sustainable Development*, 2020 (ISBN 978-94-035-2074-2).
56. A. Perulli & T. Treu (eds), *The Future of Work: Labour Law and Labour Market Regulation in the Digital Era*, 2021 (ISBN 978-94-035-2853-3).

www.ingramcontent.com/pod-product-compliance
Lightning Source LLC
Chambersburg PA
CBHW071239230926
51849CB00001B/157
* 9 7 8 9 4 0 3 5 2 8 5 3 3 *